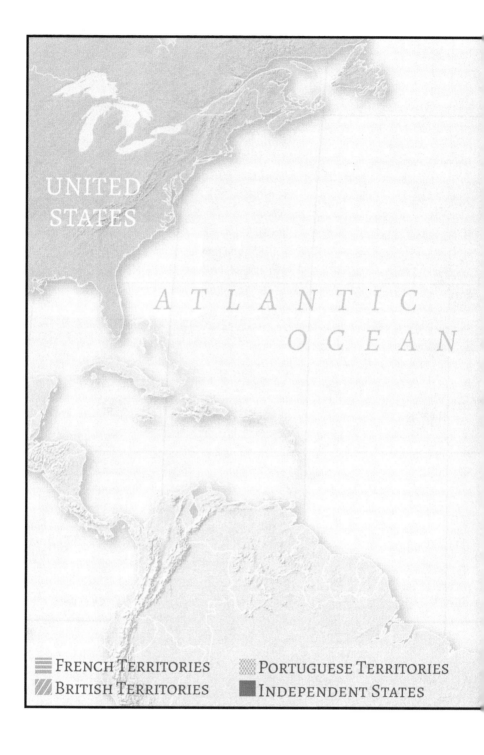

UNITED
STATES

*ATLANTIC*

*OCEAN*

FRENCH TERRITORIES  PORTUGUESE TERRITORIES
BRITISH TERRITORIES  INDEPENDENT STATES

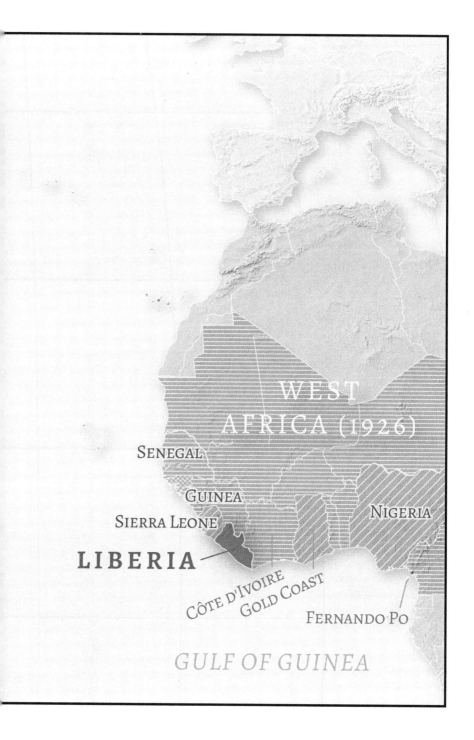

WEST
AFRICA (1926)

SENEGAL

GUINEA

SIERRA LEONE

LIBERIA

CÔTE D'IVOIRE
GOLD COAST

NIGERIA

FERNANDO PO

GULF OF GUINEA

# Empire of Rubber

# Empire of Rubber

Firestone's Scramble for Land
and Power in Liberia

Gregg Mitman

NEW YORK
LONDON

Requests for permission to reproduce selections from this book should be made through our
website: https://thenewpress.com/contact.

Published in the United States by The New Press, New York, 2021
Distributed by Two Rivers Distribution

ISBN 978-1-62097-377-6 (hc)
ISBN 978-1-62097-378-3 (ebook)
CIP data is available.

The New Press publishes books that promote and enrich public discussion and understanding
of the issues vital to our democracy and to a more equitable world. These books are made
possible by the enthusiasm of our readers; the support of a committed group of donors, large
and small; the collaboration of our many partners in the independent media and the not-for-
profit sector; booksellers, who often hand-sell New Press books; librarians; and above all by
our authors.

www.thenewpress.com

*Composition by Westchester Publishing Services*
*This book was set in Adobe Caslon Pro*
Front endpaper map cartographer: Lily Houtman, University
of Wisconsin–Madison Cartography Lab.

Printed in the United States of America

2   4   6   8   10   9   7   5   3   1

*For Emmanuel and Gomue*

# Contents

# Preface

Evening rains have flushed the heat and dust from the air. An early morning breeze brings a cool freshness to the day. It is quiet at the river's edge on the back patio of the Farmington Hotel, a $20 million, five-star luxury complex, opened in 2017 across from Liberia's Roberts International Airport, also known as Robertsfield. The hotel mostly serves a foreign-business and donor-agency clientele able to spend $200 a night in a country where half the population lives on less than $2 a day. Our film crew will be working for the next few days at the nearby Liberian Institute for Biomedical Research, which makes this hotel a convenient place to stay.[1]

Also nearby the hotel is the town of Harbel, where the headquarters of the former Firestone Plantations Company, now Firestone Liberia, is located. Harbel is a shadow of what it was in an era when the natural wealth of the land was harvested to fill the coffers of American rubber barons, steel magnates, and Liberian elites.

The hotel's patio looks out on the Farmington River, after which the hotel is named. A few miles downstream, the fresh waters of the Farmington mix with the Atlantic Ocean's saline waters to form a unique estuarine habitat of mangrove forests and barrier islands that support a diversity of life. Across the river, children are at play in Zangar Town. I can see palm and banana trees on the town's edge and, interspersed among the mud brick homes, small garden plots, likely growing peppers, cassava, and other Liberian staples. Throughout Liberia, such crops provide sustenance, cash, and a claim to land rights in a country where land is life. Nearby, a dugout canoe, fashioned from a huge log, ferries people from one side of the river to the other.

In the 1940s this area was abuzz with United States Army personnel, Firestone engineers, and Liberian workers. They labored to quickly build an airport to be operated under military contract by Pan American Airways, initially called Roberts Field, and an adjoining military base to service American military transport planes destined for battlefronts in the Mediterranean and Southeast Asia. But protecting Liberia was also a priority. Thousands of African American troops, and a smaller contingent of white officers and soldiers, had been sent to secure a valuable American supply of natural rubber in a world at war. This era of American empire is over, but its legacy lingers. Standing next to the old Roberts International Airport terminal is a shiny new terminal of glass, concrete, and steel, its $50 million cost financed by China's Export-Import Bank. Recently opened, it resembles, with a dual cantilevered roof, the wings of a jumbo jet and signifies the rise of a new era of geopolitics and resource extraction in Africa.

Less than a mile away is the main entrance gate to Firestone Liberia. The company is now operated by the Tokyo-based Bridgestone Corporation, which acquired U.S.-based Firestone Tire & Rubber Company in 1988, almost a decade after the last Firestone to manage the family company gave up control. In 1926, the Liberian government granted a concession for up to a million acres of land to Harvey Firestone Sr. to build what would become the world's largest contiguous rubber plantation. The territory that the Akron, Ohio, tire manufacturer initially claimed, as well as that on which Roberts Field was built, was once customary land of the Bassa people. They are one among a number of ethnic groups that settled in this region long before immigrants—first from America, and later the Caribbean—began arriving in the early nineteenth century to make this land their home.

Looking upstream from the Farmington Hotel, I catch a glimpse of a silver-hued water tower that marks the location of the Firestone latex-processing plant, originally built in 1940. Now, in an area covering roughly two hundred square miles, tappers awake early each morning, as they have done for generations, to extract the milky white fluid from millions of *Hevea brasiliensis* trees. Thousands of gallons of the liquid latex are transported by truck each day from the many divisions of the plantation to the factory. The smell of ammonia in the processing plant can be overpowering, as I learned when I too carelessly bent down to sniff the fast-moving latex flowing through the plant and was almost knocked unconscious. For decades, the Firestone Plantations Company used the Farmington River as a convenient sink for dumping ammonia and other waste products generated in the industrial production of "natural" rubber. Residents of nearby communities along the river who bathe, wash clothes, and fish in its waters had long complained of foul-smelling air, contaminated wells, skin rashes, and a scarcity of fish. But not until 2008 was a wastewater treatment plant built, almost seventy years after the factory began processing latex.[2]

Atop a hill in the distance, not far from the old headquarters' main entrance gate, sit the ruins of a two-story, reddish-orange brick house, its design out of keeping with the cinder block and mud brick homes in the area. I recognize it as the distinctive architectural style that Firestone used in constructing comfortable homes for its largely American—and exclusively white—management staff. Palm trees tower over the building. The surrounding landscape is bare but for recently planted rubber seedlings. Ruins like this one, found throughout the Firestone plantation complex, recall the plantation landscape of the antebellum South, where planters looked out over their property: land, crops, and human chattel. These hilltop homes assigned to white "planters," as Firestone called its division superintendents, were purposefully separate from division camps, often located in low-lying areas and swamps, where an African labor force lived. A home on a hill offered some protection from the bite of the female *Anopheles* mosquito, which avoids higher elevations. The mosquito, an important link in the life cycle of the malaria parasite *Plasmodium falciparum*, was a threat to the health and productivity of Firestone's workers and remains so for workers today.

A few miles down the road from the Farmington Hotel, in the direction away from the Firestone plantations, another aspect of the expansive reach of an American rubber empire comes into view. The buildings of the Liberian Institute for Biomedical Research are also constructed in the Firestone style. In the entrance hallway is a gold plaque commemorating Harvey Firestone Sr. The laboratory complex was erected in 1952 with a $250,000 gift from Harvey Firestone Jr. to establish an institute for research in tropical medicine to honor his father's "deep and abiding faith in the Liberian people" and commitment to "their well-being."[3]

In an outside part of the complex, empty cages, with rusting iron bars, and several painted concrete statues of chimpanzees evoke a time when both animals and humans were enrolled in experiments and clinical trials. Here, Western doctors and biomedical researchers sought treatments to combat malaria, schistosomiasis, and other tropical diseases that threatened the transformation of nature on an industrial scale. From the beginning of Firestone's venture in Liberia, the beneficence of American science and medicine, in improving the lives of a Liberian workforce, could go far in winning support for an American rubber empire in a sovereign Black republic. The fragments and remains of that empire, centered on a plantation, are everywhere around me. An industrial ecology, built to satiate

America's growing thirst for rubber at the dawn of the automobile age, reordered relationships of life and land in Liberia. These fragmentary remains give clues to past worlds remade and new ones born.[4]

I first came to Liberia in 2012 to retrace the journey of a 1926 Harvard scientific expedition to Liberia. On the flight from Brussels to Monrovia, I was among a mix of people. Some were Liberians who had fled the country during years of civil conflict, returning to visit family and provide help where needed. Others were working for Western NGOs and governments, giving their time and expertise to rebuilding a nation. American missionaries, many of whom were white women of college age, were also on board, propelled, perhaps, by a belief that Liberia needed saving.

Like so many Americans who came to this West African nation, including those on the Harvard expedition, I misread the landscape when I arrived.[5] On the drive from the airport to Monrovia, I wondered about the many half-built cinder block homes along the road, imagining them to be structures abandoned amid conflict. With images and stories of war and poverty in my head, I naively saw ruin. Later, I would learn about the value and meanings of land in Liberia, and see these structures not as ruins but as signs of renewal. They represented aspirations to claim and secure a piece of ground in a country where land has long been an important resource in securing livelihoods and self-determination. In 2018, roughly 50 percent of land had been leased long-term to foreign investors.[6] After fourteen years of nearly continuous civil conflict that ended in 2003, the Liberian government needed capital to jump-start the country's economy and remake its devastated infrastructure. Eagerly seeking foreign investment, the government gave out generous agricultural, mining, and timber concessions.

Today, a massive wave of industrial plantation agriculture washes over the world in a rush for land. It is not unlike the late nineteenth and early twentieth centuries, when American and European firms grabbed lands in Latin America, the Pacific Islands, Southeast Asia, and Africa to grow tropical fruits, rubber, and oil palm to meet growing consumer demand for pineapples, bananas, automobile tires, and more. Estimates suggest that globally 75 million acres have been sold or leased in the past decade alone to foreign investors for large-scale oil palm, rubber, and other agricultural concessions.[7] The first act in the making of a plantation world is always land dispossession. Almost one hundred years ago, Firestone secured a major land concession in Liberia to build a vast rubber plantation to break

America's dependence on the British and Dutch for what was then one of the most profitable commodities in the world.

This book is a history of America through the lens of Firestone in Liberia. It is the story of how a behemoth American company on a nationalist mission of profit, robed in beneficence, negotiated, maneuvered, and bullied its way into what was then one of only two sovereign Black nations on the African continent. Stepping outside America helps to make visible the structures of white privilege and power, buttressed by science and medicine, that drove the march of American capitalism and empire across the globe. But the story of Firestone in Liberia is more than a story of the white supremacy and racial capitalism that powered an American family dynasty for more than half a century. It is also a history of contestation, complicity, and resistance. The leaders of a struggling Black republic maneuvered to hold their ground to save Liberia from becoming an American protectorate. From across the African diaspora, Black activists, writers, scientists, diplomats, and businesspeople rallied to support or oppose the experiment that was Firestone in Liberia.

Could the plantation free itself from the violence of land dispossession, racial exploitation, and unfree labor that shaped its history in the Atlantic world?[8] Could American capital be trusted to respect the rights of a sovereign Black nation and its people in an imperial and colonial world? Would Firestone prove to be an angel or a devil to Liberia? Such questions swirled around the promise Harvey Firestone Sr. made to build in Liberia a modern industrial plantation that would bring great benefits to the country and its people. These questions remain today.

To the many elders, chiefs, colleagues, friends, and family in Liberia who have shared their stories with me, helped me out of a jam, honored me in their village, and schooled me in my misunderstandings, I owe an immense gratitude. They challenged my ideas and beliefs, opened my eyes to other ways of being in this world, and altered the direction of my work and commitments. Without them, this book would not be possible. Denied access to the Firestone company archives—which were removed from the publicly funded University of Akron after a 2005 lawsuit alleging labor rights violations on the Firestone plantations—I have pulled together bits and pieces, gathered from around the world, to make sense of a story that can and should be told from many perspectives.[9] I offer one, as a historian of science, medicine, and the environment, with the hope that understanding the past can build more-just futures.

# Empire of Rubber

# 1

# "America Should Produce
# Its Own Rubber"

"Rubber is the most important commodity in the world," Harvey S. Firestone, president of the Rubber Association of America, declared to the association's more than six hundred members and guests gathered at New York City's Waldorf Astoria hotel for an annual meeting in 1917. Many industry executives, dressed in black tuxes and white bowties, laughed at such an audacious claim as they feasted upon oysters, squab, "bisque glacé," and wine. The forty-eight-year-old Firestone was dead serious. The grand ballroom in which guests dined and where he delivered his remarks was decorated for the occasion with a lavish, patriotic display of draped American flags.

William Howard Taft, another famed Ohioan, was the guest of honor that evening. At 350 pounds, he was a giant of a man. Moreover, Taft, who became the first governor-general of the Philippines under American occupation in 1901 and served as president of the United States from 1909 to 1913, had no qualms about throwing around the weight of private capital and government to gain economic and political advantage for American firms in foreign lands. Taft's efforts to build a civilian government in the Philippines, and, in particular, to secure a place for American capital, where the rubber industry might "grow and produce its rubber under the American Flag," were welcomed with applause by the dinner guests. Noting that the United States consumed 60 percent of all crude rubber in the world, Taft reminded the attendees of "the awkwardness of being without a supply of rubber." "The increase in the demand for rubber," he observed, "emphasizes our greater dependence upon tropical products and the greater necessity for the improvement of conditions of life and business and government in tropical countries."[1] Firestone couldn't have asked for a speech more in keeping with where his own thoughts had begun to turn.

To better undersell his competitors, the Akron industrialist had done everything he could to reduce the production costs of tires coming out of his factory. But there was one cost Firestone couldn't control: the price of crude rubber. American tire manufacturers found themselves beholden to the climatic constraints of a tropical plant and to the geopolitics of empire, which put Brazil, Great Britain, and the Netherlands in control of the world's rubber supply.

Latex—white gold, as it was known in the early twentieth century—is an opaque, sticky substance exuded by thousands of flowering plant species. It is a plant's natural defense against predators. When an insect bites a leaf, a milky liquid containing a mix of defensive agents rises to the leaf surface where, upon contact with air, it coagulates. Rubber, a natural polymer, is one protective substance found in the latex of many plant species. Insects find themselves trapped or their mouth parts mired in the gummy, oozing liquid. Rubber also acts like a bandage, sealing wounds on leaves and stems.

Rubber had been valued among indigenous human inhabitants of Mesoamerica for centuries. They used latex extracted from the Panama rubber tree, *Castilla elastica*, and from other plants native to Central America, to make sandals and game balls. Latex was exchanged in Aztec, Olmec, and Maya trade networks long before it became a commodity of European conquest and empire. In 1839 American chemist Charles Goodyear learned that sulfur, combined with heat, stabilized rubber's unique elastic and water-repellent properties. The discovery transformed what was once a curiosity into what Paul Litchfield, president of Goodyear Tire and Rubber Company, described as the vital "flexing muscles and sinews" of the country's industrial infrastructure.[2]

An awakened world appetite for rubber depended in the nineteenth century on a tree growing in the Amazon rainforest. *Hevea brasiliensis* yielded high-quality rubber in concentrations double those of other latex-producing plants. But its natural habitat made harvesting rubber on an industrial scale problematic. The trees, which can reach 75 to 150 feet in height, grow interspersed among a diversity of rainforest plants, but typically there are just one or two *Hevea* trees per acre. Harvesting latex under such conditions was a grueling job. Tappers, or *seringueiros*, many of them landless peasants from northeastern Brazil, used machetes to open paths through thick jungle to prized *Hevea* trees. A tapper might have paths encircling as many as 150 to 200 rubber trees, from which he collected latex. A tapper cooked his latex over an open fire to congeal it into crude rubber. Tapping was seasonal work limited to the dry season, when rainfall amounts dipped but temperatures soared. Sweltering heat and a horde of creatures, from malaria-carrying mosquitoes to venomous snakes, took a toll on tappers' lives. So, too, did the people to whom tappers were indebted. Middlemen, the *patrão*, claimed ownership of the rainforest tracts where rubber trees grew. In exchange for tapping rights, *seringueiros* agreed to purchase their food and supplies from and to sell their collected rubber to the *patrão*. It was a system that benefited the *patrão* and impoverished the tappers.[3]

Dealers, or *aviadors*, traveled in steam-powered boats up the Amazon River's many tributaries to buy crude rubber from the *patrão*. *Aviadors* then brought their rubber downriver to the port city of Belém, in the Brazilian state of Pará. There, where the massive volume of water flowing from the largest river in the world spills out over a vast delta to meet the Atlantic Ocean, crude rubber piled up in the merchant houses. Foreign buyers from the United States, Great Britain, and elsewhere came to Belém seeking deals.

Amazon rubber, and the peonage system of labor that extracted it, yielded fortunes for the middlemen, dealers, and speculators during Brazil's rubber boom, which ran from 1879 to 1912. An extractive economy developed in which local and foreign investors secured concessions from the Brazilian, Bolivian, and Peruvian governments for large tracts of land. Wall Street investors and American rubber barons were in on the action. The Bolivian Syndicate, a charter company formed by American and British investors, including rubber magnate Charles Flint, financier J.P. Morgan, the House of Rothschild, and the heirs of transportation tycoon Cornelius Vanderbilt, used strong-arm tactics to gain access to 50 million acres of land in Acre, one of the Amazon's most productive rubber regions. The company, having pledged to support Bolivia in its territorial conflict with Brazil, had its lease dissolved when Bolivian troops ceded control of the region to the Brazilian military in 1903. The Bolivian Syndicate, nevertheless, walked away with a settlement worth £110,000.[4]

Brazil kept tight control on the rubber trade, much to the chagrin of American rubber manufacturers. Each year, they were powerless as Brazilian elites set rubber prices. Rubber wealth was on display in places like Manaus, a city in the heart of the rainforest where the lower Amazon begins. The city's opera house, the grandiose Teatro Amazonas, was built in a Renaissance style with decorated roofing tiles from France, walls of English steel, and Carrara marble from Italy. Rubber had made the city of fifty thousand inhabitants into the arts and culture capital of Brazil. In 1905, eight years after the theater opened and the same year Firestone signed a contract to make tires for Henry Ford's Model N automobile, the per pound price of Pará rubber climbed from 61¢ to $1.50. Five years later, when Model T's were rolling off Ford's assembly line at unprecedented speed, the price of Brazilian rubber skyrocketed to $3.06 per pound. Firestone fretted each year about when to buy rubber in a speculative commodities market over which he had little or no control.[5]

An act of piracy, committed in 1876 by British botanist Henry Wickham, would eventually bring Brazil's monopoly on crude rubber to a grinding halt. In 1871, Joseph Hooker, director of the Royal Botanic Gardens at Kew, who commanded the vast botanical realm of the British empire's global expanse, sent Wickham to South America on a collecting expedition. Five years later, Wickham returned to London with a surreptitious cargo of seventy thousand *Hevea brasiliensis* seeds, gathered from the Tapajós plateau in Pará where some of the best rubber trees grew. Nearly three thousand of the seeds germinated at Kew. The rubber tree seedlings then traveled from the inhospitable climate of England to the more inviting tropical habitats of the British colonial islands of Singapore, in the Malay Archipelago, and Ceylon, present-day Sri Lanka.[6]

In Singapore and Ceylon, the British successfully domesticated the wild rubber tree into a plantation crop. It was a stroke of ecological luck. In the Amazon, the fungal parasite *Dothidella ulei* was a *Hevea* disease. Young rubber trees were the most vulnerable to infection. As the fungus wormed its way through gaps in the leaf's cellular structure, it damaged tissues, blackened leaves, and deprived the tree of its ability to harness the sun's energy. The scattered growth of different-aged rubber trees in the dense Amazon jungle was a defensive strategy that allowed for an evolutionary stalemate between plant and fungus. But trying to grow *Hevea* plantation-style in Brazil gave the fungal parasite the upper hand: rubber seedlings planted in dense stands were decimated by the fungus. Henry Ford would learn this when he set out in 1927 to grow a source of American rubber on a concession for 2.5 million acres in the state of Pará. There, he carved out of the tropical rainforest his short-lived Fordlandia and Belterra rubber plantations. Ford's efforts ran into a series of disease, labor, and political problems that proved too difficult to solve.[7] In South Asia, British Malaya, and the Dutch East Indies, however, no such fungal enemy of *Hevea* existed. Consequently, the species thrived as a monoculture plantation crop, planted in neat rows roughly fifteen feet apart, making a uniform crisscross pattern of approximately two hundred trees per acre.

Early on, investors were cautious about making significant capital outlays for plantation rubber. In 1904, twenty-eight years after the British empire orchestrated a reshuffling of *Hevea*'s geographic range, a mere fifty thousand acres of rubber had been planted in South and Southeast Asia. All that changed as the price for Pará rubber soared. The first commercial sale of plantation rubber coincided with the 1905 Brazilian price hike. The huge return on investment resulted in a scramble to plant rubber trees throughout the Malay Archipelago, often on failing coffee plantations, devastated by coffee rust disease and competition from Brazil.[8] In 1910, the British colonial official Charles Braddock looked forward to a time when the "ruined coffee planters of Java, Sumatra, and the Malay Peninsula return the compliment by ruining the rubber industry of Brazil, as Brazil ruined them in the coffee business, thus evening up matters in the eternal justice of things."[9] He didn't have to wait long. In 1914, plantation rubber displaced wild rubber on the world stage, accounting for just over 60 percent of global production. By 1922, that figure jumped to 93 percent. Wild rubber could not compete with the production output and profit margins of cultivated rubber grown on industrial plantations worked by imported labor.[10]

Singapore quickly became the financial hub and knowledge capital of the world rubber trade. Among the seven largest ports in the world, this melting pot of Asia and gateway to the China Sea and Indian and Pacific Oceans was designated, under British rule, an official free market for rubber in 1911. Weekly auctions of rubber—from the finest Ribbed Smoked Sheet Grade One (abbreviated RSS 1), sought after by American tire manufacturers, to low-quality scrap—took place each Wednesday afternoon at 12:30 in the Exchange Building. Located in the vicinity of Raffles Place, the center of Singapore's Financial District, the Exchange Building was also home to the Singapore Chamber of Commerce and the Singapore Club, where only the wealthiest and most influential men of the city's white colonial aristocracy gathered. Donald Alastair Ross, a Scotsman who would become the first general manager of Firestone's Liberia operations, made a sizable sum as a planter and civil engineer in these heady days of Singapore's rubber boom. He boasted of lighting cigars with pound notes on weekend getaways with his mates at the grand Raffles Hotel, just across the harbor and a short rickshaw ride away from the Singapore Club.

By 1914, the average price of RSS 1 rubber sold at auction in the Exchange Building effectively became the world's rubber price. It was telegraphed weekly through the undersea cable that linked the rubber-producing regions of the Malay Archipelago to the large tire-manufacturing firms in Akron and smaller buyers across the globe.[11]

The B.F. Goodrich Company became in 1913 the first of Akron's conglomerates to establish a presence in Singapore. The company employed as its buying agent W.T. Easley, a New Yorker living in the Straits Settlements, the British crown colony of which Singapore was a part. Having someone on the ground negotiating prices instead of working through brokers gave Goodrich an advantage over its Akron competitors. Firestone soon followed Goodrich's lead, opening in 1915 its own buying branch in the British empire's free port. Doing so saved the company an estimated $1,500 per day. "Though the cable charges between Akron and Singapore are heavy—and no abbreviated code messages are permitted in these war times—the factories are in constant cable communications with its staff of crude rubber experts on the other side of the world," noted a reporter from the *New Orleans Times-Picayune*.[12] Four years later, to offset increasing raw material costs and to "Americanize the Far East's methods of handling crude rubber," Firestone invested $1 million in a Singapore-based plant to sort, clean, and compress crude rubber. The move sidestepped "numerous middlemen" and reduced shipping expenses. S.G. Carkhuff, Firestone company's secretary, saw other benefits. "A white man" in Singapore, he bragged, could have four servants to attend to his every need for "no more than forty American dollars each month."[13]

Controlling the buying and processing of rubber from a position near its source shaved costs. In Firestone's quest to dominate the American tire market, the next step toward vertical integration—controlling every part of the tire-manufacturing process—was growing rubber. But where? Southeast Asia held promise. But the British and Dutch had a firm grip on the region's land and labor. Their control of Southeast Asia's rubber-growing belt irked Firestone. Selecting Taft as the keynote speaker at the 1917 Rubber Association of America meeting was strategic. Taft was outspoken in his defense of "extreme measures" to protect American corporate investments in foreign lands. He also shared Firestone's disdain of legislation in the Philippines that limited corporate land holdings to 2,500 acres and curtailed indentured labor importation. Both measures impeded Firestone's ability to secure a foothold in Southeast Asia.[14]

Firestone's strident nationalism made it unpalatable for him to engage with profitable rubber-growing ventures in the Dutch East Indies and British Malaya, on which other U.S. rubber manufacturing firms had embarked in the early days of plantation rubber. The United States Rubber Company in 1910 secured a seventy-five-year lease on fifteen thousand acres of land on the east coast of Sumatra at a cost of $700,000. The rubber company formed a subsidiary, the Holland American Plantations Company, and quickly converted the former tobacco plantation into a vast rubber enterprise. By 1922, the cultivated area had more than tripled in size, stretching across seventy square miles. It was the largest of the United States Rubber Company's holdings in the Dutch East Indies and British Malaya, which together totaled 110,000 acres. "The Dollar Land of Deli," a reference to the overpowering presence of American capital in Sumatra, soon came to also include Goodyear and other American companies as well.[15] In size and labor force, the United States Rubber Company's operation in Sumatra was, at the time, the single largest industrial rubber plantation in the world. A white enclave of managers from Europe and America, along with experts—including engineers, soil scientists, foresters, botanists, and physicians—drawn largely from the United States took "scientific care of men as well as of trees."[16] Twenty thousand indentured laborers, imported from Java and China, cleared, planted, and tapped the area, supplying roughly 20 percent of the American parent company's rubber needs. Firestone liked to portray himself as an individualist and pioneer. But he would come to rely heavily on the knowledge, organizational management, and plant materials cultivated on these plantations in Southeast Asia to nurture the growth of *Hevea brasiliensis* in West African soil.

A gift for sales and a way with horses led Harvey S. Firestone into the rubber industry. But it was his understanding of the ups and downs of commodity markets that most contributed to his success in an industry where the ability to reliably source and cheaply purchase the raw materials of tire production—crude rubber and cotton—was critical. It was knowledge Harvey acquired at a young age. Born in 1868 on a farm in Columbiana, Ohio, the future tire mogul watched his father, Benjamin, successfully negotiate the sale of livestock and grain each year. The elder Firestone had developed his own keen sense of when to buy and when to sell through owning and managing a farm with four hundred sheep; a couple hundred acres of wheat, corn, and oats; and a dozen or so steers and horses. Thanks

to his father's intuitive sense of the markets and his principled commitment to saving, building up his cash reserves in productive years, Harvey
and his two brothers were spared the typical hardships of farm life in the
nineteenth century. Benjamin Firestone was the "best business man I have
ever known," remarked Harvey. It was high praise coming from the son
who by 1929, at the age of sixty-one, had built the second largest tire-
manufacturing firm in the United States, then valued at $135 million
(roughly $2 billion today). Moreover, the success of his tires, rivaled only
by those of Goodyear in the new car and truck market; his nationwide
automotive service stores; and his weekly NBC music radio program, *The
Voice of Firestone*, had made Firestone a household name in America.[17]

Farm life taught Harvey the ways of turning surplus into capital, and it
was this that most interested him. He soon learned that his love and knowledge of horses could turn a profit. As a teenager, he began swapping
horses, abiding by his father's advice "never to rush in on a deal." "By the
time I was fifteen," boasted Harvey, "I could hold my own with any one
in a horse trade." Horses were a part of Firestone's life; he was never without one. His Harbel Manor, a one hundred–acre Akron estate, included a
118-room mansion, a private polo field, and a stable of seventy-five horses.
Firestone even gifted his prized three-year-old Kentucky thoroughbred to
President Warren Harding in 1921 after the head of state, on a camping
trip with Firestone, Thomas Edison, and Henry Ford, became smitten
with the sorrel gelding. For the Ohio farm boy, horses served as a primer
in business and a path into the upper echelons of American society.[18]

Horses, or, more specifically, horse-drawn carriages, brought Firestone into the cutthroat, patent-driven, cartel-dominated space of the rubber manufacturing industry. After graduating from Cleveland's
Spencerian Business College, where oil tycoon John D. Rockefeller had
learned bookkeeping skills, Firestone first worked as an accountant for a
coal company and next as a traveling salesman, pitching flavored extracts
and patent medicines. After joining the Columbus Buggy Company,
where his uncle, Clinton Firestone, was a controlling partner, Harvey
rose up the ranks to manage its Detroit district sales office. By the 1890s,
the firm was manufacturing a hundred carriages a day, employed more
than a thousand people, and had $2 million in annual sales. For Harvey
Firestone, life was good. With $150 in monthly earnings, Harvey invested
in horses. He trained and sold trotters, bought a sulky, a lightweight cart
used in harness racing, and joined the Gentlemen's Driving Club of High-

land Park. His fancy for harness racing led him to compete on private racing tracks in Detroit, sometimes driving for himself, sometimes driving for other wealthier men. And he was the first to drive, thanks to his uncle's company, the only rubber-tired buggy in the city. Comfort didn't come cheap. It cost an extra $40 to upgrade from steel wheels, standard on most carriages, to rubber-cushioned tires. Harvey was acquiring a taste for the finer things in life. But in the midst of an economic depression, few farmers could afford the $110 carriage offered by the Columbus Buggy Company, when competing firms sold good buggies at $35. Crop failures, plummeting commodity prices, and tightening credit in the 1890s fueled agrarian unrest and saw the rise of the Populist Party, hostile to banks, railroads, and a government serving the interests of elites. Fancy carriages became a symbol of the large inequalities in wealth that marked America's Gilded Age. When the Columbus Buggy Company went into receivership in 1896, Harvey Firestone struck out on his own.[19]

With backing from a Chicago investor who was sold on the comfort that rubber tires afforded a carriage ride over the Windy City's cobblestone streets, Firestone moved to the thriving Midwest metropolis. He bought an old rubber factory and founded the Firestone-Victor Rubber Company. In Chicago, Firestone began selling rubber carriage tires to a clientele making vast fortunes investing and trading in agricultural commodities such as cattle, hogs, lumber, and grain. Here, Firestone was first introduced into the ways of finance: loans and mortgages, assets and liabilities, stocks and bonds.[20]

In the 1890s, it was not buggy tires, but those for bicycles, along with a wide assortment of other items, including boots, shoes, raincoats, aprons, condoms, hoses, belts, telegraph parts, and many more, that made up the bulk of products produced through rubber manufacturing. But in 1897, when Ohio governor William McKinley rode into the White House as the nation's new president in a parade that sported horse-drawn carriages fitted with rubber tires, interest and demand for rubber carriage tires surged. McKinley's Republican presidency witnessed rapid economic growth, protectionist trade tariffs, and, in 1898, the Spanish-American War, which gave the country a victory over Spain and ushered in the rise of the United States as an imperial power. All of these developments would shape Firestone's business prospects, as he rode the buggy-tire wave.

In 1896, the entrepreneur took out his first loan; bought a larger manufacturing plant, Imperial Rubber Company; and two years later became

part of the Rubber Tire Wheel Company. Through its patent on a fasten-
ing device to affix the rubber to a flanged steel rim, Rubber Tire Wheel
held a controlling share of the carriage tire market. But the company's
majority owner, Edwin Kelly, hoodwinked the greenhorn rubber manufacturer when he bought out Firestone's company for $125,000. In 1899,
in his efforts to build a syndicate of rubber manufacturing companies, Kelly
sold Rubber Tire Wheel to the McMillin investors group for $1.25 million,
which renamed the company Consolidated Rubber Tire Company. Firestone walked away with $45,000 in his pocket, not a bad four-year return
on his $1,000 investment. But he was chastened by being cut out of the
bigger deal. From then on, he fought vigorously against monopolies and
syndicates, vowing to go it alone.[21]

With his wife, Idabelle, their two-year-old son, Harvey Jr., and $25,000
to invest in his pocket, Firestone headed to Akron in 1900. At the turn
of the twentieth century, Akron was fast becoming the rubber capital of
the world. Approaching the rubber city, you could recognize a distinctive
smell. The pungent odor of vulcanized rubber, resulting from a toxic brew
of crude rubber, sulfur, and other compounds, wafted from the mixing
mills of rubber manufacturing companies. It bathed the city in an aroma
likened by some of the city's inhabitants to the smell of dirty diapers.[22]

When Firestone arrived in Akron, three companies—B.F. Goodrich,
Goodyear Tire and Rubber, and Diamond Rubber—had already established themselves as major Midwestern players in rubber manufacturing.
On the East Coast, rubber magnate Charles Flint commanded more than
three-quarters of the rubber market in footwear and more than 50 percent
in mechanical goods through the controlling interests of his firm, the
United States Rubber Company. At five feet, six inches tall, the slightly
built Firestone seemed no match for these corporate giants. But Firestone
was a fierce competitor. In his office, he sat in a large chair and on a thick
cushion behind an equally outsized desk. He believed the imposing desk
and elevated seating gave him a psychological advantage in negotiations
with employees and business associates who came to speak with him.[23]

Patents, not height, proved far more important in gaining a competitive
edge in the rubber business. Firestone's first lucky break came in July of
1900. He had been in Akron only a short time when a retired physician,
Dr. Louis E. Sisler, took notice of the fine pair of sorrel horses that Firestone drove about town. Sisler reckoned the horses, far superior to his
own, spoke to the discerning character of their owner: horses made the

man. When the Akron doctor also learned of Firestone's interest in tires, he arranged a meeting with a business associate, a former schoolteacher and carpenter named James Swinehart. It was a meeting that transformed Firestone's life. Swinehart held a patent on a unique way of securing solid rubber tires to steel rims that he had, with Sisler's help, pitched, without success, to Akron's rubber manufacturers. Firestone recognized the merits of its crosswise-wire design, particularly for heavy commercial vehicles: the heavy weight of such vehicles posed challenges to making a quality tire that lasted and stayed on the rim. The patent was just what the determined and driven newcomer needed to establish himself in Akron. In August that year, Firestone, Sisler, and Swinehart, along with James Christy, an Akron leather dealer, formed the Firestone Tire & Rubber Company. With $20,000 in capital, a legally solid patent, and himself anointed as treasurer and general manager, Harvey Firestone set about to make his mark in Akron, and in America's rapidly changing rubber industry.[24]

Make it, he did. For its first two years, the new company relied upon other manufacturers, with whom it competed, to make their carriage tires. Vigorous sales required acquiring a manufacturing plant or getting out of business. Harvey hit the road, selling $200,000 in stock to investors. It was enough capital to purchase a vacant foundry on Akron's south side and buy secondhand manufacturing equipment. In January of 1903, the factory started operating. Twelve men working one day could produce forty solid rubber tires, with treads three-quarters inch and four inches wide. Demand for larger tires drove initial sales. Eventually, 90 percent of commercial vehicles in Boston were equipped with Firestone tires. Thanks to Firestone, five-ton, horse-drawn Anheuser-Busch trucks delivered beer in St. Louis on rubber-cushioned wheels. In New York City and Chicago, all fire departments used Firestone tires on their horse-drawn equipment. By 1904, sales reached nearly a half million dollars, with more than $70,000 in profits. Shareholders could be pleased. But Firestone, whose motto and guiding principle was "Nature is never at rest," was not content. His sales were still less than half those of the bigger Akron rubber manufacturers. Ever looking to expand, Firestone set his sights on the growing automobile industry and a recent invention, inflatable pneumatic tires that used air, instead of solid rubber, to cushion the ride over bumpy roads.[25]

In 1905, Detroit was on the cusp of becoming America's motor town, and Akron's own fortunes would rise and fall concomitantly. In Detroit,

Henry Ford (seated on tractor) and Harvey Firestone on a visit to the Firestone farmstead in August of 1918. Harvey Sr.'s five sons accompany them, with Harvey Jr. standing next to his father, both dressed in ties. (From the Collection of The Henry Ford.)

Michigan's own farm boy and talented machinist, Henry Ford, hastily set out to make a low-cost line of passenger cars that even farmers and workers could afford. When Firestone learned of Ford's plans to introduce the Model N and sell it for about $500, he went to Detroit with his newly designed sidewall pneumatics. Firestone was eager to land a contract with Ford for two thousand sets of tires.

The two had much in common. Both grew up on relatively prosperous farms in the Midwest but shared no love of backbreaking farm work. Both were initially shut out of their respective manufacturing realms by syndicates that controlled key patents. Each portrayed himself as an individualist and an outsider fighting against cartels. Both were adamantly anti-union. Both pursued vertical integration strategies in expanding their companies. And both favored policies that supported the economic independence of the United States.

The bonds they shared deepened into a friendship in the ensuing decades, but it was the bottom line that sold Ford on Firestone's pitch. Firestone promised to undercut by $15 the $70 the G & J Clincher Tire Association charged for a set of tires. Delivering a high-quality product at more affordable prices became a mantra of Firestone and his management team. The approach sometimes meant leaving the company open to legal challenges for patent infringement. Firestone landed the tire contract for the Model N, a car that made Ford in 1907 the number-one automaker in the United States. It was just the beginning of a partnership from which Firestone reaped immense profit. In 1908, Ford released the Model T, the first mass-produced automobile—during its twenty-year production span, more than 15 million were made. Firestone secured a deal for 50 percent of the Model T's original equipment tires. In 1909, Ford's order for Model T tires amounted to more than 10 percent of Firestone's annual production. Six hundred Firestone workers were manually crafting nearly five hundred tires per day.

When the Model T was introduced, the rate at which new cars were being made and sold was doubling almost every other year. Akron had trouble keeping pace with its sister city to meet demand. Identifying and addressing bottlenecks in the manufacturing process was key to any company's success. Each year, contracts with Ford had to be renegotiated. Each year, Firestone faced stiff competition from Goodyear, Goodrich, and Diamond for Ford's business. Each year, he underbid them, sometimes below his own costs. To maintain quality while lowering prices and still preserve a chance for profit, Firestone was forced to follow Ford's lead in automation. In 1908, Firestone hired away Goodrich chemist John Thomas, created a small research laboratory, and began to adopt principles of scientific management. "Is that necessary?" "Can it be simplified?" Such questions tested every step in the production process that transformed crude rubber into the wheels of transportation and commerce.

In its first decade, tire manufacturing was labor intensive. It involved physically demanding jobs—some skilled, some not, but all requiring the brute strength and fortitude of strong men. At both Firestone and Goodyear, prospective workers were required to show their hands in job interviews. Those without calluses, with hands too smooth, were deemed unfit to become gummers, as tire makers were called. In the compounding and milling rooms, workers weighed crude rubber, which came in the early years from the Amazon jungle. Workers added sulfur, lead salts, and other chemicals to the crude rubber. Mills churned, continuously grinding together the rubber and hazardous compounds. Men scooped up the masticated rubber and chemical dust that spilled to the floor and fed it back into the mill's mechanical jaws. Next, calenders—large rolling machines with many cylinders—pressed together the rubber mix and cotton cording to make large sheets of a hybrid admixture produced by nature and machine. Men with large knives, making six cuts per minute, sliced the corded sheet rubber into strips, or plies, with which the tire builders would work. Quotas drove the speed of work in the tire room. Tire builders stretched, smoothed, and layered plies of corded fabric around a rotating drum, gluing them together with volatile coal-tar solvents, such as benzol, before adding on a final layer of tread. Tire builders were among the most skilled of rubber workers and commandeered the highest wages and respect. Before mechanization, the best could make seven or eight medium-size tires per day. Over time, the skin on their hands wore thin and bled easily: bandaged fingers were common among workers in the trade. The most grueling work was in "the Pit," where tires were heated, molded, and cured into their final shape. Factory bosses looked for large men, weighing two hundred pounds or more, who could both do the work and endure the brutal heat, suffocating conditions, and stench of hydrogen sulfide that accompanied this vulcanization process.[26]

To keep pace with Ford, Firestone, like his competitors, sought ways to streamline this craft work. In the first decade of automobile tire manufacturing, the tire-building workplace resembled a nineteenth-century shop floor. But the modern factory of a new era, running on the principles of mass production, was coming. The 1910 opening of Ford's Highland Park plant near Detroit revolutionized manufacturing. There, Ford introduced the moving assembly line and, within three years, reduced the fabrication time of a Model T from 728 to 93 minutes. The price of Ford's most popular car dropped from $825 in 1909 to $525 in 1913. Firestone, after visiting Ford's factory in its opening months, returned to Akron keen on building a tire manufacturing plant modeled on the same principles of efficiency, standardization, and scientific management on display in Highland Park.[27]

Among the Akron tire manufacturers, Firestone was the first to build a modern factory of concrete, steel, and glass. It incorporated many of the features Michigan architect Albert Kahn introduced in his design of Ford's Highland Park plant. To build his state-of-the-art factory, Firestone increased his company's stock capitalization from $500,000 to $4 million. He carefully studied the plant's scale model to ensure it would accommodate the smooth and rapid flow of materials, bodies, and work needed to assemble five thousand tires a day. The sprawling four-story, yellow-brick structure on twenty-three acres of land in south Akron took shape in 1910.

Workers in the open and brightly lit spaces of Firestone's state-of-the-art modern factory, built in South Akron, which began production in 1911. (Goodyear Tire and Company Records, Archival Services, University Libraries, The University of Akron.)

Tilted skylights and large windows brought natural light into the wide-open factory floors of the plant's four wings. A power plant and line of railroad tracks adjacent to the factory reduced energy and transportation costs. Inside, bigger milling and calender equipment and new tire-building machines, which necessitated a subdivision of the labor previously done by one man, rapidly increased production rates. Where machines once aided men, men now supplemented machines. But change comes at a cost.[28]

Firestone liked to think of his company as "a big family."[29] In some respects, it was. In 1912, Harvey owned 41 percent of the company's common stock. When a merger between Goodrich and Diamond that same year sparked speculation that Firestone and Goodyear might consolidate, Firestone made his family intentions clear. "I have five sons who will grow up and take a hand in the company's affairs," the rubber firm's president declared. "I want to have those places prepared for them."[30] Preparing them began at an early age. His eldest son, Harvey Jr., was not yet five years old when he pulled the engine switch that started Firestone's first factory in December of 1902. The company would stay in the continuous control of father and sons for more than seventy years. Harvey Sr. liked to remind himself of the family empire he had built. All of his prized possessions—his Akron estate; his fifteen-bedroom winter getaway on Miami Beach's Millionaires' Row; his prized Kentucky thoroughbred, which he had gifted to President Harding; and his Liberia rubber plantation, established in 1926—were named Harbel. It was a contraction of his name, Harvey, and his wife's, Idabelle. Idabelle, whom he had married in 1895, was a distinguished composer and lover of classical music, but she stayed in the shadows of the family business. So, too, did their daughter, Elizabeth, who would die in 1941 at the age of twenty-six. In his actions toward both employees and family members, Harvey relished his patriarchal role. In 1913, he began hosting an annual outing at the original farm homestead with the plant's superintendents and foremen. A caravan of thirty cars, led by Harvey Sr. and followed just behind by his heir apparent, Harvey Jr., traversed the backroads from Akron to Columbiana. Upon their arrival, a hot chicken dinner awaited the all-male entourage, cooked by Idabelle; Harvey Sr.'s mother, Catherine; and the women of the Ladies' Aid of Grace Reformed Church. Firestone held family loyalty, be it at home or in his company, dear to his heart. He rewarded those who dutifully followed his lead by promoting from within. And he was confident in his resolve that he knew what was best for his children and employees. "I must give as much attention to the building of men of character as to the manufacture of goods," Firestone once declared.[31]

In its first decade of existence, Firestone Tire & Rubber Company recruited workers from the surrounding region. "Our employees were Americans—country folk from the farms of Ohio—the kind of people we knew and had been brought up with," Firestone wrote nostalgically about the company's early years.[32] In 1910, Akron had a population of 69,000: 80 percent white, native-born Americans; 19 percent foreign-born whites, the majority of whom were immigrants from Germany, Hungary, and Austria; and 1 percent Black Americans.[33] Over the next decade, the size and composition of Akron's labor force changed to keep pace with the skyrocketing demand for rubber tires. More and more rubber workers were recruited, from the hills of Kentucky, West Virginia, Tennessee, and other places, to keep up with escalating car ownership, which surged from 1.1 million in 1913 to 8.1 million in 1920.[34] Firestone, always eager for new markets, was also in the vanguard of putting rubber tires on tractors and promoting the "Ship by Truck" movement. By 1920, 1.1 million trucks traveled American roads, a hundredfold increase since 1910.[35] A world at war also helped Akron become the fastest-growing city in the United States. To feed the war machine of the United States and Allied governments, the factories of Goodyear, Goodrich, and Firestone quickly turned out observation balloons, gas masks, boots, raincoats, and tires and tubes for military vehicles. When peacetime returned in 1918, Akron was a bustling city of 208,000 and annually consumed 40 percent of the world's entire supply of raw rubber.[36] Labor shortages, constant turnover, and high wages plagued the company during these boom years, as its workforce swelled to more than thirteen thousand men and women, making more than 4 million tires. Nonetheless, Firestone still performed well, recording $91 million in sales and $9 million in profits in 1919. Firestone's ideal of family togetherness strained at such economies of scale.[37]

The first sign that all was not well in the Firestone family came in 1913. By then, Firestone's new factory was chewing up and spitting out 5 percent of its labor force each day—they quit, were injured, or got fired. Those who survived their initiation into the heat, smell, sweat, and grind of the factory could make up to $6 per day as tire builders and finishers. Such wages surpassed even the $5 per day Ford would pay male workers a year later, a pay rate that would catch American industry by surprise. To further improve efficiency and reduce costs, Firestone hired a time-motion study consultant, Robert P. Holmes, whom suspicious rubber workers called Sherlock. When, on the basis of Holmes's recommendations, the company introduced a piece rate that would limit earnings of builders and finishers to, at most, $3.50 per day, the workers walked out. The Industrial Workers of the World (IWW), founded in Chicago in 1905 and having arrived in Akron in 1912, sprang into action. Bolstered by the speeches, soup kitchens, and organizational efforts of the so-called Wobblies, roughly three-quarters of the city's twenty-two thousand gummers went out on strike. It was the first collective labor action faced by Akron's rubber barons.[38] Firestone took it as a personal offense to his beloved company family. Writing to Harvey Jr., at that time sheltered in an exclusive boarding school in Asheville, North Carolina, the father expressed his dismay at the "demoralized and agitated condition" that Akron was in. "We have about half of our men out of the factory. There is no dissatisfaction among the men or any grievance," he asserted. "But the agitators are here trying to organize them."[39] Firestone laid blame for the strike on outsiders—radical "reds" and socialists hostile to capital—not on wage reductions and working conditions inside the plant.

Akron's rubber companies refused to recognize the IWW local. Within six weeks, the strike dissipated, a consequence of internal IWW politics, confusing demands, frayed worker solidarity, influence from the mainstream labor movement as represented by the American Federation of Labor, and a lack of citizen support. Akron would remain a nonunion town for the next twenty years. But the strike propelled Firestone, following Goodyear's lead, to implement a range of worker benefits—known as welfare capitalism—to better protect their companies from union organization. Firestone began by building Firestone Park, a real estate development in the housing-starved city, which would come to encompass one thousand acres of land near the Firestone plant. When the project's housing sales began in 1916, workers, with a 5 percent down payment, could select from a range of kit homes made by Sears, Roebuck and Company in Tudor Revival, Dutch Colonial, Georgian Revival, and other styles and have the home built on one of 929 lots. Planned by the same New York architects that designed Firestone's Harbel Manor home, Firestone Park featured curved boulevards, green spaces, and an athletic field and clubhouse, along with a library, schools, and churches. Seen from a bird's-eye view, the contours of the neatly arranged community duplicated the company's iconic Firestone shield. To live in Firestone Park was to be a part of the Firestone family. To add to the feeling of belonging, Firestone began offering employees the opportunity to buy into a stock savings plan, which was later made a condition of employment. To further encourage thrift and savings among employees, the company founded the Firestone Park Bank in 1916. Ten years later, the bank held $5 million in worker savings. Harvey Firestone insisted, "We do not believe in paternalism." But company actions spoke otherwise.[40]

Through its worker housing, recreational sports, stock options, savings bank, and English language classes for immigrants, Firestone implemented an aggressive program aimed at assimilating the worker into the company family and into America as a nation. But one group of Akron's residents was excluded from this plan. Firestone Park was a white enclave. Black people were barred from home ownership.[41] During the period of the Great Migration, when African Americans fled the Jim Crow South for better job opportunities in the North, Detroit became a favored destination in the decades from 1910 to 1930. Akron, one of the largest centers of the Ku Klux Klan north of the Mason–Dixon line, was and remained an unwelcoming place. White Southern migrants made up the bulk of the rubber city's labor force, and it was for more than one reason that Akron jokingly became known as the capital of West Virginia.[42] Statistics are revealing. In 1920, 79 percent of Black male workers in Detroit were employed in industrial jobs associated with the automobile industry.[43] That same year, fewer than 700 Black laborers out of a workforce of 74,000 were employed in Akron's rubber factories. The very few Black employees who worked at Firestone, Goodyear, and Goodrich were restricted to the lowest-paid, dirtiest, and heaviest jobs: the handling of bales of crude rubber arriving, increasingly, from Southeast Asia. It was not until 1955, as the American civil rights movement drew widespread national and international attention, that African Americans gained the right to be trained and employed as tire builders in Akron's rubber factories.[44]

Of the roughly six thousand Black residents of Akron in 1920, the majority worked not in the rubber industry but as day laborers or domestic servants, catering to the needs of wealthy industrialists like Firestone. At Harbel Manor, Harvey Jr. and his siblings grew up in a world of white privilege, a world where African American maids were expected to stand erect aside the dinner table, platters in hand, awaiting the beck and call of their employers. Sent as a teenager to Asheville School, in expectation that he would one day assume the company's leadership, Harvey Jr. continued his education in racism and segregation. Active in the school's dramatic society, he was immersed in the boarding school's racist culture, where young men regularly performed in blackface, playing parts that cast African American characters in comedic, infantile, and demeaning roles.[45] At home, at school, and on the factory floor, Harvey Jr. was surrounded by paternalistic and racist attitudes toward Black workers. "We have found the Negro particularly adapted to handling our raw materials," his father remarked.[46] It was the role Black workers occupied in the Firestone family for many years. Confined to cleaning spittoons on the factory floor, laboring in the mill rooms to mix raw rubber with poisonous compounds, or tapping Liberian rubber trees to make latex flow, Black laborers were relegated to service roles in the segregated spaces of the Firestone household, factory, and, beginning in the 1920s, plantations.

"Go it alone."[47] This is the business tenet Firestone gleaned, traveling by automobile on the backroads of America with Thomas Edison and

John Burroughs, Thomas Edison, and Harvey Firestone on a 1916 camping trip.
(From the Collection of The Henry Ford.)

Henry Ford. The legendary camping trips of the three friends, taken over
seven summers between 1916 and 1924, were hardly adventures in "rough-
ing it." The aged naturalist John Burroughs described them as the
"Waldorf-Astoria on wheels." Rolls-Royce touring cars and Packard lim-
ousines furnished with Firestone tires, eating tents equipped with electric
lights, fine riding horses and accompanying grooms, and an entourage of
chefs, maids, butlers, and cameramen became a staple of the caravan as it
grew in size and luxuriousness each year. Esteemed friends, like Burroughs, and movers and shakers in the Republican Party, including fellow
Ohioan Warren Harding, who became the U.S. president in 1921, and his
successor in the White House, Calvin Coolidge, accompanied the wealthy
vagabonds on one or more of their much-publicized vacations. The press
relished the wood chopping contests of the famous men. Crowds lined up
on country roads to catch a glimpse and cheer as the rich and famous passed
by. "With squads of newswriters and platoons of cameramen to report and
film," wrote Ford executive Charles Sorensen, "these well-equipped excursions into readily accessible solitude were as private and secluded as a
Hollywood opening, and Ford appreciated the publicity."[48] So, too, did
Firestone. He may have professed hating the "traveling circus." But the

cavalcade was great advertising: local Ford and Firestone dealers used the group's arrival in town as marketing opportunities.

Whatever publicity stunts these auto-camping trips supported, evening conversations around the campfire inevitably turned to pressing political and business issues of the day. Harvey Firestone Jr. was a frequent companion, often sitting with Edison by the fire long after others had retired for the evening. The Princeton undergraduate, who earned a bachelor of arts degree in 1920, had taken up flying the Curtiss JN-4 "Jenny" biplane as a hobby. In 1918, the young man enlisted in the U.S. Air Service, but never saw active combat. That summer, when more than a million American soldiers were in France, in battle on the Western Front, Harvey Jr. joined his father, Edison, and other friends on a trip that wound its way along the Blue Ridge mountain range, which stretches from its southwestern-most reach near Asheville, North Carolina, up through Virginia's Shenandoah Valley.[49] The war in Europe weighed heavy on the travelers' minds. Harvey Sr. had just turned down a request to serve as rubber "czar," directing the U.S. government's wartime rubber policy. Edison served as chairman of the Naval Consulting Board, helping to advise the U.S. Navy on ideas and innovations to improve military effectiveness. Wartime shortages and government restrictions brought into stark relief how heavily American industry depended on foreign sources of raw materials to sustain production.[50]

Of all the imported commodities essential to American manufacturing, rubber provoked the greatest worry. Firestone and other rubber manufacturers had narrowly escaped a disaster when Great Britain declared war on Germany in August of 1914. Two months later, England banned the exportation of rubber from any British port. At least half the 250,000 American rubber workers found themselves without jobs in December 1914, as manufacturers scrambled to find rubber from non-British sources. Only an act of diplomacy reopened the shipment of crude rubber from Britain's Far East plantations to Akron, at a time when President Woodrow Wilson was determined to keep the United States out of war. An offer by Secretary of State William Jennings Bryan to ban the export of contraband goods produced in the United States to England's enemies eased restrictions. Lingering anxieties about wartime shortages lifted three years later, when the United States joined the Allied fight in April of 1917. Samuel Colt, president of the United States Rubber Company, delighted in Britain's subsequent relaxation of rubber restrictions to American manufacturers as American soldiers joined the fight in Europe. For the first time since 1914, his company was able to import enough crude rubber to entirely meet its needs. "England regards us rightfully as an ally, and is showing her friendship even to the extent of helping our business interests so far as she is able," Colt declared.[51]

Firestone did not share in Colt's trust of British goodwill. He remained wary of the American rubber industry's dependence upon Great Britain for survival, even as the war ended. If he had learned anything from Edison and Ford on his camping trips, it was the importance of self-reliance and self-sufficiency in business affairs. The staunch individualist marveled at Ford's Iron Mountain complex in the Upper Peninsula of Michigan, where the trio toured the massive sawmill, hydroelectric plant, and 313,000 acres of timberland owned and developed by Ford to supply the wood needed for automobile production. "The lesson which I learned," Firestone reflected, "was that a manufacturing operation should be carried through without a stop from the raw material to the finished product, and that no man can be said to control his business unless also he can control his sources."[52]

In the wake of the war, Firestone would turn that lesson into a cause célèbre, cloaking economic independence and self-sufficiency in nationalistic and patriotic fervor as he led the charge against Great Britain's virtual monopoly on the world's rubber supply. It was the Stevenson Restriction Act, enacted by Britain in late 1922, that would rile Firestone, unite Ford and Edison behind him, and set him on a determined quest to find a suitable place to grow rubber under the American flag. The act's architects included Winston Churchill, secretary of state for the British Colonies; a committee led by Sir James Stevenson, the managing head of Johnnie Walker whiskey; and members of the British Rubber Growers' Association. The image of Churchill, the British bulldog, pitted against Firestone, who in size and temperament resembled a terrier breed—small, fearless, and wiry—made for a compelling story. Harvey Jr. boasted afterward on the *Voice of Firestone* radio show that his father single-handedly defended the nation against Churchill, "who . . . was intrigued with . . . how effectively England's monopoly of rubber could be used in extorting tribute from the United States, which was then consuming nearly three-fourths of all rubber produced." But far more actors and forces were at play.[53]

After a flurry of boom years, the American rubber industry faced a calamitous collapse in 1920. Projecting another blockbuster year, American auto and tire manufacturers overreached. Sales plummeted as a wartime economy shifted to a peacetime one. Oversupply of crude rubber sent prices spiraling downward. Firestone's company saw the value of its rubber and fabric stockpiles drop by $35 million from the start of the year, and bank notes were due. Slashing the retail price of tires by 25 percent and eliminating jobs saved the company. Firestone's contract for 65 percent of Ford's original equipment tires also helped. Other Akron manufacturers did not fare as well. Goodyear and Goodrich found themselves heavily indebted to New York banks.[54]

The 1920 slump in the American tire industry sent shock waves across the Atlantic. With American orders shrinking, crude rubber prices tumbled well below the profit margins needed to sustain British planters. The United States occupied a different place on the world stage after the war, commanding significant economic leverage over European nations. European allies owed the United States nearly $11 billion for munitions, foodstuffs, and other goods supplied during the war. The United States had become a major creditor nation and exporter of capital. Sir Frank Nelson, a former British planter, expressed how the economic rise of the United States factored into Britain's decision to implement the Stevenson Act: "There was a miasma of utter gloom and despondency over the whole rubber world, and waiting on the outskirts of that miasmic zone . . . were three or four syndicates with unlimited [American] money behind them of which I had personal knowledge. . . . They were waiting to buy up such plantations as had no alternative except bankruptcy in front of them. It was a question of days, a question almost of hours—until the restriction scheme was approved."[55] At first, Churchill hesitated to support the plea from British planters for government intervention. By the fall of 1922, however, he had come to their side. "One of our principal means of paying our debt to the United States is in the provision of rubber," Churchill explained in a defense of British imperial interests.[56] The Stevenson Restriction Act, signed on November 1, was aimed at stabilizing wildly fluctuating rubber prices. It placed production quotas on British rubber plantations. The limited output was meant to keep rubber prices above 30¢ to 36¢ per pound. Firestone was livid.

He first sounded the alarm at a stockholder's meeting in Akron in December of 1922. The company had rebounded from the 1920–1921 depression. The volume of tires sold increased 23 percent from the previous year. Stocks were up $16 per share, and Firestone had reduced the company's bank debt by $9 million, a nearly 50 percent reduction in just one year. They had weathered the storm, and Firestone was optimistic about the coming year. But, he warned shareholders and the American public, "unless the action taken by England and certain colonial governments relative to production and exportation of crude rubber is rescinded . . . the effects of this uncalled for legislation will be far-reaching." After adoption of the Stevenson Act, the cost of crude rubber had jumped from 15¢ to 37¢ per pound in less than four months. Firestone projected that the crude rubber price hikes would in the upcoming year increase rubber import costs to the United States by $100 million. Such costs would inevitably be passed on to the American consumer. The only way out of this mess, Firestone argued, was for the "United States to pass such legislation as will encourage American capital to develop rubber plantations in the Philippine Islands . . . and negotiate with South American republics to develop production in their rubber regions." Such a move would "make the Philippines one of our most valuable possessions" and ensure a "secure supply" of rubber, Firestone reasoned.[57] A few weeks later, he urged fellow manufacturers to act. Every firm, Firestone insisted, needed to meet an "invading nationalism with a defending nationalism, by informing and arousing American public opinion, and by taking steps to make sure that, in the future, Americans can produce their own rubber."[58]

With his camping companion Warren Harding as president, Firestone had direct access to the Oval Office. The tire mogul wasted no time in mobilizing influential Republican friends in Harding's administration to come to his aid. In early January of 1923, he headed to Washington, DC, to meet with Harding; Secretary of Commerce Herbert Hoover; and Illinois senator Medill McCormick, chair of the Foreign Relations Committee. Among them, Firestone found friendly ears. Rubber had become a weighty concern of U.S. foreign relations. It was the United States' fourth largest import, valued in 1923 at $185 million, representing 72 percent of world production. Only raw silk, sugar, and coffee surpassed it in value.[59] And the automotive industry, a huge driver of the American economy, was wholly reliant upon it. In cabinet meetings, McCormick and Hoover pushed forward Firestone's ideas to break the British stranglehold on the American rubber industry. Some in Harding's cabinet, like Secretary of War John Weeks, favored the cultivation of rubber in American territories, in particular, in the Philippines. McCormick saw advantages to focusing on Central and South America. American-owned rubber plantations would further stimulate trade with Latin America. Furthermore, an American rubber supply located in the Western Hemisphere would offer more protection from supply chain disruptions by hostile navies in the event of war. Both Hoover and McCormick saw merits in Firestone's suggestion of a Department of Commerce survey of suitable rubber-growing sites around the world. McCormick drafted a bill for congressional consideration to fund an extensive investigation of regions around the world suitable for growing rubber free from foreign control. Meanwhile, the arrival of a three-member British Rubber Growers' Association delegation in Washington, DC, in early February enabled Hoover to explore a strategy of using diplomatic pressure to gain assurances from the British government that crude rubber prices would be kept at fair levels. When that failed, Hoover threw his full weight behind Firestone's quest for American rubber independence.[60]

Despite support in Washington, Firestone found himself alone among American rubber manufacturers. The Rubber Association of America dismissed the dire warnings of their former president and, instead, welcomed the British delegation with open arms. The three men representing British planter interests were wined and dined at the home of Goodrich president Bertram G. Work, feted at the Downtown Club of New York City by executives from America's rubber and banking industries, and given a VIP tour of Akron's tire factories. Apart from Firestone, members of the Rubber Association were convinced by the British delegation that the Stevenson Act offered price stabilization and a sure supply of the crude rubber critical to the future success and profitability of the tire industry. The fact that Goodrich, Goodyear, and the United States Rubber Company were also beholden to New York banks, far more than was Firestone, may have prompted the manufacturers' accommodating stance. Lenders, such as National City Bank, looked favorably on any scheme that helped Britain pay off its war debt, even if it might mean higher prices for the American consumer. As far as U.S. banking interests were concerned, Churchill's linking of British loan payments to crude rubber prices held the upper hand over Firestone's concern. Within a few years, the Stevenson Act did indeed result in financial strain for ordinary Americans and profits for the banks to which rubber concerns were indebted. Firestone had been right.

Adhering to Edison's and Ford's lessons on self-reliance, Firestone broke ranks with the Rubber Association of America and struck out alone to oppose the Stevenson Act. In late February, the combative, defiant industrialist organized a two-day gathering of leaders from the automobile, rubber goods, and tire-manufacturing industries, along with government officials, to protest the British monopoly and discuss steps toward action. The Rubber Association of America organized a boycott, wiring its members to stay home. Not one executive from the United States Rubber Company, Goodrich, or Goodyear showed. But nearly two hundred businessmen did come to hear a fiery set of nationalistic speeches advocating American rubber independence. Firestone was able to rally attendees behind his cause. The group issued a resolution to work with rubber manufacturers in Great Britain to urge the repeal of the British rubber restriction. Another resolution endorsed legislation already before Congress that authorized the appropriation of $500,000 both to survey areas around the world suitable for growing plantation rubber and to explore the potential of growing rubber on American-controlled soil. The House of Representatives had approved the appropriation the day before. A few days later, the Senate did too.[61]

Despite Firestone's success in winning over Harding and his cabinet, Firestone failed to garner the support of the Rubber Association of America in either opposing the Stevenson Act or investing American capital to grow rubber on an industrial scale. In fact, the relations between Firestone and the organization he once led became an outright publicity war. In newspaper stories paid for by the Rubber Association, leaders of the American tire industry rebutted Firestone's opinions, questioned the soundness of growing rubber in the Philippines, and assured readers that the British scheme would lead to stability in crude rubber prices. Firestone was furious. He resigned from the organization in early May and took his message directly to the American public.[62] "America should produce its own rubber," splashed the headlines of newspapers across the country in the spring and summer of 1923.[63] Some writers saw companies like Goodrich and Goodyear in the pockets of "Wall Street financiers" and praised Firestone for using "piles of money and lots of nerve" in defending the interests of the American consumer.[64] Others looked optimistically to a time when the plantation growing schemes of Firestone and Ford, with their sights set on the Philippines and South America, would result in "New York or some other American city" becoming "the rubber capital of the world."[65] Draped in the American flag and targeting American citizens where it mattered most—their pocketbooks—Firestone's campaign won over the American public and further endeared his brand to motorists across the country.

With Harding's administration and the American public behind him, and with a $500,000 congressional appropriation for a rubber survey,

Firestone was emboldened by the prospect of securing a sizable amount of land somewhere in the world suitable for growing rubber. With friends in the White House, he was also brazen in his attitude that the U.S. government—by either diplomacy or force—would protect the interests of private capital. In April of 1923, Secretary of Commerce Hoover established a crude rubber division within the Department of Commerce and appointed Dr. Harry N. Whitford as its head. Whitford's appointment revealed how highly Hoover and others in Firestone's inner circle regarded the Philippines as the place to grow rubber under the American flag. As head of the tropical division of the Yale School of Forestry, Whitford had cut his teeth professionally in the Philippines. In 1910, as the United States looked to its newly acquired colonial possession as a source of natural wealth, Whitford conducted an extensive botanical survey of the country's forests, assessing their commercial importance. After Hoover tasked him with advising the U.S. government on crude rubber sources, Whitford led a group of American agents with expertise in forestry, soil science, and economics. They fanned out across the globe. Their travels took them to the rubber region of the Amazon, to Panama, and to Mexico. They journeyed to Ceylon, British Malaya, the Dutch East Indies, and the Philippines in search of climate, soil, land, and labor favorable to growing rubber. Also on their list of prerequisites was a business and political environment hospitable to American interests and needs.[66]

Firestone was not a patient man. Nor did he trust all the experts Whitford was gathering. One, David Figart, was "well known in Far Eastern circles" and had once been friendly to British planter interests. In May, even before Whitford's Commerce Department teams were fully assembled much less dispatched, Firestone put together his own survey teams. He cabled Marion Cheek, his rubber buying agent in Singapore, with instructions to hire the best planting experts he could and venture to the Philippines and Mexico. Both countries, it seemed to Firestone, had growing conditions suitable for rubber and were places persuadable by American capital, along with the threat of military force. Cheek, accompanied by his planting experts, Donald Ross and Samuel Wierman, sailed for the Philippines. There, Firestone's team members were guests of Leonard Wood, the U.S.-appointed governor-general. Wood, a Harvard-trained army surgeon, had fought in the Apache Wars and alongside Theodore Roosevelt in Cuba. Under President Taft, he had been Army chief of staff. His was a career that rode the frontiers of American empire. Wood had written to Firestone, hoping that he "would have some of his people come and look things over." When Cheek, Ross, and Wierman arrived, they explored the archipelago on Wood's yacht, investigating the islands of Luzon, Mindanao, and Basilan. The soil and climatic conditions were ideal, but Philippine laws limited foreign land holdings to 2,500 acres and barred the importation of "coolie" labor, both of which frustrated Firestone's plans. The rubber baron appealed to Wood to use his power as governor-general to help repeal the land laws. But the Jones Act, which granted the Philippine Legislature full authority to set land and immigration laws, curbed Wood's influence. Philippine legislators like Manuel Quezon and Manuel Roxas, defenders of Philippine independence, were right to be suspicious of American capital. A Firestone investment in rubber plantations could give the American government an excuse to delay its withdrawal from the affairs of the Philippine government. Unable to bend the Philippine Legislature to his will, Firestone looked elsewhere to realize his dreams of an American rubber empire.[67]

Prospects in Mexico were no better. Traveling on Firestone's behalf, Elwood Demmon and Samuel Wierman, both of whom had extensive planting experience in the Far East, had to cut short their explorations of rubber-growing conditions in southern Mexico. They got caught in an armed rebellion in the wake of the Mexican Revolution and fled through Guatemala.[68]

With his hopes for both the Philippines and Mexico dashed, Firestone again looked elsewhere, determined to grow rubber free from British control. Donald Ross, at the behest of Firestone, boarded a ship in Liverpool bound for Liberia on December 15, 1923. On January 10, 1924, he had been there just over a week when he cabled Firestone from Monrovia:

Plantation 2000 acres growth and conditions good. Labor ample excellent material wages one shilling daily. Conditions favorable . . . recommend return.[69]

It was the briefest of messages. But it would set in motion a flurry of activities and events that would forever alter the fate of a nation—both its land and people.

# 2

# Reverse Passage

On a warm day in early January of 1924, W.E.B. Du Bois looked out over an abandoned plantation, a forest of more than two hundred thousand rubber trees, in neat rows, on Monrovia's outskirts. The Harvard-trained historian, sociologist, and civil rights activist—one of America's foremost Black intellectuals and leaders—had been sent to Liberia by his president. The trees, covering thirteen hundred acres of what had once been a coffee estate, grew straight, like pillars, with gray-and-white-mottled trunks. About thirty feet in height, the branching treetops made a uniform canopy over the barren ground. Small, white latex-collection cups still hung from wire holders on tree trunks below V-shaped patterns of scars. On the edge of the forest, a few bungalows, two machine sheds, and two houses for smoking rubber were reminders of a once-worked landscape. But the Mount Barclay Plantation was empty of workers and silent. The Liberian Rubber Corporation, a British syndicate led by the British naturalist and explorer Sir Henry Hamilton Johnston, had deserted the farm a few years before. Falling rubber prices and heavy export taxes had contributed to the plantation's demise, but mismanagement deserved most of the blame. Still, the rubber trees, shipped as seeds and seedlings from Ceylon by way of England and planted between 1908 and 1911, were healthy and flourishing. Before its arrival in Liberia, *Hevea brasiliensis* was unknown to Africa, separated from its native Brazil by three thousand miles of ocean. But the plant took well to West African soil and the heat and humidity of Liberia's climate.[1]

Solomon Porter Hood, United States minister and consul general to Liberia, accompanied Du Bois. Hood, a graduate of Lincoln University, the United States' first historically Black college, had written to Firestone six weeks earlier to alert him of the abandoned Mount Barclay Plantation. Liberia had not been in the purview of crude rubber surveys undertaken by the U.S. Department of Commerce in 1923. All eyes, including Firestone's,

Mount Barclay Plantation. Image by Loring Whitman, 1926. (Courtesy of Indiana University Libraries.)

had been focused on the Malay Archipelago, and, in particular, the Philippines. Hood's reports, sent to the U.S. State Department and shared with Firestone, were replete with detailed information on topography, soil, rainfall, temperature, labor, health, transportation, duty fees, exports, and life in Liberia: everything needed to assess the prospects of cultivating rubber in Liberia.[2] The reports came at an opportune time. Unable to bend the Philippine Legislature to his will, and thwarted by revolutionaries in Mexico, Firestone was inclined to act upon Hood's information. Firestone never credited Hood for an idea that would reap great fortunes for the company and his family.

The rubber mogul dispatched Donald Ross, by now a representative of the Firestone Tire & Rubber Company, on a scouting mission to the West African republic. Ross was with Du Bois and Hood as the intense sun of the new year's dry season beat down upon the Mount Barclay Plantation and three men on an informal reconnaissance mission for a place to grow American rubber. Each imagined the world Firestone might build here.[3]

Ross saw one future. Cheap land and labor, combined with a favorable climate and soil, were the right conditions for realizing a rubber plantation in Liberia to rival those in the British Straits Settlements and the Dutch East Indies. An American rubber empire planted on Liberian soil promised to reap immense financial rewards for Firestone Tire & Rubber Company and the white planters, like Ross, the company had set out to employ.

Du Bois and Hood saw a different future. In the struggles and solidarity of African peoples and those of African descent throughout the world, Du Bois and Hood saw in Liberia hope. The West African republic may have occupied only 43,000 square miles on a vast continent of nearly 12 million square miles. But, as one of only two sovereign Black nations in Africa, its symbolic importance was large. Liberia may be poor, observed the editor of *The Crisis*, the journal of the NAACP and one of the most influential magazines of Black politics, life, and culture in America. It may be underdeveloped. But "for a hundred tremendous years," Du Bois informed *Crisis* readers, Liberians "have dared to be free." Liberia's political independence and economic success, bolstered by American capital, would, Du Bois believed, embolden and empower Black self-rule, "democratic development, and decent industrial organization" throughout colonial territories and protectorates across Africa.[4]

Ross, Du Bois, and Hood each had his own motivations and desires in attracting Firestone and American investment to Liberia. This was not the first time in Liberia's history where the interests of white capital and the desire for Black self-determination and freedom had coalesced. Competing motivations and interests lie at the very foundation of a Black settler colony on the West African coast and the eventual establishment of Liberia as an independent, free Black republic.

*Plantation.* It is a word with varied uses and meanings across time. In the early seventeenth century, it meant the establishment or planting of a colony. The original thirteen British colonies of North America began as plantations. They were speculative ventures, made by individual investors and companies, to establish permanent settlements and reap profits from land claimed in the name of the British Crown. In 1628, for example, King Charles I of England granted a Royal Charter to the Massachusetts Bay Colony to establish a "Plantation in Massachusetts Bay" for the settlement of Puritans in the New World. By 1660, all of the thirteen colonies were governed from England by a Board of Trade and Plantations. A plantation, then, originally symbolized an act of colonization. It meant the planting of a settler society in a new land. And it often meant the taking of land, by trade or by force, from its indigenous inhabitants.

A century later, *plantation* had taken on new meanings. The taking of land, the planting of people and crops, and the extraction of surplus value from nature, all inherent in the word's original meaning, carried on. However, by the eighteenth century new forms of the plantation, built upon chattel slavery, were flourishing in the Atlantic world. The plantation was an economic, agricultural, and social system of production, built upon the theft of indigenous land, and now dependent upon the labor of enslaved people imported from Africa to the Americas, driven by brutality and racialized violence. Precursors of the plantation system can be found in the cultivation of sugar in the Mediterranean region during the medieval period, and in its westward expansion to archipelagoes off the coast of Africa—the Madeira, Canary, and Gulf of Guinea islands—by the Portuguese and Spanish in the fifteenth century.[5] The cultivation of cash crops for a global market—sugarcane, cotton, and tobacco—propelled the movement of plants, people, goods, and capital around the world. In its combination of men, machines, disciplined labor, and efficient production, the plantation followed upon and paralleled other commercial systems of production, such as the massive Andean silver mines in Potosí, a vast source of wealth for the Spanish empire.[6] On the plantation and in the mine, land, labor, and capital were organized into extractive and exploitative economies upon which capitalism was built and flourished. The modern factory and its management were forged out of such systems of production and exchange. So, too, were industrial ecologies that reshaped relationships among land, people, non-human beings, and things in the manufacturing of commodities, traded and sold across the globe.[7]

The Civil War may have brought an end to the plantation economy built on slavery in the United States. But the plantation's repercussions could still be seen and felt in Du Bois's time. In *The Souls of Black Folk*, a seminal work on race in America published in 1903, the Atlanta University professor reflected deeply on the violence the South's plantation economy inflicted upon people and the land, and the harrowing racial inequalities that continued to endure in its aftermath. Traveling through rural Georgia, across forlorn, forsaken, and scarred land where cotton was once king, Du Bois wrote of the dark shadow the plantation cast over Dougherty

County. In the heart of the Black Belt, "perhaps the richest slave kingdom the world ever knew," Du Bois wrote of the sharecroppers, tenant farmers, and field laborers that worked the spent soils of the Deep South, beholden to white capital, fettered now by the slavery of debt. Ninety-four percent of farmers in the Black Belt, Du Bois observed, had "struggled for land and failed, and half of them sit in hopeless serfdom."[8] In the wake of Reconstruction, the tightening grip of white power in the South left many Black plantation laborers and sharecroppers caught in a system of spurious debt that deprived them of their land and was used by white planters as a chokehold on their livelihoods.

Across the Atlantic, the plantation may have been an unwelcome memory for Liberia's early nineteenth-century settlers, some who emigrated from the United States and the West Indies to the West African coast by choice, others in exchange for freedom. In their 1847 constitution, these settlers declared Liberia a "home for dispersed and oppressed children of Africa." Liberia prohibited all slavery and traffic in slaves. "None but persons of color" were to be granted citizenship. Only citizens were entitled to own land. These proclamations were assertions of Black independence and self-determination. They stood in defiance of exploitative labor and racialized violence inherent to plantation slavery and the systems of white capital and racial oppression that built the plantation and sustained its iterations. All were assertions of power meant to break free of the shackles of the plantation. The history of Liberia is one intertwined with the history of the plantation in all its forms and meanings.[9]

At the center of that history is land: its promise, its value, its ownership, its use, and its contestations. Liberia, or at least the political idea of it, began with the planting of a colony. In this, Liberia's history resembles earlier histories of plantation settlements such as Plymouth Colony and Massachusetts Bay Colony, settler colonial societies carving out spaces of religious and political freedom in a new land. Yet the colonization of this stretch of the West African coast differed from that of the British colonies in America in at least one important respect. For these settlers, the establishment of a West African colony marked a return to an ancestral home.

The American Colonization Society (ACS), founded in 1816 by Charles Fenton Mercer, a Virginia congressman, and Robert Finley, a Presbyterian minister from New Jersey, pushed forward the need and desire to establish a colony in Africa for America's Black population. The ACS comprised a national group of prominent white politicians, religious leaders, and businessmen, divided in their views regarding slavery, but united in their belief that an African colony for both emancipated slaves and African Americans born into freedom offered the best solution to the perceived threat free Black people posed to a young nation, whose economic fortune was still rising on the sweat, toil, and suffering of enslaved people of African descent. Thomas Jefferson, James Madison, and Henry Clay were among the nation's most prominent statesmen who considered colonization the best way to address the problem of slavery. The gradual emancipation of enslaved Black people in America, and their emigration back to Africa, ACS members argued, would cleanse the United States of the troubling elements and problems that they believed jeopardized the future of a white settler nation. And they cloaked their motivations and desires in patriotic language that paralleled the myths of freedom and colonization upon which the early American republic was founded.

In December 1820, Daniel Webster, ACS vice-president and one of its most prominent statesmen and orators, spoke before a crowd gathered at Plymouth Rock to commemorate the bicentenary of the landing of the *Mayflower*. "The progress of population, improvement, and civilization" had followed the arrival of the Pilgrims at Plymouth Rock and continued unabated in America, Webster eulogized. Webster's sermon on settler colonialism ignored the taking of land, the genocide of North America's indigenous peoples, and the capture, transport, and sale of millions of enslaved Africans upon which a "civilized" nation was built.[10]

A similar story of colonization, civilization, and progress had begun to unfold in the mythmaking of the ACS earlier that year. On a cold February day, the ship *Elizabeth* left the icy waters of New York City's harbor to sail for the west coast of Africa. Aboard were eighty-six free Black people from America destined for a new home. Dubbed the "Mayflower of Liberia," the *Elizabeth* was accompanied by a U.S. Navy war sloop, the USS *Cyane*, which patrolled West Africa's coastal waters. Private capital from ACS members supported early colonization efforts, as did $100,000 appropriated by an 1819 act of Congress to support the resettlement of Africans captured on ships intercepted by the U.S. Navy for trafficking slaves. Federal law had banned the importation of slaves into the United States beginning in 1808.

For almost two years, *Elizabeth*'s passengers waited, first on Sherbro Island, and then in the Fourah Bay section of Freetown in the British colony of Sierra Leone, for land to be secured farther down the West African coast where America's free Black émigrés and intercepted enslaved Africans could build a new colony. Tensions mounted between settlers and the white agents who, representing the interests of the U.S. government and the ACS, sought to command them. The desires of the ACS and those of the colonists seeking liberty and self-determination were hardly one and the same. A dozen settlers died of disease. In 1821, a second ship, the *Nautilus*, arrived at Freetown carrying needed supplies and new settler recruits. In April 1822, with land secured, passengers from the *Elizabeth* and *Nautilus* established a permanent settlement on Cape Mesurado, a rocky promontory surrounded by mangrove swamps on the Grain Coast, also known as the Pepper Coast, of West Africa. In honor of U.S. president James Monroe, who had authorized federal support for the colony's establishment, the settlers named the coastal town Monrovia.[11]

White ACS members imagined a renewal on African shores of the drama of colonization that had unfolded in New England two centuries before. But what sort of colony was this to be? Did the planting of a colony on distant shores represent an early foray into the overseas expansion of the United States as a settler empire?[12] Or was the venture to be instead a reproduction of Thomas Jefferson's "empire for liberty," wherein African Americans could build a republic independent of the United States on Africa's shores? This was a question debated by ACS proponents and members of Congress in the early years of the colony's founding. Ultimately, Daniel Webster, as secretary of state, settled the matter in 1843 when he answered Britain's query as to whether a settlement founded, administered, and largely financed by private American citizens, but protected by the American military, constituted a formal colony of the United States. No, was the answer.[13] Liberia was neither a formal colony of the United States nor entitled to the protections of the U.S. government, beyond military support in subduing the slave trade in its coastal waters. Four years later, this fragile settler society declared independence from the United States to become the free Republic of Liberia.

The area claimed by the ACS, however, hardly constituted unoccupied land. Many ethnic groups—Bassa, Dei, Gola, Dan, Kpelle, Kru, Mano, and Vai, among others—lived in the region, having migrated from Africa's interior along trade routes that crossed savanna and rainforest to reach the sea, while enabling movement of salt, kola nuts, and other goods.[14] By the fifteenth century, if not before, the coast and interior of what would become Liberia were already occupied by people of Mel, Mande, and Kwa language groups. When settlers from America arrived in 1822 seeking a new home, they brought with them a Western system of private property ownership alien to the customary practices and cultural beliefs of the area's indigenous inhabitants. To "sell" or "buy" land was not a widely held West African concept. Chiefs were the custodians, not the owners, of the land. Among Liberia's indigenous communities, conflicts over land, particularly territorial borders, were not uncommon. At the same time, communities considered land to be held in common; it belonged to the living, to ancestors long since dead, and to those yet to be born.

The mission of securing land for colonization and settlement led to confusion, misunderstanding, and conflict. The original land treaty for Cape Mesurado was negotiated with King Peter, a chief and spokesman for Dei leaders, who controlled the coastal territory where white U.S. government and ACS agents sought to establish a colony by trade and force. With his naval warship, the USS *Alligator*, anchored offshore, Lieutenant Robert Field Stockton, along with ACS agent and physician Eli Ayers, grew increasingly frustrated by what appeared to them obfuscations and reversals on the part of King Peter in securing a deal. Believing he was being taken for a fool, Stockton, who earned a reputation combating pirates and slave traders on the Atlantic, supposedly put a pistol to King Peter's head and demanded he "make a book," as he had promised, to give them land. The account may reflect the bravado and conquest of Stockton's naval adventures rather than actual events. Nevertheless, King Peter and five other chiefs put their marks on a document granting Dozoa Island, just off Cape Mesurado, and a section of the mainland to Stockton and Ayers in exchange for an estimated $300 worth of sundry goods, including muskets, gunpowder, iron bars, tobacco, calico, and rum. The settlers renamed their home Providence Island. But the treaty was short-lived. Plundering raids and skirmishes ensued as hostile feelings grew among the Dei people. A Mandingo leader of the Condo confederation, a powerful alliance of indigenous ethnic groups, intervened on the settlers' behalf. Perhaps Sao Boso, also known as King Boatswain, saw supporting the colony as strategic, useful for solidifying control of critical trade routes between the coast and the interior Condo stronghold in Bopolu, about sixty miles north. He was not, however, able to protect the colonists for long.[15] In November 1822, less than seven months after the colonists took possession of Cape Mesurado, the Dei people attacked the colony's fort. Thirty-five settlers, armed with muskets and a single cannon, managed to keep the warriors at bay for three weeks, before men aboard the British schooner *Prince Regent* heard the cannon fire and came to the colonists' defense. A peace settlement was reached. The first land conflict between settler and indigenous had ended, but it would not be the last as emigrants from America and later the Caribbean attempted to carve out a place of freedom and bring Christianity, civilization, and commerce to a newfound home on the African continent.[16]

Many free African Americans adamantly opposed the project of Black colonization, which championed their removal from the United States, as an affront to their rightful place as birthright U.S. citizens.[17] Few chose to uproot their lives to resettle on a distant shore that had never been their home. Roughly eleven thousand emigrants came to Liberia between 1822 and the start of the Civil War in 1860. Approximately four thousand were free people. Another seven thousand were emancipated slaves, set free by plantation masters on condition of their leaving the United States. The costs were high. More than 25 percent of settlers died within two years after arrival. Most died from "fever," likely malaria.[18] If a settler was alive after two years, prospects for survival markedly improved. The largest number of settlers came from slave states: before the Civil War, nearly 40 percent of emigrants arrived from Virginia and Maryland alone. Northern states accounted for less than 8 percent of settlers. But with the passage of the 1850 Fugitive Slave Act, which imposed federal fines on law enforcement officials and citizens in all states who failed to aid in the return of runaway slaves, and with an 1857 U.S. Supreme Court decision that excluded people of African descent from any legal claims to citizenship, the prospect of leaving the United States for Africa became more palatable, even among free Black people in the North.[19]

Stay in America, where your educational and economic opportunities, even your rights as a citizen, would be limited because of your skin color? Or leave your home and kin for freedom and opportunity, living, as your ancestors had, in Africa? These difficult choices confronted free Black people in antebellum America. Augustus Washington was one. The first in his family born into freedom, Washington built a successful daguerreotype business in Hartford, Connecticut, in the 1840s. Active in abolitionist circles in New York and New Jersey, he published in 1841, at the age of twenty-one, a letter in the *Colored American Magazine* that was critical of the ACS. However, over time his views changed. At Dartmouth, where he was the only African American student, he spoke in favor of "a

separate State for colored Americans." It was not "a choice, but . . . a necessity." "Better for our manhood and intellect to be freemen by ourselves,"
the young man wrote, "than political slaves with our oppressors." The
Mexican-American War thwarted the efforts of Washington and his fel-
lows "of superior talent and ability" to secure a tract of land in Mexico. By
1851, one year after the passage of the Fugitive Slave Act, Washington
grew increasingly fearful of the "tide [of] oppression rolling over us." With
his newborn son's future on his mind, he warmed to the promise Liberia
offered.[20]

Washington argued that African Americans would never, under "our
present social and political disabilities," be in a position "to prove to the
world the moral and intellectual equality of the African and their descendants." Excluded "from the most honorable and lucrative pursuits of industry," African Americans had neither government nor institutions of
higher learning nor capital on their side. Full citizenship required that a
citizen be allowed to approach "every avenue to wealth and respectability."
Washington was not enslaved, but he did not feel free.[21]

Earlier in America's history, an oppressed and persecuted people found
freedom in a new land. Calling up the "forgotten history of Plymouth
Rock and Jamestown," Washington urged his skeptical readers to consider
how "this powerful Republic, by her oppression and injustice to one class
of . . . people, will plant in Africa a religion and morality more pure, and
liberty more universal, than it has yet been the lot of my people to enjoy."
Liberia beckoned. In 1853, Washington packed up what he could of his
Hartford business, gathered $500 in cash, and, with his wife, Cordelia, and
their two young children, left to begin a new life in Monrovia.[22]

Washington soon found in Liberia the "style of ease, comfort, and independence" he had sought in America. During the dry season, he was making from $20 to $40 per day at his daguerreotype studio, catering to
Monrovia's elite settler class of merchants and legislators. For colonists
who came to Liberia with capital, mercantile trade could provide an avenue to wealth and power. In the 1850s, the country boasted a merchant
fleet of twenty Liberian-owned vessels. These merchant ships plied Liberia's shallow coastal waters and estuaries, delivering imported goods and
procuring palm oil, camwood, and other prized export commodities at
trading posts and towns. In Monrovia, Liberia's natural wealth was
loaded onto English and German ships anchored offshore, destined for
overseas markets. Washington frowned upon the settlers' sole reliance on

trade. It had made some rich. But many in Monrovia were petty traders, living, in his view, "from hand to mouth."[23]

Many members of Liberia's planter-merchant class had established farms along the St. Paul River, twenty miles northwest of Monrovia. Like his peers, Washington saw agriculture as the future of Liberia's wealth. Without producers, Washington feared, the country would "struggle on . . . in poverty, till it meets with some reverse, and falls as a colony into the hands of some European power."[24] A decade after coming to Liberia, he proudly proclaimed he was "at least six thousand dollars better off than I ever was in the United States."[25] Washington was a man with "scores of irons in the fire," observed his friend, Edward Blyden, after visiting the émigré's thousand-acre farm, "Deerford," in 1873.[26] Washington, as editor and publisher of the *New Era* newspaper, speaker of the House of Representatives, and a judge and senator, had amassed significant wealth and respectability. Having invested his photography profits in plantation agriculture, Washington made part of his fortune when the global market boomed in Liberian sugarcane and coffee. By the late 1860s, after the U.S. Civil War left the South's sugarcane plantations in ruins, Washington was shipping more than "one hundred thousand pounds of sugar, and a proportionate share of syrup and molasses" to Europe and America.[27] On his farm, he oversaw a labor force of fifty workers. All were paid field hands. Most were "Congo," Africans captured by the U.S. Navy from intercepted slave ships, who often became wards in settler households. Others were poor immigrants. A smaller number were indigenous—perhaps Gola or Kpelle—who possessed valuable knowledge about growing crops in Liberia's climate and soils. Indigenous and settler cultures intermixed in these changing agricultural landscapes. Washington took delight knowing that for British officers and soldiers who bought his syrup, it was likely "the first time they have used free labor sugar."[28]

Enterprising Liberian farmers—both settler and indigenous—also grew prosperous transforming Liberian coffee, *Coffea liberica*, from a forest plant into an agricultural commodity. Growing demand for the beverage in the United States and Europe, and aggressive marketing of the Liberian product by ACS agents at international fairs and exhibitions, established a niche market for Liberian coffee in the 1870s and 1880s. At its peak in 1878, some Liberian farms were exporting as much as eighteen thousand pounds of coffee per year, for which they earned 24¢ per pound. Liberian planters also shipped coffee seeds and seedlings across the world, where the plant flourished as a plantation crop in the Dutch East Indies.[29] In little more than a decade after Liberian independence, Washington could boast that "Liberia has not yet any foreign debt." When Washington died in 1875, the economic future of the country looked bright.[30]

Then the market for Liberian commodities collapsed. Global prices for palm oil plummeted in the 1870s as industrial-age petroleum replaced palm oil as a base for lubricant. Prices for camwood, prized as a source of red dye, fell with the use of synthetic aniline dyes. By the 1890s, small Liberian producers could no longer compete with large American syndicates and monopolies that controlled Cuba's sugarcane plantation economy. Once-prosperous Liberian sugarcane farms were reclaimed by the forest. Neither could Liberian coffee farmers keep pace with the global demand for and skyrocketing plantation production in Brazil of the now-preferred *Coffea arabica*.[31]

Liberia's economy was caught in a maelstrom of economic, ecological, and political forces beyond its control. The economic collapse, coupled with the scramble by European powers for control of Africa, jeopardized Liberia's sovereignty and Black self-rule. By the early 1900s, the Liberian government found itself in a vicious cycle of debt upon debt, financially beholden to Great Britain, and forced to trade concessions for land and labor in exchange for needed capital. The Mount Barclay Plantation concession that Du Bois visited was itself wrapped up in a 1906 loan to the Liberian government, $500,000 at an interest rate of 6 percent, from the Liberian Development Corporation, another British syndicate run by Sir Henry Hamilton Johnston. Desperate for money to discharge debts to Great Britain, Liberia paid dearly, allowing the British oversight of its customs revenues, its military—the Liberian Frontier Force, commanded by British officers—and access to its natural resources. Liberia was on the brink of becoming a financial protectorate, if not an outright protectorate, of the British empire.[32] It was the nightmare Washington had warned of and most feared: to be swallowed up in abject poverty by a foreign power. Political sovereignty as an independent Black nation meant little without economic independence from white control.

Throughout the nineteenth century, the United States government took a back seat to the private interests of the ACS in the affairs of Liberia. Fifteen years after Liberia claimed independence, a U.S. president, Abraham Lincoln, acknowledged its diplomatic status as a sovereign nation.

Britain's increasing economic grip on the nation, however, and the advocacy of Booker T. Washington on the nation's behalf, brought Liberia increasingly into the fold of American foreign policy under the administrations of President Theodore Roosevelt and his successor in 1909, William Howard Taft.

Central and South America, not West Africa, had been the object of Roosevelt's imperial ambitions in the Western Hemisphere. His "big stick" policy, also known as the Roosevelt Corollary to the Monroe Doctrine, asserted the right of the United States to exercise its international police power and intervene in the affairs of nations threatened by economic and political instability. It would be used as justification for American occupation of Cuba, Nicaragua, Haiti, and the Dominican Republic in the ensuing years. At roughly 10 degrees west of the prime meridian, Liberia fell under the purview of America's self-proclaimed police protectorate. But it took convincing for Roosevelt and Secretary of War Taft to entertain exercising American might on a continent carved up by European imperial powers.

Booker T. Washington, who held considerable sway over the Black Republican vote, wrote to Roosevelt in September 1907, alerting him to "information from reliable sources that both France and England are seeking to take large parts of the Liberian territory." "I am sure you will prevent this, if it can be done," he urged.[33] In June 1908, a delegation led by Liberian vice-president James Jenkins Dossen arrived in the United States seeking "moral assistance and international influence" to counter British and French territorial encroachment. Washington came to the nation's capital from his Tuskegee Institute headquarters in Alabama to personally arrange meetings with Roosevelt, Taft, and other members of the president's cabinet. The celebrated author of *Up from Slavery* presided over a public reception for the Liberian envoys at a meeting of the local chapter of the National Negro Business League, where an overflow crowd had gathered at the Lincoln Temple Congregational Church. Speaking of Liberia's commercial, agricultural, and industrial prospects, and affirming the mutual benefits to accrue from American capital investment in developing Liberia's agricultural commodities, Washington called for a "closer union between the United States and Liberia."[34]

As the U.S. State Department grew increasingly alarmed about Britain's intentions in Liberia, incoming president Taft sought Washington's counsel. A plan was laid. In April 1909, Taft sent an American commission to Liberia to assess the crisis. Emmett Scott, Washington's private secretary, was among the three-member team. It was a fact-finding mission, but with an appropriate display of U.S. military force. Two scout cruisers, the *Chester* and the *Birmingham*, accompanied the delegation to Monrovia, where they fired a twenty-one-gun salute and sat watch offshore. The commission reported back with justifiable concerns that Liberia was in peril. Without "the support of some power commensurate in strength with Great Britain or France, she will as an independent power speedily disappear from the map," the Americans observed. They also enthused about the country's untapped "stores of wealth" awaiting to be developed.[35] "Money, men, and a settled boundary" were needed if Liberia was to be saved, remarked Ernest Lyon, U.S. minister plenipotentiary to Liberia, later that year at a banquet that was "billed as one of the greatest events in the history of the colored race" by the *Washington Bee*. Here, Booker T. Washington, Ernest Lyon, Emmett Scott, and other African Americans with "national reputations" from almost "every profession" and "every walk of life" had gathered to speak on behalf of their solidarity with Liberia's struggle and lend their "moral influence to secure the integrity and independence of its territory."[36]

What Liberia most needed, Lyon noted, was capital. Lots of it. And, in 1909, that was largely in the hands of white institutions. The Taft administration eventually brokered a deal in 1912 for a $1.7 million loan at 5 percent interest over forty years that would retire Liberia's foreign debt. The monies came from a conglomerate of U.S. and foreign banking houses and institutions: J.P. Morgan & Co., Kuhn, Loeb & Co., and National City Bank in the United States; Robert Fleming & Co. in England; and M.M. Warburg & Co. in Germany, among others. In exchange, Liberia ceded financial control of its customs revenues to foreign hands. A general receiver, appointed by the U.S. president, was granted authority to oversee the country's finances, with assistance from three receivers appointed by France, Germany, and Great Britain. Through the dollar diplomacy embodied in President Taft's new foreign policy motto, "Substituting dollars for bullets," the U.S. government was assured a place in the affairs of Liberia. American influence also extended to Liberia's military. Training and leadership of the Liberian Frontier Force came under U.S. control and the command of Captain Charles Young, a West Point graduate and distinguished commissioned officer in the U.S. Army's Ninth Cavalry Regiment, one of the Black units that fought against Native Americans in the West and served in Cuba and the Philippines during the Spanish-American War. Young was also a lifelong friend of W.E.B. Du Bois.[37]

Through the influence of African American leaders like Booker T. Washington, a struggling Liberia had garnered the economic, military, and political support of the U.S. government. But Washington, whose "Tuskegee Machine," as Du Bois called it, included a network of newspapers and magazines inclined to promote his views, warned that the 1912 loan was only a stop-gap measure. Writing to the editor of Monrovia's *Liberian Register*, Washington, who in the 1880s had transformed a former plantation into an agricultural and industrial school to further Black economic advancement, offered his well-practiced advice to Liberia. Its leaders needed to develop "scientific, technical, and industrial" expertise that would enable the country to "understand and master" its natural resources. As a former slave, educator, and businessman, Washington had been witness to the boom and bust of the South's plantation economy and the ways that white capital, through instruments of credit, debt, and foreclosure, continued a system of racial oppression long after slavery ended. Only through economic empowerment, through the generation of Black capital from the land, he argued, could Liberia's independence and sovereignty be maintained.[38]

This was the Liberia into which Du Bois arrived in December 1923. He had been sent as the personal representative of President Calvin Coolidge to honor the second inauguration of Charles Dunbar Burgess King, seventeenth president of Liberia. Du Bois, officially the envoy extraordinary and minister plenipotentiary to Liberia, considered the trip one of the greatest occasions of his life.[39] Never before had the United States sent a diplomat with such a high rank to Africa. It was a symbolic gesture, but not devoid of incentive. In 1922, the U.S. Congress failed to pass a $5 million dollar loan to Liberia. The economic consequences of the 1914–18 World War, during which Liberia had pledged support to Allied Powers, were disastrous for the African republic. Germany had been one of the country's most significant trading partners, with the German-owned Deutsche-Liberia Bank controlling Liberia's banking industry. When Liberia severed ties with Germany, trade revenues plummeted, the Deutsche-Liberia Bank dissolved, and the Bank of British West Africa swooped in. Beset anew by foreign debt and its borders threatened by France and Great Britain, the

W.E.B. Du Bois, Atlanta University, 1909. (W.E.B. Du Bois Papers (MS 312),
Special Collections and University Archives, University of Massachusetts Amherst
Libraries.)

Liberian government had looked again to the United States for much-
needed capital and protection.[40]

The First World War had stalled efforts to advance American business
interests, and, thereby, American influence, in Liberia. When the U.S.
Congress failed in 1922 to deliver on the loan proposal, State Department
officials worried that plans to secure a place for the United States in Africa
had been dashed. A decade earlier, George Finch, secretary of the American Commission to Liberia, warned that in "the rapidly approaching time
when the continent of Africa will have come into its own in the world's
commerce and politics, the little sphere of influence at and round Monrovia will be the only door through which American enterprise will have a
chance to enter."[41]

Leaders among the African American community likewise feared
what the failed loan proposal meant for Liberia's future. In January 1923,
Du Bois contacted Secretary of State Charles Hughes expressing alarm
at the lack of American financial support for Liberia. British banking in-

terests were watching, threatening to make the country a British protectorate.[42] When Du Bois wrote Hughes, he did so as an Executive Board member of the Pan-African Congress, a gathering of leading intellectuals and political activists from Europe, North America, and Africa. Members of the organization, which met periodically between 1900 and 1945, were united in their opposition to colonialism and the exploitation and oppression of people of African descent across the globe. Liberia's independence had become a cause among supporters of the Pan-African movement in the 1920s. Solidarity with the struggling Black republic was also foremost in William Lewis's mind when he wrote his former Amherst classmate, President Calvin Coolidge, recommending Du Bois as the president's special representative to King's inauguration. A graduate of Harvard Law School, Lewis had served under both the Roosevelt and Taft administrations and was the first African American to hold the post of U.S. assistant attorney general. In sending Du Bois to Liberia, Lewis advised, the president would be showing the country's leaders that despite the "failure of the five million dollar loan in the Congress," the U.S. government still "continues to maintain a kindly and friendly interest in that Republic."[43]

On a December afternoon in 1923, the envoy extraordinary and minister plenipotentiary to Liberia first beheld Africa. Looking across the water from the deck of the German freighter *Henner*, Du Bois saw Liberia's Cape Mount in the distance. Once a supply post for British, Dutch, French, American, and Portuguese traders, Cape Mount had also been one of the largest slave ports on Africa's Windward Coast in the latter years of the Atlantic slave trade.[44] By evening, the freighter, with Du Bois and just five other passengers aboard, dropped anchor. Four degrees north of the equator, the constellations appeared twisted to the New Englander far from home, while the twinkling lights of Monrovia pierced through the dark night. Five wooden boats, propelled by the muscles and song of Kru oarsmen, arrived out of the dark shadows and glided up alongside the ship. On one of the boats was Captain Moody Staten, who followed in Young's footsteps as U.S. commander of the Liberian Frontier Force, dressed in the official brown khaki uniform of the Liberian military. The officer boarded the *Henner* to greet his fellow American. Moody had served in a segregated Black regiment on the Western Front during World War I and was on assignment in Liberia to help organize and discipline the country's military. At the request of President King, Moody would serve as special attaché to Du Bois in Liberia.[45]

A view of Monrovia that greeted W.E.B. Du Bois upon his arrival. Image by Loring Whitman, 1926. (Courtesy of Indiana University Libraries.)

How familiar and yet strange were the sights and sounds that greeted Du Bois! The Liberian flag flew at the stern of the long boat that carried him to shore. Its design—eleven horizontal red and white stripes with a blue rectangle bearing a lone white star in the canton—was reminiscent of the flag of the United States, a place that had been home, albeit an uncomfortable and oppressive one, to many of Liberia's early colonists. Monrovia's architecture reflected characteristics of that of the American South. Music emanating on Christmas Eve from Monrovia's streets bore striking resemblance to the mission revival hymns Du Bois had heard as a student in Nashville almost forty years before. In the rhythms, cadences, and harmonies, Du Bois heard the sounds of cultural traditions rooted in both Africa and America.[46] In Liberia, where so many strands of the African diaspora—threads woven through West Africa, the Caribbean, and the United States—came together on the promise of freedom from racial hostility, Du Bois found a place to guide his evolving Pan-African vision.

Du Bois delighted in the formal ceremonies, decorum, and intellectual conversations Liberia's ruling elite afforded. President King had spared no expense. A company of Frontier Force soldiers, sporting red fezzes and carrying Krag and Peabody rifles, escorted the envoy extraordinary down Ashmun Street in central Monrovia to the Executive Mansion. There,

A home in Monrovia, incorporating architectural styles of the American South, from which many of Liberia's early settlers came. Image by Loring Whitman, 1926. (Courtesy of Indiana University Libraries.)

The Executive Mansion on Ashmun Street. Image by Loring Whitman, 1926. (Courtesy of Indiana University Libraries.)

Du Bois first met the Liberian head of state. At King's inauguration, Du Bois was a guest of honor. The pomp and circumstance of the president's procession impressed Du Bois: a spectacle of top hats, topcoats, military dress, and floating arches in different hues carried by flower girls dressed in white.

Du Bois's sojourn into the interior—with all the trappings of a colonial African safari, including pith helmets, hammock-carrying porters, and men with guns on alert for leopards prowling the dark jungle night—also left an impression. In the hinterland, Du Bois reveled in the simplicity and elegance of African village life.[47]

In his four-week stay, Du Bois had seen enough to counsel President King and advise the U.S. government on a path forward. "Liberia can become a great, rich, and successful self-ruling black democracy," he told U.S. secretary of state Hughes. But it needed foreign capital and experts—in anthropology, business, economics, education, and public health—to aid Liberia in achieving its destiny. First and foremost, he argued, wherever possible, such experts should be "colored American citizens." "Nothing would go further to reassure the colored peoples of Africa, Asia, and all America, . . . than to see the United States in her attitude toward a struggling, but promising Negro Republic, eschewing the temptation of conquest, domination, and profit making and seeking to be a guide, friend, and protector," Du Bois maintained.[48]

Du Bois's call for a "Talented Tenth" of educated Black Americans to journey to Liberia and help lift it up as a nation echoed the ideas of Edward Blyden, a founder of Pan-Africanism.[49] Born free into the slaveholding plantation society of St. Thomas, once a sugarcane center of the Danish colonial empire, Blyden grew up with parents who taught him of his African heritage. They were of the Igbo people, an ethnic group in what is now southeastern Nigeria. When Blyden was unable to gain entrance to a U.S. theological college, he became appalled by the treatment and plight of Black people in America. In 1851, at the age of nineteen, he emigrated alone to Liberia under the auspices of the New York Colonization Society. He enrolled as a student in Monrovia's Alexander High School, run by the Presbyterian Missionary Board. A quick study, he had a particular gift for linguistics. Over the course of his life, he mastered Arabic, Hebrew, Spanish, and dozens of African languages. In 1858, he was appointed head of the school. Three years later, he became Professor of Greek and Latin at Monrovia's Liberia College (now University of Liberia). Blyden believed that an "African nationality" could be forged from the fledgling republic of Liberia. Without "some great center of the race where our physical, pecuniary, and intellectual strength may be collected," Africans and their descendants throughout the Atlantic world would never be granted the respect and dignity owed to them, he held. Traveling along America's eastern seaboard in the summer of 1862, while the American Civil War divided and tore the nation, Blyden preached to African American congregations that their future lay not in America, but in Africa. Providence, proclaimed Blyden, called the descendants of Africa in America to return to the land of their ancestors to help build a Black nation that would rival those of their white oppressors. This was Liberia's offering.[50]

Blyden's Pan-African vision was born out of a civilizing mission, one in which people of the African diaspora would "uplift Africa" through Christianity, commerce, and civilization. Enterprising, educated, and pious African Americans had a spiritual obligation and moral duty to return to the land of their forefathers. They alone could "roll back the appalling cloud of ignorance and superstition," which Blyden believed held back the people of the African continent.[51] On its own, Blyden argued, Africa could not rise. Its prosperous future, its salvation, he believed, awaited the return of its descendants, "who having learned the arts of civilization will introduce them."[52] The "future material welfare and moral progress" of Liberia also depended, Blyden argued, on the "extraneous help" of Anglo-Saxon nations. Reflecting, perhaps, his West Indian roots, as well as the ascendancy of Arthur Barclay, an immigrant from Barbados, to the Liberian presidency, Blyden, in 1908, suggested that Great Britain, not America, was a more well-intentioned partner in the "economic development of the country."[53]

What place did Liberia's indigenous inhabitants occupy in this vision? "Without the aborigines in our domestic, social, religious, and political life, there is nothing before this State but death," Blyden prophesied. He had, over the course of his life, come to understand and appreciate how central the livelihoods of Liberia's indigenous peoples were to the success of the country. For Liberia to thrive as "one great, strong, populous [and] prosperous African State," it needed its settler population to "coalesce with the aborigines like kindred drops of water . . . incorporating and being incorporated by them." A merged African identity, Blyden believed, would arise through the intermixture of Western and African values. He

Edward Blyden. Published by Dalton and Lucy, Booksellers to the Queen, 28, Cockspur Street, S.W. London, between 1866 and 1900. (Courtesy of Library of Congress, LC-USZ62-135638.)

championed Liberia, not as a little America in Africa, but as an aspiring African nation, whose future depended upon the study and embrace of African religious, social, and industrial systems, such as "the collective ownership of land," by Liberia's settler population as they sought to govern and guide the future course of the country.[54]

In the decades after Blyden's call for people of African descent to return to, redeem, and rehabilitate the land of their ancestors, traces of his Pan-Africanist vision surfaced in Du Bois's recommendations for Liberia. Those in the African diaspora, Du Bois argued—in particular, African American experts—needed to come to Liberia's aid to help achieve its promise as an aspiring Black nation on a continent controlled and governed by European imperial powers. Liberia also needed capital to place it on a solid economic foundation. To where should the country turn? Nationalistic interests seeped into Pan-African visions as Du Bois urged Li-

Liberian President Charles D.B. King, circa 1919. (Courtesy of Library of Congress, LC-USZ62-114796.)

beria to look toward America, not Europe, as Blyden had once suggested, in her hour of need.[55]

Hood agreed with Du Bois's view. "Liberia would be redeemed and put on its feet through the agency of the black man," the U.S. minister to Liberia argued.[56] Hood, a missionary in Haiti before taking up his Liberia post in 1922, firmly believed in Liberia's future. President King, in his 1924 inaugural address before the crowd gathered at Government Square, affirmed Liberia was "a Republic founded by Black Men, maintained by Black Men, and which holds out the highest hopes and aspirations for Black Men."[57] Seated by his side, Hood and Du Bois concurred. Liberia had the resources: untold mineral wealth; commodities, including palm oil, coffee, camwood, and rubber; and an abundant supply of labor. What was needed and awaited was "some force strong enough to develop them."[58]

A force, a source of investment capital, was needed to harness industry and science to transform nature's bounty into an engine of growth and

development. This force should do so without leading to a path of conquest and exploitation. Du Bois imagined a company, small at first, financed and run by African Americans, that would supply Liberia with
technical experts to develop the country's natural resources and facilitate
commerce and trade. Hood thought his friend failed to grasp the scale
and urgency of the problem facing Liberia. Five million dollars in capital
would be needed, preferably from Black financiers in the U.S. Moreover,
Hood insisted, the investors must be a "class of men" such that their "names
are absolutely free from any connection" to a man and a movement the two
friends looked upon with skepticism: Marcus Garvey and his Universal
Negro Improvement Association (UNIA).[59]

From his UNIA headquarters in Harlem, Marcus Garvey, a Jamaican-
born journalist and publisher, had been building a Black separatist Pan-
African movement increasingly at odds with the elite, integrationist ideals
espoused by Du Bois and the NAACP. By the 1920s, the *Negro World*, the
official organ of the UNIA, reached a readership of two hundred thousand,
rivaling that of *The Crisis*. Garvey boasted a following of more than 3 million
UNIA members across the globe, although Du Bois would dispute the
claim. Garvey caused an international stir in 1919 when he announced
the incorporation of the Black Star Line, a shipping company and business
venture meant to fulfill his dream of creating a Black Zion in Africa.
Within three months, the company had raised sufficient stock to purchase
a crumbling thirty-year-old passenger and cargo ship, the SS *Yarmouth*,
which was rechristened as the SS *Frederick Douglass*. With an all-Black
crew, the ship was commissioned to transport goods and people throughout
the Black Atlantic.

Garvey, while working as a timekeeper on a large banana plantation of
the United Fruit Company in Costa Rica, had become all too familiar
with the racial inequities built into the white structures of capitalism, its
exploitation of Black labor, and its snaring of local elites. His experiences
working on the plantation enclave of an American company operating in a
foreign land constituted an important political awakening.[60] The lot of
people in the African diaspora, he believed, could only be improved by
building up their own autonomous economy, independent of white institutions and capital. A symbol of Garvey's Back-to-Africa movement, the Black
Star Line appealed to UNIA members—many of them domestics, farmers,
tradesmen, and plantation laborers. Many were willing to give five dollars

of their hard-earned money to help build a Pan-African empire, where the oppressed Black workers of the world might find a home and a place to look for "moral and physical support." On August 1, 1920, the first International Convention of the Negro Peoples of the World opened in Harlem. Twenty-five thousand UNIA supporters, including delegations from Bermuda, Jamaica, Nigeria, Panama, and St. Lucia, had gathered. To a packed house in Madison Square Garden, the anointed leader, elected as "provisional president of Africa," and bedecked in a cap and gown of purple, green, and gold, stood before those assembled and called upon UNIA members to "organize the 400,000,000 negroes of the world into a vast organization to plant the banner of freedom on the great continent of Africa."[61]

Garvey looked to Liberia as the promised land upon which a "great industrial and commercial commonwealth" would be built, a staging ground from which a free Africa would be demanded of Western imperial powers.[62] The U.S. government, in contrast, viewed Liberia as a beachhead for expanding American economic and political interests in Africa. At the grand parade through Harlem that marked the opening day of the UNIA convention, seated in a motorcar beside Garvey, was Monrovia mayor Gabriel Johnson. Later that evening, Garvey announced to the Garden audience Johnson's election as the "Supreme Potentate," the second highest ranking position in the UNIA. The Liberian guest had a distinguished lineage among the colonial settlers who emigrated back to Africa. His grandfather, Elijah Johnson, was among the passengers aboard the *Elizabeth*, and he fought defiantly against the Dei attack on their Cape Mesurado settlement. It was all the more fitting, then, that Johnson would play a part in Garvey's new Back-to-Africa plan.[63]

That same summer, in the hopes of winning over the Liberian government to the UNIA's cause, Garvey dispatched Commissioner Elie Garcia, a Haitian immigrant to the United States, to meet with President King and his cabinet. Garcia informed King of the UNIA's wish to move its headquarters to Monrovia. The organization also requested a concession of land to pursue business, agricultural, and industrial interests. In exchange, UNIA financial assistance would help "to liquidate" the country's "debts to foreign governments." UNIA would also, he promised, encourage immigration of "Negroes" in the African diaspora to "develop Liberia," and would assist in building hospitals, institutions of higher learning, and infrastructure for the benefit of the Liberian people. From where would the capital come? Garcia boasted of the organization's Black

Star Line, capitalized, he claimed, at $10 million. He also offered the UNIA's service in soliciting subscriptions from around the world to raise sufficient funds to supplant the $5 million American loan that was under debate in the U.S. Congress but not yet secured. Black capital, used to pay off foreign white debt, would secure Liberia's economic autonomy, political sovereignty, and prosperous future.[64]

Liberian secretary of state Edwin Barclay cordially listened to and responded receptively to the plans Garcia professed. But the polite decorum of diplomacy hid a mutual and growing contempt and mistrust. President King bristled at the idea of his father-in-law, Gabriel Johnson, being elected second-in-command to a man who proclaimed himself the "ruler for all black people."[65] Family connections aside, the Liberian leader reprimanded the Supreme Potentate for accepting both the title and the pledged $12,000 salary. King then exiled Johnson from the True Whig Party's seat of power in Monrovia and sent him to serve in a government post on the far-off Spanish island of Fernando Po.

Meanwhile, Garcia disclosed his disdain for Liberia's ruling oligarchy in a confidential report to Garvey, in which he described the leaders as "the most despicable element in Liberia," prone to graft and guilty of treating the country's indigenous inhabitants as "slaves." Garcia advised Garvey that whatever political interests he had in Liberia, he should keep quiet. "Modesty and discretion" were the most prudent course of action to "remove any possible idea of opposition" within King's administration. Nor would such a strategy prevent the UNIA, he suggested, "after having a strong foothold in the country to act as we see best for [Liberians'] own betterment and that of the Race at large." Unbeknownst to Garcia, the inflammatory report fell into the hands of King's cabinet. The Liberian leaders sat on it, waiting for the right moment to pounce.[66]

By the fall of 1920, the UNIA had sold $137,500 in bonds to help finance the Liberian scheme. The Liberian government played along, even while King, on a visit to Washington, DC, in March of 1921, discreetly made known to the Harding administration his distaste for Garvey's imagined empire. Regarding the UNIA's fundraising prowess, King's administration understood that it would require real power brokers to ensure Liberia's sovereignty. The country had maintained its independence as a sovereign Black republic through Europe's scramble for Africa by becoming adept at navigating the interests of white capital and power. Garvey's anticolonial talk did little to ease Liberia's relations with its European neighbors. Nor did it help in advancing King's cause to win American aid and support in neutralizing British and French aggression toward Liberia. The Liberian president had come to the United States to try and secure the assistance of President Harding's administration in delivering the $5 million loan he sought for Liberia, a loan that would get European creditors off its back. Meanwhile, Barclay assured UNIA commissioner Cyril Crichlow that land would be forthcoming. He also suggested that Garvey tamp down his public bravado.

Du Bois, who had grown impatient and suspicious of Garvey's class antagonism and business claims, invited President King in the spring of 1921 to make his thoughts about Garveyism known in *The Crisis*. King complied, with an open letter published that June. While King welcomed "strong young men trained as artisans, engineers and merchants who can bring with them some capital for investment" in Liberia, he chafed at any plot to "allow her territory to be made a center of aggression or conspiracy against other sovereign states."[67] Barclay reinforced King's public stance, denouncing Garvey's "proposal . . . to use the Liberian Republic as a centre from which to launch propaganda to drive the white people out of Africa." It was a message meant to assuage growing French, British, and American concerns.[68]

Garvey and his representatives had ignored Barclay's instructions to keep their intentions secret. "We don't tell them what we think," Barclay told Garvey's operatives. "We only tell them what we like them to hear— what in fact they like to hear."[69] It was sage advice, learned by a small Black power accustomed to dealing with the intimidating and aggressive ploys of Western imperial nations. The UNIA might have been wise to listen. By early 1922, Garvey and three associates were facing federal indictment on alleged mail fraud charges and conspiracy. An anxious U.S. government declared the UNIA had failed to show sufficient progress on promises it made to its shareholders regarding the Black Star Line, the Liberian loan project, and other UNIA ventures. Africa's vast natural wealth was too large a prize for Western powers to risk losing to Garvey's growing Black separatist movement. Garvey was convicted and received a five-year sentence in June 1923 but was released on bail in September, pending appeal.

Meanwhile, Du Bois and Garvey exchanged increasingly vitriolic barbs. In February of 1923, Du Bois had placed a stinging essay in *Century Magazine*, lampooning Garvey as a "little, fat black man, ugly, but with intelligent eyes and a big head, . . . who . . . was deluding the people and taking their hard-earned dollars."[70] Privately, he also wrote to U.S. secretary of state Hughes, denouncing Garvey as a "criminal, with grandiose schemes of conquest." Might not the U.S. government seize Black Star Line stock and put it in the trust of a "private company, headed by men of highest integrity, both white and colored," to advance commercial enterprise between America and Liberia? Du Bois asked.[71]

The UNIA returned insults. In 1924, at the August convention of the UNIA in Harlem, Garvey identified Du Bois and the NAACP as "the greatest enemies the black people have in the world." This was only two years after the UNIA had named Du Bois one of the "twelve greatest living Negroes."[72] Within the UNIA ranks, suspicion had grown regarding Du Bois's real intentions, particularly after his return from Liberia in 1924. Three delegates representing the UNIA, Henrietta Vinton Davis, Robert L. Poston, and James Milton Van Lowe, had arrived in Monrovia in early February of that year, shortly after Du Bois had left. A cordial reception of Liberian dignitaries awaited them at the Methodist Church in the nation's capital. Ex-presidents Arthur Barclay and Daniel Howard, Chief Justice James Dossen, and members of the Liberian Legislature socialized with the Garvey team. A few days later, the visitors were warmly received by President King. The UNIA delegation left the meeting at the Executive Mansion elated. The president, they reported, had promised concessions of land in Maryland, Sinoe, Grand Bassa, and Grand Cape Mount counties. Here, UNIA members would be welcome to establish settlements and begin the task of agricultural, industrial, and educational development.[73] Arrangements were made for a shipment of building materials, including a sawmill, water filtration plant, and four tractors, to the Cavalla River region in the southeastern corner of Liberia. A group of civil and mechanical engineers, contracted by the UNIA from the United States and the West Indies, left for Liberia in June 1924 to prepare for the anticipated arrival of the first group of UNIA colonists in September. What a shock it was when the team of technical experts, upon landing, were arrested, detained, and deported by the Liberian government.[74]

President King justified his action in the uproar that followed. The "apparent intention" of the UNIA "to use Liberia as its base for the dissemination of its propaganda of racial hatred and ill will," he asserted, "compelled the Executive Government" to deport the UNIA emissaries and to henceforth deny visas to anyone connected with the UNIA wishing to emigrate to Liberia.[75] In Liverpool, England, Consul General of Liberia C. E. Cooper told readers of the *African World* that Garvey's "aim is to make Liberia the dumping ground for his army of propagandists in Africa." "My people will have none of Garvey," Cooper insisted. "Liberia is content to have the sympathy and support of the white man."[76]

To Garvey, the shunning of UNIA investment in and emigration to Liberia by the country's leaders all could be attributed to one person: W.E.B. Du Bois. "Do you wonder why Du Bois was in Liberia part of this year?" he asked his compatriots gathered in 1924 at Liberty Hall in Harlem for the Fourth International Convention of the Negro Peoples of the World. "Go and find out among the capitalists' class who are paying Negroes to keep down Negroes," he implored.[77] Du Bois and Hood, Garvey claimed, had sold the UNIA out to Liberia in favor of Firestone. Delegates of the UNIA rallied behind their leader, who now faced another federal indictment, this time for alleged income tax fraud. At the convention's close, they issued a petition to President Calvin Coolidge, deploring the Liberian situation and alerting him to "the unfriendly attitude" of his representatives in Liberia, Hood and Du Bois. Together, the delegates declared, the two had conspired to derail the interest of the UNIA in Liberia and had "used their official positions to create prejudice against" the organization's aims.[78]

There was, in fact, some truth to Garvey's claim. The day before Du Bois left Liberia, Donald Ross, the Firestone agent who had joined Du Bois at the Mount Barclay Plantation, left on a Spanish ship bound for Cadiz, and was back home in Great Britain by late February. There, he composed a report to Harvey Firestone Sr. It included an assessment of the Mount Barclay Plantation, a report on confidential talks he had with Hood and Sidney De La Rue, the American financial adviser and general receiver of customs. He also included notes on the soil, labor, and political conditions in Liberia. He wrote his boss, "I see no reason why with experienced management," the Mount Barclay Plantation "should not hold its own with the crack estates of Malaya."[79] In March, Ross was a guest at Firestone's winter home in Miami Beach, where the two discussed next steps. Meanwhile, Hood set in motion negotiations in Liberia to transfer the Mount Barclay estate, which was in debt to the Liberian government for £7,000, to the Firestone Tire & Rubber Company.[80]

As the UNIA made plans to ship equipment and personnel to Liberia, a team of Firestone negotiators had already arrived in Monrovia in late

May 1924, with $20,000 worth of automobiles and tractors, ready to be-gin building their own version of an African empire. Among the negotia-tors was Bill Hines, who served as Firestone's trusted personal secretary. Hood and Hines found themselves literally on two ships passing in the night. The ailing minister was on his way back to the United States for a much-needed leave when, upon arriving in Hamburg, he received an ur-gent cable from the State Department. Hines was in London headed to Liberia. Could the two arrange to meet? Hood spent two days with Hines in Brussels, educating the Firestone representative about all aspects of life and politics in Liberia. He also supplied Hines with a letter of introduc-tion to President King.[81] In Liberia, Hines was accompanied by Ross and Firestone's Singapore agent, Marion Cheek. They had come on Harvey Firestone Sr.'s behalf, eager to strike a deal for land with the Liberian government.

Members of Firestone's team, as well as American government officials, believed Secretary of State Edwin Barclay was the most suspicious among King's cabinet and likely to present the most difficulty. Barclay had good cause to be suspicious. The U.S. invasion of Haiti was a mere decade in the past and the United States still occupied the country. Barclay feared Libe-ria could be opening the door to a similar fate.[82] King appeared less wary. Foreign loans came with "too many political entanglements." The coun-try's future, he believed, rested in private foreign capital, provided it came with safe and agreeable terms. King was savvy to the fiscal realities of Garvey's proposed venture and keenly aware of the challenges a small, sovereign Black nation faced in a world where white capital largely con-trolled the purse strings of global finance. Confronted with the choice between Garvey and Firestone, the Liberian president opted for an Amer-ican company backed by a nation that rivaled the colonial powers sur-rounding his country on all sides.[83]

Through most of June 1924, Barclay, King, and Firestone representa-tives hashed out tentative agreements. The first solid agreement granted Firestone a one-year lease, with a renewable option, on the Mount Barclay Plantation to allow the company to determine the feasibility of growing rubber in Liberia on an industrial scale. In exchange, Firestone would pay in gold annual rent to the Liberian government at the rate of one dollar per acre. The company also agreed to not import unskilled labor and to pay a revenue tax of 2.5 percent on all rubber sales. Should Firestone build roads or other public utilities of benefit to the country, the revenue tax would be reduced to 1.5 percent. In addition, a provisional agreement was drafted for a ninety-year lease for up to 1 million acres of land in the country to grow rubber, as well as another agreement that pledged Firestone to the improvement and construction of a harbor in Monrovia. Hines left for America on June 20. Ross set to work on the Mount Barclay Plantation. Cheek headed up country to survey soil conditions and the labor supply. Much remained to be sorted out, but the company had, with the help of Hood and Du Bois, successfully planted itself in Liberia.[84]

In helping to bring Firestone to Liberia, Hood sincerely believed he had the best interests of the country at heart. "As a Negro, I had to be absolutely true to these Negroes," he confided to Du Bois. He imagined all that would flow from Firestone's investment: roads, wharves, harbors, wages and employment, and money for education. He was certain that "the only way to save Liberia from further territorial aggression was by getting some great power so interested and involved as to make it to that power's interest to defend Liberia."[85]

Du Bois, too, believed, that Firestone had within his purview the potential to achieve "one of the greatest and far reaching reforms in the relations between white industrial countries like America and black, partly developed countries like Liberia." On Liberian soil, Firestone had an opportunity to germinate a new relationship among the capital, land, and labor that comprised the plantation, one resting not on exploitation and extraction but on mutual dependence, growth, and prosperity. It all depended, Du Bois wrote Harvey Firestone, on whether the rubber executive gave "educated black men a chance to work up in your industrial system."[86] In an essay in the *New Republic*, Du Bois shared his thoughts with the public at large. "White capital in America" had the potential in Liberia "to do a fine and unusual job in imperialism," he wrote. Firestone "can build a local organization of control, without a rigid color line. They can allow in Liberia decent and increasing wages: they can yield to the Liberian government satisfactory revenue. This is possible. This is what Liberia and black America hope."[87]

For its part, the State Department was glad to have Du Bois and Hood on its side. The failure of Congress to pass the loan to Liberia had been for some officials in the Coolidge administration a diplomatic disaster, as well as a moral failing. Firestone offered a means to salvage the administration's relationship with Liberia and the Black vote in the United States. William Castle, then chief of the State Department's Division of Western

European Affairs, shared his opinion with colleagues that "Hood would promptly get the negro element on the side of the Department and on the side of the Firestone projects should it go through." Furthermore, Du Bois had said that "he would push the Firestone project if it gave an opening for colored graduates of some of the technical schools." If Firestone delivered, Castle jubilantly wrote, "we should have all the radical press controlled by Du Bois also on our side."[88]

Garvey had promised much to Liberia, but Du Bois thought the numbers in the UNIA proposal didn't add up. None of the movement's business ventures had, in his opinion, succeeded. In the choice between private white capital and a man he considered a charlatan preying upon the dreams and savings of people in the African diaspora, Du Bois cast his lot with an American captain of industry.

The UNIA urged the Liberian Legislature in 1924 to think twice before granting a concession to Firestone. "As time goes on," the organization forewarned, the company's interest will "seek to further tighten its hold upon the republic."[89] Garvey himself believed that it was the UNIA's internal critique of Liberia's class structure becoming known to the King administration that had led to the undoing of the UNIA's plan. He consequently grew increasingly outspoken in his hostility toward Liberia's elite and their alleged exploitation of indigenous labor. "They keep the Natives poor, hungry, shelterless and naked," he lashed out, "while they parade themselves in the tropical sun in English frock coats and evening dress."[90]

In Liberia, public opinion in Monrovia rallied behind King's actions. Those in Liberia who invested money in the Black Star Line "soon found themselves losers," the *Liberian News* declared.[91] "We are Africans," another Liberian correspondent remarked. "The Foreign Negro of the Garvey type lacks this. He knows not what he is."[92] Harsh words flew back and forth across the ocean. Liberia's objective was, King told his fellow citizens, the making of a strong African nation, not becoming the seat of a Pan-African Black empire.

Firestone kept quiet. But he could delight in winning the support of Hood and Du Bois. Just days before Garvey's team of experts was cast out of Liberia, Du Bois wrote his new friend, Liberian president Charles Dunbar King. The question of Firestone weighed on the president's mind. "Liberia must have capital for her development," Du Bois exhorted. Faced with a choice among England, France, and the United States, Liberia would be wise, Du Bois advised, to choose white American investment, which Du Bois believed posed the least threat to the country's sovereignty and self-determination. King could rest assured that he would have behind him the "Negroes of America," who had "enough political power to make the government go slowly," Du Bois declared. It was a devil's bargain, one that traded land and labor for the promise of development and freedom. But at what cost? The question would come to haunt Du Bois in a few years.[93]

# 3

# Missionaries of Capital

"America was built on Africa," Du Bois wrote in *The World and Africa*, published later in his life. Stolen and enslaved African labor had made the United States "the center of the sugar empire and the cotton kingdom." Slavery was the foundation upon which the "Industrial Revolution" was built and "the reign of capitalism" flourished. In the taking of land, in the extraction of raw materials, and in the exploitation of cheap labor, "the rape of Africa" continued, Du Bois observed. Chattel slavery may have ended. But the legacies of racial and geographic difference born of plantation economies endured in the global flows of capital and labor that built modern industrial nations and structured the geopolitics of the world. Liberia, since its founding, was caught in this bind of a global political economy built on racial capitalism, in which patterns of extraction and exploitation continued to thrive on the making of racial difference.[1] How could the country remain sovereign in a world ruled by the power of white capital and Western imperialism? Du Bois and Hood held hope that the Black vote in the United States and a reliance on African American expertise would ensure that the plantation Firestone built would benefit Liberia and its people.

Firestone, however, was a corporation that grew up in a town, in an industry, and in a nation where growth was sustained by the inequalities of capitalism buttressed by racism.[2] In looking to erect a "colossal enterprise" in the jungle of West Africa, Firestone turned not to African American experts, as Du Bois and Hood had urged, but to the people and places of white privilege and power: Ivy League institutions and mindsets, labor and management structures, and scientific disciplines that both aided and profited from plantation slavery and American empire.[3]

Richard Pearson Strong, head of Harvard University's Department of Tropical Medicine, was one key white expert Firestone looked to in bringing his modernist visions of an industrial plantation into being. Strong had survived many harrowing adventures on behalf of American economic, military, and political interest in foreign lands. He served as an army physician in the campaign in the Philippines during the Spanish-American War. He conducted autopsies on pneumonic plague victims in Manchuria, working for the American Red Cross and the U.S. government. He had been dispatched there in 1911 to assist an international effort to quell a worrying outbreak that had killed upward of sixty thousand people. He voluntarily threw himself into the relief efforts of the American Sanitary Commission during the First World War as it fought to alleviate the suffering of a devastating typhus epidemic afflicting civilians and soldiers behind the battle lines of war-torn Serbia. He also launched many an expedition, from the upper reaches of the Amazon to the interior of Liberia, at the behest of U.S. firms such as the United Fruit Company and Firestone Tire & Rubber Company, to assist in their commercial expansion into the tropics. But never in his travels across the globe in the name of science, medicine, and American empire had he faced an incident like the one he witnessed one November morning in 1926.[4]

Strong had just returned to Monrovia, as a guest of the Firestone Plantations Company, after an exhausting journey to complete the first biological and medical survey of Liberia ever undertaken. For four months, Strong and his seven-member team, which included some of Harvard's best minds in medical entomology, botany, mammalogy, parasitology, and tropical medicine, had trekked by foot for nearly seven hundred miles, east, west, north, and south, through Liberia's dense tropical jungle on trails and uncompleted roads during the worst of the country's rainy season.[5]

At a long journey's end, after months of trudging as many as twenty miles a day in the tropical heat, sleeping in tents, and suffering bouts of malaria, the men delighted in the luxuries Monrovia offered. Harvey Firestone Jr. and his wife, Betty, were in town. It was the first of many visits the eldest son would make to Liberia on behalf of the Firestone dynasty. The Akron couple treated the Harvard scientists to a lavish dinner, with champagne, fine food, and music at the home of Firestone Plantations Company manager Donald Ross. White expatriates, of which there were about a hundred in a city of roughly ten thousand inhabitants, stuck together like flies. They were, as Lady Dorothy Mills described it, a "white colony" in Monrovia. Mills, daughter to the Earl of Orford and heiress to the fortune of Daniel Chase Corbin, an American mining and railroad tycoon, had also traversed Liberia's hinterland, preceding the

The Harvard African Expedition team. Seated, left to right: Joseph Bequaert (medical entomologist), George Shattuck (physician), Richard Strong (tropical medicine specialist, the expedition's leader), Glover Allen (zoologist). Standing, left to right: David Linder (botanist), Max Theiler (bacteriologist, who would go on to win the Nobel Prize for the development of a yellow fever vaccine), Harold Coolidge (assistant zoologist), Loring Whitman (photographer). Firestone capitalized on its support of medical humanitarianism in building a plantation world. Image by Loring Whitman, 1926. (Courtesy of Indiana University Libraries.)

Harvard team and covering much of the same ground while being carried in a hammock on the shoulders of porters. The promise of plentiful land, abundant resources, and adventure attracted the mix of white customs officials, diplomats, bankers, businessmen, scientists, and explorers. A shared moral conviction of the superiority of white expertise and capital to guide Liberia down a path of development united them. They moved in the same circles of lunches, picnics, and dinner parties, often frequenting each other's homes in the evening, sharing in whiskey, racist innuendos, and the latest Victrola records imported from America or Europe. They were a white enclave, made up mostly of Americans, British, and Germans, protective of each other in a country where, as noncitizens, they had few legal rights and claims.[6]

Firestone Bungalow No. 1 was one such gathering place for the city's white residents. Home to Firestone Plantations Company physician Dr. Willis and his wife, it was more mansion than bungalow. Built on a hill in Monrovia overlooking the Atlantic Ocean, the three-story, white-plastered building also served as a Firestone dispensary and clinic: the lower floor contained six hospital beds for white staff only. Balconies wrapped around the upper floors of the residence. Four large corner bedrooms and a magnificent sitting room on the second floor opened on both sides to the sea breeze. The home's comforts were a welcome relief for Strong; his close colleague, George Shattuck; twenty-two-year-old assistant zoologist Harold (Hal) Jefferson Coolidge Jr.; and the young expedition photographer, Loring Whitman, while they were in Monrovia.[7]

On Saturday morning, November 6, just before dawn, Shattuck and Coolidge, along with Firestone representative Marion Cheek, also a guest at the Willis home, had gathered outside to set off on a quail hunt. The Firestone driver was late. They waited for their ride for an hour. Cheek grew edgy. He claimed items in his room had been stolen in the night. When the Liberian chauffeur finally arrived, Cheek was furious. While Shattuck held the driver, Cheek struck the man repeatedly. People hearing the young man's cries saw the scene from their windows. The three Americans then pressed the abused and shaken Firestone employee to transport them to their quarry. Coolidge recounted the incident in his diary, replete with racial slurs denigrating the driver, and Liberians in general. But mostly he wrote of his delight with both his marksmanship and the birds they had bagged: francolins, a cuckoo, a nighthawk, and a number of pigeon-like birds. The hunt a success, the group arrived home three hours later, its members each in a good mood.[8]

While the hunting party sat down to breakfast, Strong went out to take his regular brisk morning walk. To his surprise, a group of police officers had ascended the stairs to the front door and were demanding to enter the Willis home. Although Strong was known among the expedition team as the chief, he held little authority in this situation. Harvard prestige, military rank, and white privilege mattered not to the officers. Liberia, after all, was their country. Strong and his team, and the Firestone company that helped support them, were there by permission of the Liberian government.

The police informed Strong that they had come to arrest two men in the house, who were accused of violating the country's laws earlier that morning. When Strong asked to see a warrant, a policeman pushed him aside. Three officers stood with Strong at the foot of the stairs. Two others entered the house and came out with Shattuck. Hines was in town on Firestone business and arrived at the scene. He pleaded with law enforcement to permit him to drive Shattuck to the police station. A growing crowd had assembled, and Hines feared for Shattuck's safety. The police dismissed his pleas. As they marched Shattuck down the street to police headquarters, a crowd, according to Strong, "hurled" epithets "at Americans, white men, and the Firestone Plantations Company." Strong could barely contain his outrage. In an affidavit sworn before Reed Paige Clark, chargé d'affaires of the American Legation, the U.S. diplomatic mission in Liberia, Strong recounted how it took great discipline and resolve not to strike out in his friend's defense as he accompanied him to the city jail. But Strong said nothing of the young Liberian man whom Shattuck had hurt and humiliated.[9]

With Shattuck secured in the city jail, the police returned to the Firestone bungalow to also arrest Cheek. The Firestone agent had grown up in and out of Southeast Asia, where his father served as a medical missionary and teak industry entrepreneur in Siam (now Thailand). "A missionary at heart," Cheek parlayed his knowledge of Southeast Asia, commodity markets, and plantation forestry to Firestone's advantage in its search for seeds, soils, and governments friendly to growing rubber on an industrial scale. Strong, ever quick to judge a person by their climatic constitution, regarded Cheek, who had spent much of his life in the torrid zones, to be "too high strung for the tropics." An aficionado of music and sport, he was the proud father of Dolph Cheek, the captain of Harvard's 1925 winning football team. He also loved to hunt. Cheek's passion for shooting game, and his alleged nervous temperament, had gotten the Harvard crew into their present predicament.[10]

The Cheek-Shattuck affair was a flashpoint. For more than a year, suspicions among Liberians of all walks of life—from those in the Liberian Legislature to the crowd that gathered that day—had been growing regarding the real interests and intentions of Firestone in Liberia. Harvey Firestone Sr. bemoaned earlier in the year that "it is just absolutely impossible to do business with an individual or a Government when they are afraid of you, and if they have the idea that I am going to ruin their country."[11] But Liberians had cause for concern. At issue was a demand that Firestone added to the initial agreements drafted in the summer of 1924. Three agreements gave Firestone a lease on the Mount Barclay Plantation for experimental purposes; a ninety-nine-year lease for up to 1 million acres of land to grow rubber; and provisions to improve the port of Monrovia. Unbeknownst to President King or Secretary of State Edwin Barclay, Firestone executives added a twist to the agreement version, signed by Firestone, that landed on the desks of King and Barclay in February 1925. A new clause authorized the company to seek a loan to Liberia for between $2.5 and $5 million from either the U.S. government or private interests. The terms were similar to the proposed 1920 U.S. loan to Liberia, which had died in 1922 on the floor of the U.S. Senate. The new clause required Liberia to accept the loan if it were secured for them within five years.[12]

Ever the diplomat, Barclay barely contained his indignation at Firestone's bait and switch. In a letter to U.S. minister Hood, who sided with the Liberian government's cause, Barclay expressed his consternation. Firestone had, "without notice to the Liberian government," Barclay emphasized, "attached to the Agreement for economic exploitation by private means, a suggestion for the flotation of a public loan which was represented as an indispensable prerequisite to the plantation operations."[13] The Liberian government would have none of it. It flew in the face of public sentiment in Liberia and the policy of King's administration to resurrect the country's finances, not through debt but through foreign investment in the development of the nation's resources. Liberia had no interest in a loan. Its interest in Firestone, Barclay asserted, was to encourage American investment "as a counterpois [sic] to other menacingly aggressive interests already established in this country," namely, France and Great Britain.[14]

The suspicions went beyond financial matters. The very name of Firestone Plantations Company elicited distrust. The word *plantations* inflamed apprehensions among Liberians, noted Clifton Wharton, the African American vice-consul serving under both Hood and his successor, William Francis, in Liberia. "When you consider that most places other than Monrovia, are small towns, peopled by descendants of freed American slaves just from plantations, few or no newspapers, little information from the outside world, inadequate schools, etc., we can appreciate that a plantation is something to be abhorred, particularly one brought by white Americans into a country proud of its conception, founded to do away with plantations, and lauding its history of freedom and independence," Wharton wrote.[15]

The fears plantations evoked were unsettling, but it was the politics at play that threatened Liberia's sovereignty. Sidney De La Rue, the U.S.-appointed general receiver of customs and financial adviser to Liberia, had perpetrated the loan maneuver. De La Rue had made a career in the tropical circuits of American empire. He arrived in Liberia in 1921 by way of the Dominican Republic. Years on the Caribbean island of Hispaniola, where two nations—Haiti and the Dominican Republic—had governments, people, and land subject to hostile takeovers by the U.S. military, were preparation for De La Rue's designs on Liberia. American firms like the United Fruit Company, amassing fortunes off banana and sugarcane plantations in the Caribbean and Central America, profited greatly from the willingness of the U.S. government to protect American private capital, by force if needed.[16] But guns were not the only means by which to secure American influence and control over foreign lands. Debt was a powerful weapon in the armament of Yankee imperialism. Political instability and rising debt, both threatening to American investments, offered a convenient justification for the U.S. military occupation of the Dominican Republic in 1916. De La Rue arrived two years later, working as an auditor, accountant, and purchasing agent in the U.S. Treasury Department. Financial experts, put in place to manage receiverships indebted to the United States, likened themselves to doctors and missionaries. They healed "sick" economies, rid the body politic of inflation, and restored financial order to promote economic health and well-being.[17] They saw themselves as the civilizing hands of American empire. De La Rue was no exception.

De La Rue inhabited a world of white power, disparaging and dismissive of people of color. In a letter to Castle, he referred to Liberians as "idiots," accusing them of fiscal ineptitude. He directed his most racist remarks at his fellow American, Hood. "You never really know where you are with a negro," he wrote, in an extended effort to undermine the American minister's credibility among State Department officials.[18] De La Rue sought to position himself with Firestone as someone in the know in Liberia, a key ally and power broker who could bend King's cabinet to the interests of American private capital. In the summer of 1924, De La Rue arranged a meeting in Akron with Harvey Sr., Bill Hines, and Firestone consultant Samuel Wierman. Here De La Rue first proposed the idea of a $10 million loan to Liberia to protect Firestone's capital investment.

Without it, De La Rue implied, Firestone could expect little support, either moral or military, from the U.S. government should political instability threaten his planned operations. Firestone, in turn, shared with the general receiver his paternalistic desire: "doing welfare work on a national scale" in Liberia. Imbued with Kiplingesque ideas of the white man's burden, Firestone, according to De La Rue's summary of the meeting, spoke of his vision of a rubber empire that would do more than supply Americans with a source of rubber. It would help uplift a nation, "establishing schools, hospitals, agricultural training schools, and so forth, for the development" of Liberia's indigenous inhabitants.[19] A loan, De La Rue advised Firestone, was the best way to make his dream a reality. It should be independent of Firestone, "mortgage the assets of the whole of the country," and be administered by an adviser nominated by the U.S. government. The loan scheme would give the adviser, whom De La Rue aspired to be, complete control of the country's finances, making him "practically a Governor of Liberia."[20]

In negotiations, Harvey Sr. increasingly grew suspicious of De La Rue's interests and ambitions, calling him "either a crook or a fool."[21] Yet the seasoned horse trader was convinced that De La Rue was right about one thing. Contrary to the counsel of Hood and Wierman, Firestone hardened his position on the demand for a loan tied to the planting agreements. Rubber trees needed seven years to mature before they could be tapped and profits could flow. During the wait, the tire manufacturer would "be gambling with a heavy capital investment," Hines observed, if "he had no assurance that the Liberian Government might not go to pieces within the next few years."[22] Firestone told members of Congress that a private loan, supported by American diplomatic pressure, and guns if necessary, was the best means to ensure adequate protection of his "large capital investment" in a "far-off country."[23]

By October of 1925, after a six-week visit by Barclay to the United States, Firestone believed a deal had been reached. Harvey Sr. wrote to his brother Elmer that he had "closed a concession with him [Barclay] for a million acres of land in Liberia for which I pay six cents an acre, and I also arranged for a banker's loan in New York for the Liberian government of five million dollars." The loan, he boasted, "made through our State Department, . . . gives us full control over Liberia."[24]

A few weeks later, newspapers across the United States announced the signing of an agreement to plant a $100 million commercial empire in the

West African republic of Liberia. At a press conference at the Plaza Hotel in New York City, the Akron businessman declared himself a "pioneer" in the development of Africa. "Doctors, sanitary workers, civil and mechanical engineers, architects, builders, foresters, and soil experts" would soon be on their way to clear the jungle and bring "civilization" to "darkest Africa." Malaria would be "stamped out entirely." Three hundred thousand "natives" and "a great organization of whites" would furnish the manpower to transform 1 million acres of land into the "greatest rubber plantation in the world." It would be, Firestone proclaimed, "America's greatest investment in the tropics, involving practically the physical remodeling of a whole country—the building of harbors, roads, towns, hospitals, and other public works."[25] Harvey Jr. had already set sail for London to establish an office of the Firestone Plantations Company, which he would head. On November 21, 1925, in an area a dozen miles southeast of Mount Barclay, so began the felling of the forest with ax and cutlass.

Celebrated tire tycoon, friend to the most influential power brokers in American business and government, Firestone was, at the age of fifty-seven, a man full of confidence and bravado. His bullishness about having closed a deal with the Liberian government did not square with conversations in the U.S. State Department, as no deal was final until approved by the Liberian Legislature. Firestone's assertion that Barclay's signature constituted a definite and binding contract was wrong.[26]

Tremors of unease over the Firestone deal escalated within King's cabinet and the Liberian Legislature when news got out in the December 1925 edition of the *Firestone Non-Skid*, Firestone's company newspaper, via the London *Morning Post* that Firestone was planning on a management force of thirty thousand whites in Liberia.[27] When the Liberian Legislature took up consideration of the agreements in the new year, it made two important changes to the planting and loan agreements signed by Barclay and Firestone. First, fearful that an American occupation could turn Liberia into another Haiti, the legislature restricted the number of white employees the Firestone Plantations Company could bring into the country to a maximum of fifteen hundred men. Second, any disagreements arising between the company and the Liberian government would be adjudicated by an arbitrator appointed by the Liberian Court. King was savvy to the Liberian judiciary's importance in keeping a check on Firestone's power in Liberia. Should the corporate giant get out of hand, Liberian judges could be a thorn in Firestone's side, making it intentionally irritating, if not painful, to conduct business in ways arrogant or dismissive of Liberian law. The resolution of disputes on Liberian soil by Liberian courts was an important safeguard against an American corporate empire making Liberia a puppet state. Legal sovereignty was not to be given up.

Firestone was outraged. Clearing was well underway on twenty thousand acres along the Du River, thousands of Liberian laborers were on the payroll, and a contingent of white experts—planters, soil scientists, foresters, and engineers—had arrived in or were on their way to Monrovia. "I am not in humor to negotiate," Firestone told the State Department's Castle. The Liberian government "must accept agreements without [a] single change," he insisted. Or Firestone would pull out.[28] Firestone sent dispatches to slow preparations in Liberia, ordering the return of equipment and staff already in transit. And he pushed some more on making the Philippines a place to grow American rubber.[29]

De La Rue was desperate upon hearing of Firestone's brash threats. His plans for control over Liberia's economy were crumbling. Immediately he cabled William Hoffman, vice-president of National City Bank: "Confidential—"Try to stop Firestone and Department acting too strongly. Situation can be handled by persuasion. Just now people very badly scared off by Firestone freehand."[30]

Whether Firestone was bluffing or not, King would not bend. The arbitration clause and the number of white employees remained sticking points. With the 1927 presidential election coming up, King could not risk losing face. His political opponents were sharply critical of the proposed loan agreement, which, under its initial terms, they saw as a selling off of the country for $5 million. Meanwhile, Firestone had his own troubles. Despite his political influence in Washington, he could not get the Philippine Legislature to pass an act that would allow the American company to lease up to a half-million acres of land in Mindanao to grow rubber.

In May 1926, just as Richard Strong's Harvard expedition was setting sail for Liberia, an opening appeared in the negotiations with King's cabinet. Through backdoor channels, Barclay suggested a compromise on the arbitration clause. With unpromising prospects in the Philippines, Firestone's vice-president and heir apparent, Harvey Firestone Jr., left Akron with Betty in early September 1926 and traveled for the first time to Liberia. He hoped to personally close a deal.

Harvey Jr. grew up around a campfire with three of America's most iconic businessmen, industrialists, and inventors: his father, Thomas Edison, and

Harvey Firestone Jr. and Firestone Plantations Company manager Donald Ross at the Mount Barclay Plantation, 1926. (From the California Historical Society Collection at the University of Southern California.)

Henry Ford. He knew nothing of the hardscrabble, cutthroat life that had taught his mentors to survive and succeed in business during America's Gilded Age. He had been groomed and educated for a life among the rich: boarding school, Princeton University, and polo tournaments defined his entrance into manhood. He had entered his father's company as head of the Firestone Steel Products division. The young executive could be suave, diplomatic, and gracious in ways his father was not. Richard Strong, upon meeting Harvey Jr. in Monrovia that November, immediately took a liking to him. In meetings with King and Barclay, the Firestone Plantations Company vice-president could be cordial, courteous, and accommodating. In correspondence, he could be equally placating, assuring Barclay of Firestone's sincere "interest in the development and progress of Liberia," and closing correspondence to him with "Your obedient servant." Behind his outward charm was a shrewd businessman. Harvey Jr. was determined to leave Liberia with a deal favoring the interests of the multinational corporation his father had built from scratch, and which he and his siblings would one day control.[31]

Almost three years had elapsed since Du Bois, Hood, and Ross looked out upon the Mount Barclay Plantation and imagined a future for Liberia and Firestone. By late October, Harvey Jr. was close to finalizing a deal. The company acquiesced to the limit of fifteen hundred white employees. A compromise on arbitration preserved the sovereignty of the Liberian courts but left an opening for the U.S. State Department to intervene should Liberian Supreme Court–facilitated arbitration not be resolved in a timely manner. As he listened to President King's annual message to the Liberian Legislature on October 20, Harvey Jr. grew hopeful that the deadlock was broken. Gesturing toward Harvey Jr., the "genial and charming gentleman" in his midst, King appealed to every "patriotic Liberian" to recognize "that the admission into the Country of a Company of this character, with the necessary safeguards, will afford the greatest opportunity that has ever been presented to us for the use of American Capital in the Development of Liberia."[32] King's cabinet was, in fact, unsure that the safeguards were adequate concerning the $5 million loan to Liberia, payable to the unknown Finance Corporation of America over forty years at an interest rate of 7 percent per year. More onerous than the interest payments were attached terms that put not judicial but monetary constraints on Liberian sovereignty. In part, the loan agreement demanded a U.S. government–appointed auditor be given significant power to shape Liberia's budget. It also forbid the Liberian government to issue any debt other than that purchased by the Finance Corporation of America. And it required that both the Liberian Frontier Force and collections of customs and revenues be overseen by American-recommended officials. Firestone was determined that no nation other than the United States and no business other than his own exercise control over certain essential functions of the Liberian government.[33]

Harvey Jr. wrote his father that he felt sure the Liberian government would ratify the agreements as long as the U.S. State Department assured King that the loan agreement was "fair to all parties."[34] But the Firestone agreement was foundering and threatening to sink King's administration. The State Department, long quietly involved in the negotiations, was suddenly caught in the middle. Firestone and the King administration both beseeched State Department officials for help in finalizing the details. Castle, in his State Department diary, expressed his hopes that the loan agreement would give the United States a larger role in West Africa. But State Department officials hesitated to be anything but neutral in a deal being brokered between a private American company and a sovereign government.[35] Strong expressed disappointment with what seemed like State Department inaction in pushing the loan through on Firestone's behalf, inaction that he believed was "mixed up with politics and the American negro vote in the United States."[36]

The Cheek-Shattuck affair marked an oddly fortuitous turn in a protracted dance of interested but reluctant partners. The tumult created when a distinguished Harvard doctor was hauled off to jail, while taunted by an angry crowd, created an embarrassing situation for King's cabinet at the very moment they were cautiously courting American capital. It was the kind of diplomatic incident that played into Firestone's hands. The way Strong, the rest of his Harvard team, and Firestone representatives saw it, a respected white American doctor had been disgraced. Shattuck wasn't just any white doctor. His father, Frederick Cheever Shattuck, had helped found, bankroll, and recruit Strong to lead Harvard's Department of Tropical Medicine in 1913. Four generations of Shattucks, including George, were Harvard professors of medicine. It was, in the opinion of Strong and William Castle, himself a Harvard College graduate and former assistant dean to students, an embarrassment undeserved and unbecoming of one of Boston's most distinguished medical families.

The involvement of a Harvard physician in an incident where Liberian law was broken proved fortunate for American interests. If "Cheek had been the only one involved or Cheek and some other Firestone employee," Castle confided to Strong, "it would have put the Department in an exceedingly difficult position, but as the Liberians attacked also people who were in Liberia for purely humanitarian and scientific reasons, it enabled us to take a very different stand from what we might have taken otherwise."[37]

Barclay and King feared the incident would grow into an international dispute. Diplomatic cables went back and forth across the Atlantic. The U.S. State Department pressed the Liberian government to make amends. Within a matter of days, Shattuck and Cheek were released. King invited Strong to the Executive Mansion, where the president offered an official apology. The incident was, King told Strong, "a demonstration of a few people against the Firestone Plantations Company and the proposed loan by people who do not wish the loan to go through."[38] Barclay also convened a meeting with the Liberian Legislature to discuss punitive actions to be taken against what he described as an "uncivil act of the police and certain rabbles of this city." An investigation was launched. The $50 fine paid on Shattuck's behalf for his violation of Liberian law was refunded.[39] Within a matter of weeks, the Liberian Legislature ratified the Firestone planting and loan agreements, ushering in an era of transformational economic, environmental, and social change.

The injuries the Liberian chauffeur suffered had been a sacrifice to a larger cause. As Clarence Simpson, a distinguished Liberian statesman, later recalled, Liberia was caught "between the devil and the deep blue sea." The country must either risk a takeover of territory by France or Great Britain, which would bring an end to the Black republic, or "accept the lesser evil—that of veiled economic domination by a company belonging to a traditionally friendly country."[40] In the end, safeguarding the political sovereignty of a Black nation outweighed whatever economic freedoms might be lost in striking a deal with Firestone. The Firestone investment offered Liberia the promise of development and a guarantee of American protection from the threat of European imperialism. Even so, King and Barclay did their best to limit the powers of an American corporate empire seeking access to land and labor in their sovereign nation.

In her travels across Liberia, Lady Dorothy Mills suggested that many people she spoke with, from "intelligent Liberian officials" to indigenous porters who carried her loads, were against the Firestone enterprise.[41] But opinion was divided. Some among the country's educated elite—both settler and indigenous—celebrated the Firestone achievement. Plenyono Gbe Wolo was one. Wolo was the son of a Kru paramount chief. In Liberia, a paramount chief is the highest-level tribal authority of a chiefdom and serves as the official representative to the Liberian government on behalf of the town chiefs, clan chiefs, elders, and people in his chiefdom. Wolo was also a graduate of Harvard College. He came away from a meeting with Harvey Firestone Jr. in Monrovia in the fall of 1926 impressed. "I believe his ambitions toward the Liberian venture is a praiseworthy one," he wrote. Rejecting claims of American imperialism, Wolo later wrote of Liberia's "selfish reasons for accepting the loan."[42] It was a matter of nationhood, he argued. The *Liberia Express and Agricultural World*, which represented the interests of Liberia's planter class, was also an unabashed Firestone proponent. In entering Liberia, Firestone's purpose was "not to impair its independence but to redeem it," the newspaper assured its readers. The initial $2.5 million of the $5 million loan granted to Liberia enabled the country to pay off its foreign debt. A "Bee Hive of American industrial activity, . . . the very thing we need and must have," had come with Firestone's arrival in Liberia, the newspaper exclaimed.[43]

The ink had barely dried on the agreements when Firestone's publicity machine kicked in. A full-page article appeared in the *New York Times*, written by James Young, who would become a public relations consultant for Firestone, celebrating the rise of an American rubber empire in Africa. Young's prose had all the trappings and clichés of a frontier narrative featuring white, Western explorers conquering the jungle and bringing modern civilization to "darkest Africa."[44]

Firestone sold his project to the world by wrapping it in a veneer of humanitarianism and development. The celebrated Harvard expedition, whose good reputation had enabled the U.S. State Department to pressure the Liberian government, had already proven the worth of American science and medicine in advancing Firestone's interests. American capital, guided by moral prescriptions and scientific goodwill, would help transform Liberia into a modern industrial nation. The promise of roads, harbors, electricity, machinery, telephones and radio, along with many other wonders that American science and medicine would bring, made for good publicity. The *Chicago Defender* heralded Firestone as "the greatest missionary Liberia ever welcomed from this country. What prayer and song has failed to do, he intends to accomplish with pick and shovel. Liberia, rich in mineral resources, can be redeemed by no other. Churches sending thousands each year to 'foreign fields' to 'spread the gospel' will see their mistake when Mr. Firestone makes his report after five years trial," the Black newspaper confidently asserted.[45] Not all African Americans were sure benefits would accrue to Liberia. A heated debate between two historically Black colleges—Virginia Union and Morgan College—on the question of whether the "Firestone interest in Liberia is detrimental to the natives" resulted in an overwhelming victory for Virginia Union. Arguing in the affirmative, the Virginia Union debaters predicted the Firestone experiment would result in land dispossession, low wages, and forced labor for Liberia's indigenous inhabitants.[46]

When the SS *Wadai* anchored off the shore of Monrovia on July 7, 1926, a bustle of activity erupted. Twenty 30-foot whaleboats, empty of cargo, rowed out from the harbor to crowd alongside the six-thousand-ton German steamer. Men aboard the *Wadai* tossed ropes to the Kru oarsmen manning the open boats below. The *Wadai* belonged to the Woermann shipping line, formed in 1849 to conduct trade with Liberia by Hamburg merchant Carl Woermann. Tons of expedition gear were on board: guns, a three-month supply of boxed food, photographic chemicals, medical supplies, experimental drugs, tents, cots, canvas bathtubs, two hundred white mice, and fifty guinea pigs. The expedition participants were there too. Once ashore, Strong would need to secure more than 250 porters to carry the weight of an expedition that marched under the flags of both Harvard University and the United States. American newspapers touted the expedition as an epic journey, one which, when completed, might result in the "saving of millions of lives."[47] But in the opening pages of his expedition diary, Strong privately disclosed intentions that extended far beyond those of humanitarian concern. With the arrival of Firestone in Liberia, he hoped the United States would "exercise a more stimulating influence upon the development of the interior of the country and its people" just as, in his view, the American government had done when it acquired "territory in the Philippine Islands, Guam, Panama, and Puerto Rico."[48]

Strong's journey to Liberia followed a circuitous path in the expanding reach of American empire. In 1898, as a new graduate of Johns Hopkins University's first class of physicians trained in the scientific, laboratory research methods of modern medicine, Strong, in the service of military and political conquest, traveled to the Philippines to work as a U.S. Army surgeon during the Spanish-American War. After the war, Strong helped establish and head the Biological Laboratory of the Philippine Bureau of Science. Enamored with medical breakthroughs and vaccines ushered in by the relatively new science of bacteriology, Strong focused the laboratory's attention on diseases such as cholera and plague that threatened the health of the islanders. His inoculation of twenty-four Filipino inmates of Manila's Bilibid Prison with an experimental cholera vaccine without their consent placed him at the center of a public scandal and investigation in 1906. The vaccine was contaminated with a virulent strain of bubonic plague. Thirteen prisoners died. Strong was found innocent of criminal negligence.[49] Any questions about his medical experimentation on colonial subjects were quickly swept aside in the missionary zeal and rhetoric of a supposedly benevolent American empire.

In the tropical environs of Manila, on polo playing fields and in officers' clubs, Strong cultivated a set of friendships that catapulted his career and access to those of wealth and influence in the Republican Party. Strong saw his good friend William Cameron Forbes appointed as governor-general of the Philippines. The two men shared a vision for the future of America's role in the tropical world. As governor-general, Forbes implemented programs aimed at the "material development" of U.S. overseas possessions. American expertise would bequeath to the inhabitants of supposedly "backward" countries the most modern and up-to-date physical, medical, economic, and political infrastructure. Armed with technology and know-how, engineers would build roads, bridges, and dams to improve transportation and industry; biologists would introduce improved methods of agriculture; medical doctors would implement modern sanitary principles to stamp out "exotic" diseases; and financial advisers would lay the foundation for economic growth and progress, implementing currency and fiscal reforms and ultimately putting the country on the path to the gold standard, which would dramatically facilitate free trade and financial exchange with the rest of the world.[50] Many of these appeals to benevolent paternalism would be appropriated by Firestone's company in enlisting the support of American diplomats, politicians, and scientists as its interest shifted from the Philippines to Liberia as a promising place to plant an American rubber empire.

The tropics, however, could wear on American colonial officials, even those who, like Strong, adhered to a strict regimen to keep mind and body

fit. Strong and other doctors believed fraught nerves and worn-out bodies were symptoms of whites being ill adapted to the tropics. In the early
twentieth century, the belief that climate largely determined civilization
found "scientific" support in popular works like *Civilization and Climate*
(1915), written by the Yale geographer Ellsworth Huntington.[51] Biological ideas of racial difference, shored up by climatic determinism and Dar-
winian theories of evolution, conveniently placed the Anglo-Saxon race at
the top of an evolutionary racial hierarchy. In northern climes, the struggle for existence in nature was posited to be fiercest. Superior intelligence
and fortitude evolved as traits among the Anglo-Saxon race who lived
there. By this logic, whites were intellectually fit to rule, but not adapted
physically to toil in the tropics. Scientific racism conveniently justified
racial capitalism. White administrators, regularly rotating in and out of
the tropics, managed and controlled Black and brown workers laboring in
the equatorial heat and humidity. This structure of labor management was
bolstered by scientific and medical theories with troubled histories born of
the plantation slavery era. Firestone's company would adopt the same design to regulate work on its "modern" industrial plantation in Liberia.

Forbes and Strong both left Manila for Boston in 1913. Strong returned
to the United States to create and head a tropical medicine department,
one of the country's first, at Harvard University, studying the "exotic" diseases that afflicted humans in hot and humid tropical environments. Forbes
became an overseer to Harvard University and a director of United Fruit
Company, the agricultural products marketing conglomerate best known for
its extensive holdings of banana plantations throughout Central America.

In the founding and flourishing of Harvard's Department of Tropical
Medicine, Strong was indebted to American businessmen, people like
Forbes and the New England sugar baron Edward Atkins, many with ties
to Harvard, who were making their wealth in the banana and sugarcane
industries in Central America and the Caribbean.[52] In creating the department, Strong brought together an interdisciplinary team of Harvard
faculty in tropical biology and medicine that looked upon "tropical America" as "one of the few large areas of the world now awaiting development."[53]
For many Harvard faculty, along with the businessmen sponsoring their
research, the tropics became the El Dorado upon which they built their
professional careers. As someone who concurrently served as Harvard department head and director of the Laboratories of the Hospitals and of
Research Work of United Fruit, Strong planned almost every American

expedition to Latin America in the 1910s and 1920s to areas of expressed or potential interest to U.S. commercial expansion abroad.

As gunboat diplomacy gave way to dollar diplomacy, Strong recognized that the tropical knowledge being advanced at places like Harvard's Department of Tropical Medicine could be a significant asset in the dual goals of U.S. commercial expansion and economic development. Companies like United Fruit were at the forefront of this economic expansion, striking deals with countries across Latin America for access to land for plantations, favorable tax treatment, and reduced duties on their export products.[54] In the 1920s, Strong fostered a business model for the department that relied upon modest annual subscriptions from commercial firms, including United Fruit, the American Chicle Company, and the International Petroleum Company, all of which had significant landholdings and investments in the tropics. The department offered expertise in the diagnosis, treatment, and prevention of tropical diseases affecting both human labor and commercial commodities, training of company medical staff, and advice on organizing company medical services. Tropical diseases such as malaria, yellow fever, and river blindness came to be seen as parasites of capital, sucking the profits out of American firms establishing their presence in the tropical world. In turn, the Harvard department received not only financial donations. It also gained unrivaled access to new diseases, unknown species, and diverse habitats. This access was facilitated by the transportation and communication networks of American commercial firms in their expanding global economic reach after the First World War. It is no coincidence that Strong referred to the work of the department as one of industrial hygiene. Virtually all of the department's expeditions occurred on industrial landscapes in the making.

Firestone's experiment in Liberia was of great interest to Strong. As a shareholder in two British rubber plantations, the Harvard professor recognized the threat that Britain's rubber monopoly posed to America's economic interests. In February 1925, Strong received an inquiry from the Firestone Tire & Rubber Company. In it, the company acknowledged that the efficiency and success of the plantations in Liberia would in "no small way" depend "upon the health" of its workers and asked Strong to recommend well-qualified men who could "provide medical services for our Executive Staff as well as native labor."[55] Little happened until December, when Frederick Cheever Shattuck, using his Harvard connections, set up a meeting between Strong, his protégé, and Harvey Firestone Sr.

When they met at New York City's Plaza Hotel in January 1926, Strong pitched the value of his department's expertise to Firestone's enterprise in Liberia. Harvey Sr. expressed interest and offered the expedition logistical support, but he offered no money to Harvard. As Strong set sail for Monrovia, Shattuck wrote to assure Strong that soon, "Firestone will open his pocket."[56] In late August, shortly after the Harvard expedition left the Firestone plantation area for Liberia's hinterland, another letter arrived from Shattuck. "Firestone has his hand on the plow and I don't doubt that we will help him to keep it there," Strong's benefactor stated confidently. From his perch of white privilege, Shattuck wrote, "8,000 Afro-American[s] can't run things indefinitely."[57] It was a derogatory, racist dismissing of Black self-rule. Soon Firestone's pockets did open, paying $20,000 to publish the expedition's two-volume report. The partnership with Harvard University was a boon to Firestone public relations and would prove critical to the making of an industrial plantation.

It took multiple acts of destruction to build a new world. Clearing the forest and tilling the soil to plant the seeds of a rubber empire began with the taking of land. Firestone bragged that they had "literally invaded the wilderness."[58] Strong boasted that he and his men were venturing into one of the most unknown parts of West Africa. This was terra nullius, "nobody's land"—at least in the eyes of Firestone and those advancing his interests in Liberia. A 1916 map of Liberia, furnished to the Harvard team by the U.S. State Department, underscored this impression. The map, as British novelist Graham Greene described in his own Liberian travelogue, was so "inaccurate—large blank spaces were filled with the word 'Cannibals'—that it would be useless, perhaps, even dangerous to follow."[59]

Such portrayals of Liberia's hinterland were violent acts of erasure. They failed to acknowledge the relationships of people with the land that had shaped the region's ecology. These were people whose knowledge and labor Strong and the Firestone Plantations Company would come to rely upon. Firestone and his acolytes projected a future of development on a map made blank by ignoring or belittling ways of life and interrelations among people, animals, plants, and spirits that had dwelled in the Upper Guinean rainforest for centuries. The Harvard team was part of an "expeditionary force of pioneers"—white engineers, doctors, botanists, soil scientists, and anthropologists, among others—sent by the Akron benefactor to conquer the jungle and bring its "natives" into the fold of industrial capitalism and a Western, Christianized civilization.[60] It was a familiar narrative that had justified the taking of land and the extermination or assimilation of indigenous peoples in the westward march of American empire in the nineteenth century and its overseas expansion in the twentieth. In its embrace of this narrative, the Firestone Plantations Company aligned with the interests of Liberia's original settlers, who had come from America with a mission to "introduce into degraded and benighted Africa the blessings of Civilization and Christianity," as the country's first president, Joseph Jenkins Roberts, declared.[61]

The "civilized" versus "native" framework had structured the very legal foundations of the Liberian Republic. The Declaration of Independence recognized "we, the people," as those who "were originally inhabitants of the United States of America." Mention of the country's indigenous occupants is relatively absent in the country's founding documents. The few references that do exist give them little recognition. Yet, over time, as Liberian settlers interacted with indigenous Liberians, pushback grew against what Blyden criticized as a tendency to legislate in Liberia "as Americans in America for Americans," with little regard to the customs, laws, and rights of the country's indigenous inhabitants.[62]

Throughout much of the nineteenth century, Liberia's indigenous territory, governed by multiple polities and ethnic groups, was vital to settler trade and commerce. But it was largely outside of Monrovia's political control: a sphere of influence that extended little more than forty-five miles from the coast into the interior. France's and Great Britain's consolidation and control of territory in West Africa by the close of the nineteenth century had put Liberia in a bind. The principle of effective occupation, adopted at the Berlin Conference in 1885, which was held, in part, to divvy up Africa, utilized international law to subordinate indigenous claims to sovereignty to the interests of European colonial powers, who claimed the right to take possession of territory on the African continent in the name of civilization.[63] Monrovia's settler government lacked economic, political, and military control over the country's hinterland, which France and Great Britain increasingly used to challenge Liberia's territorial claims. Partly in response to these pressure tactics, and spurred by an urgent need for increased internal revenues to address Liberia's failing economy, President Arthur Barclay in 1905 enacted a series of reforms meant to bring the country's indigenous population and its territory into the administrative, economic, and legal fold of the nation.[64] A system of indirect rule modeled after British policies was established in the interior, by which local chiefs were installed as the arms of the central government. Indigenous inhabitants deemed sufficiently "civilized" were granted voting rights and made eligible for land allotments. The Liberian government also instituted a hut tax that demanded each town or village pay the government's district commissioner an annual levy in cash and goods based on the number of houses present. Should a village fail to comply, the Frontier Force, organized in 1908, offered the state a military means to exact its revenue by physical might.[65]

Insurrections against the government were frequent in the two decades before Firestone's arrival. For example, the 1915–16 Kru Rebellion, one of the most significant acts of indigenous resistance in Liberian history, arose out of growing animosity toward taxes that the settler government imposed on the Kru people. Their labor, seafaring knowledge, and trade in palm oil, piassava, and other products had long been essential to Liberia's coastal economy. Yet they received "no protection, no justice, and no benefits" from the Liberian state, they told American investigators. These investigators had arrived aboard the USS *Chester*, a destroyer ship sent by the U.S. government, along with American military officers commissioned to take charge of the Liberian Frontier Force, to help quell the coastwise revolt. Thousands of Kru houses were burned to the ground. Many Kru were killed. Forty-seven Kru chiefs and headmen were hanged on government charges of murder and rebellion. The American military sided with the interests of the Liberian state in the clash over indigenous claims to economic and political self-determination.[66]

Terra nullius? Such conflicts, as well as sporadic dissent against the government's treatment of the country's indigenous inhabitants, suggest otherwise. So do the reports of the Harvard expedition, which began by surveying and collecting life in the region Firestone had selected for a vast experiment in reordering the area's ecology on an industrial scale. Birds and mammals, reptiles and insects, plants and fungi, and especially parasites that threatened the well-being and productivity of workers and the prized, imported rubber tree, *Hevea brasiliensis*, were all subjects of the expedition's study. David Linder, the expedition's chief botanist, marveled at the verdant and impenetrable jungle he passed through on a flat-bottomed, mahogany launch. The expedition made its way thirty miles up the Junk and Du Rivers to Firestone Plantation No. 3, which would become the expedition's base camp. Along the riverbanks, the tangled, aerial prop roots of the screw pine, *Pandanus candelabrum*, and the arched canopy of its long, sword-like leaves gave Linder the impression that he had entered "a restored forest of the carboniferous period."[67] Farther inland, as the elevation began to rise, swamp gave way to mixed forest. Here, the silk-cotton tree, *Ceiba pentandra*, with its majestic winged buttresses supporting a gray columnar trunk reaching upward of 160 feet, towered above the forest. The cotton tree, "Ghuo chu" in the Bassa language, was recognized among indigenous Liberians as a sacred marker of ancestral occupation. Planted by prior occupants, whose spirits still dwell there, the tree marks a continuing customary claim to the land.

Traveling up the Du, Linder imagined journeying back in time to a primeval era, before humans had arrived and reshaped life in the forest. But as the Harvard expedition passed through the Firestone concession area, it was clear this was not some American idea of pristine wilderness, despite Firestone's claim. It was a patchwork of primary forest, secondary growth forest, cultivated land, and interspersed villages. From within an expanse of 100,000 acres to which Firestone initially laid claim, 20,000 acres along the Du River were selected for clearing.

This area Firestone first claimed and felled was the homeland of the Bassa people. They were among the initial group of Kwa-speaking peoples to migrate, from the northeastern edge of the Upper Guinean rainforest to a region stretching from the West African coast to fifty miles inland within what is now present-day Liberia.[68] Before Firestone's arrival, this was a landscape managed to sustain a diversity of life. Working in a multi-year cycle and in an area near their village edge, men would selectively chop and burn a clearing in the forest to let in light and release nutrients. Oil palm and cotton trees were left standing, a reflection of the integral part they played in the lives of some of Liberia's indigenous peoples. Women would then plant and harvest rice, cassava, and other food staples in the opened area. After a few years, a nutrient-depleted clearing would be left fallow and a new clearing prepared. Such practices and rhythms, known as swidden agriculture, shaped life in the region.

Tree crops—including coffee, cacao, kola, orange, and oil palm—were planted amid the returning second-growth forest. Planting tree crops did more than supply food and trade. For the planters' descendants, they physically substantiated in the land both the memory of ancestral occupation and the powers and benefits associated with land held in common. Harvard expedition members noted these forms of swidden agriculture visible

Photos and motion picture footage of a Bassa cultural performance on Firestone Plantation No. 4, taken by Harvard expedition photographer Loring Whitman in 1926, of which this is an example, served as a reminder to elders in Queezahn in 2018 of the displacement their ancestors experienced with the arrival of Firestone. Image by Loring Whitman. (Courtesy of Indiana University Libraries.)

throughout the concession area. But Strong saw little of value in the economic, social, and spiritual relationships Bassa people cultivated with the land and life around them and regarded them as not "particularly intelligent as a race."[69] The taking and destruction of Bassa customary lands was a first step in Firestone's development of a new economy of nature that would, in Strong's estimation, "bring great benefit to the country and redound to the welfare of its people."[70]

Technically, the Firestone agreements excluded "tribal reserves of land set aside for the communal use of any tribe within the Republic of Liberia." But the government ran roughshod over customary land claims nevertheless.[71] Stories of land dispossession wrought by Firestone and the Liberian government abound. Motion picture footage taken in 1926 by Loring

Whitman, the Harvard expedition's official photographer, depicts cultural dances performed by Bassa and Grebo peoples on land being developed on the first divisions of the plantations. When our research team shared this footage with elders in Queezahn, a small village to the southeast of the Firestone concession area, it elicited powerful responses. Images of their ancestors dancing brought up memories of displacement, crops destroyed, cultural traditions lost, and promises broken. The place name Queezahn means the "White (or civilized) people took us from there." Elders claim the name implicates both Firestone and the settler government in the taking of Bassa land and the displacing of their ancestors from, they assert, the area where the Firestone Staff Club now sits. Several years ago, the Queezahn community gathered under cover on a rainy afternoon. An elder remarked that they are still waiting for Firestone to rebuild their village, more than ninety years after the company took their land. Laughter erupted. The joke cuts to the bone with the pain of past deeds that destroyed intimate relationships with the land.[72]

Another place name recalls the violence of land seizure. Firestone's clearing of the land that became Division 22 required torching thousands of acres of cut wood, desiccated in the intense heat of Liberia's dry season. Firestone took care to notify town chiefs in nearby villages that they would assume no responsibility for losses incurred by fires that got out of their control.[73] Elders suggest that these fires are the origin of "Wolowoennie," a name that refers to a part of Division 22 and means "baboon burning." As recounted by a second-generation Firestone worker whose father came in 1926 to work on the plantations: "People refused to move, so the whole area got burned. So the people that got burned, they name them wolo (baboon)."[74]

The Harvard expedition members make no mention—not in personal letters, diaries, or official publications—of the devastating effects of this ecological violence, its destruction of life and lifeways.[75] From their vantage at base camp on Plantation No. 3, they instead marveled at the creative destruction. Sounds reverberated around them: work gangs chopping trees in unison to drums and song, and the trees, some 150 feet tall and 4 feet wide, crashing to the ground. Among Liberia's indigenous inhabitants, many of these trees, including Jru (sasswood), Fauh (red ironwood), and Kut-wahn (*Cassipourea firestoneana*), had medicinal or ritualistic value. To Firestone, they were worthless unless sawn into timber or converted to nutrients by fire. At Plantation No. 1, Whitman reflected in amazement at

For the Harvard expedition members, the clear-cutting of Liberia's rainforest represented not ecological violence, but the foundations of modern industrial development. Image by Loring Whitman, 1926. (Courtesy of Indiana University Libraries.)

how "this whole clearing was virgin forest in November."[76] His friend Hal Coolidge, the expedition's assistant zoologist, was similarly in awe of the transformation, remarking, "The great forest is as bare as a good lumbering job in the U.S. and between the stumps are sticks in straight lines, cuttings of rubber trees already planted."[77]

Clear-cutting the rainforest, reordering life, and importing labor on an industrial scale created opportunistic conditions in which certain pathogens thrived. One such disease was smallpox, a threat to the health and productivity of Firestone labor. After setting up base camp, the Harvard team learned of a smallpox case on Plantation No. 2. With thousands of workers living together in close quarters, a contagious virus could burn through the plantation, killing and scarring untold numbers. Strong located and isolated the infected worker, and the Harvard medical team sprang into action. Led by Strong and Shattuck and with key contributions from Max Theiler, the expedition's chief bacteriologist, and Firestone physician

Firestone relied upon the labor, knowledge, and experience of Liberia's indigenous inhabitants in felling and clearing the rainforest for agriculture in its making of a rubber plantation. Image by Loring Whitman, 1926. (Courtesy of Indiana University Libraries.)

Dr. Willis, the expedition team vaccinated more than one hundred men per hour until their work was done. A disaster had been averted. The Harvard team's impressive medical work made for great press, underscoring the assistance coming to Liberia from the "civilizing hand" of American

science and medicine, now that Firestone was planted in the country. Time and again, Firestone used the modern medical expertise provided through his company to paint a picture of a munificent American corporation advancing the interests and welfare of a "backward" nation, as branded by the white, Western world.[78]

The routes the Harvard expedition followed on their journey through the Liberian interior were not drawn on an official Liberian map, but they were well known by Mandingo traders; nineteenth-century Liberian explorers; missionaries; and the Bassa, Kpelle, Mano, and Vai peoples, among others.[79] The paths upon which Strong and his team trekked had long transported slaves, kola nuts, and other commodities from Liberia's interior to coastal markets. More recently, they served as paths of conquest, used by Liberia's Frontier Force and district commissioners to subdue Liberia's indigenous population and bring it into the fold of an emerging nation-state.[80] Conflict continued in the messy process of state formation. For example, in 1921 the Jorkwelle clan of the Kpelle people attacked a military post in Naama, a town in north-central Liberia, through which the expedition would pass five years later. American-led Liberian Frontier Forces of about seven hundred men suppressed the armed attack, marking the beginning of the end of indigenous insurrections.[81] By the time Firestone arrived, internecine warfare and ethnic conflicts with the Liberian government had largely subsided. In 1927, President King confidently asserted that "thanks to the all-wise direction of Providence, feelings of hostility and periods of conflict between the government and the native population in the interior . . . are now considered things of the past, and let us hope the irrevocable past."[82] The Liberian interior was open to the "civilizing mission" of Christianity and Firestone, despite pockets of indigenous resistance that persisted beyond King's administration (1920–30).

Strong conveyed to the American press that the expedition was on a mission to conquer the jungle, uplift the "natives," and bring light to "Darkest Africa." But these Western scientists were completely dependent upon the knowledge and skills of local hunters; the good graces of town, clan, and paramount chiefs; and the guidance and labor of hundreds of porters to find their way and carry their loads. A disgruntled Strong recognized early on that Glover Allen, the expedition's chief zoologist, and his assistant, Coolidge, were both rather hopeless at tracking and shooting the mammals the expedition intended to collect. Strong had to hire, at some expense, indigenous hunters. The first, on his first day, killed three of the largest Colobus monkeys Strong had ever seen. The expert skills of indigenous hunters put to shame those of the Harvard crew, and contributed to the expedition's success. But these men are not mentioned in the expedition reports.

The ignoring and, thereby, erasure of indigenous knowledge, like the erasure of indigenous land claims, helped legitimate the expedition's interventions into the landscapes and lives of people outside the marketplace of

A young Liberian expedition worker posing with a bagged crocodile. In collecting wildlife for Harvard's Museum of Comparative Zoology, Strong and his team were reliant upon the skills of local indigenous hunters. Image by Loring Whitman, 1926. (Courtesy of Indiana University Libraries.)

American science, medicine, and industry. In encounters along the expedition's path, Strong and his men often expressed annoyance at the unwillingness of people to have their pictures taken or blood drawn. When, for example, a town chief refused to give up his "charming little tumor, we cajoled, we threatened, we vowed he would die," wrote Whitman, "and still he coyly refused to part with that most . . . cherished treasure."[83] The chief had grounds for suspicion: the taking of bodily things and the administering of experimental drugs probably seemed not unlike the local witchcraft he feared. Such acts of resistance, in the eyes of Harvard physicians, were superstitious, irrational impediments to progress. Strong believed that if only Liberia would embrace the vision of Harvey Firestone and the promise of American science and medicine, then "a new era of prosperity in the development of the country and the welfare of its people as a whole" could arrive.[84]

Plenyono Gbe Wolo, the son of a Kru paramount chief and a Harvard graduate, with his wife, Djua. This published Harvard expedition photograph had the erroneous caption, "Plenyono Wolo, son of a Vai chief, and his wife." Image by Loring Whitman, 1926. (Courtesy of Indiana University Libraries.)

The population view that informed the Harvard expedition, wherein people were potential vectors of disease and pools of labor, meshed with the tools, language, and projections of economic development used by the Firestone Plantations Company. Strong saw Liberia's indigenous people primarily as resources for American science and industry. But Whitman's camera captured the lives of individuals, people who were much more than laboring bodies, reservoirs of biological specimens, or objects of a scientific curiosity. Among the 476 still photographs of people, customs, crafts, diseases, and landscapes that appear in the published account of the expedition, only one contains a caption with a person's full name. The caption reads, "Plenyono Wolo, son of a Vai chief, and his wife." The Harvard University archives has another photograph of Plenyono Wolo, taken in 1917. In it, Wolo is dressed not in tribal costume but in Harvard graduaation robes. The elision of Wolo's Harvard pedigree and the fabrication, or perhaps misapplication, of his ethnic identity in the expedition photo reveals the ignorance and accompanying erasure that were the hallmark of the Harvard expedition as it trekked through Liberia.[85]

Wolo was the son not of a Vai chief but of an esteemed paramount chief of the Kru people. He was educated by Methodist missionaries and completed studies at the College of West Africa. He worked his way on a boat to America and graduated from Massachusetts's Mount Hermon School for Boys in 1913. Kru advocate Didhwo Twe, himself a Harvard student, had filled out Wolo's application.[86] Wolo earned a BA with honors from Harvard University in 1917; completed an MA in 1919 from Columbia University's Teachers College; and received a bachelor of divinity degree at Union Theological Seminary in 1922. Through contacts made by Harvard president Abbott Lawrence Lowell, he helped conduct a 1919 economic survey in Liberia for American commercial interests. Among Harvard and Columbia faculty and his classmates, Wolo was known, perhaps sometimes facetiously, as the "African prince." While working as a waiter in Harvard dinner clubs to pay his way through college, he realized no white students were among the waitstaff. It struck him as impugning the dignity of his Kru people and of African peoples in general, so he quit. He understood that as a Black Harvard student, he was not equal in the eyes of many. He spent a summer in North Carolina working as a common laborer to experience firsthand the realities of inequality and segregation that Black Americans faced in the Jim Crow South.[87]

With a $750 check from the Phelps Stokes Fund and another $2,000 from private donations, Wolo returned in the early 1920s to his village of Grand Cess to live, as he stated, "quietly among my people, as one of them, without being under any obligation to any board."[88] Wolo was critical of education of the "urban type, which prepares the gentleman who wears gloves to keep cool in tropical Africa," making some "black men" so "westernized in their notions that one would find it difficult to believe they were black except for the accident, in their case, of exterior pigmentation." He also critiqued colonial educational systems that banned the teaching of native languages in schools. "To deprive a people of their language," he suggested, "comes well nigh to deracializing them." Africa was, he argued, largely a "continent of villages," desperately in need not of prodigious orators, lawyers, and statesmen but of doctors, nurses, farmers, trained mechanics and skilled laborers "who alone can conquer and make the environment obey their creative powers and trained gifts."[89] Toward this end, he built a day school in Grand Cess, with enrollment quickly surpassing two hundred pupils. Its training program focused on practical techniques of raising foodstuffs and the introduction of native crafts. Certainly Virginia's Hampton Normal and Agricultural Institute, where Wolo likely spent a summer, and Alabama's Tuskegee Institute were models for the agricultural and industrial training schools he envisioned to foster rural education in Liberia. But with no foundation behind him and under pressure from the local Catholic Church, which ran a competing school, his larger aspirations were thwarted.[90]

Like Harvard alumnus Strong, Wolo held out great hope for the prospects of Firestone in Liberia. Again at the request of Harvard president Lowell, Wolo aided Cheek in his initial visit on Firestone's behalf to Liberia. Wolo took Cheek to Sunday services at Kru Town, introducing him to Kru people and to members of other ethnic groups from which Firestone would likely draw laborers. Cheek was "carried away with the physical appearance of the people," exclaimed Wolo.[91] For several months, Wolo advised the company on employees and suitable housing styles. He hoped for a managerial position that would involve "welfare work" and implementing and overseeing a "commissariat" for employees. Wolo was eager to have his "finger in the pie" in industrialization's initial stage in Liberia, which, he believed, would provide a foundation for "moral, intellectual, and religious" development. In 1926, he secured an assistant manager position on the Firestone plantations, overseeing a workforce on the Du plantations and brokering labor relations between different ethnic groups.[92] After Harvey Firestone Jr. completed his first trip to Liberia in December that year, Wolo expressed confidence in the young executive's "keen and sympathetic" regard "to the social welfare of the laborers" and their right to a "fair wage."[93] Wolo's work on the plantations, however, was short-lived. Firestone soon established a policy of whites-only management, which would continue for almost forty years.

Although Wolo brokered many of the arrangements in Liberia for the Harvard expedition, walked with Strong through the streets of Monrovia, and sat among his Harvard "brothers" at a dinner organized by President King, Strong failed to acknowledge what Whitman documented on film: the traces of Plenyono Gbe Wolo's lived life. Wolo's biography did not fit in Strong's view of Liberia's indigenous ethnic groups, wherein the Kru people are spoken of disparagingly and represented in photographs only as medical subjects.[94] Maybe Strong saw the Kru lineage as not suited to a Harvard alum, and so, whether purposefully or born of disregard, he dressed Wolo in a different life.

In misidentifying Wolo, Strong perhaps revealed his prejudices regarding the suitability of different indigenous groups for Firestone's needed labor force. The Harvard doctor was no anthropologist. But he had opinions regarding labor, and he let his scientific credentials back his advice to Firestone. His valuations of different ethnic groups considered a host of components—blood relations, dress, literacy, religion, and craft skills—to create an explicit hierarchical classification of people. This formula appealed to science for support in reinforcing notions of racial superiority and difference. The Vai, a subgroup of the Mandingo, Strong reasoned, were "superior intellectually" and "one of the most progressive groups in the native population." Their knowledge of Arabic, their own written language, their skills in farming and weaving—all made them, he argued, "an important civilized and important civilizing element in Liberia."[95] Strong gave Wolo the ethnic belonging he saw as best suited to a Harvard graduate and a Firestone plantations assistant manager. Vai religious beliefs, knowledge, and skills came closest, in Strong's racialized ladder of development, to the characteristics of white civilization, which occupied the highest rung. That highest position unquestionably legitimated white supremacy and the missionary reach of American empire across the globe. In contrast to the Vai people, Strong had little positive to say about settler immigrants. They are not "good agriculturalists or gardeners," and "physically they are lazy," he opined in the two-volume expedition tome published by Harvard University Press and dedicated to Harvey S. Firestone. "Liberia," Strong asserted, "cannot be successfully developed without the aid of interior tribes."[96]

As the Harvard expedition moved through the Liberian interior, members' observations and accounts were suffused with judgments about which indigenous ethnic groups held the greatest worth to Firestone. Their views interested Firestone, who was eager to find productive plantation workers and to learn "what in native life is worth preserving and what can be eliminated or improved upon." Firestone again reached out to Harvard University to "unofficially" hire a qualified anthropologist to continue where Strong's party left off.[97] Earnest Hooton, curator of Harvard's Peabody Museum, was a physical anthropologist dedicated to the study of anatomy

to discern supposed biological differences in racial types. He recommended his student George Schwab for the task. Schwab had spent the
better part of his career as a Presbyterian minister and missionary in Cameroon.[98] In Liberia, the neophyte anthropologist set to work. He carefully
measured 382 indigenous men and women to assess their value to Firestone. Assisting Schwab was George Way Harley, a Yale-trained physician
who had just established a Methodist mission among the Mano people
in Ganta, a trading post on the Liberian border. Schwab compiled a list
of characteristics he thought "common to all primitive Negroes." The list
included sensitivity to pain, capacity for smell and taste, conception of
truth, sense of loyalty, humor, and intelligence.[99] The list drew upon racist
caricatures and stereotypes that served to affirm superiority of the white
race. Anthropometry, as this measurement science is called, has a sordid
past. Measurement and quantification of Black bodies originated on the
plantation. The accounting practices of white plantation owners violently
rendered enslaved Black people into commodities. Black bodies were valued solely for their productive and reproductive capacity, for the physical
labor they performed in transforming life into capital.[100] Slavery was out-
lawed in Liberia, but the accounting of bodies and the racial ordering of
labor that structured work on the Firestone plantations hardly represented
a radical break from the past.

Schwab thought it would take "some years of experimenting" to determine "which tribe would be most suited for any particular branch of plantation work."[101] But Strong had his own opinions. The Kpelle people, whose
territory occupied the central region of the country, stood out. Strong
greatly valued the skills of Kpelle hunters he hired. They were far more
adept at tracking and shooting game in the forest than any member of his
team. Without the knowledge of these indigenous hunters, the bird,
mammal, and reptile collections that the expedition sent back to Harvard
University's Museum of Comparative Zoology would have been sparse. In
addition, the Kpelle were an agricultural people. Strong, with great interest, took note of the "many plantations" they passed through on the
journey from Plantation No. 3 to the town of Gbarnga. "Rice, cassava,
and millet, plantains and sugar cane," and "bananas, coffee, cotton and
tobacco" were "cultivated extensively."[102] And the Kpelle were also, in
Strong's view, peaceful.

This impression was confirmed for Strong as they passed through Suakoko, a town 110 miles northeast of Monrovia. This was a region con-

trolled by a powerful woman chief named Madam Suakoko. A renowned Zoe, the title for a respected elder of the women's secret Sande Society, Madam Suakoko reportedly commanded legendary healing and spiritual powers. Elders today speak of the hospitality she showed strangers traveling on the important trade route through her domain.[103] In the 1910s, when the last battles to control the interior were being fought, her diplomatic skills brought her people and territory into alliance with the Liberian government. The Harvard men met with the kindness of Madam Suakoko, who furnished them a dinner of country rice, chicken, and squash and supplied the expedition with needed porters.

Strong painted a picture of the Kpelle as best suited to plantation life: allies of the Liberian government, "peaceful and industrious," and formerly "principal purveyors of slaves."[104] Within a few years, the path through the central interior upon which the Harvard expedition trekked would become the rubber corridor of Liberia: a 100-mile stretch of road, initially built with corvée labor, reaching from Harbel, the center of the Firestone plantations, to Gbarnga, the hub of Bong County and the Kpelle people.

Bound for the Belgian Congo aboard the SS *Wolfram* on the last day of November 1926, Strong drafted a letter to Harvard University president Lowell reciting the expedition's accomplishments in Liberia. They had traversed almost every part of the country and made observations "among almost all of the important tribes." They collected approximately 500 bird and mammal skins. They obtained 1,300 specimens of flowering plants, 36 species of blood-sucking insects, and "15 species of fleas, lice, bugs, ticks and other sundry parasites." They set up numerous medical clinics, performed diagnostic laboratory work, and compiled a medical survey of diseases—including malaria, schistosomiasis, onchocerciasis (river blindness), hookworm, leprosy, and elephantiasis, among others—that afflicted Liberia's population. They took more than 675 photographs and shot 7,700 feet of motion picture film that documented Liberian life along the coast and within the interior. All in all, Strong summarized, it was a successful expedition, one that Harvard could be proud of.[105]

Strong, who was relieved the expedition ended with its members in good health, concluded his letter with a concern he felt a responsibility to address. He asked Lowell to discuss with him at length "some of the political and social questions regarding Liberia" encountered by the expedition.[106]

Men, conscripted by the Liberian government, building a road by hand. Strong instructed Whitman to document the use of forced labor by the Liberian government on film to convince the U.S. government to take a more active stance against alleged labor abuses in ways that would benefit Firestone. Image by Loring Whitman, 1926. (Courtesy of Indiana University Libraries.)

As he departed Liberia, Strong also wrote to Assistant Secretary of State William Castle to express his dismay at the "distressing conditions found to exist here, particularly in the interior."[107] The "questions" and "distressing conditions" mentioned in these two letters were thinly veiled references to the issue of forced labor in Liberia. During the expedition, Strong had grown increasingly incensed about labor conditions. He realized Firestone's plan to secure a labor force of 300,000 men was grossly ignorant of prevailing conditions. Male labor was in short supply. Strong recognized it firsthand while in southeastern Liberia when the expedition had to use women as porters. Doing so pained Strong's sense of morality and masculinity. But the villages they passed through in that region were bereft of men. The men had been subsumed by the Liberian government's forced labor scheme that supplied contracted workers to the cocoa plantations on Fernando Po, an island of long-standing strategic importance in the Atlantic slave trade, occupied successively since the fifteenth century by the Portuguese, Dutch, and Spanish. Strong increasingly instructed Whitman to document conditions of oppression and coerced labor with photographs and film—men building roads, women in pawn, women working on government farms, and porters carrying district commissioners by hammock through the interior. Such images added to the increasing weight of documentary evidence Strong amassed, hoping to convince U.S. government officials to take an active stand against labor abuses in Liberia.

When Strong returned to the United States, his connections to the highest echelons of the Republican Party opened the door to the White House. Chief Justice of the Supreme Court William Howard Taft welcomed his friend from the Philippines to his home in Washington, DC, to hear the doctor's concerns.[108] In February 1928, another friend and patron, William Cameron Forbes, arranged for Strong to be an overnight guest of President Coolidge at the White House. Strong attempted to impress upon the president the "excessive abuses" inflicted upon the people in the country's interior by the government's Liberian Frontier Force, without any "redress."[109] Although Strong welcomed the idea of Liberia becoming an U.S. protectorate, he thought such an intervention was "impracticable at the present time." Instead, he believed the loan to Liberia required by the Firestone agreements gave the United States powerful leverage over Liberia. Castle replied shortly after the meeting that the "President was most interested and that those talks have very much roused his concern for that country."[110] Strong also went public with his accusations, arguing in a *Boston Herald* editorial that the conditions of forced labor "are not such as would receive either the approbation or the respect of the civilized world."[111]

In making moral accusations in public against the Liberian government, Strong did not disclose his ties to Firestone. It likely appeared that the concerns of a Harvard physician were born of humanitarian intentions and goodwill toward Liberia's indigenous population. But Strong's interactions with and descriptions of Liberia's diverse ethnic groups suggest more complicated motives. Indeed, Strong himself resorted to forced labor practices while in Liberia. As the expedition reached Towya, a town near the southeastern coast, his team grew desperate. Few men could be found in the villages, and those hired often ran away, abandoning their cargo. At

times, Whitman alone transported the loads across rivers that proved un-
manageable for shorter women and children. When they did finally secure a group of men, they tied them up with strings or vines. "It was quite
a merry caravan," Whitman wrote in his diary. "Eighteen men in chains
(I mean ropes) with three white men armed to the teeth—ready to shoot
to kill—a pretty picture." Whitman couldn't help but reflect on how the
image was not unlike "years ago when many such scenes took place," where
"whites with whips and crude guns" drove their way thru the forests . . . the
"slave traders."[112] But it was an image neither he nor his boss chose to
document on film.

In speaking out against the most blatant instances of forced labor in Liberia, Strong benefited Firestone immensely. The rubber company's success in
securing workers depended greatly upon pressuring the Liberian government to abandon its domestic use of and export trade in forced labor.[113]
Moreover, such an action would resonate with the Firestone-promoted
ideology of corporate welfare and benevolence in which science and medicine played an important role. While Firestone staunchly opposed
unionization in his factories at home, he nevertheless saw himself as a
pioneer in labor relations, providing his employees with numerous benefits like housing and health care. Images of plantations worked by forced
labor simply did not fit with this carefully crafted image of benevolent
capitalism.

Science and medicine proved critical allies in planting an American corporation in Liberia and in nurturing the seeds of a growing plantation
world. Tropical medicine and botany, entomology, and anthropology, among
other sciences, helped to transform relationships of land and life in Liberia
to benefit an introduced tree, *Hevea brasiliensis*, and a system of production
out of which rubber and profits would flow. In this massive industrial
undertaking, Firestone looked to scientific expertise and knowledge that
advanced not racial equality but white supremacy and racial difference.
Scientific statements and moral prescriptions went hand in hand in ways
that had legitimated both Jim Crow policies within the United States and
the interventionism of American empire across the globe.

# 4

# An American Protectorate?

Harvey Firestone's Miami Beach vacation home, Harbel Villa, an Italian Renaissance–style mansion built along sixteen hundred feet of oceanfront, was separated from his budding industrial plantation in Liberia by five thousand miles of Atlantic Ocean. Each February, Firestone reunited with his fellow vagabonds in Florida to mark Edison's birthday—Thomas Edison and Henry Ford had adjoining homes 150 miles away in Fort Myers. On February 11, 1929, Fort Myers was abuzz with parades, fireworks, and picnics. Newspaper reporters and photographers came from across the county. Children lined up at the Edison estate gates, hoping to be part of the festivities honoring Edison's eighty-second birthday. In a photograph taken that day, Edison, his features chiseled by age and success, looks into the camera with a confident swagger. To his left, Firestone poses self-assuredly. On his right, automotive king Ford converses with former secretary of commerce and recently victorious Republican presidential candidate Herbert Hoover. The president-elect, whose victory had been aided by the purse strings and endorsements of the three men photographed with him, had arrived that day by yacht: when the behemoth *Saunterer* pulled up to Edison's pier, the inventor shouted up to Hoover, "Hello fisherman."[1] Edison's birthday celebration, his esteemed guests and their projects, and the president-elect's penchant for big-game fishing—he planned a few days of tarpon fishing before his March 4 inauguration—made good newspaper copy.

Rested and relaxed, basking in their financial and political success, the privileged friends had good reasons to look forward.[2] Firestone's anti-restriction campaign, backed by the U.S. government under Hoover's auspices as commerce secretary, had helped convince Great Britain to repeal the Stevenson Act in November of 1928. Increasing production on the rubber plantations of the Dutch East Indies also helped by breaking the British

Herbert Hoover, Henry Ford, Thomas Edison, and Harvey Firestone celebrating
Edison's eighty-second birthday in 1929 at Fort Myers, Florida.

stranglehold on the world's rubber supplies.[3] Firestone claimed that the
British rubber restriction had cost the American consumer $625 million.
His Liberian venture, he boasted to reporters, "assured" the United States of
"an independent rubber supply."[4] In truth, American-owned rubber planta-
tions provided just under 5 percent of U.S. rubber consumption in 1929.[5]
Facts be damned. This triumphant gathering of friends spoke of good times
to come. Firestone predicted that under Hoover's administration, the United
States "will have the most prosperous four years it has ever had."[6]

To the press who flocked to Edison's birthday gala, Firestone described
a vast enterprise underway in Liberia. He credited his son Harvey Jr. for
his foresight in selecting Liberia as a suitable place to grow American
rubber and for sealing the deal for a million-acre concession. The rubber
magnate rattled off the company's supposed accomplishments. "We have
125 white American college graduates in charge of the 20,000 black

employees," he said. "We are cooperating with the missionaries in the establishment of a public school system." "We have cleared 50,000 acres" and planted roughly 6 million trees. "The country was passing out of existence when we took hold," a fervent Firestone claimed, revealing his underlying attitude and intentions toward the sovereign Black republic. "Our going into Liberia has saved that country, which is more or less a protectorate of the United States," he crowed.[7]

Firestone's introduction of wage labor, amounting to an annual payroll of more than $1 million, along with $2 million investment in infrastructure, including roads, bridges, water supplies, and rubber seeds, did have a noticeable impact on the Liberian economy. Imports in 1928 skyrocketed to more than $4 million, a value more than triple that of three years earlier. Government revenues soared. Merchants and traders, anticipating future Firestone investments, "were feverishly occupied in filling their shelves with merchandise for expected business."[8]

Yet in 1929, the picture on the ground looked quite different from the salesman's pitch. Behind the statistics trumpeted at the company's headquarters, Firestone's dream of building an American rubber empire in Liberia was fast becoming a nightmare. Liberian officials knew how to frustrate Firestone and remind the company that it operated in a sovereign nation. Arrests and lawsuits, stalled radio communication licensing requests, land disputes, and conscription of labor for government work projects irritated the company. By 1929, open hostilities and veiled resentments toward the foreign company's presence were escalating, outbreaks of yellow fever were erupting up and down the coast of West Africa, and labor continued to be in short supply. Problems over land, labor, and disease, coupled with a downturn in profits, led Firestone to retrench its operations in 1929, drastically shrinking its labor force and reducing its investment by a half-million dollars.[9] Almost three years into its operations, Harvey Firestone Sr. wrote to Harvey Jr., angry and discouraged by the Liberian government's treatment: "[The leaders seem] to continually persist in penalizing and making it difficult for Firestone to establish a rubber plantation and do business in Liberia. . . . They feel we are taking something away from them, instead of it being entirely the other way—that we are doing for them."[10] But giving and taking rested in the eyes of the beholder. If Firestone's ambitions were to succeed, he needed a stable and sympathetic government, ready to bend to his will. With his friend Herbert Hoover now in the White House, Harvey Sr. would stop at nothing to use his influence and power in the Republican Party to try and secure control of a nation.

Despite agreements that guaranteed the company access to land—1 million acres of it—land conflicts were a perpetual thorn in the American giant's side. A dispatch from William Francis, Solomon Hood's replacement as U.S. minister to Liberia, received at the State Department in early 1929 listed a number of land disputes and other complaints that had precipitated the curtailing of the company's operations. To augment the company's main operation outside Monrovia along the Du River, Firestone established a second plantation on the Cavalla River in Maryland County in southeastern Liberia, near the Côte d'Ivoire border. But a conflict over a hundred-acre section of land cleared and planted by the company, which a Liberian citizen had claimed title to, left the future of Firestone's Cavalla River plantation in the hands of President King. Firestone also clashed with the Liberian government over the company's efforts to claim land on both sides of a new government road, built by government-conscripted labor under the supervision of a Firestone engineer, that stretched roughly fifty miles from Monrovia to Kakata.[11] This had been Kpelle land, under the custodianship of paramount chiefs. However, citing the need for development, the Liberian government readily seized customary lands, integral to the sovereignty and self-determination of Liberia's indigenous people. It took the lands for public works projects, like roads, and private interests, such as independent rubber farms. On more than one occasion, Firestone's clearing of land, later revealed to be a tribal reserve, offered the Liberian government a means to remind the American company of whose country and by whose laws they operated in.

Disease, too, imperiled Firestone's precarious foothold in Liberia. In late February 1929, Everett Vinton, a Firestone planter, developed symptoms of an illness that struck fear in the medical director of the Firestone Plantations Company, Justus Rice. Black vomit and tarry stools issued from the Iowa man's body. Jaundice cast a yellow pale over his skin as his pulse rate dropped and his temperature climbed. Rice, an expert in tropical medicine who had seen the disease while working in Panama, knew Vinton's symptoms were telltale signs of yellow fever.

The appearance of yellow fever in the Liberian capital and port city of Monrovia spelled trouble. Yellow jack, as it was once popularly known, had long been a threat to global trade. Prevailing medical opinion in the nineteenth century located the source of yellow fever in the filth and bad air—miasma, as it was called—emanating from open sewers, festering garbage, and uncleanly behaviors thought to characterize port towns in the tropics. In 1929, more was known about yellow fever's cause, but defensive strategies hadn't changed much. Quarantine was one defense, but it was costly. An 1878 epidemic originating in Havana, Cuba, for example, cost the American South an estimated $100 million in lost revenues as the disease swept up the Mississippi River from New Orleans to St. Louis. The outbreak killed twenty thousand people and struck fear before and behind its wake.[12]

Firestone was anxious about the crippling effects of quarantine. Yellow fever outbreaks had been erupting along the West African coast since the company's arrival in Liberia. Epidemics in 1926 and 1927 in Accra and Dakar, port cities, respectively, of the Gold Coast and Senegal, left British and French colonial health officers struggling to protect foreign white residents, who seemed to die at much higher rates than the local population.[13] If France, Germany, Great Britain, and the United States prevented their ships from unloading and loading cargo in Monrovia because of a confirmed or even suspected yellow fever epidemic, Firestone's operations would come to a grinding halt. Rice had no way to clinically verify that Vinton's affliction was caused by the yellow fever virus. The virus had only recently been isolated and identified in laboratories of both the Pasteur Institute in Dakar and the Rockefeller Foundation's International Health Division in Lagos, Nigeria. Monrovia had no public health laboratory, nor did the country have a qualified bacteriologist, pathologist, or entomologist who could assist with diagnosis. The Liberian Government Hospital, a thirty-bed facility with an operating room but no X-ray machine, electrical equipment, or running water, was improvised in 1928 from a former German clubhouse, cable-station, and residence quarters. Rice's medical facilities on the Du plantation were not much better.

Given the deleterious impact that news of a yellow fever outbreak could have on the company's operations, Firestone did its best to keep the outbreak quiet. Freetown, in neighboring Sierra Leone, had already in March of 1929 issued quarantine regulations restricting passengers from Monrovia, in response to spreading rumors of a yellow fever outbreak. Andrew Sellards, who successfully brought back an isolated strain of the live virus from Dakar to the United States (which he achieved with the financial support of Firestone), confided to his mentor, Richard Strong: "I feel sure that Mr. Firestone would not want any note of appreciation even in [the journal] Science that might suggest yellow fever work."[14] William Francis kept the early signs of Monrovia's 1929 yellow fever outbreak a close secret, fearful of the damage it could cause Firestone. By the time Vinton became sick in February, anxieties among foreign residents living in Monrovia were already escalating. By early April, Rice estimated, twenty-five people had died. Four were American citizens.[15]

As the outbreak escalated, the Firestone Plantations Company became a hideout for foreign residents seeking shelter from yellow fever lurking in Monrovia. An entourage of American government officials, including William Francis, his wife Nellie, U.S. financial adviser John Loomis, and U.S. supervisor of customs Conrad Bussell and his wife, sequestered themselves on the Du plantation. Foreigners who stayed in the city proper were encouraged to confine themselves indoors by 3:30 p.m., before *Aedes aegypti*, the mosquito responsible for transmitting the virus between humans, became active.[16]

Moving the city's white foreigners to the Firestone plantation compound was not enough, Rice feared, to guarantee their safety. He consequently dispatched a telegram to Dr. Edward Hindle at the London School of Tropical Medicine to request that 110 doses of a yellow fever vaccine developed from Sellards's live virus be sent, in haste, to Monrovia. The vaccine, a mix of ground liver from an infected monkey suspended in a glycerine-and-phenol solution, had yet to be tested on humans. Strong wrote to Harvey Firestone Jr., strongly recommending against its use. "We do not think that we can conscientiously recommend to you that you should have your employees inoculated with Dr. Hindle's vaccine," advised the Harvard physician. It was far more important, Strong believed, to get Firestone staff out of Monrovia and do everything possible to eradicate mosquitoes.[17] Rice was desperate. Two fatal cases had already appeared among laborers on the plantations.

Ignoring Strong's advice, the bold doctor, in an act of either selfless heroism or stupidity, injected himself on April 1 with 3 cubic centimeters of the vaccine. A German surgeon, Dr. Wehrle, working at the Liberian Government Hospital, also agreed to participate in the first human trial. When neither doctor exhibited ill effects, Rice used his power as company physician to next test the vaccine on three indigenous Liberians employed as plantation workers.

Firestone billed its rubber plantation in Liberia as an enclave of modernity in a sea of the "primitive." From its capital investment, Firestone promised, benefits would come to the country and its people—but the worlds of its Liberia plantation were already forming along racial and class divides. The use of plantation workers as experimental subjects in a vaccine trial showed these fault lines. So, too, did the dispensing of the vaccine, once Rice deemed it safe. With the vaccine in short supply, highest priority went to "whites of European descent," forty-nine employees of the Firestone Plantations Company. All received inoculations. William and Nellie Francis, although of African descent, were also treated with the vaccine by virtue of their diplomatic rank and American citizenship. The U.S. minister described the resulting symptoms: eyes a little bloodshot, some nausea, a little stiffness, but he otherwise felt fine. By late April, fear of the yellow fever threat among foreigners, buoyed by their faith in Hindle's vaccine, subsided. That assuredness proved to be misguided.[18]

With the arrival in June of the rainy season, yellow fever struck with a vengeance in Monrovia. James Sibley, American educational adviser to Liberia, became afflicted. To American religious and philanthropic groups with an active interest in Liberia, Sibley was a beloved figure. He had been long enough in Liberia to know the disease would likely take him. He wrote his will and died eight days later. In the third week of June, William Francis, despite being inoculated with the Hindle vaccine, lay bedridden in his Monrovia home, suffering the early symptoms of yellow fever. That same week, the disease claimed the lives of the acting French consul and a British trader. When the news reached Harvey Firestone Jr., he telephoned the State Department. He urged officials to put diplomatic pressure on the Liberian government to hire a sanitary engineer, preferably American, "to clean up conditions in Monrovia." On the Du plantation, Harvey Jr. proclaimed, "where the sanitation has been properly cared for, the disease has been practically eliminated, but Monrovia seems to have been suffering more and more and such efforts as the Liberians make are spasmodic and not scientific."[19] A few days later, Sir Esme Howard of the British Embassy wrote to U.S. secretary of state Henry Stimson to make a similar call for an increase in joint international pressure by the British, American, and French governments to impress upon the Liberian government "the necessity of improving health conditions in Monrovia."[20]

The Liberian government was not easily intimidated. To the dismay of the American, British, and French governments, King's administration thwarted international efforts to impose foreign sanitary interventions and control. Liberia was a sovereign nation, unwilling to bend to an act of imperialism, cloaked in the guise of health considerations and humanitarianism. Control of epidemics had been a pretense for American intervention in foreign lands in the past. Yellow fever, for example, was as much an overriding concern as was the liberation of Cubans from Spanish colonial rule when the U.S. declared war on Spain in 1898. By the 1890s, 90 percent of Cuba's sugar exports went to the United States. Protection from yellow fever went hand in hand with protection of U.S. interests in the Cuban sugar industry. What would prevent the U.S. government from doing the same to protect its fledgling rubber supply in Liberia?[21]

What's more, the Black republic had microbes on its side. Liberian officials knew that yellow fever more readily panicked Westerners than it did longtime inhabitants. Loomis, the U.S. financial adviser who was sequestered on the Du planation, admitted as much in a private meeting with King after Sibley's death. Foreigners, who largely had never been exposed to yellow fever, were more likely to die of the disease than were Liberians, many of whom, having survived childhood exposures to yellow fever, had acquired natural immunity to the disease. Sanitary interventions sought by the international community looked to protect foreign residents and capital at the expense of political self-determination and independence. The American vice-consul Clifton Wharton confided to his superiors back home that one high Liberian government official "is said to have remarked that the Germans had their submarines, Great Britain has her navy, and the United States, money with which to turn out war supplies, but Liberia has her mosquitoes."[22]

King eventually acquiesced to a cleanup campaign. But he stalled on doing anything more. The Firestone agreement had already mandated that Liberia employ a U.S. financial adviser to oversee the health of the country's finances.[23] Now, the Liberian government was being asked to cede control of its public health and sanitation to an American expert at its own expense. Each concession whittled away at Liberia's economic sovereignty and independence. Each insertion of American expertise into the Liberian government furthered the protection of Firestone's interests. For a country resisting what might become a colonial takeover, fostering the image of Liberia as "the white man's grave" offered certain advantages.[24]

Firestone championed the introduction of an eight-hour workday and wage labor as a hallmark of its "civilizing mission" in Liberia. Such pronouncements, however, were merely a smokescreen that clouded the con-

Firestone worker housing, circa 1937. Liberian workers resisted the tenement-style housing that Firestone initially provided. From Firestone Plantations Company, *Views in Liberia* (Chicago: Lakeside Press, R.R. Donnelley & Sons, 1937).

tinuing labor challenges the company faced. Labor was in short supply, even after, in the wake of a worldwide economic depression, the workforce on its Liberia plantations was slashed from 18,000 laborers in 1928 to 2,700 men in 1930. The different attitudes among workers, some of whom had come of their own choosing while others were sent by chiefs to fulfill Firestone quotas, made a strong impression on some staff. One white supervisor wrote to General Manager Donald Ross that "to try to work men that do not care to come to Firestone . . . is a dangerous thing as these men will not do good work here and so will not receive good pay. They will then only return to their homes and tell all other country people unpleasant news and stories regarding Firestone."[25] Ross suggested to Firestone that "breaking in the tribes will have to be done by supervision accustomed to handling primitive people."[26]

Liberians who came to work the plantation, however, did not bend so easily to the demands and racist attitudes of the company's white management staff. Laborers resisted, for instance, the "coolie line" housing, which Firestone sought to impose. Imported from worker housing designs found on rubber plantations in British Malaya and the Dutch East Indies, such tenement-style living conditions provided each worker a room in "a contiguous row."[27] Liberian plantation workers preferred instead to build their own housing of mud walls and thatched roofs, like the village housing they knew. That they did so on company time infuriated management. Men's work rhythms, honed in the communal clearing of land to make farms, also frustrated Firestone staff. The daily and seasonal experiences of making agricultural livelihoods in Liberia's hinterland did not match with the time-clock regimens and quotas that structured work on the factory floor in Akron, and which Firestone tried to bring to its Liberia plantations.

The impediments posed by land, disease, and labor cut into the profits of Firestone's foreign investment, which by 1930 had reached $6 million. Nature, too, constrained the production of a plant grown on an industrial scale. It took seven years from the planting of a rubber seedling to the moment tapping of latex could begin. A lot could change in seven years, making the planting of rubber a risky bet on the future. And the future's prospects looked increasingly dim as Hoover's first year in the White House ended.

The rosy forecast that Firestone shared in early 1929 of a bright economic future ahead turned dark later that year. In October, stock prices on Wall Street plummeted, sending the industrialized world into a devastating economic tailspin. The American rubber tire industry saw more than a billion dollars of market value disappear in the first years of the Great Depression. Rubber prices plunged from 21¢ per pound in 1929 to 3¢ a pound in 1932. Tire production also shrunk by half as car sales dropped from more than 5 million units in 1929 to less than 1.4 million in 1932.[28] In a stroke of luck, Firestone had sold $60 million in preferred company stock just ten days before Black Tuesday wreaked financial havoc. The cash on hand helped the company pay its bills and take advantage of depressed real estate prices in hard times. Wary of both New York bankers and of pushing his credit to the limit, Firestone had sold the stock to secure the capital needed for expansion. The ambitious entrepreneur was eager to spread the Firestone name across America, not just on tires but on retail stores and service stations. Within a few years, Firestone had retail outlets and complete auto care service stations in more than four hundred cities throughout the United States.[29]

Depressed rubber prices, deflated tire sales, and the unanticipated challenges of building a plantation in a foreign land led Firestone to put growth
of his tropical rubber empire on ice. During the Depression years, the
company invested just enough to keep the plantations on life support. A
dozen white staff remained, only four of whom were planters. Tapping at
Mount Barclay ceased. A skeletal management crew and a couple thousand laborers kept the planted acres of rubber seedling free of weeds. They
were aided in this task by *Pueraria*, also known as tropical kudzu, used as a
cover crop on the rubber plantations in Southeast Asia. Firestone purchased fifteen kilograms of seed from the Tjikasintoe Rubber Estates in
Java, where *Pueraria* was used to minimize weeds and to stabilize and enrich soils denuded of vegetation. Like *Hevea brasiliensis*, the aggressive le-
gume, now found throughout the country, took well to Liberia's laterite
soils and tropical climate. It also reduced labor costs at a time when the
company was slashing its investments.[30]

In a big gamble on the future, Harvey Jr. also ordered that more than
3 million young rubber trees, covering sixteen thousand acres, be cut down
to three-foot-high stumps. Apprised of the latest developments in the rubber industry, the Princeton graduate decided to try grafting buds from
high-yield Sumatran rubber trees onto the Liberian root stock. If successful,
the manufactured clones, once mature, would double the plantation's yield.

Clones were a new technology in rubber production. The first experiments with bud grafting of high-yielding rubber trees onto established
root stocks occurred in 1918 in Sumatra. Results were uncertain, but
promising. Unable to get enough seed from the Mount Barclay Plantation for expansion, Harvey Jr. sent John Le Cato, a young graduate in hor-
ticulture from the University of Illinois, to Sumatra in the fall of 1928. He
was directed to purchase ten thousand plants of three different clones recently developed at a private research station in the Dutch East Indies.
Each certified clone promised yields upward of one thousand pounds per
acre when mature, twice the yield coming out of Mount Barclay. None of
the Sumatran planters or scientists believed that Le Cato could successfully transport the rubber tree clones to Liberia. "If the venture is successful," they claimed, "it will rank with the feat of [Henry] Wickham," who,
in an act of biopiracy, had taken *Hevea brasiliensis* from Brazil and placed
it into the hands of the British empire.[31] On a six-week journey across the
Indian Ocean, over the Red Sea, through the Strait of Gibraltar, and on to
Monrovia, less than 4 percent of the plants died. Transported by truck

and surfboat to Division No. 7, the seedlings were planted in three separate "Mother Tree Seed Areas." A quiet revolution was underway on the
plantations. A small crew of staff and laborers engineered and constructed
upward of 3 million bud-grafted rubber trees. Harvey Jr. would need to
wait seven years for the clones to reach maturity, when their prized "white
gold" could be tapped, to know if his bet had paid off.

Growing rubber was, in short, a risky business. Harvey Firestone Sr. had
raised horses. He had watched his father run a successful farm, trading in
sheep, corn, oats, and wheat. But a tree crop like rubber was a quite different venture. The Firestone company neither owned the land nor controlled
the labor where the rubber trees had taken root. Protecting its investment
became an obsession with Harvey Sr. and Harvey Jr. during the Depression years. The father often claimed Liberia to be a "moral protectorate, if
not a direct protectorate" of the United States. Together, father and son
would use their money, influence, and power, to try and turn that misguided
belief into a reality in their scramble for land and power in Liberia.[32]

In the late 1920s, the company whose designs for success depended on un-
savory labor practices decided to consolidate its position in Liberia—through
an attack on forced labor.

Strong, whose work on Firestone's behalf had ingratiated himself to
father and son, had no qualms about using his Harvard position and ties to
the Republican Party to advance Firestone interests by meddling, on "humanitarian" grounds, in the affairs of Liberia. Strong's accusations of labor
abuses in Liberia, his ties to White House inner circles, and his friendship
with Firestone all played decisive roles in Assistant Secretary of State
William Castle's instructions in June 1928 to William Francis to begin an
"absolutely secret" and "strictly confidential" investigation into the use of
forced labor in Liberia.[33]

Castle was hardly ignorant of the labor challenges posed by industrial
plantations. His grandfather, Samuel Northrop Castle, was a founding
partner in Castle & Cooke, one of Hawaii's Big Five sugarcane growing
and processing corporations. Although Castle expressed confidence that
Firestone was conscientiously operating in Liberia so as "to avoid any charge
of peonage or forced labor," he nevertheless asked Francis to include the
practices of Firestone, as well as those of the Liberian government, in his
intelligence gathering. Castle worried about a time when the State Department and Firestone might be held responsible for conditions under which

forced labor prevailed, particularly with respect to work on the plantations. "When that day comes," the Hawaiian-born diplomat warned, "it
seems highly important" that the U.S. government "be in a position to show
beyond question where the responsibility for such conditions rests and be
able to show that American influence has been exerted . . . against such
conditions." That day came sooner than even Castle perhaps anticipated.[34]

Francis's undercover work had barely begun when Raymond Buell, a
young, left-leaning, Princeton-trained political scientist, delivered a
speech at Williams College in western Massachusetts. Buell had recently
published *The Native Problem in Africa*, a comprehensive two-volume study
of the economic, political, and social conditions arising from colonial rule
that Africa's indigenous peoples faced. Commissioned by the Committee
of International Research of Harvard University and Radcliffe College,
with funding by the Rockefeller Foundation, the book was based on a
fifteen-month investigative trip Buell made to Africa, where he visited
eighteen territories, each occupied by Britain, France, or Belgium, and
the Republic of Liberia. His analysis of the Firestone concession and the
U.S. State Department's role in influencing the company's negotiations
with the Liberian government was particularly hard-hitting. His remarks,
prepared for a conference hosted by the Williamstown Institute of Politics
in August 1928, elaborated on the charges outlined in his book. Buell, an
international relations expert, accused then secretary of commerce Herbert
Hoover of using his power in the U.S. government to pressure Liberian
officials to accept a deal greatly beneficial to an American manufacturer
but costly to Liberia. Everywhere in Africa where Buell had observed the
plantation system, confiscation of indigenous land and coercion and mistreatment of laborers had occurred. "The United States may soon find itself
in the position of fostering conditions in Liberia which will make forced
labor for private profit inevitable," Buell declared, "and at the same time of
shielding Liberia from the efforts of the outside world to protect the native population."[35] A company and a government had colluded to throw its
"influence against the native farmer in favor of the outside capitalist."[36]
This was blatant economic imperialism. It was a scheme, Buell predicted,
that might "sooner or later make Liberia into another Haiti or Nicaragua,"
a reference to the U.S. military occupation of both countries that was carried out, in part, to protect American private investment.[37]

Somehow, government officials had gotten wind of Buell's plans and
alerted Firestone. Behind the scenes, the State Department and Firestone

worked furiously at damage control in the two weeks leading up to Buell's lecture. Should President King be willing to issue a rebuttal to Buell's accusations, the State Department advised Francis, the Associated Press was primed and ready to publish it. Strong had also contemplated going to Williamstown to refute Buell's claims. In the end, he told Castle, he thought it "better not to call any further attention to his expressed ideas."[38]

On the day of Buell's speech, the State Department obtained an advance copy of Buell's remarks and excerpted and telegraphed the most stinging assertions to Harvey Firestone Jr., urging him to wire the text to Bill Hines in Monrovia. Meanwhile, Castle alerted Francis and called upon him to meet with King and Hines to arrange a press release for publication in the next day's papers. Together the Firestone manager and the U.S. minister convinced King to come to the defense of both Firestone and the State Department. Hines, a former newspaper reporter, undoubtedly advised King on language sure to persuade the American public. King's statement, sent out over the Associated Press wire, categorically denied any influence on the part of the State Department in "compelling the granting of the Firestone concessions." The Liberian president also declared Buell's allegations that the scheme involved the "control of Liberia by American officials" to be "untrue and mischievous." Furthermore, in an added embellishment, King flatly rejected any suggestion of forced labor. "Far from suffering a dearth of laborers the Firestone plantations are suffering from an embarrassment of riches," proclaimed the savvy politician. King took particular offense that an outsider, who spent no more than fifteen days in the country, had the arrogance to "predict Liberia's future and impugn the soundness and integrity of its statesmen." Needless to say, Firestone and the State Department were pleased by President King's statement and the reception it received.[39]

A disaster had been averted. But the Buell episode made clear that if Firestone's operations were to succeed in garnering favorable public opinion and producing a needed rubber supply for America, the company had to distance itself from labor practices that had the whiff of plantation slavery. If conditions of forced labor existed, the blame needed to be placed not on Firestone but on the Liberian government.

Francis spent nine months gaining the trust of Liberian confidants, perusing available government documents, reading Liberian newspapers and confidential radiograms, listening to rumors, and carefully observing business dealings, shipping manifests, and government revenues. Through these intensive efforts, he had privately amassed enough evidence of forced labor by Liberian government officials to recommend action. In a strictly confidential report, which he delivered to Castle in early March 1929, Francis concluded that "officials of the Liberian Government have knowledge of, are engaged in, and are making large sums of money by the exportation of forced labor which has developed into a condition analogous to slavery."[40]

Francis had focused his attention, in particular, on an export labor scheme, agreed to by Liberia and Spain, in 1914. Provisions of the agreement required the Liberian government to supply a certain number of laborers each year to work the cocoa plantations on the Spanish colony of Fernando Po, an island in the Gulf of Guinea. The terms of employment were for one to two years. In exchange, the Spanish government guaranteed payment of the laborer's wages plus a head tax of $4 per man to the Liberian government. Liberian recruiting agents were also paid $5 for each laborer they brought forth.

In a country desperate for cash, labor became an important export commodity. But contracting out labor by the government created a system open to widespread abuse.

Word of one such case of abuse reached Francis, shortly after his arrival in Liberia from the U.S. in November 1927 to take up the post of U.S. minister resident and consul to Liberia. Samuel Ross, former vice-president under King, obtained an "executive sanction" that enabled him to secure a contract with the Spanish chargé d'affaires for a thousand laborers for Fernando Po. Unable to recruit workers in southeastern Liberia voluntarily, Ross wove a web of entrapment: his agents would enter a village with soldiers and demand that the chief send rice, along with porters to carry it, to the coast to be sold to pay off the town's hut taxes. When the approximately three hundred porters arrived at the coast, the Liberian Frontier Force placed them in barricades to await transport to Fernando Po. Liberian postmaster general Reginald Sherman, who happened to be in the coastal area at the time, implored Secretary of State Edwin Barclay, nephew of former Liberian president and Firestone lawyer Arthur Barclay, by radiogram to deny the former vice-president permission to ship the imprisoned men. "Shall we whose fathers founded this country to secure liberty for their sons encourage this blighted and cursed practice which is ruining our country?" Sherman asked. Barclay complied with Sherman's request, but a few months later the postmaster general was stripped of his position and Ross was appointed in his place.[41]

Stories of the coercion and mistreatment of laborers for export in Liberia had been relayed on occasion to Washington, DC, more so after the United States helped finance a 1912 international loan and became more vested in the country. But after Firestone arrived in Liberia, the U.S. government paid much closer attention to such allegations of abuse. Two issues were at play. First, rubber had a—quite recent—bloody past. The atrocities committed under the command of Belgium's King Leopold twenty years earlier claimed an estimated 10 million lives in the brutal extraction of wild rubber from the Belgian Congo. International headlines galvanized a worldwide movement against slave labor.[42] Given the strong-arm tactics often used by labor recruiting agents, Firestone could, knowingly or unknowingly, easily find itself caught up in a forced labor scandal. Second, Firestone's need for voluntary, free labor competed with the kickback schemes that profited Liberian government officials and chiefs. Putting an end to forced labor practices in Liberia could free up workers, in short supply, that Firestone desperately needed. It could also help distance the company from any innuendo of building a plantation on unfree labor.[43]

In the original Firestone agreements, the Liberian government agreed to "encourage, support and assist" Firestone "to secure and maintain an adequate Labor supply."[44] But the company's presence posed challenges for the government's own labor needs. To facilitate development and extend the government's reach into the interior, President King had undertaken a series of road construction projects not long after the end of the First World War. These projects relied on compulsory labor, in accord with the terms of the 1926 Slavery Convention, an international treaty brokered by the League of Nations among its member states to eliminate slavery, the slave trade, and forced labor, but with an exception for public works. Each chief was required to furnish the government, through its district commissioners, with a certain number of men for up to nine months each year to help build roads by hand without pay, food, or supplies. Young men, and sometimes boys, moved massive tree roots, rocks, and heavy red clay soil with nothing more than sticks, raffia mats, and baskets, working in unison to rhythms played and songs sung by musicians among them. Many young men assessed their options: stories abound of young men fleeing government road work for paid employment on the Firestone plantations. The Liberian government, to better address labor supply problems and prevent every able-bodied man from the hinterland "floating towards the sea-coast," established in late 1925 a Labor Bureau to supply Firestone with ten thousand men.[45] But American advisers, such as U.S. financial adviser Sidney De La Rue, feared what might become of the scheme. It left, in his opinion, "certain opportunities for graft" and at the same time left Firestone open to allegations that it was using the government to recruit what might be seen as forced labor.[46]

Daniel Walker was one such paramount chief who received orders from the Interior Department and Labor Bureau informing him of responsibilities under this new plan. Walker had a large and powerful frame, an impressive mustache, and was purported to have two hundred wives. He held a commanding reach over Kpelle lands, which included the Kakata area adjacent to the Du plantation, and held sway over the people and clan and town chiefs there. He was to supply one hundred men, along with two proper headmen, to work on the plantations for one to three months. Each man was to be paid one shilling per day. Walker, and each town chief under him, would also be compensated by Firestone. No money was to be taken from the laborers, and no part of their service was to be unpaid. De La Rue had reason to be anxious.[47] The payments to town and paramount chiefs created incentives for coercion. One Firestone manager reported seeing 150 men in "an exhausted and emaciated condition" arrive on the plantation, escorted by armed government guards. Within a week of their arrival, twelve had died.[48]

Rumors of deceit and intimidation swirling around Firestone made labor recruitment difficult. In an effort to ameliorate the situation, Firestone agitated the government for permission to use its own recruiting agents. But the plan, implemented in 1927, still relied on a quota system in which each district was responsible for supplying thousands of men. Each chief would be compensated by the company one shilling for each worker serving three months and twelve shillings for each laborer working one year on the plantations. Chiefs were also obligated to return "runaway laborers" or supply Firestone with "fresh ones to serve out the term" of anyone who fled.[49]

In his 1929 report to Castle, Francis absolved Firestone of any wrongdoing in knowingly recruiting labor through means of coercion. Yet the report weighed heavily on the American diplomat. He appealed to Castle to keep his sources in strictest confidence, wishing to bring no harm to his Liberian friends who freely shared their knowledge and were "innocent of harmful intention."[50] One such friend was Didhwo Twe. The Fernando Po scheme had most affected his people, and Twe was an outspoken advocate, both in Liberia and internationally, in defense of the Kru and the rights of indigenous people in Liberia. Born on the Kru coast in 1879, Twe came to the U.S. in 1900, studied at Columbia and Harvard, and for a time served as a valet for Mark Twain, with whom he shared an intimate and lengthy correspondence about race in America. A gifted and effective speaker, Twe introduced an act into the Liberian Legislature in November 1928 outlawing the exportation of labor, which passed the House but was killed in the Senate. Twe was a critical source in Francis's investigation. He had confidentially informed Francis, for example, of how Kru men were being forcibly shipped to Libreville, a port town in French Gabon, where they were detained as ship hands. The private scheme involved the Danish owner of a steamship line operating on the coast of West Africa and officials in President King's cabinet who received $5 per ship hand.[51]

In a moving letter to Castle, Francis despaired of how such "money-mad" men, "so calloused that they have lost all sense of right and wrong," had jeopardized Liberia's future. "I hold the deepest sympathy for Liberia and no one regrets her errors more than I," he wrote. In delivering his report, Francis sought not to injure the government but to find a way "before it is too late to save the country from itself."[52] He sincerely believed that unless the United States, or some other equally friendly country, stepped in, the republic would not succeed.

Six days before Francis fell ill with yellow fever, the U.S. minister, at Castle's direction, sent a dispatch to Liberian secretary of state Barclay. His letter was crafted in polite diplomatic language, but stinging in its accusations. Under orders from U.S. secretary of state Henry Stimson, Francis alerted Barclay to "reliable evidence" gathered by the U.S. government that a system of export labor existed in Liberia that was indistinguishable from an "organized slave trade." The letter drew specific attention to the regular shipment of thousands of men from Liberia to work the cocoa plantations on Fernando Po. But even within Liberia's borders, Francis suggested, Liberian government officials, aided by the Liberian Frontier Force, had been complicit in using forced labor for their benefit. "It would be tragically ironic if Liberia, whose existence was dedicated to the principle of human liberty, should succumb to practices so closely akin to those which its founders sought forever to escape," noted the former Minnesota lawyer and defender of Black civil rights in America. "Because of its century old friendship for Liberia," Francis wrote, the United States was compelled to alert the Liberian government of this evil in its midst. He ended by expressing his government's confidence "that the Republic of

William T. Francis, U.S. Minister Resident and Consul General to Liberia, 1927–29. (Courtesy of the Minnesota Historical Society.)

Liberia will act promptly and effectively to vindicate its good name" and work "to eliminate a condition which if continued threatens grave consequences to Liberia."[53]

Francis did not live to see the international repercussions that his illness and his actions as a diplomat working on behalf of American interests would have on Liberia. Bedridden, plagued by the high fever the virus unleashed, Francis still held out hope for the promise of Firestone and his country's goodwill in helping a nation that he believed needed saving. In early July, the *New York Times* reported encouraging signs of the American minister's recovery. But on Monday, July 15, in the early hours of the morning, with Nellie by his side, William Francis died in Monrovia of heart complications arising from his month-long battle with yellow fever.[54]

President King put aside the tense relationship brewing with the U.S. government to honor the minister's death. He sent a telegram to President Herbert Hoover with his condolences, finding in "this poignant grief, consolation . . . in the high sense of loyalty and devotion to duty" that characterized the minister's life. Hoover, for his part, thanked the Liberian leader and expressed his sorrow for the loss, not only of one of America's "most devoted public servants" but "of a sincere and loyal friend" to Liberia. Hundreds attended Francis's state funeral in Monrovia. At the time of his death, Francis was the only Black minister serving in the American diplomatic corps. His body was returned from West Africa on a freighter ship across the Atlantic and laid to rest in Nashville, Tennessee, where Nellie was born and would live until her death in 1969. In its tribute, the *Chicago Defender* impressed upon its readers the importance of the minister's position in Liberia owing to the "vast rubber plantations and holding of the Firestone Rubber company." Tributes from Mr. and Mrs. Hines, Mrs. Harvey Firestone, and Harvey Firestone Jr. underscored Francis's loyalty in endeavoring to see white foreign capital succeed in the service of a sovereign African nation.[55]

As Francis lay dying of yellow fever in Monrovia, Strong fired off a letter to Assistant Secretary of State William Castle, volunteering to use his influence with the Health Section of the League of Nations to secure greater U.S. influence over the affairs of the Liberian state in their efforts to protect Firestone's interests. Because Liberia was a member of the League of Nations, Strong suggested, he and Castle might use the yellow fever outbreak to bring League and State Department pressure on the Liberian government to allow American expert advisers to intervene.[56]

Castle welcomed the Harvard physician's "ideas concerning Liberia." The two men often shared opinions on the country and both believed Firestone could play a beneficial role in Liberia's development. Castle, however, urged Strong "to go a little slow about appealing to the League." Behind the scenes, he confided, the State Department was pursuing "the whole slavery situation in a very vigorous manner." Strong welcomed the news. He had, after all, been outspoken, privately and publicly, about his moral indignation toward what he regarded as gross labor abuses in Liberia, even though he made no mention of forced labor, like prison chain gangs, operating in the United States and in its overseas territories. Confidentially, Castle also shared that the Liberian government would soon request that a committee investigate the U.S. State Department's allegations of a system of forced labor, akin to an "organized slave trade," operating, knowingly or not, under the King administration.[57]

Castle enthusiastically supported Firestone's designs to mold Liberia into a banana republic. The assistant secretary of state's family background in plantation agriculture and his Harvard pedigree poised him to be sympathetic to private capital's role in securing American hegemony in resource-rich regions of the globe. From his position in Washington, DC, Castle discreetly sent Harvey Firestone Jr. confidential information contained in American Legation dispatches from Monrovia. The information was damning of the company's operations in Liberia.[58] The diplomat did whatever he could to give advantage to the Akron firm. Castle believed, as he wrote to his superior, Secretary of State Henry Stimson, that Firestone's success would mean "fewer inherent dangers than there would be in either turning Liberia over to the League of Nations or in accepting a mandate ourselves which would inevitably lead to military control of the country for a long time."[59]

Timing became critical as Castle worked to help Firestone achieve a secure foothold in Liberia. In May 1929, as he deliberated over the U.S. minister's report, Castle learned from Francis that a Liberian citizen, Thomas J.R. Faulkner, had left Monrovia for Europe to bring the matter of forced labor in Liberia before the League of Nations.[60] Faulkner planned to then travel to the United States to drum up sympathetic publicity for his cause.

Faulkner, along with Didhwo Twe, was an outspoken critic of the Liberian government's treatment of its indigenous population. Faulkner, who had emigrated to Liberia from North Carolina in the 1880s, first tangled with King's administration in 1925 when it hindered his plans to bring electric lighting to Monrovia through a partnership with Westinghouse Electric.[61] In Liberia's 1927 presidential election, Faulkner dared to run against King as the People's Party candidate. For decades, Liberia had been governed by the True Whig Party, an unopposed political machine controlled by a handful of elites within Liberia's settler society. Faulkner ran on a platform defending the rights of the country's indigenous population. At its inception in 1869, the True Whig Party aspired to do the same thing. In their opposition to the ruling Republican Party, founding members of the True Whig Party had denounced the treatment of the country's indigenous inhabitants and the class and caste hierarchies that favored Liberians of lighter-skinned complexion. Faulkner lost the election. He next took up the issue of forced labor as a cause célèbre in an effort to topple King's administration.[62] Perhaps "a quiet but careful observance" should be made of "Mr. Faulkner's movements" in Geneva, wrote Francis to a diplomatic peer in Switzerland.[63] If Faulkner's accusations got a hearing in Geneva or in the American press before the State Department could act, Castle feared, it would neutralize the United States' leverage over the situation. Just weeks after Castle received the U.S. minister's memo alerting him of Faulkner's departure for Europe, Francis received instructions from U.S. secretary of state Stimson on June 7, 1929, to deliver the letter to Liberian secretary of state Barclay that would send shock waves across the world.[64]

Barclay quickly responded to the American minister's damaging claims. It was, in brief, a letter of "solemn and categorical denial."[65] The use of compulsory labor for the building of public roads, the Liberian secretary of state pointed out, was permissible under the Slavery Convention of 1926. Although the convention's precepts had been adopted by the League of Nations, fewer than thirty nations had ratified the agreement in 1929.[66] The United States, unlike Liberia, was not even a member of the League. Barclay also rightly noted that Liberia was hardly unique in its use of compulsory labor for public works projects. In fact, European powers used forced labor for infrastructure development throughout their colonies. Barclay assured Francis that the Government of Liberia did not "underestimate the serious character of international public opinion" brought forth by the U.S. government's warning. And he welcomed an investigation "on the spot by a competent, impartial and unprejudiced commission."[67]

The State Department's assertion that labor conditions orchestrated by the Liberian government bordered on slavery was meant to put Firestone's operations in favorable light. Shifting blame for forced labor practices to the Liberian government was the State Department's veiled attempt to undermine the country's sovereignty, turn international public opinion against the republic, and promote Firestone as Liberia's savior. It would also, if successful, permit Firestone to more easily recruit labor, in short supply, to the plantations.

Three months later, in September 1929, Liberia's chargé d'affaires and permanent delegate to the League of Nations, Antoine Sottile, asked the League Council's president to assist in establishing an International Inquiry Commission. It should determine by "means of an impartial, serious, and detailed investigation . . . whether slavery or forced labor is or is not practiced" in Liberia. Sottile proposed the commission include three members: one appointed by the U.S. government, one nominated by the

Council of the League of Nations, and one selected by the Liberian government.[68]

The State Department discussed who should be the U.S. representative on the inquiry commission. Secretary of State Stimson advised President Hoover that it would "be preferable to recommend a colored man for this position." Castle concurred. But who could meet Stimson's criteria of "a suitably qualified colored man of sufficient standing and prominence"?[69] And who would be sympathetic to the interests of Firestone and white capital? Before his death, Francis had recommended that Emmett Scott be considered should an international investigative committee materialize. Scott was a former chief aide to Booker T. Washington and had traveled to Liberia as part of the 1909 American commission. But Scott, despite Hoover's personal plea, refused the offer, asserting that his duties at Howard University, where he served as secretary-treasurer, required his attention, regardless of his wish to render "service in behalf of my country and people."[70] W.E.B. Du Bois was also considered, but the suggestion never left Castle's desk. Instead, Hoover chose Charles Spurgeon Johnson.[71]

Johnson had qualifications and experience suited to the challenging assignment. He had been the first African American student to work at the University of Chicago with the renowned sociologist Robert Park, a former ghostwriter and adviser to Booker T. Washington. Johnson shared Washington's conciliatory stance toward the white establishment. As Johnson advised readers of the *Chicago Defender* at the height of his career, better to consolidate one's "position by strategic cooperation with . . . liberal members of the majority," than "by increased self-consciousness and racial chauvinism."[72] Johnson's earlier work on Black migration and race relations in Chicago led to many appointments on prominent white liberal boards and investigative inquiries. During the First World War, he conducted with Scott a study on Black migrant conditions on behalf of the Carnegie Endowment for International Peace. He was also director of research and investigations of the National Urban League, where he founded and became editor of its journal, *Opportunity: A Journal of Negro Life*. In 1928, he became professor and head of the Department of Social Science at Fisk University. From Fisk, he would produce classic works on American race relations, including *The Negro in American Civilization*, *Shadow of the Plantation*, and *Growing Up in the Black Belt*. Johnson's cultivation of white philanthropic organizations, from the Laura Spelman Rockefeller Memorial to the Julius Rosenwald Fund, in support of race relations research drew skepticism and critique from Du Bois. Johnson may not have been a "complacent black man," as Du Bois once accused him of being. But charitable organizations, whose benefactors were the nation's most famed captains of industry, supported him. To Firestone's champions, Johnson was the perfect man for the job: possessing impeccable academic credentials, respected across the color line, and not averse to the reputed beneficence of white capital.[73]

Johnson accepted Hoover's invitation to serve as the U.S. representative on the International Inquiry Commission in early December 1929. Shortly after, he was in Akron, accompanied by Emmett Scott, determined to meet with Firestone company representatives before Harvey Jr. left for Christmas holiday at his family's Miami Beach compound.[74] Two months later, Johnson was in Monrovia, where he took residence in quarters leased by the Firestone Plantations Company. Along the journey, the data-driven sociologist spent time in Washington, London, Paris, Bern, and Geneva to consult documents and interview people familiar with Liberian affairs. An opportune meeting occurred in London. At the home of wealthy British aristocrat and aspiring anthropologist George Pitt-Rivers, Johnson met Bronislaw Malinowski, whose recent book, *Argonauts of the Western Pacific*, was transforming the field of anthropology. Malinowski's two-year immersion in the life of Trobriand Islanders in Melanesia introduced participant-observation methods as the sine qua non of ethnography. His interest in exchange relations and reciprocity in forming the bonds, meanings, and structure of social life shaped his ethnographic approach and field observations, likewise with many of his students. Malinowski pressed Johnson on the methods he planned to use in his investigation into labor conditions in Liberia. The London School of Economics professor urged the Fisk sociologist to expand his inquiry beyond relevant documents, "intimate visits inland," and investigative hearings. Malinowski urged Johnson to consider also the values, meanings, and economies that shaped life among the country's indigenous inhabitants. Johnson left London in agreement with both Malinowski and Pitt-Rivers that "our sympathies are first with the natives in getting their confidence and trying as nearly as any European can to see things from that point of view."[75] He arrived in Monrovia predisposed to examine the predicament of Liberia's indigenous inhabitants regarding the economy and governance of the republic.

At thirty-six years old, Johnson was half the age of other members of the International Inquiry Commission. Dr. Cuthbert Christy, the League of Nations appointee, was a seventy-year-old British medical officer whose investigations in the service of the British empire covered a broad swath from India to East and Central Africa, where he researched plague, sleeping sickness, and other diseases. Christy arrived in Liberia two weeks after Johnson, convinced that he would die there of poisoning but that Liberian officials would ascribe his death to yellow fever. The Victorian-era colonial physician was deeply suspicious of Firestone, believed in the superiority of white rule, held condescending attitudes toward Black people, and proved temperamental and inept. Unsurprisingly, discord characterized interactions between Christy and Johnson. Arthur Barclay, the former Liberian president and Firestone lawyer, was the third member of the commission. At seventy-five years of age, Barclay had little interest in making the journey up country during the rainy season, where the commission would gather testimony from indigenous chiefs and villagers on their treatment by district commissioners, the Frontier Force, and other arms of the Liberian state. Nor did the elder statesman care to travel by boat to southeastern Liberia to investigate allegations concerning the export of forced labor to plantations on Fernando Po. "Cheerful noncooperation" is how Johnson described Barclay's role in the inquiry.[76]

In the company of two aged men, each of whom, for quite different reasons, took a halfhearted approach to the task at hand, Johnson threw himself into the commission's investigation. Shortly after Christy and Johnson arrived at Kakata, a town roughly fifty miles inland at the edge of the Firestone concession area, Christy took ill. The League of Nations representative was taken to the Firestone company hospital to be attended by Firestone physician Justus Rice. The seasoned British explorer had succumbed not to poisoning but to schistosomiasis, a disease caused by a parasitic flatworm. As Christy faced a six-week course of treatment, Johnson pursued the investigation without him.[77] Harvey Firestone Sr.'s right-hand man, Bill Hines, frequently accompanied Johnson on his investigative journeys. The Firestone company provided transport and treated the American commissioner to tours of the Harbel and Cavalla plantations. When Christy rejoined Johnson in Maryland County, both men were again housed by the Firestone Plantations Company. Stuck in Cape Palmas by a yellow fever quarantine imposed on Africa's West Coast after the Monrovia outbreak, the commissioners also relied on the use of Firestone's wireless cable messages to arrange ship transport to near Monrovia. After two months' travel, Johnson returned to Liberia's capital "dirty and tired." An evening's entertainment at the home of Firestone manager Donald Ross refreshed him. As Johnson noted in his diary, Hines "was efficiently cordial as usual," Rice treated everyone to parlor tricks, and "everybody was drinking whisky and sodas and smoking Lucky Strikes."[78]

Over a four-month period, the commission secured hundreds of depositions about labor conditions from government officials, paramount and town chiefs, indigenous laborers, and other interior and coastal residents from all walks of life. In Kakata and Maryland County, groups of from eight hundred to three thousand people assembled to listen, verify, and add to the testimonies of chiefs and elders. Johnson implemented a card system to handle the abundance of data produced by gathered statements. Christy dismissed the social scientist's methods and sought to sideline Johnson in the writing of the report. The Fisk sociologist held firm. The bulk of the 130-page report, completed in August 1930 and submitted to the League of Nations, the U.S. State Department, and the Liberian government, was crafted by Johnson, even though it became known as the Christy report.[79]

To the question of whether slavery as defined by the League of Nations existed in Liberia, the commission answered with a qualified "no." No evidence of "classic slavery carrying the idea of slave markets and slave dealers" existed. But the commission reported that pawning—the practice of loaning out a family member to pay a debt, which the commissioners regarded as "domestic slavery"—persisted in "the social economy of the Republic." The commission absolved the Liberian government of any active wrongdoing and acknowledged that the courts, in fact, "discouraged" pawning as a practice. On the question of forced labor, the commission had harsher things to say. Widespread abuse of compulsory labor for public projects existed, they asserted. Labor recruited by county superintendents and district commissioners for road building was often "diverted to private use on the farms and plantations of high Government officials and private citizens." The commission directly accused Vice-President Allen Yancy and other high government officials of using the Liberian Frontier Force to intimidate and physically coerce laborers into service. It reserved its most stinging charges for the Liberian government's revenue-generating contract labor scheme that exported workers to Fernando Po. The export labor arrangement was, the commission argued, "scarcely distinguishable from slave raiding and slave trading."[80]

Firestone emerged squeaky clean. Despite Christy's antagonism toward the American company, the commission found "no evidence that the

Firestone Plantations Company consciously employs any but voluntary labour on its leased plantations."[81] For abuses in the recruitment of labor to the plantations, the commission placed blame solely on Liberia's district commissioners and Labor Bureau. In the commission report, Firestone came across as a naïve and innocent bystander. Still, the company had knowingly participated in quota systems that were open to coercion: chiefs would profit when laborers were sent—voluntarily or not—to work for pay on the plantations. That the Christy report downplayed how Firestone benefited from such labor schemes led Montserrado County representative and House speaker Clarence Simpson to "entertain doubts" for the first time regarding the "motives of the State Department to Liberia."[82]

In Liberia, Johnson came to sympathize with and defend the country's indigenous inhabitants. "The zeal of the natives for education, their tradition of labor and ready adaptability to new forms of work, their vitality and surprising mental acuteness," Johnson would later write, "seem to mark them as the ultimate salvation of the country."[83] He had heard hundreds of people describe exploitative labor practices and abusive power relationships that district commissioners and government officials imposed on people in the hinterland. In Johnson's eyes, the inequalities he observed between settlers and indigenous people resembled race prejudice in America: both were the consequence of struggles for economic and social status. In *Bitter Canaan*, a posthumously published historical and sociological study of Liberia, Johnson suggested that "settler elites eschewed labor as degrading with a prejudice no less marked than the 'poor Whites' of America exhibited in their attitude toward slave labor."[84] In the U.S., the doctrine of "Anglo-Saxon superiority," Johnson argued, "originated not among the common workers," who embraced it. Rather, it was a myth devised by capitalists to legitimize their need "to keep Negroes enslaved" as a source of "cheaper and cheaper labor."[85] In Liberia, Johnson saw a similar process at work. Economic class and social caste combined in ways to produce difference, leading to a stratification around a "civilized" and "native" divide that produced the greatest benefits for settler elites.

Johnson viewed Liberia's development in the tradition of race relations cycles that informed the Chicago school of sociology in which he was trained. A successful, harmonious Liberian future, he believed, would come when the dynamics of competition and conflict that defined relations between settler and indigenous peoples developed into one of accommodation and assimilation. The future president of Fisk University looked favorably upon Firestone in aiding that transition. Johnson was already part of a network of American white philanthropic and missionary boards, such as the Phelps Stokes Fund, with interests in Liberia, who looked to Firestone as the country's savior. The country needed capital and agricultural experts. Markets needed to be developed. Education needed to be expanded. To the scholar of race relations in America, wage labor offered a means by which the status of Liberia's indigenous population could rise. When Hines explained his difficulties attracting labor to the plantation, Johnson recommended showing "moving pictures" of Firestone workers getting "rice issues, pay, etc." When rural people saw their kin purchasing goods with plantation wages, Johnson advised, "it might help and also stimulate want" to exchange one's labor for a shilling per day.[86] Johnson never lived among Liberia's indigenous inhabitants, as he had hoped and Malinowski had advised. Perhaps, as a consequence, the immense importance of land in sustaining the flourishing economies and lifeways of the interior never rose to prominence in Johnson's analysis. Yet access to and control of land animated much of life and social relations within and between the many ethnic groups that made up the Republic of Liberia. Land, as much as labor, was what Firestone needed to plant, produce, and profit from.

The commission report ended with recommendations meant to foster the acculturation and assimilation of Liberia's indigenous people into the nation-state, but these overstepped the bounds of the inquiry. They urged a reorganization of the political divisions and administration of the republic to bring hinterland inhabitants onto a more equal footing in Liberian society. Political boundaries separating the coast from the interior only reinforced the "civilized" and "native" divide. The League of Nations report advised that boundaries be replaced by districts extending from the sea to the interior's upper reaches to promote freer movement of labor, goods, and trade. Corruption, the report alleged, was rampant among district commissioners. The commission advocated they be removed and replaced with American or European senior commissioners. In addition, export labor should cease, pawning should be made illegal, and education should be extended to all. These changes, the commission argued, would teach "market values" to the "unsophisticated native," stimulate their "wants," and encourage them to "make money, with the result that trade increases, the coast merchant flourishes," and "the revenue of Government expands." Both Firestone Sr. and Jr. were very pleased. The commission's recommendations were a recipe to transform Liberia's peasant farmers into a proletariat class, eager cogs in the industrial machine. Furthermore, if American advisers friendly to the interests of American capital oversaw the country's interior administration, Firestone's supply of labor would be secure.[87]

In early September 1930, three days after handing the International Inquiry Commission report to President King, Johnson and Christy sailed from Monrovia. King, according to interim U.S. chargé d'affaires Samuel Reber, "expressed . . . his 'mortification' over the conditions which had been found."[88] Harvey Firestone Sr. immediately pounced on King's vulnerable position. Speaking from the United States by radio, Harvey Sr. dictated to Hines in Monrovia the reforms he wanted King's administration to implement. They were largely identical to those the commission recommended: reform the interior's administration and judiciary, appoint foreign experts, and open the hinterland to commerce, among others. American financial adviser John Loomis stood behind Firestone's demands. So, too, did the U.S. State Department. If King did not agree, the State Department warned, he could not expect the U.S. government's support or assistance in navigating the brewing international scandal. King assured the U.S. government of impending reforms. But Firestone and the State Department regarded members of his cabinet with suspicion. Secretary of State Barclay, in particular, was frequently maligned within an inner circle of diplomats supportive of Firestone's Liberian venture. Reber, in Monrovia, suggested to his superiors in Washington "that Barclay . . . would never consent to the appointment of white district commissioners."[89] Reber echoed Harvey Firestone Jr., who expressed on more than one occasion that Barclay was "anti-foreign in general and anti-American in particular."[90]

In Monrovia, the atmosphere stiffened as the findings of the international inquiry leaked to the public. Led by former Liberian president Daniel E. Howard, a large citizens' gathering on October 2 called for the resignation of King and the establishment of a provisional government. Howard had helped to orchestrate a similar protest the previous June with Faulkner, both of whom led the opposition People's Party. Then, as the commission investigators heard more and more troubling testimonials, upward of five hundred people from Monrovia, Careysburg, White Plains, Congo Town, and other places in Montserrado County expressed condemnation and disapproval of the government. In the wake of the commission's report, civic unrest continued to escalate. The Citizen's Non-Partisan League planned a mass demonstration for October 20 to demand action by the Liberian Legislature.[91] The American Legation, worried that an "anti-white faction" had taken hold of the group agitating for King's impeachment, grew increasingly concerned. Great Britain sent a small warship to patrol waters off the West African coast, to be ready should violence erupt. While the protest took place without incident, the increasing political turmoil heightened racist anxieties and fears already prevalent among Monrovia's white expatriates.[92]

At the end of October, President King delivered a defiant address refuting, in part, the commission's findings. It was the Liberian government, he reminded citizens, that had requested the League of Nations inquiry. He rejected the assertion that the government had been complicit in the coercion and abuse of workers sent to Fernando Po. Regarding the mistreatment of laborers conscripted for public works, he castigated that "unpatriotic citizen" Thomas Faulkner for seeding the foreign press with "propaganda concerning slavery and forced labor" that had so harmed the place of Liberia in "the ranks of civilized and Christian States of the world." In Tanganyika, Nigeria, the Gold Coast, Togo, and the Cameroons, he pointed out, the British and French had used compulsory labor. Why, he asked, was Liberia being singled out? The criticisms and outcries, King suggested, were "an excuse on the part of the enemies of our race to blot out of existence a State in Africa which holds out to the millions of Negroes in Africa, the United States, and the West Indies, the brightest hope for the realization of their highest political and social aspirations."[93]

U.S. secretary of state Stimson was not pleased. He penned a missive harshly critical of the Liberian government and telegraphed it to the chargé d'affaires in Monrovia to hand to President King. Stimson conveyed profound shock at revelations in the commission report, advising King that its release will "cause a revulsion of feeling throughout the civilized world against the Republic of Liberia" unless reforms were instituted with "sincerity and effectiveness." Stimson timed his telegram with a press release that summarized the commission report conclusions.[94] King complained that publishing the summary was deeply disrespectful to the Liberian government, which initiated the League inquiry. Stimson escalated his punitive tone and rhetoric. A cutting letter delivered a few weeks later through diplomatic channels admonished, "International public opinion will no longer tolerate those twin scourges of slavery and forced labor." Unless they were abolished and reforms were made, Stimson warned, "friendly feelings which the American Government and people have entertained for Liberia since its establishment nearly a century ago" would end.[95] Harvey Firestone Sr. applauded the secretary of state's strong stance.[96] The Republican Party's major donor pushed hard on Hoover's administration to pressure Liberia to accept reforms advantageous to his company and protective of his foreign investment.

Firestone was either arrogant or naïve thinking he could control the aftermath of the League of Nations investigation. On December 2, the Liberian Legislature, facing mounting public pressure, called for King's resignation and impeached Vice-President Allen Yancy. It expelled two members of the House of Representatives and recommended a number of district commissioners, superintendents, and Frontier Force commanders implicated in the commission's report be removed from office and prosecuted. King abdicated the presidency the next day. He would later serve as legal counsel for the Firestone Plantations Company. In the falling house of cards, the next in line for the presidency was Liberian secretary of state Edwin Barclay. This was not what Firestone wanted. Five months later, on the eve of the May 1931 election that would likely give Barclay another four years, Harvey Jr. telephoned Castle to insist that the U.S. government not recognize a Barclay presidency. Firestone feared Barclay would "make local political capital out of American recognition."[97] The State Department agreed. The U.S. government refused to recognize Barclay as head of state when he became the eighteenth president of Liberia.

Firestone hoped the fallout from the League of Nations investigation would force Liberia to become a U.S. protectorate. Short of that, a puppet government would suffice. Firestone, fond of polo and Indy car racing, relished competitive play. Barclay, who had ably negotiated for Liberian protection in the Firestone agreements, was a formidable foe. Before entering politics, the Liberian president had been a professor of mathematics at Liberia College. An adept logician, he was admired by his cabinet for his ability to think "several moves ahead" of his opponents.[98] If Firestone thought he could quickly checkmate Barclay in their strategic chess match, he was deeply mistaken.

In late January of 1931, the American chargé d'affaires, along with British and German representatives, met with President Barclay at the Executive Mansion. They issued an ultimatum. In light of the president's unwillingness to accept the commission's recommendations in full, they

Edwin J. Barclay, eighteenth president of Liberia. From Firestone Plantations Company, *Views in Liberia* (Chicago: Lakeside Press, R.R. Donnelley & Sons, 1937).

demanded that the Liberian government appeal to the League of Nations for "aid, assistance, and possible international supervision." Should Barclay refuse, he could anticipate the end of "friendly relations" with the nations represented in the room.[99] Two days later, Barclay, expert in diplomacy and international law, agreed to ask for League of Nations assistance and advice regarding Liberia's economics and finance, judicial organization, sanitation, and "native administration." But, so long as Barclay was in power, the country would not surrender to any form of international control. To do so, Barclay asserted, would be a "violation of the constitution of the Republic" and "would also be tantamount to surrender of its sovereignty and autonomy."[100] Speaking publicly, the Liberian president took issue with the "peculiar suggestion . . . that for reforms to be effective in any group, they must be supervised by forces alien to that group." Such a demand was "not only false to truth," he warned, "but has hidden in it certain imperialistic implications against which we have to guard."[101]

The next month, the League of Nations established a committee to take up Barclay's request for advice and assistance. British lawyer and cabinet minister Lord Robert Cecil, one of the League's architects, assumed the committee chair and was joined by representatives from Germany, Italy, Poland, Spain, Venezuela, and Liberia. Technically, the United States, not being a member of the League, had no power to insist it be included, but the League extended a courtesy invitation to participate. Stimson instructed Samuel Reber to leave his post in Monrovia and go to Geneva to represent American interests in committee deliberations.[102]

A team of experts in administration, finance, and public health were appointed by Cecil's committee to survey the situation in Liberia. This commission was to advise committee members on technical steps to strengthen the republic and its standing in the world. Henri Brunot, a seasoned colonial administrator and former governor of the Ivory Coast, was appointed head of the expert commission. The appointment flagrantly violated Liberia's request that no experts be chosen from countries whose African colonies were its neighbors. The whole of the Brunot Commission consisted of white colonial officials, used to representing the interests of European imperial powers, who had little regard for the rights and self-governance of a Black republic.

After just six weeks in Monrovia they concluded their investigation. Before departing, they told an American diplomat that "Liberia's rehabilitation" depended greatly "upon the collaboration of both the United States and the Firestone Company." They urged renegotiation of the terms of the $5 million loan from the Finance Corporation of America. How Firestone would obtain the "extra labor needed to cultivate their vast areas in a few years" was, they opined, a "momentous question" yet to be answered.[103]

The Brunot Commission report, delivered to Lord Cecil's Liberia Committee in November 1931, was far-reaching and threatened the country's independence and sovereignty. It called for handing the country's entire administration of finances, interior governance, education, and public health to a group of foreign experts at a cost of $400,000 annually for salaries, natural resource surveys, and infrastructure development. Liberia's total revenues for 1931 barely exceeded $480,000. The Liberian government insisted slavery and forced labor allegations had been already addressed and took particular offense to the Commission's suggestion that Liberia had "no citizens sufficiently capable" of undertaking proposed reforms. In its request for assistance, Liberia had never contemplated that "proposals would be made to substitute the native organisation wholly by foreigners," or place its indigenous population "entirely under the direction of an alien race." Barclay's administration refuted the commission claim that the government had squandered money and instead blamed Liberia's economic woes on the Depression, the subsequent fall in commodity prices, the Firestone Plantations Company retrenchment, and the punishing loan agreement inflicted upon Liberia by the Firestone agreements.[104]

During ensuing months, meeting upon meeting of the League's Liberia Committee sought to devise an assistance plan to which Barclay and the Liberian Legislature would agree, recognizing that little could be done without Liberian consent. The Firestone agreements, particularly the $5 million loan from the Financial Corporation of America, hobbled Liberia's future development. The terms of the agreements completely favored Firestone. On this point, the Brunot Commission and Barclay agreed. The commission's financial expert calculated that five years hence, when the fifty thousand planted acres reached full production, Firestone would reap $4 million if rubber prices rose to 20¢ per pound. Liberia would receive $43,320. That return would not cover administrative salaries for servicing the loan, let alone the loan payments. It was a "vicious circle" of sinking debt. Only a renegotiation of the loan's terms, the experts argued, would help Liberia escape its deplorable economic conditions. If that were done, the experts argued, and if Firestone "introduced a labour policy which would attract the necessary native labour to the plantation and keep it there," the problem "could be solved."[105]

The colonial officials imagined a future Liberia where "model native villages were erected near the plantation, cultivable land allotted, and seeds and machinery advanced." White experts predicted "numerous natives would leave their miserable forest haunts and become regulation plantation workers." Liberia would be a "country of small, well-to-do cultivators, with a prosperous industrial plantation into the bargain." The dream was born of racial capitalism, paternalism, and blinding white privilege, ignorant and disparaging of practices, values, and beliefs that sustained lifeways in Liberia's hinterland.[106]

Not all Brunot Commission members were sympathetic to Firestone's role in Liberia. Salvador de Madariaga, Spanish ambassador to the United States, urged his colleagues to "consider the difficult problem presented by the existence of the powerful capitalist organization in a weak state."[107] At a meeting with commission members in Geneva in January 1932, Firestone representatives insisted that Firestone and the Finance Corporation of America were unwilling to revisit the terms of the 1926 agreements, but they would consider floating Liberia more money if proper "administrative safeguards" could be assured. Harvey Sr.'s position was well known to Hoover's administration. He would revisit the loan agreement only if the League plan recommended that an American chief adviser control Liberia's administrative affairs. Stimson privately supported Firestone's position.[108] But publicly he would not assert terms that would make the United States unilaterally responsible for overseeing the Liberian state. Accusations of American imperialism, he had told an American radio audience the previous year, "have damaged our good name, our credit, and our trade far beyond the apprehension of our people."[109] The United States could not repeat the mistake of military invasions into Haiti and Nicaragua. Extension of the Monroe Doctrine to Africa, in Stimson's view, was beyond consideration.[110] It would look far better if American involvement in the Liberian assistance plan was invited by the League.

Barclay well understood that the egregiously unfavorable loan terms could help him enlist international sympathy and support for Liberia's predicament. The League's Liberia Committee revised its assistance plan in May 1932. It reduced the number of foreign experts, halved the budget, and left open the nationality of the chief adviser. The most significant change, however, recommended a moratorium on loan payments to the Finance Corporation of America until Liberian government revenues reached $650,000. Further, the plan proposed that the Finance Corporation pay out the remaining $247,000 of the first $2.5 million loan installment. Renegotiation of the loan terms would occur upon Liberia's acceptance of the League plan. Finally, the plan called for the rent Firestone paid for its Liberian land concession to be increased from 6¢ to 50¢ per acre.[111]

Harvey Sr. was livid. In an angry letter to Hoover, he declared the League of Nations had no right to "suggest that we increase our payments" to Liberia in what was strictly a "commercial enterprise." In the lengthy appeal to the president, the Akron millionaire, who supported Hoover in his reelection bid, listed all that the company had accomplished and invested in Liberia. It did so, he complained, "in the face of every conceivable opposition by the Liberian Government and European Countries." Firestone thanked Hoover for "freeing the United States from a foreign monopoly" that had hamstrung the American tire industry. But the "Liberian question," he implored, needed to be taken out of the hands of the

League of Nations. If it was not, Firestone warned the president, Liberia's strategic importance to the United States as an independent source of rubber "will be placed in great jeopardy, and eventually taken away from us." In a further twist, Firestone advised that only a firm stance against the League would prevent the administration's embarrassment before African American voters in an important election year. Little evidence backed Firestone's claim that African Americans were on his side. Yes, Firestone had the support of some conservative Black intellectuals like Charles Spurgeon Johnson who were friendly to the interests of white capital, philanthropic organizations, and charitable missions. But nothing in the company's actions, neither in the United States nor in Liberia, suggested Firestone's particular concern for the plight of Black workers. In Akron, African Americans were relegated to the lowest-paid and most-demanding jobs on the factory floor. In Liberia, Hines told a State Department official, all Firestone cared about was "cheap labor."[112] The optics going into a presidential election certainly concerned Hoover's cabinet. Jay Pierrepont Moffat, chief of the Western European Division of the State Department, lamented that appeasing the competing interests led to a complicated "mental gymnastics" of "trying to carry two pails, one filled with negro votes and the other filled with Firestone campaign contributions."[113]

A few months later, Barclay's government made a brilliant, calculated move in the winner-take-all game that Firestone seemed determined to play. Firestone had, in the fall of 1932, rebuffed Lord Cecil's invitation to meet with Liberia Committee members in Geneva. Harvey Sr. deeply distrusted European interests and had little patience for the League. He instead sent the vice-president of the Finance Corporation of America, L.T. Lyle, to Liberia to meet directly with Barclay. Firestone's act of "bad faith" played into the Liberian president's hand. The same week that Lyle arrived in Monrovia, the Liberian Legislature passed a joint resolution, the Moratorium Act, that unilaterally reduced the number and salaries of foreign fiscal personnel, suspended interest on the loan for two years, and declared a moratorium on loan payments. The legislature also called for the resignation of the American financial adviser, P.J. Fitzsimmons, for failing to comply with the resolution.[114]

The Firestones were furious. Time was short to convince Hoover to take more aggressive action against the Liberian government. Franklin D. Roosevelt had won the November election in a landslide and would be inaugurated in a matter of months. The Democrats controlling the White

House and both chambers of Congress meant uncertainty for Firestone's Liberia operations. In the final days of Hoover's presidency, Firestone was losing favor even among friends like Stimson. The secretary of state admitted that he had "relied to such an extent on the good record of the Firestones" that he perhaps had erred in speaking "out very strongly on their behalf." Stimson realized Firestone was not "playing ball" fairly; his position with Lord Cecil and the Liberia Committee was awkward.[115] Although Stimson believed that the new Liberian legislation had violated a contract with an American corporation, whose rights and interests he was obliged to defend, Firestone's go-it-alone behavior had diminished the American diplomat's bargaining power. How could he appeal to Lord Cecil to bring international pressure on the Liberian government to withdraw the legislation that flouted the loan agreement terms? Cecil had little sympathy for the company's predicament. The Liberia Committee had invited Firestone on several occasions to assist it "with information and advice." Firestone declined each offer. Several committee members, the British vice-consul confided, thought that Firestone, "by insisting on the rigid execution . . . of a very onerous agreement," meant "to drive the Liberian Government into such straits that they would be at the mercy of the corporation."[116] To Stimson, the accusation unfairly disregarded the "humanitarian record of the Firestones made by the slavery investigation," which showed, he suggested to Cecil, that Firestone had "no oppressive intentions toward the Liberian government."[117]

As Stimson deflected the League's oppression charges, the Firestones were trying to orchestrate the corporate takeover of a foreign government. In a series of revolving-door meetings in Washington, DC, during Hoover's final days in office, father and son escalated their rhetoric and threats. Barclay "will sell out his country to . . . Europeans, unless the United States takes hold," the elder Firestone told Hoover in early February 1933.[118] A "condition bordering on anarchy" prevailed in Liberia, Harvey Sr. declared. "Armed and turbulent young men, countenanced by the President of Liberia," had imperiled the lives of Firestone management, he charged. Beseeching the president and secretary of state out of a "personal sense of responsibility toward our American employees in Liberia," the company patriarch urged that an American battleship be sent to protect American interests.[119] When Hoover and Stimson did not comply, Firestone petitioned the chair of the Republican National Committee to pressure them to do his bidding. Meanwhile, rumors circulated in Monrovia that Firestone's Hines was plotting revolt among Barclay's political foes, hoping for a Liberian government more favorable to Firestone's interests.[120]

The contest between a self-made American millionaire used to getting his way and a savvy statesman defending the rights and sovereignty of his country ended here. In 1932, at the age of sixty-four, Harvey Sr. relinquished the presidency of the Firestone Tire & Rubber Company. The future of the Firestones' rubber empire no longer rested solely in the hands of the father. Perhaps Liberia had always been less a reality and more an image, a fanciful dream, for the Akron businessman. He had never visited the country, and never would. As chairman of the board, he would continue to wield power and influence, but with thoughts turned more toward his legacy. His good friend Thomas Edison had died the year before. Brazened by wealth, power, and fame, Harvey Sr. in his power play with Barclay had backed himself into an untenable position without clear moves forward. The heyday of the Republican Party had ended and, with it, much of Firestone's influence. As Roosevelt took office on March 4, 1933, Liberian president Barclay, the masterful tactician, had the upper hand.

# 5

# Contested Development

At New York City's Prince George Hotel, fifteen men, all white but one, met the week before Christmas Day, 1932. With Harvey Firestone Jr. among them, they represented a century of white philanthropic, religious, and business interests in Liberia. All held concerns that the Black republic's present economic and political instability threatened their investments. They felt that assisting the Firestone rubber company to better secure and expand its Liberian investment would aid their own ambitions for the country. The men had gathered to hear the reconnaissance report of Henry West, president of the American Colonization Society and veteran *Washington Post* reporter. West had just returned from a three-month trip to Europe and Liberia. Just that week, the Liberian Legislature had introduced the Moratorium Act, which would suspend loan payments to the Finance Corporation of America. The move threatened Firestone's undertaking in Liberia—the future of white capital in a Black republic hung in the balance. West's reconnaissance report was anticipated as a timely and informative take on the Liberian crisis in world affairs.

Ensconced in the splendor of the opulent, Beaux Arts–style hotel, West reported on his conversations in London, Geneva, and Monrovia. He told how he had carried abroad the message of the like-minded men to whom he now spoke. In Monrovia, at a reception in his honor hosted by President Barclay, West compared Liberia to a ship in need of expert piloting through a harbor's dangerous waters. West made clear that the pilot Liberia needed "to steer her 'Ship of State' through the present crisis" should be an American chief adviser. That the man to chart Liberia's course to better days should be a white man was a given among those gathered in New York City. West also told the assembled men that his meeting in Geneva with Liberian secretary of state Louis Grimes had done little to further his diplomatic mission. That meeting had confirmed for West what his conversations with Barclay led him to believe: "The Liberian

Government has no goodwill toward the Firestone Company . . . and are generally anti-American."[1]

After West spoke, Harvey Jr. gave a spirited defense of the company's operations and intentions in Liberia. Firestone was at the meeting to summon the help of supporters. He vigorously denied rumors that the family company wanted to establish an "American dictatorship" in Liberia. Yes, their interests in Liberia were economic, tied to the production of rubber. But they were also, he insisted, "interested in the stability of the country and desired it to succeed." He insisted the company was not extractive like oil and mining. "Instead of taking anything out of the country," he argued, the company was "actually putting something into it." It had imported supplies and equipment, built roads, and employed up to twenty thousand laborers. The 55,000 acres of planted rubber trees being nurtured for latex production would soon be "an asset . . . comparable with the cocoa industry in the Gold Coast." Despite the board of directors' advice that Firestone pull out of the country, Harvey Sr. remained committed to "the Native people of Liberia" who, like their company, Harvey Jr. claimed, were being persecuted by Barclay's government. The rousing speech won the approval and support of those in the room, men of influence on philanthropic and missionary boards, among religious organizations, and in the U.S. federal government.[2]

When the president of the ACS spoke at the reception given in his honor before President Barclay and other Liberian officials, he had dared, eighty-five years after Liberia had declared itself a sovereign Black republic, to invoke the paternalistic attitude of his white predecessors who had sponsored the Liberian colony's first Black settlers.[3] West's speech was tone deaf to Liberia's political sensibilities and to the national and race pride held among the audience. West spoke as a white man ready, yet again, to save Liberia, a country whose very existence both substantiated and challenged a world in which twin oppressive forces, white supremacy and racial exploitation, sustained global flows of capital. Firestone, upon setting foot in Liberia, had wrapped its rubber venture in a missionary rhetoric of salvation through American capital, science, and medicine. And in this garb, it justified the taking of land and the securing of cheap labor in a country that did not see itself as either a "ward" or "moral protectorate" of the United States, however much Firestone portrayed it to be. At stake was Liberia's development, but also Liberia's independence. Who would determine the course of the country's development? The stakeholders in the contest included representatives of white capital, African American voices and expertise, and Liberians themselves.

The meeting at the Prince George Hotel had been organized by Thomas Jesse Jones, educational director of the Phelps Stokes Fund, head of the newly revived New York Colonization Society, and chairman of the charitable Advisory Committee on Education in Liberia. The Phelps Stokes Fund, established by Caroline Phelps Stokes's bequest in 1909 to improve housing for New York City's poor and to aid in "the education of negroes, both in Africa and the United States," had strong ties to the New York Colonization Society and to Liberia. Phelps Stokes's grandfather, Anson Greene Phelps, a New York merchant made wealthy by his mining and shipping enterprises, founded the New York Colonization Society and in 1858 bequeathed $50,000 to Liberia College, established in 1851.[4]

Cultivating the Phelps Stokes Fund's educational and Liberian interests, Jones harnessed social science tools to bring supposedly objective scientific rigor to the study of Black education in America's South and in Africa. In truth, he bolstered preconceived views of Black education using field research and survey methods he learned while earning a sociology doctorate at Columbia University. These were views touted by industrial philanthropists, white Southern professionals, and conservative Black leaders in the United States and by white European experts in colonial Africa. Jones's work on Black education ingratiated him to philanthropic organizations like the Phelps Stokes Fund and the Rockefeller-funded General Education Board, often founded with the wealth of northern industrialists to promulgate the moral precepts of Christianity and commerce. W.E.B. Du Bois looked upon such northern boards of philanthropy with great suspicion. They had "long ago surrendered to the white South," Du Bois wrote in a scathing critique of Jones's published study, *Negro Education*, sponsored by the Phelps Stokes Fund and the General Education Board. Men like Jones, and the organizations he represented, "find it so much easier to work *for* the Negro than *with* him," Du Bois argued, such that the "Negro [is] unrepresented and unheard."[5]

A system of industrial schooling focused on agriculture and the mechanical trades promoted by Jones's study of Black education matched Firestone's interests in developing a labor force in Liberia.[6] Critical of Jones's work was Carter Woodson, a leading scholar-activist, educator, and public intellectual. Woodson lambasted Jones's "capitalist education" policies, which he saw as selectively using social science research to devise a narrow vision of educational opportunity for Black people, limited to labor in the service of white rule. Through the Association for the Study of Negro Life and History, which he co-founded in 1915, Woodson pioneered rigorous scientific, historical studies of Black life in America. His 1933 book, *The Mis-Education of the Negro*, took issue with missionary educational philosophies that taught and reinforced the history, ideas, and life of white oppressors, instead of the history and culture of those they oppressed. "The education of the Negroes in Africa, . . . as in America," Woodson wrote, "must be carefully worked out and directed by the exploiters of the race." Now that missionaries and "some far sighted businessmen" had rethought exterminating "the natives" from Africa, Woodson observed, they were introducing and financing schools of industrial education to "properly" train a workforce for "lazy Europeans" who got their "bread from the sweat of another's brow."[7] Woodson regarded Jones as "an evil in the life of the Negro," who was "nevertheless catapulted into fame among . . . capitalists and government officials."[8]

While Jones's ideas on industrial education for Africans suited Firestone's objectives, it was the vision of U.S. educational adviser to Liberia James Sibley that best aligned industrial and agricultural education with Firestone's workforce needs. Sibley espoused a benevolent paternalism as the key to educational and economic progress. Agricultural training and knowledge was best acquired, in Sibley's view, not from generational experience cultivating Liberian soil but from American experts. Before his untimely death from yellow fever in 1929, Sibley had brought the Phelps Stokes Fund and the Advisory Committee on Education into Firestone Jr.'s orbit while encouraging their support of the company's work in Liberia. Sibley also recognized how Firestone could advance his vision for educational development in Liberia. With the backing of the Phelps Stokes Fund, the American and New York Colonization Societies, and the foreign mission boards of the Protestant Episcopal, Methodist Episcopal, and United Lutheran Churches in the United States, Sibley spent seven months in Liberia in 1926 surveying the status of elementary, secondary, and postsecondary education in government and mission schools. The white Southerner trekked through Liberia along many of the same paths followed by Strong and his Harvard team. Like Strong, Sibley had traversed the circuits of American empire from the Philippines to Liberia. A former state agent for Negro Rural Schools in Alabama, Sibley sought to export Booker T. Washington's model of industrial education to the tropics. In the Philippines, he taught "modern" agricultural methods to the country's rural population, firm in his belief that the guiding hands of American capital and empire would improve people's lives.

Upon his return to the United States, Sibley persuaded Olivia Egleston Phelps Stokes, sister to Caroline, that it was a propitious time to establish an agricultural and industrial training school in Liberia. It should be modeled after Tuskegee, which both sisters had generously supported.[9] Olivia died later in 1927, leaving a bequest to establish a Tuskegee in Africa. Securing a suitable location was the next task. Sibley had hoped President King would grant an allotment to expand the small St. Paul River Industrial Institute in White Plains, a farming community fourteen miles from Monrovia that had prospered in the nineteenth-century heyday of Liberia's coffee economy. The vocational school had received support from Phelps Stokes and was run by the Foreign Missions Board of the Methodist Episcopal Church. But King had other plans. He granted a thousand-acre parcel to establish the Booker Washington Agricultural and Industrial Institute (BWI) in Kakata.[10] Fifty miles from the capital, connected by a new dirt highway built with the aid of Firestone engineers, Kakata was an important center of trade and a favored gathering place for chiefs to air grievances with the Liberian government. It was also close to Firestone's main Du plantation and adjacent to land Firestone had claimed for expansion. As Sibley drove African American architect and Tuskegee vice-president Robert Taylor and his wife to the new school's site in Kakata, he noticed "new country homes" being built along the highway. Elites were taking ownership of newly accessible land and planting their country estates with profitable rubber seedlings.[11]

At the BWI's Founder's Day ceremony in March 1929, just months before his death, William Francis spoke of the new vocational institute's promise of a diverse agricultural landscape. Before an estimated crowd of three hundred chiefs, government dignitaries, and members of Monrovia's settler society, the U.S. minister painted a picture of the region's future: "The smoke of thrift issuing from the chimnies [sic] of Kakatown's many factories; here perhaps a pineapple canning factory, there an orange or grape juice bottling plant, and yonder perhaps a building housing modern equipment for preparing Liberian coffee for the world's market." Francis saw a diverse agricultural economy, rooted in traditional cash crops, scaled up to furnish an export trade. Yet, in the distance, where the green leaves of rubber seedlings grew from a scorched earth, a different agricultural landscape was taking root. A monoculture tree crop, previously unimportant to Liberian lifeways, was displacing people from the customary lands where the cornucopia of foodstuffs that sustained them grew.[12]

Sibley welcomed Firestone's coming to Liberia, and with it the "advent of large outside capital" and "all that it would mean."[13] So, too, did Tuskegee Institute's Taylor. He left Liberia "amazed at the magnitude of the development" of the Firestone Plantations Company and impressed by the "favorable attitude of the native employees" with whom he spoke. To Harvey Firestone, Taylor expressed his hope for forging a partnership with the Tuskegee Institute, the Phelps Stokes Fund, and the rubber company to create an industrial school of "benefit to the future welfare of the country."[14] Harvey Jr. joined the BWI's Board of Trustees and his company began to donate expertise, equipment, and funds in the building and running of BWI, which had a class of seventy-one boys in 1931.

The school's agricultural education program that Taylor outlined focused on silviculture—the cultivation of tree crops—including rubber, coffee, oil palm, and cocoa. The latter three had all been important to Liberia's settler and indigenous economies. Planting tree crops was also an established practice, used by generations of agriculturalists in Liberia to secure customary land rights. Taylor sought to couple education in farming techniques with religious education, and to offer a course of instruction for girls on domestic skills such as sewing, cooking, and cleaning. Firestone undoubtedly hoped BWI would train and furnish a steady supply of subservient plantation laborers, educated in efficient hard work, religious piety, and family life modeled on American ideals. In a yearlong program on "The Romance and Drama of the Rubber Industry," aired on the NBC radio show *The Voice of Firestone*, Harvey Jr. justified the company's presence in Liberia through an appeal to white superiority. In "operating a modern plantation," he assured millions of American listeners, the white superintendent, "chosen by us for his tact as well as his efficiency, . . . soon gains the respect and love of the trusting and childlike people working under him."[15] Firestone's segregated workplace vision sprung from attitudes of white superiority mixed with racist policies; it mirrored the structures of industrial agriculture that were born of plantation slavery and sustained in the sharecropper system of the Jim Crow South. Not surprisingly, early on few students showed interest in BWI's agricultural program, knowing they could make more money as carpenters, masons, and mechanics than as skilled rubber tappers. Our "greatest tragedy," reflected the school's first superintendent, was "doing the very thing we came to Liberia not to do—taking the boys away from the farm instead of back to the soil."[16]

Among the group of fifteen gathered at the Prince George Hotel, Lester Walton was the only African American. He was a newspaper man, invited to the meeting by Jones. Three years earlier, Walton had published an article in the popular magazine *Current History*, extolling the virtues of American enterprise in Liberia. In it, Walton denounced Raymond Buell and others who argued that Firestone was engaged in "a nefarious plot to exploit the republic" of Liberia. Walton's piece instead painted a rosy picture of Firestone's operations in Liberia, one supported by a willing and cooperative Liberian government. Motor roads, machinery, and "unprecedented prosperity" had accompanied the company's transformation of the jungle into "a kaleidoscopic picture of industrial life," Walton maintained. Meanwhile, great improvements were underway in Liberia's educational system, which Walton credited to the "conspicuous service" of American mission boards and philanthropic organizations, such as the Phelps Stokes Fund, in advancing vocational training in the hinterland.[17]

Race and political affiliation made Walton a minority among the power brokers at the Prince George Hotel. But he had significant influence and standing, and had already shown himself to be well disposed toward Firestone and the Phelps Stokes Fund before meeting Harvey Jr. that day in December 1932. Influence and sympathy with their cause was what the Firestones—facing waning influence in the White House, Liberian government defiance, and growing suspicion of the company's intentions in Liberia—needed in their present crisis.

Born in St. Louis, Walton was a graduate of Sumner High School, the first Black public high school west of the Mississippi. Walton's writing talents earned him a reporting job with the *St. Louis Star*. In 1906, he headed to New York City where he became a drama critic and theatrical editor for the *New York Age*, the largest circulating Black newspaper in the nation.[18] In 1912, Walton married Gladys Moore, the daughter of Fred Moore, the paper's owner and editor. Gladys's father had purchased the *New York Age* in 1907 with the help of Booker T. Washington, and had earlier partnered in purchasing the Colored Co-operative Publishing Company and its monthly periodical, the *Colored American Magazine*.[19]

Walton agreed with his father-in-law on the importance of business in empowering African Americans and advancing their rights in a segregated society. He had little patience for critiques of capitalism calling for liberation of Black labor from white oppression through working-class revolution, championed by the Communist and Socialist parties. "Capital," he wrote, "has done more for" African Americans "than labor, which bars members of my race from trade unions."[20] But Walton did not share in his father-in-law's nor much of Harlem's allegiance to the Republican Party. As his success as a journalist grew writing for the *New York Age*, the *New York World*, and the *New York Herald Tribune*, so too did Walton's political aspirations. In 1913, he began a movement to push the Associated Press and the white newspapers it represented to print the word *Negro* with a capital *N*. It was a necessary change in journalistic standards, Walton argued, in keeping with the "individuality and dignity worthy" of his race and its "place in the ethnological classification of the world."[21] He became active in the New York Democratic Party and served as publicity director of the Colored Division of the Democratic National Campaign Committee in the 1924, 1928, and 1932 presidential elections. With Franklin Delano Roosevelt's 1932 win, Walton hoped his decade-long effort to bring part of the Black vote to the Democratic Party would earn him a political job.

One month after the Prince George Hotel meeting, Walton was a Firestone guest at Harbel Manor. Walton wrote to his friend Claude Barnett, founder of the Associated Negro Press, that he had been at the "PALACE of senior," where "before a big fire-place [and] crackling logs, No. 1, No. 2 . . . discussed with me the situation."[22] The "situation" was the Firestones' plan to make a final appeal to the outgoing Hoover administration to use force to back their position in Liberia. Walton's connections to influential leaders in and supporters of the Democratic Party, the Tuskegee Institute, and the Associated Negro Press made him a critical ally in the Firestones' fight with Barclay and their efforts to install a U.S. chief adviser to oversee the League's proposed reforms. On February 14, Walton left New York City on a midnight train to meet the Firestones in the capital the next day. Between their meetings with officials in the State Department and the White House, father and son spoke with Walton. Walton embraced the Firestones' belief that Barclay was "pro-British" and that "Great Britain, also France, has its sinister eyes on Liberia and would gobble it up upon the least pretext in the guise of friendship." Walton thought an American gunboat would have "the desired psychological effect" on a Liberian president who was "running wild."[23]

In the quiet of the Firestones' hotel room, Walton proposed a plan that he and Barnett had been discussing in confidence. The two newspaper men, both pro-business, both with deep ties to Tuskegee and its donors, would use their influential connections in the Black press to publish stories that portrayed the company and its work in Liberia in a favorable light. "Either we have a good and righteous cause or we have not," Barnett wrote Walton. "If we have then let's go ahead and make capital for it," he advised.[24] Barnett hoped for financial compensation for the public relations campaign he and Walton would render the company.[25] But Walton wanted a different benefit. Merit and position mattered more to Walton than monetary reward. As he and Barnett discussed the likelihood of a political appointment, perhaps even the ministership to Liberia, Walton confided that he was certain he had won the father's and son's "confidence" and could count on "their influential backing" should a "certain proposition" arise.[26]

Walton and Barnett represented one camp in the divided opinions among Black writers, journalists, intellectuals, and activists in the United States and across the African diaspora after the League of Nations investigation into slavery in Liberia and the ensuing political fallout.[27] Viewpoints differed regarding the roles of capital, labor, and imperialism. Walton and Barnett backed Firestone's vindication by the League's International Inquiry Commission and squarely laid the blame for the forced labor scandal and the country's financial woes on Liberia's ruling elite. They saw Firestone as a promising force for Liberia's economic development and championed the company's introduction of wage labor as a benefit for the nation's indigenous inhabitants. Further, they believed that the United States had a moral obligation to intervene in the affairs of the Liberian government, given America's historical colonization efforts in Liberia.

Walton and Barclay found common cause not only with Charles Spurgeon Johnson, who drafted the League's initial investigative report, but also with George Schuyler, a prominent and prolific African American journalist and author. Schuyler was an iconoclast and master satirist whose essays, in magazines such as the *American Mercury*, and novels, including *Black No More* and *Slaves Today*, parodied both white supremacists and Black elites.[28] In 1931, Schuyler traveled to Liberia, financed by the *New York Evening Post* and his book publisher. He returned to pen a series for the *New York Evening Post* and the *Washington Post*, along with a spate of vitriolic columns for the *Pittsburgh Courier*, that disparaged Barclay's regime and the True Whig Party, which he likened to the "system of corruption, chicanery, persecution, and terrorism" once rampant in New York's Tammany Hall and persisting in the rigged election systems of Mississippi and the Jim Crow South.[29] His columns were so complimentary of the Firestones' enterprise in Liberia and so favorable to the idea of an American protectorate that William Jones of the *Baltimore Afro-American* accused him of being on the Firestone payroll and "the most brazen defender of the imperialistic slave driver our group has produced."[30]

Schuyler was not one to take ridicule of his pro-Firestone stance lightly. He grew up in a working-class family in Syracuse, enlisted in the U.S. Army at the age of seventeen, and worked at various jobs in New York City in the "fetid world of steam, odors, dirty dishes, and twelve-hour days."[31] He joined the Socialist Party in 1921 and became a member of the Black socialist group Friends of Negro Freedom. A ten-month assignment for the *Pittsburgh Courier* investigating the conditions of African American life below the Mason–Dixon line led Schuyler, as he reflected in his autobiography, *Black and Conservative*, to decidedly shift his political stance. He became convinced that Black people would be "worse off under any collectivist system." Self-help, achieved through Black-owned businesses, consumer cooperatives, and educational institutions, "in cooperation with willing whites," would, he believed, prove more effective for realizing racial equality in American society than a proletariat overthrow of the bourgeoisie.[32] So, when the *Baltimore Afro-American* reporter denounced Schuyler for his defense of Firestone and scathing critiques of Liberia's ruling settler elite, Schuyler ruthlessly schooled the Communist reporter on his Marx. Liberia's indigenous population was the working class, Schuyler explained. He found it unconscionable that Jones would fail to defend them under the "Red banner of revolution." "It seems that the white American capitalists who grind down the proletariat are ogres ripe for extermination, whereas the black Liberian capitalists, whose exploitation is cruder, more brutal, and less efficient, are angelic philanthropic souls," he chastised. "I greatly fear I shall have to wrap up my three volumes of 'Das Kapital' and mail them [to Jones] for his perusal and digestion," Schuyler quipped.[33]

In embracing the professed savior power of American capital, the pro-Firestone, anti-Barclay group paid little heed to Liberia's situation on the world stage. The small, weak republic was caught in a battle with colonial and corporate empires. But Schuyler, Walton, and others focused on the country's domestic politics and on what they regarded as an exploitative system that profited settler elites at great cost to the country's indigenous inhabitants. They argued that the introduction of wage labor on the Firestone plantations would economically benefit Liberia's working class and thereby empower its indigenous people to secure equal standing and rights in the nation's governance. In short, they championed American capital to furnish aid in what they deemed to be Liberia's critical hour of need.[34]

But did Liberia need saving? Barclay had made no such request, certainly not in a form that would jeopardize his country's sovereignty. Nor had paramount and clan chiefs in Liberia's central hinterland that stretched from Kakata to Gbarnga, the principal region of Firestone's tentacular reach for land and labor. At a large gathering in Gbarnga, Kpelle and Mandingo chiefs collectively signed a decree to be delivered to the League of Nations, along with forty-eight white kola nuts as a sign of respect. "We do not want White Men OVER US to RULE US, but we want our OWN BLOOD, OUR KITH, AND KIN," they declared. "According to our Father's Customs, we are fixing our Palava ourselves, as we know our Peoples, the Americo-Liberians and they know Us."[35] The notion that people needed to be saved had long been a motivating force in the intrusion of missionaries into foreign lands. Firestone's corporate incursion into Liberia was little different.

Calls to "save Liberia" could be seen as a ploy to justify American intervention. Barnett worried about "a hue and cry" being "raised against" the push for an American chief adviser "on the grounds that white capital is seeking to dominate the situation."[36] But the outcry that Barnett feared would subvert their efforts to sway Roosevelt's administration toward backing Firestone in Liberia had been smoldering for some time.

W.E.B. Du Bois stoked the fire with a column published in *The Crisis* in the fall of 1932, a month before the U.S. presidential election. In an essay reprinted in the Black press, Du Bois listed reasons why Black voters would be wise not to reelect Hoover. The Republican president's "Lily-White" policies, appointment of officials with "anti-Negro attitudes," and "failure to recognize or appreciate the plight of the Forgotten Black Man" were reasons enough. But, citing the incumbent's policies toward Haiti and Liberia, Du Bois suggested Hoover was a puppet of Firestone, who was "demanding a dictator who will destroy the independence of Liberia."[37]

Du Bois's reference to Liberia in his column was likely prompted by a telegram that Walter White, executive secretary of the NAACP, had received and shared with Du Bois just weeks before. Dorothy Detzer, an anti-war activist and the U.S. secretary of the Women's International League for Peace and Freedom (WILPF), had sent the cable from Geneva. She was troubled by the League of Nations plan. It violated, she thought, a nation's sovereign rights and also ignored the Liberian government's request that the chief adviser be neither an American citizen nor from a colonial power in Africa. After receiving a lukewarm reception at the League of Nations headquarters from Lord Cecil, who dismissed her remarks as "extreme and radical," Detzer dispatched a cable to the WILPF's Washington office.[38] "Negro protests against American plan needed," she urged.[39] Soon, the WILPF and the NAACP, with support from the Foreign Policy Association, a nonprofit organization founded in 1918 dedicated to educating the public on international affairs, joined forces to fan the flames of an anti-imperialist, anti-Firestone campaign.

Du Bois's anti-Firestone campaign was a reversal of the opinion he had formed when he visited Liberia nearly a decade before. At that time, he had cautiously held hope that white American capital, working in partnership with "black educated men, both African and American," might create an industrial plantation of "mutual dependence and prosperity" like none yet seen.[40] "I had not then lost faith in the capitalistic system," Du Bois admitted.[41] After seven years of operation, however, Firestone's intentions were clear to Du Bois. The company was engineering an industrial system in Liberia built on a segregated workforce of white management and Black labor; it was no different from the other extractive industries that the European colonization of Africa had built, in Du Bois's words, on the "theft of her land and natural resources."[42] Du Bois had specifically warned Harvey Sr. in 1925 against following such a path. The Akron industrialist had never replied. Now, as the company sought to tighten its grip on the country, Du Bois became one of Firestone's most vocal critics.

By the summer of 1933, Detzer intensified the WILPF's lobbying efforts, asking Du Bois and the NAACP's White for support as the League of Nations Liberia Committee met in London to finalize its plan. Earlier that year, Hoover had refused the Firestones' request to send a gunboat to Liberia. But he did, with the incoming administration's approval, dispatch Major General Blanton Winship to Monrovia to find a solution that would safeguard "American rights" and advance "efforts to assist Liberia."[43] Detzer didn't trust Winship and warned White that he held "the point of view of a southerner of the old south in a kindly, paternalistic attitude toward Liberia."[44] In Liberia, in advance of the League's committee meetings in Geneva and London in May and June of 1933, Winship had brokered an agreement with Barclay, Firestone, and the Finance Corporation of America. The Finance Corporation, with Harvey Jr.'s consent, agreed to modify the 1926 loan agreement. Interest on the loan would be cut from 7 to 5 percent and salaries of American fiscal officers would also be reduced. The terms, however, were contingent upon the Liberian government rescinding its Moratorium Act, which suspended loan payments, and accepting the League's final plan.[45]

Winship had not mentioned the demand of a U.S. chief adviser position to Barclay while in Liberia. But the issue exploded at the League talks in London. Both Harvey Jr. and Henry West were there to represent the interests, respectively, of Firestone and U.S. missions in discussions with Lord Cecil and the Liberia Committee. To Winship's dismay, West distributed in London a pamphlet published by the American Colonization Society, "The Liberian Crisis." The piece was blatant propaganda, meant to raise suspicion against British interests in Liberia and drum up support for a League plan supportive of Firestone and the appointment of an American chief adviser. Harvey Jr. had advised on the pamphlet's content, and the Firestone company underwrote some of its cost. Thousands of copies were sent to American religious and philanthropic organizations. Another five hundred copies, each in a stamped envelope, were sent to Dr. Robert Russa Moton, Washington's successor as president of the Tuskegee Institute. West hoped the influential African American educator would distribute the pamphlets to Black colleges and leaders. In the edition targeted to Black audiences, Harvey Jr. and Henry West followed Walton's advice: *Negro* was spelled with a capital *N*. In the edition aimed at white churches and philanthropic boards, the word appeared in all lowercase letters.[46]

"The Liberian Crisis" depicted a paternalistic history of Liberia as a "ward" of the United States, a script straight from Firestone's publicity department. American missions and philanthropic organizations contributed a "quarter of a million dollars each year" to advance religion and education in Liberia, the pamphlet claimed. Should not the "American government . . . act as a protector in safeguarding their labors?" The greatest praise went to Firestone, whose $8 million investment had transformed "an unproductive wilderness" into "a revenue-producing plantation." Firestone had come "not as conquerors to destroy," the document declared, but "as harbingers of a new era of economic development in Liberia." Dismissed were those who decried American imperialism: unlike Great Britain and France, the United States had no territorial ambitions to seize control of Liberia's valuable natural resources. "We are not land-grabbers," the American capitalists insisted. The pamphlet concluded by asserting that Liberia's "only salvation" lay in "repealing its repudiating legislation," re-negotiating the loan terms with its creditors, and accepting an American chief adviser.[47] Meanwhile in London, Harvey Jr. let it be known to a League official that the company would "not advance money to support any plan unless the Chief Adviser were American."[48]

Liberian secretary of state Louis Grimes, representing his country in London, promptly rejected the U.S. chief adviser demand. The Liberian government had never wavered on this point, and it would not now. Detzer urged White and Du Bois to act. In a telegram sent on behalf of the NAACP to President Roosevelt and Lord Cecil, White strongly defended the Liberian government's position, urging appointment of a Dutch or Scandinavian national as a neutral adviser. The League talks, White said, gave the impression that the U.S. government was "upholding Firestone interests in Liberia." "Does the new deal not include Liberia?" he asked. White also told Roosevelt that he had appealed to prominent African American organizations and newspapers, whose constituencies represented millions of Black votes, to support Liberia and its rights as a sovereign nation.[49]

In July, Du Bois publicly delivered the blow that the WILPF and NAACP had hoped for in their fight against Firestone and imperial ag-gression. In a stinging critique, commissioned by and published in *Foreign Affairs*, an organ of the Council on Foreign Relations, Du Bois brought historical and economic analysis to bear, mustering a brilliant defense of Liberia and its sovereignty. Du Bois was a skilled economic historian. In the 1890s, as a doctoral student at Harvard University and Frederick Wilhelm III University in Berlin, Du Bois specialized in history, eco-nomics, and political economy. He was adept at using social science tools to make visible the dark underbelly of capitalism, revealing its dependence on and perpetuation of racial inequality and oppression. Liberia's "chief crime," Du Bois wrote, was "to be black and poor in a rich, white world; and in precisely that portion of the world where color is ruthlessly exploited as a foundation for American and European wealth."[50] Liberia was rich in raw materials. But it needed capital to develop, capital largely held in the hands of white men and imperial nations. For fifty years, it had been caught in a vicious cycle of foreign loans and escalating debt. The Firestone loan was among the most recent and egregious, and Du Bois's account exposed it unequivocally.

The Firestone planting agreements had demanded that Liberia pay off its foreign debt by securing a $5 million loan to protect the company's investment. Liberia had received half the loan, but had used legislation to stop making payments. However, deceit in the loan's financing surfaced in the League of Nations inquiry. As Grimes reminded White, the King administration had been clear that they "did not want any loan from any company doing business in Liberia."[51] Du Bois made public what the Liberian government learned through the League's investigation: the Finance Corporation of America and the Firestone Corporation were one and the same, one a shadow of the other. The deal was one-sided. Firestone profited not only off Liberia's land and labor but also off the loan. Du Bois found, after adding up interest, amortization expenses, and salaries of American fiscal officers, Liberia was paying not 7 percent on the $2.5 million borrowed so far, but an egregious 17 percent. In Du Bois's reckoning, Liberia was justified in renouncing its loan payments and rejecting Firestone's demand for an American chief adviser. Du Bois argued that, contrary to the "querulous criticism" meant to denigrate Liberia, her "jealous and proud" independence and her fight "to be let alone" constituted "one of the most heartening efforts in human history."[52]

Du Bois's *Foreign Affairs* attack on Firestone was just the beginning. At the end of July, Howard University president Mordecai Johnson scheduled a meeting with Acting Secretary of State William Phillips in Washington, DC. The attendees represented the causes of civil rights, anti-imperialism, Pan-Africanism, and Black education in America. They included Johnson, Du Bois, and Detzer, along with representatives of Howard University, the Association for the Study of Negro Life and History, and the International Council of Women of the Darker Races. They meant to challenge the State Department's position on Liberia and its selection of Winship, a white Southerner, to represent American interests in the League of Nations' ongoing negotiations.

Du Bois, as spokesperson, delivered the opening salvo. Twenty-three thousand African Americans had attended college the previous year. Despite their educational accomplishments, they found "no increase of opportunity and no essential softening of deep-seated racial prejudice," Du Bois told Phillips. When such talented Black youth "see in the whole white world, . . . a disposition to shut the gate of opportunity in their faces and to reduce every colored country where possible to complete vassalage to white countries," they are left, Du Bois asserted, "astounded and embittered." Black people in America saw "no 'New Deal.'" Instead, they saw old tactics at play: "loaning money to small countries, encouraging them to buy and spend beyond their ability to pay, finding or inventing moral excuses for intervention, and then taking charge of the country in the name of some white country and in the interest of commercial organization whose chief and only object is profit." This is how Haiti landed in economic bondage to the United States. The "same process" was now "incubating" in Liberia, Du Bois informed Phillips.[53]

If the Roosevelt administration was sincere in its resolve to not "participate in the exploitation of disadvantaged people," Du Bois and his colleagues warned, it must reconsider its Liberia position: recognize Barclay's regime, drop its threats and ultimatums, and appoint the chief adviser from a neutral country as the Liberian government requested. Educational assistance should be done in cooperation with the Liberian government, not channeled through American missionary organizations, which too often served as "the hand-maiden of capitalistic and imperial designs."[54] Immediately after the meeting, the NAACP issued a statement calling the Firestone loan "fraudulent and based upon the use of slave labor." Du Bois and Detzer, confident that a contingent of American public opinion was on their side, also telegrammed Grimes in Geneva: "Don't yield."[55]

Phillips was shaken. Both *The New Republic* and *The Nation* published pieces favoring the group's demands. Phillips wrote a lengthy, apologetic letter to President Roosevelt. On one side, he claimed, "aggressive negroes, including Dr. Dubois . . . as well as certain groups such as the WILPF and the Foreign Policy Association," accused the State Department of "selling out Liberia for the benefit of the Firestone interests." But others, Phillips said, backed the State Department's policy, including the Phelps Stokes Fund, the Boards of Foreign Missions, the Colonization Society, and "more conservative negro elements," including "Dr. Moulton [*sic*], President of Tuskegee," George Schuyler, Charles Spurgeon Johnson, and Lester Walton. Phillips asked how they should proceed. The decision was not trivial. Because the Firestone plantation in Liberia was the only major source of American rubber outside the Far East, Phillips clarified, it represented "a very important consideration in our national defense."[56] Roosevelt replied: "Continue the present policy." Further, the president said, remind Firestone that he "went into Liberia at his own financial risk." Roosevelt added, "It is not the business of the State Department to pull his financial chestnuts out of the fire except as a friend of the Liberian people."[57]

The attack organized by the WILPF and the NAACP rattled the State Department's inner circles and those who held common cause with Firestone. Barnett was vexed that he and others who supported the interests of Firestone had not attended what was referred to as the "Washington Conference." If they had, Barnett asserted, "those opposed to American interests" likely would have "refused to participate" or taken a different approach.[58] The NAACP press statement undermined completely his and Walton's efforts to portray Firestone favorably in the Black press.

On the day after the "Conference," Walton left for Liberia. Officially, Walton traveled "in the capacity of newspaperman and observer." But before leaving, he mailed Barnett a letter captioned "PLEASE DESTROY AFTER READING." In it, Walton told his friend that he had arranged for "certain people" to contact him while away. Walton's cryptic communication plan strongly suggests he was in Liberia furtively advancing the interests of Firestone. Walton also divulged to Barnett that a confidant of Roosevelt's had assured him he would be "given consideration" for the diplomatic post of American minister to Liberia "when time comes."[59]

In Liberia, Walton's negative opinion of Barclay dissolved. The Liberian statesman's gracious hospitality and his "frank discussion on many subjects" left the American "immensely impressed" and "optimistic to Liberia's future welfare." Walton found Barclay very much "alive to the problems confronting" him and "desirous of solving them." Barclay also trusted Walton, and asked him to serve as Liberia's press agent in America to "disseminate accurate information" and counter malicious statements about his government in the Western press. Walton agreed to do so without charge.[60] Moreover, Barclay told Walton that he would reject the League's Plan of Assistance and instead seek assistance rebuilding Liberia from the U.S. government.

The Liberian president was an astute politician. He certainly knew Walton would repeat to confidants what he learned in Liberia. Barclay likely saw advantage in leaking this information to Firestone, who might be prompted to reconsider the demand for an American chief adviser. In early September, Walton sent a dispatch to the Phelps Stokes Fund's Leo Roy telling him of Barclay's plan. Roy relayed the information to Barnett, on the condition that this "new move by Liberia" be kept from Du Bois and the "opposition groups."[61] While the U.S. State Department seemed unaware of Barclay's strategy, Firestone was not. In late September, Harvey Sr. told Roosevelt's secretary of state, Cordell Hull, that he would accept a non-American chief adviser.[62] The stunning position reversal would cost Firestone little if Barclay refused the Plan of Assistance. But by acquiescing to State Department and League pressure regarding the adviser, Firestone acquired favor.

In Geneva on his return home, Walton walked with Liberian secretary of state Grimes, discussing whether the Liberian government favored a Black man or white man as U.S. minister. Grimes ended, Walton disclosed to Barnett, "saying if a man of my caliber were named, he would be warmly welcomed."[63] Grimes had also befriended Detzer in Geneva. His letters to her and Du Bois were as gracious and flattering as Barclay's were to Walton. For her efforts aiding Liberia, the Liberian government awarded Detzer the Humane Order of African Redemption.[64]

In January 1934, three months after the League finalized its Plan of Assistance, and almost four years after its investigation into forced labor and slavery in Liberia, the Liberian Legislature authorized Barclay to accept the plan, but only if twelve conditions were met.[65] The League retorted that the plan be accepted without reservation. Barclay wired Walton that the conditions, all protective of Liberia's political and economic independence, effectively ended negotiations. The Liberian president, true to his word, had not accepted the plan. For the Firestones, every condition the Liberian Legislature demanded directly affronted their terms for remaining in Liberia. They pleaded with Walton to do something to sway African American sentiment to support the League plan. Walton wrote to Barnett bewildered. How, he wondered, could the Firestones be so obtuse to the fact that "race sentiment is positively and emphatically with Liberia"?[66]

On May 18, after more than three years of negotiations, the League of Nations formally withdrew its Plan of Assistance. As a Liberian citizen described it, Barclay "knew enough 'book' to outwit the white man who was trying to take his country."[67] Barclay had, so far, thwarted Firestone's remaking of Liberia into an American protectorate and protected the country's sovereignty. He now needed American government recognition and assistance to complete his strategic development plan.

Liberia, in the spring of 1934, was politically isolated. Walton was angered by the ongoing smear campaign by European countries intent on "blackjacking Liberia to accept" the League plan and to "mandate if it does not," authorizing a League of Nations member to take over Liberia governance.[68] He struck back in early June, publishing an opinion piece, "America, Save Liberia!," in the *New York Age* that defended Liberia's rejection of the League plan. The plan was tainted with the "secret longing" of European powers eager to mandate "the little West African republic" when the "time was deemed propitious," Walton wrote. To whom in its "trying hour" should Liberia turn? "Turn to the United States, which is responsible for Liberia's birth, which has been her traditional friend and protector and whose benevolence has materially furthered Liberia's educational and economic development," he answered.[69] Behind this statement stood American corporate, philanthropic, and religious interests in Liberia with whom Walton had allegiance. Walton also reached out to Du Bois. They sharply disagreed about Firestone. But the friends found common cause in the need to protect Liberia's sovereignty and independence. Du Bois agreed to help and recommended "a formidable appeal be made to President Roosevelt" to come to Liberia's aid.[70]

Meanwhile, against Walton's advice, Harvey Sr. and Harvey Jr. kept pushing behind the scenes for a hostile American takeover or an internal coup to topple Barclay's regime.[71] The British government, infuriated by Liberia's rejection of the League plan, also pressed Secretary of State Hull on the U.S. government response. "A corrupt and inefficient oligarchy of Monrovia," the British ambassador implored, threatened the "slaughter and maltreatment of two million natives." The British diplomat urged American action, since Liberia's "financial machinery" was already in "American hands," and assured Hull of the British empire's cooperation. Hull expressed dismay over "the deplorable conditions in Liberia" and its resistance to the League plan. But abandonment was not warranted, he acknowledged, because Liberia's fate mattered too much to Black Americans and to U.S. philanthropic and religious organizations, not to mention Firestone.[72]

In August 1934, Hull sent special assistant Harry McBride to Liberia to assess the situation. After six weeks in Monrovia, the former U.S. fiscal adviser to Liberia told Hull he saw encouraging changes. In just over a decade, he reported, Monrovia had become a modern city of ten thousand

Monrovia, capital of Liberia. When Harry McBride, former American fiscal adviser, visited Monrovia in 1934, he reported back to US secretary of state Cordell Hull that he was impressed by what a modern city it had become. From Firestone Plantations Company, *Views in Liberia* (Chicago: Lakeside Press, R.R. Donnelley & Sons, 1937).

inhabitants with "leveled and cleared" streets, "dozens of cars and trucks in operation," "electric lights, at least one or two good schools, a creditable waterfront, an excellent new customs house and a main trading street lined with well-stocked stores." When McBride first visited in 1919, one abandoned rubber plantation existed. But now he saw "over 60,000 acres of flourishing rubber trees offering the country's greatest economic resource." Liberia had achieved all this, McBride recognized, with "few weapons, little administrative experience, and . . . with a pitifully restricted pocketbook."[73]

Further, Barclay had shown McBride his three-year plan of proposed administrative, economic, educational, and public health reforms for which he would seek legislative approval. His plan guaranteed Liberia's sovereignty in overseeing its affairs and included many League recommendations.[74]

McBride's report, contrary to portrayals in the foreign press of a degenerate, "primitive," and "backward" country, offered a favorable impression of Liberia to which Hull warmed.

Eventually a rapprochement between Barclay and Harvey Firestone Jr. would also help break the political logjam that blocked the flow of capital, goods, equipment, and personnel between the United States and Liberia during the early years of the Great Depression. Economic and political pressure changed Firestone's view. When the British and Dutch in April 1934 again tightened the world's rubber supply, Firestone grew eager to resume tapping and planting operations. Furthermore, the State Department grew tired of Firestone's bullying. When Harvey Sr.'s right-hand man, Bill Hines, confronted the chargé d'affaires in Monrovia, boasting of Firestone's political power and threatening to "unleash a newspaper campaign" against Roosevelt's administration if it failed to assist Firestone's efforts "to control Liberia," Jay Moffat of the State Department had had enough.[75] In early October 1934, after receiving McBride's report, Moffat summoned the father and son to Washington. The career diplomat, who had served under five American presidents, made it clear that the United States would no longer intervene in "small countries, bending governments to their will, particularly on behalf of commercial interests."[76]

Moffat's words had an impact. Harvey Jr. arrived in Monrovia in late January of 1935. The debonair executive was thirty-seven years old. He had keen interest and knowledge of business and international relations and possessed the social graces befitting a tête-à-tête with a foreign head of state. In meetings that lasted into the morning's early hours, Barclay and Firestone spoke frankly on a broad range of subjects touching on their respective interests. Barclay impressed upon the younger Firestone that it was within his power to halt the company's operations without "violating the terms of the Planting Agreement." He could, for example, with a word to chiefs in the hinterland dry up the plantations' labor supply. Barclay added that it had been himself, not then president King, who had most favored granting Firestone permission to operate in Liberia.[77]

For five years, the Firestones had tried intimidation, mudslinging, and political maneuvering to discredit Barclay and remove him from power. Harvey Jr. now had to cast the lot of the rubber empire that rested increasingly in his hands. Barclay was facing an election against former president King. Whether swayed by interactions with Barclay, Walton's influence, Hull's admonishment, or the fate of millions of maturing rubber trees,

Harvey Jr. forged a mutual accord with the formidable Firestone adversary. In the weeks before the May election, he and Barclay privately renegotiated the terms of both the loan and planting agreements. Loan interest was reduced from 7 to 5 percent on outstanding bonds. Annual interest payments would be waived if yearly government revenues dropped below $450,000. Revenues above that amount would pay off annual interest, amortization, and outstanding debt. In addition, the Liberian government agreed to pay the salaries and expenses of foreign specialists and fiscal officers included in Barclay's three-year plan. Firestone agreed to prepay $400,000 for sixty years of rent on 110,000 acres and $250,000 in exchange for tax exemptions. As additional revenue, the Liberian government would receive a 1 percent tax on the value of rubber and commercial products shipped from the plantations. In exchange, Firestone could operate in the country at no other cost and with its foreign employees exempt from all income and personal taxes. The 1935 agreement also granted Firestone exclusive mineral rights to the land it leased. It was a good deal for Firestone. Time would tell its value for Liberia.[78]

Barclay had thwarted the power-grabbing actions of father and son, bending a corporation and the American government toward his side. His achievements, popular with the Liberian Legislature and people, easily won Barclay an extension of his presidential term. In early June, the Liberian Legislature ratified Barclay's revised loan and planting agreements and repealed the Moratorium Act. The following week, on June 11, Secretary of State Hull instructed the chargé d'affaires in Monrovia to convey formal recognition of Barclay's government by the United States and to "express the good wishes of the American Government and people for the welfare of Liberia."[79] After five acrimonious years, President Barclay found himself in the good graces of the American government and on candid terms with Harvey Firestone Jr., sixteen years his junior.

On June 18, Walton received a long-distance telephone call from Washington, DC. President Roosevelt offered him the post of U.S. minister to Liberia.[80] Endorsements in favor of Walton for the ambassadorship had flooded the State Department from across the country in the weeks before his appointment. They came from Democrats and Republicans, from businessmen and religious leaders, from educators and journalists, and from community organizations and philanthropic boards that reached across America's color line. Harvey Firestone Jr. was among his supporters, as were all who had been present in December 1932 at the Prince George

Lester A. Walton, U.S. minister and envoy to Liberia, accompanied by his wife
Gladys and daughters Marjorie and Gladys Odile, en route to Liberia, 1935.
(Courtesy Photographs and Prints Division, Schomburg Center for Research in
Black Culture, The New York Public Library.)

Hotel meeting that had instigated so much machination.[81] Walton's appointment received widespread publicity and praise, from *Time* magazine
to the *Daily Herald* of London. Two years later, "pajama-clad" at 7:30 in
the morning on his veranda in Monrovia with his "trusty typewriter," he
reflected on the proud moment. He confided to Barnett that with a
$10,000 annual salary, including a house and entertainment and travel
expenses, his material compensation was more than that of any other African American holding a political job in any branch of federal, state, or
municipal government.[82]

Walton came to Liberia already a "conciliator."[83] He had won the support of both a white rubber baron who sought to shape a small West African republic into an American protectorate, and that republic's Black
president who was determined to protect his country's independence.

When the newly appointed United States envoy extraordinary and minister plenipotentiary was preparing for the transatlantic move with his wife Gladys and their two daughters, he received a letter from Du Bois. It offered hearty congratulations and words of wisdom. Du Bois proclaimed the appointment "a great chance" and, either accidentally or intentionally, "a touch job." But the "villain in this play is the Firestone Company," Du Bois warned. "They are going to be so nice to you and your family in a country where entertainment and society is scarce that you will have a hard time escaping them. Nevertheless, if you play your game right," Walton's friend counseled, "you can save the independence of Liberia."[84]

Harvey Jr. missed the inaugural ceremonies in Monrovia in January 1936 for the reelected Liberian president. Nine days and nights of activities created a festive atmosphere in the capital, "the liveliest in all its history," Walton observed. People from all walks of life, and from all parts of the country—some dressed in traditional country cloth, others clothed in suits and ties—jostled to see the country's leading dignitaries, sporting top hats and tuxedos, Walton among them, parading down Broad Street, the main thoroughfare. An inaugural ball, diplomatic dinners, an agricultural fair, and a day celebrating Liberia's indigenous cultures and chiefs occupied Walton, his family, and the thousands gathered to take part in the festivities.[85]

As atonement for missing the inauguration, Harvey Jr. entertained Barclay and nearly fifty Liberian legislators at Duside, the initial headquarters of the Du plantations, at the end of February. Harvey Jr. spared no expense, putting on an extravaganza that included an airshow and banquet. The accord Barclay and Harvey Jr. reached initiated a new wave of company investments. In 1936, Firestone spent $1 million (roughly $19 million in 2020 dollars) to ramp up plantation operations. Seedlings planted in the first divisions cleared along the Du River in 1926 had matured. Tapping could begin. Wooden bungalows that housed management were replaced with two-story brick homes, and the tin-roof tract houses shunned by workers were rethought to mimic the thatched-roof homes in circular layouts found in their home villages. A new hospital, constructed of steel and concrete, featured an operating room, laboratory, X-ray room, and dispensary. It gestured to the benefits that modern industrial development might bring to Liberia, as did the company's landing

Aerial views of the mature rubber trees on the Du plantation and new Firestone management housing. These were just a few of the images that adorn the book *Views in Liberia*, produced by the Firestone Plantations Company in honor of Barclay's presidency. From Firestone Plantations Company, *Views in Liberia* (Chicago: Lakeside Press, R.R. Donnelley & Sons, 1937).

Harvey Firestone Jr., Liberian president Edwin Barclay, and U.S. minister Lester Walton stand together, surrounded by Liberian government officials at an airshow and banquet hosted by Harvey Jr. at Duside. From Firestone Plantations Company, *Views in Liberia* (Chicago: Lakeside Press, R.R. Donnelley & Sons, 1937).

field and airplane, the first in Liberia. The airplane gave Barclay a bird's-eye view of Monrovia and made possible aerial photographs that captured the stunning scale of landscape change being driven by plantation forestry. Pictures of the felling, clearing, and burning operations that displaced people and denuded hilltops and valleys were, wittingly or not, both triumphant framings of industrial capital on the move and elegiac tributes to loss. Lands deemed unproductive in the eyes of a corporation had through the wonders of American science, medicine, and technology been reengineered into a monoculture plantation with seemingly endless rows of rubber trees and miles and miles of roads. These scenes populated *Views in Liberia*, a limited-edition, large-format photo book privately published by the Firestone Plantations Company as a gift in honor of Barclay's presidency. The images were meant to celebrate the people and events heralding a new era of friendly relationships between Firestone and Liberia, and the benefits to come. A group portrait in the book features the three men largely responsible. Harvey Firestone Jr., Liberian president Edwin Barclay, and U.S. minister Lester Walton stand together, surrounded by Liberian government officials invited to the plantation's headquarters at Duside that February day.[86]

Walton worried "friends like Du Bois" could get "the wrong impression" from such scenes, but he resolved that "to socialize with Firestone" was not to hinder his neutrality in ironing out affairs between Firestone and Liberia.[87] In the West African republic, Walton and his family found welcome relief from the "demon-prejudice" that impinged opportunities in America. In Monrovia, he joined the "Northern Athletic Club," which was supposed to be "Lily White." As the U.S. minister to Liberia, not the "Negro Minister," he emphasized, he delighted in "every respect and consideration" given him and Gladys by the "Diplomatic Corps at Monrovia."[88] With Barclay, Walton developed the most "cordial and confidential relations," and would drop in at the Executive Mansion or at the president's farm near the Firestone concession on the Farmington River. Walton felt at home and welcome in Liberia.[89]

Harvey Jr. forged social relationships with Barclay and Walton that proved mutually beneficial while solidifying and deepening the Firestone Plantations Company's commitment to expansion. Banquets at Duside were one way Firestone ingratiated himself to Barclay and Liberia's ruling elite. Gestures like selling difficult-to-obtain Ford automobiles and hosting visits to Akron smoothed Firestone's relationships with Liberian officials. But the single most important courtesy the company extended to both settler and indigenous elites, which fostered mutualistic relationships, was to supply rubber seeds and root stock, scientific advice, and a market for the rubber of independent Liberian farmers, whose fortunes became enmeshed with those of Firestone Tire & Rubber Company and its Firestone Plantations Company.[90]

In the 1930s, many of the most recognizable among Liberia's ruling class and indigenous leaders began to cultivate large rubber estates, some of several thousand acres, at the edges of the Firestone concession along the Du and Farmington Rivers. Among them were former president King and many in his cabinet, including former interior secretary John Morris and former treasury secretary John Cooper.[91] Didhwo Twe also owned a farm. As an indigenous man, Twe had been among the most vocal critics of the Liberian government, and was outspoken in defense of the country's indigenous inhabitants during the forced labor scandal. For his efforts he was expelled from the House of Representatives in 1929. A student of agriculture at Harvard and Columbia, he took a keen interest in the Firestone plantations. In the early 1930s, a Liberian legislator published a scathing attack on Firestone in Thomas Faulkner's Monrovia-based newspaper, *The Voice of the People*. He charged Firestone with expropriating indigenous lands and destroying cash crops on local farms without compensation. Twe wrote a vigorous rebuttal absolving Firestone of wrongdoing and instead blaming the Liberian government, "the sole protector of the native's rights." Twe believed the knowledge that indigenous laborers gained handling "machines and mechanical tools" on the Firestone plantations would do more to "accomplish for the advancement of the native" than "what the Missionaries have been trying to do for more than a century without results commensurate with the money spent."[92] Twe sent employees from his own rubber farm to the Firestone plantation to learn bud-grafting techniques, borrow tools, and seek scientific advice on diseases that affected the rubber trees.[93]

Barclay, too, owned a farm. Agriculture was at the center of the three-year development plan presented in Barclay's 1936 inaugural address.[94] He envisioned his Mount Olive Farm Estate, on the Farmington River, would be a "show place for his political friends and followers" of what agriculture might achieve for Liberia. Barclay's farm, managed by his nephew and adopted son, George Padmore, relied on roughly 150 laborers who resided with their families in two villages on the farm that included a school and a church. Sections of the estate grew rubber, cocoa, and sugarcane; fruits, such as pineapple; and traditional staples, like cassava. This was an experiment not in monoculture plantations but in diversified agriculture, a microcosm of what Barclay envisioned for Liberia. While Barclay was more interested in cultivating annual cash crops, his nephew planted and focused on the high-yielding clonal rubber trees furnished by Firestone. Barclay's Mount Olive farm was located in the Firestone concession area on what was becoming prime real estate, especially as the plantations company expanded its operations toward the Farmington River. Harvey Jr. knew Barclay intended to retire to his farm after public life and worried that the proximity of Firestone's "factory operations to [Barclay's] farm might be increasingly annoying."[95] In November 1937, Harvey Jr. offered Barclay $25,000 and concession land across the river in exchange for the farm, which had five thousand rubber trees at that time. Barclay refused to sell. In 1944, when Barclay did retire to his farm, he was shocked by what he earned selling his estate rubber to Firestone. One month of revenues paid out more than his entire yearly salary as president of Liberia.[96]

In their 1935 negotiations, Barclay had pressed Harvey Jr. hard on how Firestone might aid Liberia in achieving self-sufficiency in agricultural production. Rice was of particular concern to both men as Firestone resumed operations. It was, and is, a staple of the Liberian diet. Firestone was adamant that Liberia's supply of "country rice," traditionally grown in dry, upland areas through swidden agricultural methods, could not meet the demands of an expanding industrial plantation. As tapping commenced, the company would need to feed a workforce of more than fifteen thousand laborers. Early in his second term in office, Barclay introduced a rice embargo act that prohibited rice importation. It was meant to stimulate domestic rice production. Firestone strenuously objected. He argued that the slash-and-burn agricultural methods practiced by Liberia's subsistence farmers severely damaged Liberia's forests. Harvey Jr. either failed to see or chose not to mention the destruction wreaked by the company's own agricultural methods. The two men sparred over why domestic rice production did not meet Firestone's needs: was it swidden methods or the lack of transportation networks? Eventually, Barclay withdrew the rice embargo in exchange for Firestone's investment of technical expertise to determine if Liberia's climate and soil could support wet rice cultivation.[97]

Reciprocal relations, at least on the surface, replaced the strong-arm tactics old man Firestone had used to try and bully his way into a country. Exchanges around land, labor, capital, and politics enabled a plant to take root and the industrial ecology of a plantation to thrive. Two years after Firestone and Barclay came to a mutual understanding, Firestone could "lay claim to operating the largest single rubber development in the world."[98] In 1937, more than 5 million pounds of rubber, valued at more than $1.1 million ($20 million in 2020), left the company's Liberia plantations. It went to Firestone's tire factories in Akron, Memphis, and Los Angeles and the company's latex division plant in Fall River, Massachusetts. Firestone purchased 5 million pounds of rice, one-sixth of it from Liberia, to feed a labor force of more than ten thousand workers. That year, workers tapped more than 3 million rubber trees and planted an additional eight thousand acres of clones.[99] The big gamble that Harvey Jr. had made would pay off, it seemed. The bud-grafted clones planted during the company's darkest days were almost ready to tap. Preliminary harvests gave latex yields nearly three times those of standard trees grown with seeds retrieved from the old Mount Barclay Plantation.[100] In 1937 the value of rubber exports equaled that of all other commodities combined, including cocoa, coffee, gold, ivory, palm kernels, piassava, and palm oil. The Liberian government achieved a balanced budget, with a surplus, for the first time in years.[101]

Walton wrote to Du Bois in 1937, enthusiastic about the state of affairs. Liberia's economic future looked bright, Barclay's three-year plan was a success, and the "American government is giving" Barclay "100 percent moral support," reported Walton. For his role in reconciling relations, the American government had pledged $100,000 for a new Legation building in Monrovia. Du Bois replied, happy about the improving situation. "But I am still deeply suspicious of the Firestone monopoly," he disclosed. "They did all they could to hurt Liberia in Europe, and of course their chief object is to make money," he warned.[102]

Flying over Firestone's Du and recently installed Harbel plantations in 1936, doctoral student George Brown did not see an exultant scene of transformation and development ushered in by American capital, industrial agriculture, and wage labor. He saw "an undesirable monopoly over the most valuable industrial territory in the country." He saw "here and there" an "African village completely surrounded by the rubber forests." He saw communities adapting indigenous economies "to meet living conditions in a forest no longer ripe with palms, coffee, cocoa, wild game, bamboo, cotton, woods for canoes and herbs for ceremonial and medicinal purposes." He saw "low wage employment" driving "young people" to the city or the plantation. In short, he saw violence wrought by the extraction of land and labor by a Western economic system alien to the "spirit, philosophy, and benefits" that, he argued, animated the economies and "communal labors" of Liberia's indigenous peoples.[103]

Brown went to Liberia in 1935 and rang in the 1936 new year at Duside with Firestone manager Donald Ross. A few days later, he accompanied Walton at sunrise to the military review of the Liberian Frontier Force at Barclay's inauguration celebration. Brown benefited from Phelps Stokes Fund support and from Firestone hospitality. Nevertheless, the intellectual course he traversed, combined with his travels through Liberia's interior and his interactions with its people, led him to a unique perspective on Firestone's impact on land and life.[104] It was a perspective his fellow Americans Lester Walton and Charles S. Johnson, who embraced industrial capital as a device for economic and educational uplift, and Du Bois, who had few encounters with Liberia's indigenous people, did not ascertain.

George Brown, an American doctoral student at the London School of Economics, in the field in Liberia, circa 1936. (Courtesy of Loma Flowers.)

Intellectual curiosity and structural racism shaped Brown's peripatetic life. Brown was born in 1900 in Missouri but grew up in Kentucky where his family moved after his father, a Methodist pastor, narrowly escaped lynching for defending his wife from the taunts and sexual advances of a group of white men. When Brown was sixteen, his family moved again, to Cleveland, once an important stop on the Underground Railroad. When he was seventeen, the young man set off for Howard University in Washington, DC. There he became an understudy to Carter Woodson, who had founded the *Journal of Negro History* in 1916. No one influenced Brown's early intellectual life more than Woodson. Brown absorbed his mentor's passion for using historical social science tools to document, record, and interpret the past and present experiences of Black people across the African diaspora. Like Woodson, Brown used those findings to combat scientific racism and white oppression. Upon completing his MA in history from Adelbert College in 1922, Brown filled Woodson's former post at West Virginia State College, teaching history, economics, and political life. In 1934 he earned a PhD in history from Western Reserve University for a dissertation on the history of African Americans in Cleveland during the nineteenth century.[105]

Brown's physical journey to Liberia was not direct, and neither was his ideological one, which resulted in a political awakening to imperial aggression and racial oppression operating through the global economy. In both cases, the path led not through America but London. In 1934 he enrolled in a PhD program at the London School of Economics (LSE), taking graduate courses in anthropology, economics, and history. In the 1930s, London became a vibrant center of Black internationalism and anticolonial thought. Brown attended gatherings of the League of Coloured Peoples, founded in London in the early 1930s by Jamaican physician Harold Moody to promote unity and welfare among all people of African descent. There he met renowned Black intellectuals, activists, and performers who were united in opposing the racial order of capitalism and empire: men like Jomo Kenyatta, who would help lead his country to independence from British colonial rule and become Kenya's first president, and Trinidadian historian C.L.R. James, then formulating groundbreaking work on the Haitian revolution and the history of Black resistance movements. In this intellectual ferment, Brown renewed his close friendship with singer and actor Paul Robeson and his wife Eslanda, both of whom shared his commitment to labor rights and socialist causes.[106]

At the LSE, Brown interacted with an international cadre of African, Afro-Caribbean, and African American graduate students. They shared experiences and ideas and challenged and confronted the colonial perspectives and institutions of their white professors. The tools of anthropology, economics, and history—used to buttress empire and white supremacy— were taken up by students of African descent and, as LSE anthropologist Bronislaw Malinowski said, turned into "weapons against us," that is, against European colonists and oppressors.[107] In the autumn of 1935, as Italian troops invaded Ethiopia, sparking anti-imperial and anti-racist critiques among Black intellectuals, Brown left for Liberia. Liberia was, thanks to Barclay's handling of Firestone and the League of Nations investigation, the one country on the African continent that had not fallen to Western imperial conquest. Writing from his position as head of history and political science at Lincoln University in Pennsylvania, future Nigerian president Nnamdi Azikiwe looked to Liberia in 1934 as "the nucleus of a black hegemony," where the "hope of an African civilization" emphasizing African ideals "of hospitality, of friendliness, of honesty, of truth, of justice, and of the brotherhood of man" might be realized.[108] Brown, armed with a Kodak camera, steeped in anthropology and history, energized by anticolonial and socialist struggles, and supported by Paul and Essie Robeson, traveled to Liberia in search of not Western but African values and ideals.

Brown's interest in the exchange relations of indigenous economies took him to Liberia. This was the project that Malinowski had recommended Charles S. Johnson undertake while in Liberia as a League of Nations investigation member. As part of his doctoral dissertation research, Brown combined the participant-observation methods of economic anthropology with the historian's penchant and quest for archives and documents. He sought to understand the different economies at work on the Firestone concession, within Liberia's settler society, and among Liberia's rural indigenous population. Among the Gola and Vai people in Liberia's Western District, the American stranger was welcomed by current and former paramount chiefs, including Momo Passay, Momo Fahnbulleh, and Komo Tiffa. Brown observed, even then, the reach and influence of the embryonic Firestone plantations, roughly two hundred miles south. When someone from a remote village asked for permission to build a hut, the local chief asked, "Which stranger are you? Rubber stranger or cotton tree stranger?" The question was meant to elicit whether the stranger was someone "who 'comes soon, goes soon,' like rubber" or who would, as symbolized by the sacred cotton tree, put down roots and become part of the community.[109]

Brown keenly observed the activities of life in Liberia's hinterland. He wanted to understand how different forms of exchange—of land, of goods, of labor—structured social interactions and meanings within and among communities. He followed the movement of rice with intense scrutiny: harvested from fields by women, carried to town by boys and men, stowed in the village storehouse by women and boys, and divided into shares among chiefs, elders, "witch doctors," and "medicine men." In Voinjama, a major trading hub in Liberia's northwestern corner, Brown observed market day in detail and the intricacies of bartering and trade. In Bendaja, near where the Mano River marks the Liberia–Sierra Leone border, he noted the elements and rhythms of the rice harvest festival.[110]

Through his interactions among the Vai and Gola peoples, Brown came to understand the central place of land in the meanings, values, and social relations that shaped rural Liberian communal life. Brown sought to document a communal set of relationships among people, non-human others, and land that fostered ways of being and values not readily subsumed by industrial capitalism. These were not "primitive" economies, he argued, but were cooperative industrial systems. They depended upon a set of exchange relations that upheld the community rather than the individual and informed the collectivist nature of social and spiritual life in Africa.

At the base of such indigenous economies was land, Brown argued. Land, and its communal uses, dominated and structured the rhythms of life in the village, the farm, and the forest. Together, Brown observed, village, farm, and forest formed "an African social trinity," each part of which was integral to and played an important function in the "social order of indigenous Africa." Brown left Liberia enamored with the communal values and lifeways of his hosts, values which stood in contrast to the individualism of American culture and the capitalistic economic system upon which it thrived.[111]

Land dispossession, driven by concessions to white foreigners, Brown argued, threatened Liberia's development. It did so, he believed, because it undermined the very foundation upon which the "communal collective economy" of African heritage rested. This was the danger that Brown saw in 1936 as rubber trees took root and men and machines resumed clearing forest land in a march toward the Farmington River. In Brown's view, the Firestone concession, through its alienation of indigenous land, risked shunting Liberia down an economic development path that would "destroy and replace communal self-sufficiency with the possessive, individual, competitive western forms of economy," a result that, from a cultural and political standpoint, Brown scorned.[112]

Time and again, Firestone and its supporters cloaked the transformation of "untouched land" and "unproductive wilderness" into an industrial plantation as a benevolent process that would bring wealth and prosperity to Liberia. American missionaries, philanthropists, and scientists had imposed Western values related to work, productivity, and land use, buttressed by scientific ideas of service to capital, to justify the Firestone enterprise. Brown utilized the social sciences to instead question and challenge Western economic assumptions and ideals. "No land was vacant," no land was wasteland, in the "economic system of the indigenous Liberian Africans," Brown observed. Categorizing land as wilderness or wasteland was a Western imposition that aided land dispossession. Such land alienation was well underway, visible by airplane or by car along a road reaching from Kakata to Gbarnga, referred to today as Liberia's rubber corridor.[113]

In his book *The Economic History of Liberia*, first titled *Black Communism, White Concessions*, Brown argued that the "parasitic capitalism of Liberia's ruling class; and, the financial exploitation of the American and European industrialist" fed upon Liberia's indigenous economies and the land and labor that sustained them.[114] As Barclay began an eight-year term as president, it was too early to say whether parasitic relationships might evolve into mutualistic ones. Brown expressed hope for Liberia's future under Barclay's leadership. The Liberian president had successfully protected Liberia's independence against Firestone and the League of Nations. Brown applauded Barclay's ideal of a "united Liberia where neither Africans nor civilized exist, only Liberians," and "a country raising itself from amongst the least important nations by its own efforts." Undeniably, Liberia's economic independence was still greatly constrained by foreign white capital. But Brown praised Barclay's agricultural plan, which proposed developing agricultural cooperative societies, as an important step toward encouraging practices of mutual aid and polyculture, alive in Liberia's hinterland, to offer insurance against the "economic disaster" that "one-crop commercial cultivation" threatened.[115]

In this new era of reconciliation in Liberia, a relation of mutualism among a plant, a company, American interests, and Liberian elites had formed and begun to grow. In 1936, as latex began to flow, the pathways along which these symbiotic relations would develop remained indeterminate. Would, as Brown hoped, "a modified form of African self-sufficiency . . . carried out by all the citizens of Liberia" take hold under Barclay's push for the diversification and development of the country's resources? Or would a species of a tree, native to the Amazon rainforest, deepen and expand a plantation economy, beneficial to some but parasitic to others, on African soil in the transformation of life into capital?[116]

# 6

# Plantation Lives

On October 29, 1938, the USS *Boise*, a brand-new, 10,000-ton U.S. Navy cruiser, steamed into the harbor of Monrovia on its shakedown cruise (a test voyage), dropped anchor offshore, and fired a salute of guns. The boom of its forty-seven-caliber Mark 16 guns, and the friendly exchange of cannon fire from Fort Norris, perched atop Ducor Hill, reverberated along the city's busy waterfront on an early Saturday morning. At a reception later that afternoon in the honor of *Boise*'s commander Captain McCandlish, held at Ducor Hall, the temporary home of the American Legation, Lester Walton toasted a new era of "international accord and friendship," which the arrival of the American naval gunboat symbolized. Before a crowd that included Liberian vice-president James Skivring Smith Jr., members of the Liberian Legislature, the Consular Corps, and more than a hundred Americans, the majority of whom were white management staff of the Firestone Plantations Company, Walton spoke of the significance the *Boise*'s goodwill mission carried "at a time when the peace of the world is seriously threatened by armed conflict, suspicions, hatreds, and divergent political ideologies."[1]

Just weeks before the *Boise*'s arrival in Monrovia, Adolf Hitler had signed a pact with the United Kingdom, France, and Italy, known as the Munich agreement, which gave Nazi Germany the right to annex the western territory of Czechoslovakia without threat of retaliation. It was a gesture of appeasement that many hoped would avert a war in Europe. Barclay feared, however, what such acts of accommodation toward totalitarian aggression meant for Liberia. At a meeting with Walton and the *Boise*'s State Department representative, Henry Villard, the Liberian president shared his growing concerns. The League of Nations did little to aid Ethiopia when the Italian military rained chemical weapons down on its army and citizens and took control of the country, forcing its emperor, Haile Selassie, into exile. Barclay, as the leader of Africa's last independent nation, "could not," according to Villard, "view with equanimity the position of Liberia in a predatory world." Who knew, asked Barclay, if "colonial appeasement" was discussed among Germany, Great Britain, France, and Italy in Munich? Germany had been one of Liberia's major trading partners. And the Dutch had recently discovered major iron ore deposits in Liberia. Barclay had grown uneasy about Germany's designs on Liberia. The country's rich natural resources in agriculture, iron ore, gold, diamonds, and timber invited development. Far better, Barclay told Villard, that it be "undertaken by American" rather than European interests, particularly given the rise of warmongering fascist states greedy for territory.[2]

To Barclay, the arrival of the *Boise* was a welcome sign. The new atmosphere of friendliness and solidarity that Barclay and Walton had worked to achieve permeated the *Boise*'s six-day stay in Monrovia. Cocktail parties and receptions throughout the capital and on the Firestone plantations made for a busy social schedule for the ship's commander and officers. Seven hundred American seamen, granted shore leave, frequented Monrovia's markets, bars, and nightspots without incident. Monrovia's expatriate community, along with Liberian guests, were welcomed on board the *Boise* for tours and an ice cream social. At a dedication for the planned $100,000 American Legation building on Mamba Point, where some of the most stunning views of the city's oceanfront and beaches could be had, Walton proudly referred to the ceremony as a "climax in a series of historic events during the year," including the recent Treaty of Friendship, Commerce and Navigation that he had advanced. Soon, the American Legation site would be home to the "most modern structure on the West coast of Africa." Its sleek horizontal lines, flat roofs, and walls of glass and concrete symbolized, in Walton's words, "a forthright expression of optimism in Liberia's strength and will to prevail as a separate, independent state in the community of nations."[3] A new chapter in the "spirit of good-will and economic cooperation" between the two countries had begun, he asserted.[4] As the American battleship departed Monrovia for Cape Town, Villard expressed confidence that the *Boise*'s visit was "deliberately interpreted as a notice to Herr Hitler to keep hands off in Liberia and as a step to reassure Liberians of the continued interest and friendship of the United States."[5]

Walton had accomplished what Harvey Firestone never could. The Akron rubber magnate had tried to mobilize American military might to secure his Liberian investment. He had urged the State Department to send a naval gunboat when the control of his rubber empire appeared uncertain. But Firestone never saw an American warship on Monrovia's shores. On February 7, 1938, eight months before the *Boise*'s arrival, the founder of Firestone Tire & Rubber Company unexpectedly died. He had been in winter residence at his Harbel Villa estate in Miami Beach. His son Russell and a niece were with him. The 69-year-old millionaire had gone to church in the morning, taken an afternoon drive, and complained of indigestion after dinner. Later that evening, a coronary blood clot ended his life. Firestone was buried in a small village cemetery in Columbiana, Ohio, his birthplace, and was memorialized in the city of Akron and in obituaries across the nation as "a pioneer in industrial welfare," the camping companion of Thomas Edison and Henry Ford, and the man who broke the British monopoly on rubber. All pointed to his Liberia rubber plantations as one of his greatest legacies.[6]

Firestone's five sons—all of whom worked for their father—had inherited the controlling interests of a company and a plantation at an auspicious moment. The company was ideally poised to reap great profits from a world at war. An army "not only marches on rubber, but fights on rubber as well," declared Harvey Jr., two years later in a speech delivered before a group of American businessmen gathered in Boston to discuss distribution issues.[7]

Crude rubber, in terms of dollar value, was then the single most important commodity imported into the United States. In 1939, the U.S. consumed nearly 500,000 tons, valued at nearly $179 million. It was the basis of an American industry that employed more than 120,000 workers and that manufactured goods with an estimated worth of more than $900 million. But the large number of plantations in Southeast Asia still accounted for more than 98 percent of all rubber produced in the world.[8]

The declaration of war on Nazi Germany by Great Britain and France in September of 1939 precipitated a federal effort to stockpile available rubber supplies from Southeast Asia, speed up research on and production of synthetic rubber, and enhance and expand rubber sources in the Western Hemisphere. It also prompted a nationwide campaign, through tire recycling and lower speed limits, to conserve domestic rubber use.[9] In response, Firestone ramped up expansion of its plantations in Liberia. By 1940, 72,500 acres of land had been cleared and planted in rubber, three-quarters of which was in high-yielding clones. Four million of the roughly 8 million trees that made up Firestone's rubber empire had reached maturity, ready to be tapped by a workforce that had swelled again to nearly fifteen thousand Liberian laborers.[10] It was, Harvey Jr. promoted, just one facet of the company's patriotic contributions to war preparedness and defense of "the American way."

In May 1941, as the United States prepared for war, Walton wrote to his boss, Roosevelt's secretary of state, Cordell Hull, urging that "Liberia, America's African outpost," be considered in the "world of tomorrow" being envisioned by the American president. Given the country's wealth in "undeveloped natural resources," and its "strategic geographic importance" to the United States, Walton believed American government investment in a program to advance Liberia's "future welfare" was warranted. Such a program, he recommended, would include technical assistance in agriculture, forestry, public health and sanitation, road infrastructure, and geological surveys, among other areas of economic and social development.[11] The plea followed on the heels of a discussion among Roosevelt's Joint Chiefs of Staff on the possibility of occupying an air and naval base on the coast of West Africa as part of a strategic plan to defend the Western Hemisphere should the Allied Powers fall. Monrovia had not even registered among the top four locations in a feasibility study undertaken by the U.S. military. Instead, military commanders had zeroed in on Dakar. Given, however, that the Vichy French government controlled Senegal and heavily defended its capital, a military invasion was summarily dismissed.[12] Roosevelt, contrary to his advisers, saw merit in Walton's plan. He wanted an air base that would allow American military aircraft to hop across the Atlantic from Natal, Brazil, to land in West Africa.

By September of 1941, construction crews began work on a U.S. military airport base in Liberia. Built by Pan American Airways under subcontract to the Firestone Plantations Company, the airfield was (and is) conveniently located adjacent to the plantations' Division 45 entrance gate, near the Farmington River and just downstream from the hydroelectric plant and main Harbel administrative headquarters and factory completed that same year. The *New York Daily News* viewed construction of the airfield as evidence that the United States had "entered Africa for keeps."[13]

Three months later, in December of 1941, the Japanese military bombed Pearl Harbor and began its sweep across the Malay Peninsula. By February of 1942, the Japanese had seized control of Singapore. The United States' worst fears were realized. In a matter of weeks, a region that supplied

90 percent of the world's natural rubber supply had fallen to the Axis Powers. Bernard Baruch, assigned by Roosevelt to assess the country's rubber shortage and recommend a path forward, argued that rubber was the resource that posed the "greatest threat to the safety of our nation and the success of the allied cause." A single battleship consumed seventy-five tons of rubber in its manufacturing. One ton went into an armored tank. The American military demanded six times the amount of rubber per person than it had in World War I. Suddenly, Ceylon, Liberia, and a handful of countries in Latin America—the remaining strongholds of Allied natural rubber production—took on strategic importance in a world at war.[14]

Wartime rubber shortages demanded faster production, both on the plantations and in American factories. In 1941, Firestone's Liberia plantations yielded 9,000 tons of rubber, representing an almost tenfold increase in production in six years. But it met a fraction of America's wartime rubber needs, estimated at 600,000 tons annually.[15] The crisis spurred a concerted, coordinated effort across American industry, government, and academia to meet the pressing shortfall. Thousands of industrial chemists and engineers, dozens of government agencies, and a host of companies, industrial laboratories, and research universities set a goal in 1942 to ramp up annual output of synthetic rubber, which in 1941 amounted to a mere 231 tons, to 700,000 tons per year.

"Plantation factories rose like magic mushrooms out of the earth," Harvey Firestone Jr. wrote in the *Saturday Evening Post* in 1944.[16] But the rubber these plantation factories produced was not by way of *Hevea brasiliensis*. Rather, the wonders of chemistry and a $700 million government investment in the alchemical forges of the petroleum and rubber industries had, by early 1942, developed a recipe for synthetic rubber. GR-S rubber, as it was known, was made of a mix of butadiene and styrene, organic chemical compounds toxic to human health, derived from byproducts of the oil refining industry. In April of 1942, the Firestone Tire & Rubber Company boasted production of the first bale of GR-S rubber. Within a matter of months, Goodrich, Goodyear, and United States Rubber had followed suit. In 1945, the four American companies, once completely at the mercy of British and Dutch rubber plantations, had come close to achieving their wartime goal, manufacturing 547,500 tons of GR-S rubber.[17]

The development of synthetic rubber did not spell the end of Firestone's Liberia plantations. Instead, the research and innovation propelled by wartime needs sped up production and increased yields of natural rubber, maximized human labor, and decreased costs. Transformations in natural rubber cultivation were, like that of synthetic rubber, a feat of scientific research, industrial engineering, and corporate management.

The industrial ecologies that arose in wartime on Firestone's Liberia plantations reshaped life in the region and on the plantations themselves that endured long after the Second World War ended. Wartime demands for rubber helped to lock in place a set of relationships—between Liberia and the U.S., between white managers and Black laborers, and between humans and the natural environment in this small West African nation that had emerged as a pivotal place in the wartime global economy. The intimate relations forged on the plantations among people, trees, parasites, chemicals, and machines brought benefits and burdens that differentially affected lives in ways that reveal the racial logics and values of Firestone's corporate culture that persisted under Harvey Jr.'s leadership.

"Latex is the initial harvest of natural rubber," voiced a narrator in a 1947 Firestone promotional film. It is "the white blood, which, flowing through the veins and arteries of Liberia, nourishes its growth and sustains its progress." In the film, the white American male's voice accompanies a close-up shot of the natural mechanism of the rubber tree's defense against insects being transformed into "an essential material of modern life."[18] A thin white line of milky substance flows down an angled channel cut into the dark and mottled bark of a rubber tree and into a metal spout at the bottom of that channel, from which the latex drips slowly into a glass cup hanging below.

Latex was the thread connecting *Hevea brasiliensis* to the global economy for rubber, but within Liberia itself, the world of the plantation also bound together Liberians and white foreigners. When the film was made, more than 25,000 indigenous Liberian laborers worked under a foreign white management staff, made up of roughly 160 botanists, foresters, plant pathologists, engineers, chemists, and accountants, almost three-quarters of whom were American. During Harvey Jr.'s reign as the president and CEO of Firestone Tire & Rubber Company, the Firestone plantations exuded whiteness, from the precious latex to the segregated policies and structures of plantation life. At the end of the Second World War, Du Bois, further disillusioned by the promise of Firestone in Liberia,

The Firestone Plantations Company's white management enclave, circa 1937.
Harvey Firestone Jr. stands in the center. From Firestone Plantations Company,
*Views in Liberia* (Chicago: Lakeside Press, R.R. Donnelley & Sons, 1937).

believed that the company's sole object in the country was "to build up a
white cast of colonial rulers who have their own housing, their own society, and their own rates of wages."[19]

Gene Manis, like many of the young, single white American men who
came to work for the Firestone Plantations Company, looked forward to
his initial two-year contract as a junior planter. He had arrived in Monrovia on Christmas Eve in 1939, along with dozens of frozen turkeys, destined for the Firestone plantations. "I am really delighted with the
opportunity and experience," he wrote his mother and sister soon after his
arrival in Liberia. "I have some difficulty, even now, making myself realize
I am really in Africa, several thousand miles from Montana," he exclaimed.
The streets of Monrovia, Manis told his family, were "not much more than
cow trails and as rough as fourth street used to be" in Hamilton, a town
near western Montana's Bitterroot Mountains, where his interest in science
began as a volunteer for a biological field station. But once he neared the
plantation on a "very good road" built by Firestone, passed through the

security gate, and made his way to Harbel Hills, the recently built headquarters of plantation management that replaced Duside, he could have been in any segregated white resort town in America.

On Christmas Day, the entire white management staff were treated to a Christmas turkey dinner with all the trimmings at the Firestone Overseas Club, reserved for whites only. It featured a large lounge, barroom, juke box with the latest hits from America, and a huge "veranda for dancing" that, at that time, "overlooked a native labor camp with mud and thatch houses."[20] Plays that were produced and performed by management and their families, along with American movies, were among the entertainment options. Ping-pong, a nine-hole golf course, tennis courts, and a swimming pool comprised the available recreational activities. At the Christmas Day festivities, Santa Claus passed out mail and toys to everyone in front of a large Christmas tree improvised from a local conifer species, decorated with tinsel, balls, and lights. Manis had been welcomed to a white Christmas, on his first full day as an employee of the Firestone Plantations Company in tropical West Africa.

Like many of the American staff, Manis relished in the luxury that the privilege of whiteness afforded on the Firestone plantation enclave.[21] The house he lived in, and the servants who waited on him, were perks he could never afford in the United States as a young agricultural scientist pursuing a PhD in forestry at the University of Wisconsin–Madison. Noticeably, most of the white "planters" Firestone hired as divisional superintendents came from Midwestern land-grant colleges, located in America's heart of whiteness. When the Firestone Plantations Company offered Manis an entry-level position at an annual salary of $2,100, when the average income in the United States was $1,368, he took it.[22] But many additional benefits came with the job. White American staff who were bachelors often shared the typical Firestone bungalow assigned to management, free of charge. The red-brick and metal-roofed bungalows were large, well-furnished homes built on eight-foot pillars and strategically located on hilltops to catch breezes and give views of the plantation. Each bungalow had a 600-square-foot living room with floor-to-ceiling double French screened windows; two, sometimes three, large bedrooms; a modern, fully equipped kitchen; and a bathroom with both a shower and bath. Most had domestic servants' quarters below. Most white households had anywhere from two to five servants, many of whom were local Bassa people, upon whose customary lands the Firestone concession laid claim. Manis shared the bungalow with Pat Littell, who had a farm in eastern Oregon and had previously worked on the plantations of United Fruit Company in Panama. Together, the roommates had a cook, steward, gardener, dishwasher, and two car valets working for them. The "boys" are at "our beck and call at all times and expect to be," Manis told his family.[23]

Out on the divisions, where Manis worked, the precise planting, disciplined surveying, and wholesale accounting of life imposed scientific order on what had once been, in the eyes of American industrialists and white scientists, unruly and unproductive nature. Each division, cleared, planted, and tapped by indigenous Liberian labor, was laid out in a specific grid system of forty-acre blocks, separated by lines running east to west, and north to south. Bud-grafted trees were planted in holes seventeen feet apart, in straight rows, also seventeen feet apart. The system created a checkerboard pattern of rubber trees, each of which was individually marked and recorded. No variation was permitted, and each step in the process of laying out and planting a division adhered to strict geometric standards and measurements, aided by the precision of a surveyor's theodolite. "By building a Plantation up through the use of the block system and incorporating a good inspection road system with it, all parts of the Plantation will become easily accessible," advised a Firestone planting manual. "Field organization and control will be better, and production will be higher," it affirmed.[24]

Such imposed order did more than improve the control of labor and increase production. It also alleviated white anxieties, born of racist fears. Trepidation of tropical life—of deadly diseases, poisonous snakes, and untrustworthy "natives"—percolated up and animated the writings and conversations of white planters. Many, like Manis, grew up in places, and were educated in institutions, that perpetuated belief in white superiority. Like all white planters, Manis oversaw a hierarchically structured Black workforce of two overseers, fourteen headmen, and three hundred tappers.[25] Order helped to rein in fears of chaos, confusion, and labor unrest that lived just beneath the surface of the idyllic world that Firestone sought to create and project for its white foreign staff.

It was a world strictly segregated along racial lines, and the Firestone Overseas Club became its center. From all parts of the plantation, which, by 1947, had expanded to eighty thousand acres connected by 195 miles of roads, its white staff and their families would gather there to enjoy in the benefits of plantation life. Saturdays and Sundays were filled with ca-

Firestone's nine-hole golf course, circa 1943. The adjoining Firestone Overseas Club
was the center of the plantation's white management world. George and Katy
Abraham Papers #6777. (Courtesy of Division of Rare and Manuscript Collections,
Cornell University Library.)

sino nights, dinner dances, golf tournaments, movies, or minstrel shows
performed in blackface. American wives socialized over drinks and
games, on the tennis court, at the pool, or on the golf course. Picnics at the
nearby beach and fishing excursions for barracuda rounded out the range
of social activities. *Planter's Punch*, the Firestone Overseas Club's newslet-
ter, kept the company's white families abreast of monthly activities and
comings and goings. It was filled with racist caricatures and jokes intended
to keep their world apart from the worlds of those they depended upon to
cook, clean, wash, iron, and shop for them, not to mention harvest latex,
upon which their generous salaries and comfortable lives were built, and
for which they paid no taxes to the Liberian government.[26]

The management staff may have been living in Liberia, but they were
not of it, nor did most care to be. At the United States Trading Company,
the company store owned by Firestone, which imported items duty free,

American brands of food and household goods could be purchased at subsidized prices. "For most of us," acknowledged Kenneth McIndoe, editor of *Planter's Punch* and director of the company's Botanical Research Laboratory, "knowledge of Liberia is limited to the environs of the Plantation, a passing acquaintance with the outward aspect of Monrovia, and some familiarity with a strip of country bordering the road between the two places."[27]

This was also largely the only world in Liberia that Lester Walton knew. In his ten years as U.S. minister to Liberia, Walton never mentions venturing beyond the corridor that linked the Harbel plantations to Monrovia. At Harbel Hills, Firestone's top executives frequently entertained Walton and his family; President Barclay and his wife; President William Tubman, who succeeded Barclay; and members of the Liberian Legislature.[28] Class and position could break the color line that rigidly separated social life on the Firestone plantations if advantageous to the company's interests. In turn, Firestone executives enjoyed the exclusive cocktail and dinner parties of Liberia's ruling elite in the capital city.[29] A comprador class, which mostly turned a blind eye toward the Jim Crow policies structuring life on the Firestone plantations, enjoyed the benefits and luxuries brought by an increasingly lucrative American enterprise.

Despite the perks, many white American personnel chose not to continue at the conclusion of their two-year contract and three months' paid home leave. "We have been told that the rapid turnover of white personnel presents a problem for Firestone," observed a B.F. Goodrich study in 1953, at a time when the Firestone competitor was about to establish its own rubber plantation in Liberia. Goodrich aimed for even higher salaries and more generous leave policies on its Liberia plantation as an "answer to a difficult climate and civilization for white men," which the company considered to be among its greatest challenges.[30]

Esther Warner, who arrived in Liberia in 1941 with her husband, a new Firestone employee, found neither the climate nor the cultures foreboding, and she threw herself into the experiences that Liberia's hinterland and its peoples offered. This openness was rarely seen among the lily-white Firestone management or their family members. An unlikely path had brought her to Liberia. She grew up on an Iowa farm, was active in 4-H, and excelled academically in high school. After two years of study at Iowa State College, she took up a position as a home demonstration agent at West Virginia Agricultural College, where she worked for six years introducing rural women to "scientific" methods in cooking, food preservation, nutrition, family health, home management, and other domestic activities. In 1936, she returned to Iowa State, completed a degree in home economics, and then in 1938 headed off to New York City to study sculpture at Columbia University. At an art exhibition in New York City, she recalled, "I saw some 50 or 60 carved ritual masks from the interior of Liberia. They took a deep, almost hypnotic hold on me and I made up my mind that I simply had to get to their source to find out how the people [who made them] thought and believed and lived."[31] Three years later, her husband, a horticulturist trained at Iowa State, was offered a position as director of the Botanical Research Laboratory on the Firestone plantations. The couple arrived in Liberia one month before the bombing of Pearl Harbor.

Warner found the social life of the Firestone enclave—"about a hundred and twenty-five white men and perhaps forty wives"—stifling.[32] In her novel, *Seven Days to Lomaland,* one of a handful of books she wrote drawing upon her relationships and experiences in Liberia, she remarked: "Whenever I have been in foreign places where there has been an effort to transplant intact a slice of westernized living, something dismal hangs over the place, a pall of ennui. The graft never quite takes. Days lack purpose, go limp. After sundown life is crisped up with rounds of iced drinks, only to wilt again when sunrise presages another hot and useless day."[33] One "old Coaster," a reference to white expatriates who had lived much of their lives on the West Africa coast, told Warner: "You have to have either God or Bols gin to keep from going crazy."[34] Yet those who never ceased complaining of jiggers, tropical ulcers, the help, boredom, and a thousand other irritations that closed their world to life around them, stayed. After three months' leave back home, they were longing for the leisurely life of servants, free housing, medical care, and all the other pleasantries that the white enclave on the Firestone plantations provided.

Warner certainly profited from the same white privileges. But she expressed ambivalence about them, and instead sought to better understand and explore indigenous lifeways. She made multiple treks across the interior of Liberia with the aid of young Bassa, Kpelle, Loma, and Mano men, among others, whom she employed as domestic workers. She made a long journey by foot, through and beyond the rubber corridor to Ganta in the northeast corner of Liberia, to meet Dr. George Way Harley, a medical missionary. Harley's wooden mask collection and knowledge of Mano healing practices was unrivaled among Western scientists and collectors. But he betrayed the trust of Mano elders, upon whose knowledge he relied, when he donated sacred ceremonial objects of the secretive Poro and Sande societies to Harvard University's Peabody Museum.[35]

From "Johnny," "Sammi," "Poor Boy, "Willie," and many others who worked for her, Warner learned of the traditions of the Poro and Sande in her search to better understand indigenous cultures in Liberia. She also learned from elders, like "Chief Kondea" and other artisans, the skills of woodcarving, pottery, weaving, and other West African craft traditions. One could easily criticize Warner for her own extraction and appropriation. The designs, colors, and patterns of Liberian handicrafts she observed and collected were later incorporated into the ceramic dinnerware she produced and sold in America. She and her husband also sold baby chimpanzees bought in Liberia to a breeder in Florida, at a time when trade in chimpanzees for biomedical research was taking off. If she romanticized "the primitive," her writing nevertheless reflects a respect and appreciation for lifeways not her own, views largely not shared by her American colleagues on the plantation.

Warner, like fellow American George Brown, came to understand how much the arts, culture, and livelihoods of Liberia's indigenous inhabitants were connected to, and animated by, the land. The taking of land, initially by the American Colonization Society, and later by Firestone, was a recurring theme in her novels. She often reflected upon land dispossession with sadness or as a forewarning. Life on the plantations as a white American could be grand. But it could also be deeply unsettling, if one opened one's eyes, as Warner did, to other worlds and to the injustices upon which the plantation was built.

Arthur Hayman, too, had his world shaken in the two years he spent on the Firestone plantations. The company hired Hayman, an American engineer, to supervise the construction of a dam and hydroelectric plant on the Farmington River, completed in 1941. Hayman admitted that he had come to Liberia with a feeling of white superiority, "part of the poisons," he wrote, "breathed in by men of the so-called 'dominant race.'"[36]

The injustices toward and treatment of common laborers that Hayman witnessed on the Firestone plantation led him to publish *Lighting Up Liberia* in 1943. Written with Harold Preece, a white Texas journalist who penned investigative stories on racial oppression, American imperialism, and civil rights for newspapers such as the *Chicago Defender*, the book was a scathing critique of Liberia's ruling settler elite and Firestone. Hayman and Preece minced no words in their condemnation of Barclay, Supreme

Court Justice Tubman (who would become Liberia's nineteenth president in 1944), and others whom they viewed as part of a "Monrovia clique." They were, in the authors' opinion, "feudal barons," who suppressed the rights of indigenous peoples in the interests of keeping a "peon" class of laborers working on their estates. One of the most inflammatory accusations they made was to compare Liberia's ruling regime to "the politically mediaeval commonwealth" of Mississippi, where two-time governor, U.S. senator, and Ku Klux Klan member Theodore Bilbo used his power to subjugate poor Black and white farmers to the benefit of wealthy, white landowners in a sharecropping system of plantation agriculture. These were harsh words. Nor did they spare Walton in their critique, "a man," they contended, "who had leaned toward the Monrovia clique too often."[37]

The U.S. State Department could not remain quiet in the face of such serious slander. Henry Villard told the *Chicago Defender* in response to a synopsis of the book's arguments published in *Tomorrow* magazine that he "failed to see the comparison made in Hayman's article between Liberia and Mississippi." Furthermore, while he admitted that much of the article was "based in fact," he found it "twisted in interpretation and meaning, in order to produce an effect of sensationalism."[38]

The most harrowing and horrific event that Hayman recounted in the book was the arrest and punishment of a Bassa man who worked for him. In the account, the worker had walked off with two planks from the Firestone grounds to repair the door of his home. A policeman, "hired by the company to protect its property down to the last rusty nail," confronted the man, arrested him, and threw him into a local jail.[39] The next morning, Hayman drove the police officer and the accused in his Ford to the Bondiway Court, located on Division 3, along the Du River in the vicinity of the first 1926 clearing. Hayman likened the Bondiway police and judge to the "Negro straw boss on the plantation," but who, in this instance, served the interests of "Firestone's rented empire."[40] After a few brief questions, the judge sentenced the man to "twenty-five lashes."[41]

Firestone labor's policy explicitly prohibited the use of corporal punishment by white management to discipline Liberian staff, but the Liberian courts, acting on Firestone's behalf, were another matter.[42] When the whipping was over, Hayman took the brutally beaten man to his "dresser" to be cared for. "Underneath the high-powered advertising and shrewd promotion of the Firestone Company," Hayman decried, "I was seeing in pitiless operation the civilization represented by all such companies who have built colossal, private empires upon lacerated, overworked human flesh."[43]

Hayman came to see injustice upon injustice layered deep in the land claimed by an American corporation for which he worked. Versed in the writings of Nigerian journalist Nnamdi Azikiwe, and a supporter of the push by the West African Students' Union for a West African federalist state, Hayman urged for land reform, unionization of Firestone workers, the development of agricultural cooperatives, and an American economic and social mission to Liberia. A tone of self-righteousness, nevertheless, appears in his accusations and words, particularly in his criticism of Barclay's regime, suggesting that the feelings of white superiority he carried to Liberia lingered. Needless to say, Hayman didn't renew his two-year Firestone contract. The publishing of *Lighting Up Liberia* would make him persona non grata in the world of Firestone and that of Barclay's administration as well.

White planters like Gene Manis lived comfortable lives in homes atop the rolling hills of the Firestone plantation complex, situated apart from the villages and lives of the company's Liberian workers. In the division's lower-lying areas, too wet for rubber trees, tens of thousands of Liberian tappers, some with their families, inhabited a radically different world. Men from almost every ethnic group and district in Liberia, some hundreds of miles away, came to work on the plantations. Firestone's Harbel plantations were "a veritable tower of Babel-babble," observed Plenyono Gbe Wolo, as Kpelle, Bassa, Dan, Mano, and Loma men, among other ethnic affiliations, recruited largely from Liberia's Central and Western districts, gathered together, speaking many different languages and dialects.[44] The ethnic groups recruited for employment matched closely the recommendations that Harvard scientists Strong and Schwab made to Firestone in their pseudoscientific estimations of who, among Liberia's ethnic groups, would make the best plantation workers. Consequently, Kpelle men composed the largest ethnic group working as tappers at Harbel, and Kpelle, along with Liberian English, became the lingua franca of plantation life.[45]

Tappers are the lifeblood of any rubber plantation. Without their valuable skill, knowledge, and labor, latex will not flow. Harvey Firestone Sr. imagined a future where three hundred thousand Liberians, roughly 20 percent of the country's entire population, would be at work on the

A young tapper and a mature rubber tree, with the tapping panel visible. Tappers were the most essential, but least compensated, workers on the Firestone plantations. From Firestone Plantations Company, *Views in Liberia* (Chicago: Lakeside Press, R.R. Donnelley & Sons, 1937).

plantations. That was the number of tappers needed to harvest the "white gold" from 1 million acres of rubber trees. But even at peak employment, when, "in Liberia, *Hevea* had gone to war," less than 30,000 Liberians worked on the Firestone plantations.[46] The majority of them—roughly 24,000—worked as rubber tappers, headmen, and overseers. Another 3,000 were employed as mechanics, machinists, carpenters, truck drivers, lighter crewmen, clerical staff, laboratory technicians, and factory workers in the latex-processing plants, among other occupations.[47] It was a fraction of the labor force the Akron rubber mogul had boasted about when he first promoted his venture.

When Fred Helm took over as head of Firestone's Labor Department in 1943, he had his job cut out for him. A graduate in agriculture from Ohio State University, Helm had run a floral business with his brother before joining the Firestone Plantations Company in its early years. He started out on the Mount Barclay Plantation, and then supervised the felling and clearing of the first division at Duside. In 1928, after completing two contracts, he went back to Ohio State, where he earned his MA degree. Six years later, he returned to the plantations with his wife and their two children. He and his family had been part of Firestone's white management enclave ever since. He was, in Warner's words, an "old Coaster."[48]

Wartime shortages in rubber turned the Liberia plantations into an experimental laboratory. Harvey Jr., a firm believer in scientific research and innovation, encouraged experimentation with different tapping systems and clonal varieties to increase production. On most rubber plantations workers tapped a rubber tree for fifteen days, and then allowed the tree to rest for another fifteen days. During the war, Harvey Jr. authorized a double-tapping system on the company's Liberia plantations, under which workers tapped a tree continuously. No one knew what plant stresses a double-tapping system might introduce or how it might affect the life of the tree. It was a necessary risk, declared Firestone, who also served as chairman of the United Service Organizations, to ensure that "precious rubber went to our fighting forces when and where it was most needed."[49] It also required a doubling of the labor force in areas where the experimental system was introduced.[50] Speeding up *Hevea* in the service of war required much more human labor. Helm needed many more tappers than Firestone had ever secured.

Tappers were the most essential but least valued workers in Firestone's operation. Classed as unskilled labor, Firestone tappers earned 18¢ per

Tappers with empty buckets headed out for their day's work, circa 1940s.
© USA TODAY NETWORK.

day up until 1950. It was a wage rate less than half of what unskilled laborers earned across much of colonial West Africa and 1 percent of what a factory worker earned in Firestone's Akron plant, where, in 1948, workers averaged $1.73 an hour.[51]

A tapper's day began well before dawn. At 3:30 a.m., the first muster bell rang. A half hour later, the headman passed through the camp. Gbe, a retired headman interviewed by our research team in 2018, had been responsible for waking up his gang, going "from house to house in the darkness with no light." "Togbah, you!, Flomo, you!, going just like that," he said.[52] If his entire gang didn't show, the headman faced a loss in pay. By 5 a.m., all the men had lined up on benches, arranged according to the headman they worked under. Each had his buckets, tapping knife, and *ganga* bag—a cloth sack to hold tools and coagulated rubber—displayed in front of him. Each tapper placed in his *ganga* bag a "stout bottle." Given to him each morning, it contained an ammonia solution, a critical element in aiding the flow of latex from tree to factory. Other essential tools included spouts, glass latex-collection cups, bark gauges, and *picule* sticks, thick five-foot lengths of bamboo on which tappers balanced full buckets of milk-white latex. "By 5 o'clock, Mr. white man come and check the bucket," recalled Gwi, who worked for Firestone for thirty-two years.[53] Gene Manis was one such "Mr. white man," arriving at his division camp by 5 a.m. to inspect the crew. He noted the number of tappers, made sure each had his complete set of tools, and sent them off promptly by 5:15 a.m. A tapper needed daylight, but tapping as early as possible let more latex flow before the heat of the equatorial sun slowed it. After muster, Manis went back to his bungalow to sleep, waking at 6:30 a.m. to a breakfast cooked by his Liberian chef. While he slept, tappers like Gwi set off in the dark, some walking several miles, to their assigned tile of rubber trees.[54]

When a stand of rubber trees matured, usually six years after planting, the overseer produced a stand map. He and his crew checked the size of every tree trunk with a metal-U caliper on a long stick and painted a black dot on the tree if its trunk surpassed five inches in diameter. A black dot earmarked a tree for tapping. As crew members called out the status of each tree, the overseer transferred the information onto the stand map in color codes that indicated whether a tree was of tappable size, wind damaged, or not yet ready for tapping. Swamps, streams, buildings, and other obstacles were also noted on the map. In this way, the size, status, and production values of millions of trees could be accounted for. Stand maps also helped lay out the task—or "tile," as the tappers called it—for each worker. The geometrical renderings of stands within the plantation's division helped determine the most efficient path for each tapper to follow through the set of trees that fell within his task.[55]

The task structured a tapper's day. It set the "average quota of work" expected of each man. The task, Firestone Plantations Company manager William Vass advised, was "one of the most important factors in the development and operation of a plantation."[56] Tasking had a long history. When cotton was king in the American South, plantation owners used it to organize the work and calculate the value of enslaved people. In the early twentieth century, the task became a defining element of modern scientific management in industrial factories.[57] In the tire-building rooms of Firestone's factories, and particularly on its rubber plantations, the task took on ever-greater scientific precision.

Opening up a stand began by laying out a tapping panel on each tree newly ready for tapping. This commenced an intimate relationship between tapper and tree. A tree tapped with attention and care could yield latex for up to twenty-five years. A tree's first tapping panel was always laid on its north side. With utmost skill, the tapper sliced a shallow cut, less than one-sixteenth of an inch wide, into the bark of the tree. The cut, which ran from left to right at an angle of thirty degrees to maximize the number of severed latex vessels, was a controlled wound of the tree. Cuts mimicked the harm caused by insects and thereby stimulated the plant to release its insect defense, which manifests as latex, the hydrocarbon contained in specialized cells just beneath the outer bark. A cut any wider than one-sixteenth of an inch wasted the tree's energies regenerating bark. A cut any deeper than one millimeter, the thickness of a dime, risked damaging the tree. If a tapper cut into the cambium, he risked injuring the vital xylem and phloem, the tree's transport highways that carry water, minerals, and sugars where they are needed. A wound too wide or too deep, and the tapper could shorten the life of the rubber tree. Firestone invested more in the life of a tree than that of a tapper. It didn't take too many deep wounds before a tapper found himself without a job.

The task set for a tapper in the years Harvey Jr. commanded Firestone's rubber empire averaged three hundred trees per day. Each morning, a tapper cleaned off the thin line of latex—tree lace—that had coagulated and dried in the cut made the previous day. He also cleaned out the *cuplump*, the latex that had congealed in the collecting cup overnight. Every drop of latex, liquid or coagulum, had value. Every drop, the company laid claim to. The tapper put the coagulated rubber into the *ganga* bag, and then opened up a new wound in the tree to start the flow of latex anew. Opening his ammonia bottle, he shook a few drops of the pungent chemical into the collection cup to make sure the "latex don't sleep."[58] About 40 percent of latex is composed of rubber. The rest is a mix of water, sugar, proteins, and salts. When exposed to air, bacteria act on the sugars and proteins, producing acids and putrefying substances that cause the liquid latex to congeal. Keeping latex awake—that is, keeping it in its liquid state—involves ammonia, a powerful base.[59]

Concentrated natural latex, more versatile than crepe or smoked sheet rubber for producing specialized items such as foam mattresses, surgical gloves, and other goods, commanded the highest commodity prices. During the Second World War, Firestone's Liberia plantations were the only Allied source of concentrated natural latex.[60] By 1949, when, in just a matter of a decade, Firestone had nearly tripled production on its plantations in response to the war, Liberia supplied 22 percent of all concentrated natural latex imported into the United States.[61]

If you were a fast tapper, like Gwi, you had time to return to camp to cook and eat a meal before the next bell rang at 10:30 a.m. At the sound of the Bong Bong, a huge gong crafted from a circular saw blade, tappers, with their *picule* sticks and empty buckets, quickly headed back to their rubber tree stands. Working fast, they went from tree to tree, dumping the milky, ammonia-infused fluid latex into their buckets, wiping each cup out with bare fingers. Three hundred trees later, each tapper carefully positioned one of his two nearly full six-gallon pails on each end of his *picule* stick. With the stick and the nearly one-hundred-pound load of fresh latex balanced across his shoulders, the walk from his tile to the collecting station could be body-crushing work. "Oh!" one elder tapper remarked. "Some people can suffer, some people, their tile, they not be near with it," referring to the distance they had to walk with their latex loads.[62] Weigh-in began at noon at the division's collecting station. Hundreds of men, with their pails in hand and *ganga* bags stuffed with coagulum rubber, waited in line for their turn at the scale, where the amount of latex and coagulum each collected was weighed and carefully recorded. Often, after eight hours of muster, a tapper's day was not yet done. During the rainy season, tappers would return to their stands to spread fungicide with their fingers across each tree's wounded bark. They also might return to weed an area around each tree or to open a new stand. To earn the maximum wage rate, a tapper could work an eleven-hour day, twenty-six days or more per month.[63]

Many tappers were not as quick as Gwi. His speed enabled him to earn extra cash, sometimes working two tiles in a day, when a spare tapper was needed. Those who struggled to meet their task faced the harsh consequences of a task system. At first, the headman docked the pay of those who couldn't keep up. If a tapper continued to falter, he would find himself on the list of spare tappers—reserve laborers who worked irregularly, only when a regular tapper on a headman's gang didn't show up for work. Women might come to the aid of their men if they struggled to meet their task. Key described how she would help her husband collect the *cuplump* and *earthscrap*, latex that had leaked onto the ground and solidified. She did so without pay. It was the only way that they, as a family, could ensure her husband's full wage under the weight of the task system.[64] Male tappers rarely, if ever, spoke of coming to the aid of a fellow member in their

Tappers carrying collected latex, circa 1966. Pails full of latex transported on the shoulders long distances could be hard on the body. Image by Frederick McEvoy. (Courtesy of Indiana University Libraries.)

Tappers wait at the collecting station for their latex and coagulum rubber to be weighed, circa 1940. (W.E. Manis Collection, Special and Area Studies Collections, George A. Smathers Libraries, University of Florida, Gainesville, Florida.)

Making bud grafts in the plantation nursery in 2012, very much like women have done for decades. (Image by Gregg Mitman.)

gang to achieve his quota. The tapper's task system incentivized individualism over communitarian values in a male tapper's world.

Among women who found work on the plantations, a different set of incentives and values prevailed. Firestone began to officially employ women in the 1960s, although in much smaller numbers than men—a 1961 survey counted seventeen female workers. Skills women honed cultivating crops assisted them in germination, grafting, and nurturing rubber seedlings in the plantation nurseries. Planting bud-grafted trees also became part of women's work on the plantations. Group contracts, rather than an individual task system, structured women's work. The system was more reflective of and reinforced communal labor practices, known as "ku" among Kpelle people, common to the making of farms in the interior. The rainy season was planting time on the plantations, as it was up country. Woman planters worked in groups, each group supervised by a headman. Each woman was given four to six bundles of rubber tree seedling, called stumps, with twenty-five stumps in each bundle, and assigned a cleared area to plant. It was laborious and careful work, supervised by white managers who would suspend or fire someone if their rows were not straight or their trees planted too loosely. Inexperienced or slow workers could find it challenging to plant all their bundles. Fast planters came to the aid of slower ones, Lo-malon recalled. "If you are strong," she said, "you will leave your friends behind and finish soon. If you are slow, your friends will help you to plant your remaining stumps before you can go home."[65] Mutual aid among women laborers ensured the contract was met and helped to nurture tree crops. Retired women workers spoke with pride of cultivating and caring for seedlings now matured into productive trees, much like they would speak of the cash crops grown on their individual farms back home. "Most of the rubber trees you see, my hand work is on many," Siawa-Geh said, who, like Lomalon, dated her start on the plantation to the early 1960s.[66]

Drivers and factory workers were classified as skilled labor and, during the 1940s, earned anywhere from 25¢ to 85¢ per day.[67] Drivers trans-ported latex in trucks carrying fourteen hundred gallons along the planta-tion's extensive road system to the processing plant at Harbel. There, factory workers operated large centrifuges to separate the precious rubber hydrocarbon from the aqueous solution in which it was suspended.

Only the "cream of the crop" became the concentrated natural latex shipped in barrels to Firestone factories in the United States. The remain-ing latex was made into different grades of dry rubber. Workers added formic acid to large vats of latex to speed up the coagulation. They then chopped the resulting white blubber into thick slices with large machetes. Large washing, mangling, and rolling machines transformed the solidified latex into lace like sheets, resembling long woolen fleeces. Giant hydraulic presses heated and compressed the sheets into 224-pound bales of crepe rubber, also bound for America. The *treelace*, *cuplump*, and *earthscap* collected by tappers, as well as coagulated rubber purchased from independent Libe-rian rubber farmers, went through similar chemical treatments, washings, and machinations in its transformation into marketable rubber.[68]

In the final leg of rubber's journey, men loaded barrels of concentrated latex and bales of dry rubber onto lighters docked at the Harbel processing plant. These flat-bottomed barges carried the strategic resource down the Farmington River, to freighter ships anchored in the Atlantic. Much like the cheap land and labor upon which Firestone relied, the Farmington was a key component in the industrial life and ecology of the Harbel planta-tions. The company harnessed the river's energy to power the machines in its processing plant, light the offices and homes of management, and fur-nish ice and cool drinks to the white clientele who frequented the Fire-stone Overseas Club. Firestone also, free of charge, dumped chemical waste

The Harbel latex processing plant on the Farmington River, circa early 1940s.
George and Katy Abraham Papers #6777. (Courtesy of Division of Rare and
Manuscript Collections, Cornell University Library.)

from its processing plant into the river, with little regard for the multitude
of lives dependent on the Farmington River for their existence.

Firestone publicized its free housing, education, and medical care for
employees as evidence of its "desire to contribute to the social and human,
as well as the economic progress of Liberia."[69] But such pronouncements
failed to account for the differential costs borne by Liberia and Liberians
in the making of Firestone's plantation world. To partially compensate
for a tapper's paltry wages, the company sold workers rations of rice, palm
oil, soap, and sometimes canned fish at subsidized rates. The term *pussawa*,
the Kpelle word for "thirty," came to be associated with the weekly eight-
pound allotment of imported rice a worker received, for which he paid out of
his wages roughly 30 percent of the retail rate.[70] Tappers could purchase
additional rice from the company store at local retail rates, which in the
late 1940s averaged around 10¢ per pound, more than half a day's wage.

Classified employees, including headmen and overseers, with wages considerably higher than those of tappers, received sixteen pounds of rice a week. Wage deductions, either as a form of punishment, or for lost or broken tapper tools or the purchase of rice, palm oil, soap, or other goods from the company store, could lead to misunderstanding and confusion at the end of the month when workers were paid. Some workers basically "owed their souls" to the company store, unable to quit with unpaid debt.

Wages and food subsidies were not compelling reasons for workers to permanently settle on the plantations. Those rewards offered fewer material benefits than did making a rice farm in the interior. It is one reason why recruiting labor was one of the most difficult and critical jobs within the organization. Everywhere Helm and his recruiting agents went, the *palava* ended with the same story. Chiefs would "send boys as soon as their farm work was finished."[71] For each male worker sent to the plantation, Firestone paid a paramount chief 15¢ per month from January through June as compensation for the loss of male labor when it was needed to make farms. During the planting and harvest season up country, from July through December, when women did much of the farm work and village life required less male labor, Firestone compensated paramount chiefs 10¢ per man. However, these payments were made only if quotas set for individual districts were met. A U.S. Department of Labor study found that this labor procurement practice continued well into the early 1960s. Firestone's "method of recruiting obviously results in a certain amount of involuntary labor," it noted.[72]

Men that chose to work on the plantations voluntarily often did so to earn just enough cash to pay the government's hut tax, purchase the dowry needed to secure a wife, or to achieve some other goal. Na-Fallon, a spry old Kpelle man, remembers well doing *kwi* work, which involved the conscription of young men to carry loads, build roads, or make farms on behalf of the government. "When the forced labor was hard on us, we ran away and went to rest at Firestone," he recalled. Like most tappers, Na-Fallon moved in and out of the wage economy when Barclay and Tubman were president. Sometimes he would spend three, four, or five months tapping trees, earning enough to pay his family's hut tax, before returning to help his parents with their farm in the village where he was born. Other times, he would spend a year.[73] Few looked to tapping as a permanent vocation. Only a third of tappers and other "unskilled" workers had permanently settled on the plantations in the 1950s.[74] Most, like Na-Fallon, worked for a time, left during the dry season to help make farms up country, and, if a tapper's life suited them, returned again to the world of Firestone.

Access to education for their children and medical treatment for their families enticed some workers to stay. In the 1940s, Firestone initiated and expanded its public education and health care programs for its employees. A school system, run by the Liberian Department of Education, but with teacher salaries, books, and supplies paid for by the Firestone Plantations Company, provided both free education, up to eighth grade, for children of employees and adult literacy classes.

All employees were eligible, but schools were segregated. The 150 or so children of white foreign staff had separate buildings, teaching staff, and curriculum. Of the Liberian workers who sent their children to Firestone schools or attended adult evening classes, the majority were headmen, overseers, and classified employees. The company operated a bus service, but with just fifteen schools spread across the plantation, access was difficult. A tapper's child, like Jaweh-teh, had a one-in-ten chance of attending school.[75]

In addition to formal education, the company also provided on-the-job vocational training to selected unskilled laborers. Gwi was one tapper who was promoted up the ranks. After a few years of moving back and forth between the plantation and his family's farm, he was offered a classified job driving a tractor at Harbel. "Oh! I was happy . . . , I am not tapper again . . . we were bigger boys," Gwi said. The wage increase allowed him to pay his wife's dowry and bring her to settle on the plantation. But what he appreciated the most was that his wife did not die in childbirth and all of their ten children finished high school. Some "people not get time for that," he said. And some people, when their children finished eighth grade, told them to "go take bucket so you can work for few years so you can carry yourself to college." He was one of the fortunate ones, valued for his tapping and other skills, which offered opportunities for his children beyond plantation life.[76]

Millions of *Hevea brasiliensis* trees, cloned via bud grafting from a couple dozen high-performing, wind-resistant individuals, had come to maturity in the war years. These engineered clones yielded more than triple the amount of latex harvested from trees planted in the earliest years of Firestone's operation in Liberia. The health of those clones and of the human workforce hired to plant, tend, and harvest the valuable latex posed some of the greatest challenges to Firestone's grand experiment in industrial engineering. The company's investment could easily be wiped out by a fungal blight of black thread or brown root rot sweeping through stands of genetically identical trees. On the divisions, where thousands of laborers and their families lived in close-knit quarters and where tappers assembled by the hundreds each day, conditions were ripe for widespread viral infection. An outbreak of smallpox or measles could decimate the company's labor force, already in short supply.

Firestone made significant investments in its medical services and support of biomedical research to keep pathogens at bay. Fungi and viruses or protozoa and flatworms could sap the productivity of plants and people, and consume the income of a Firestone subsidiary that in the 1950s accounted for 10 percent of the company's total net income, yielding gross profits that could average 150 percent over cost.[77] Its Harbel plantation hospital, located at Duside, grew from 60 beds in 1940 to 167 beds in 1959. The white, two-story building had the best diagnostic equipment and laboratory services in the country and a surgical ward with a modern operating room. A maternity clinic, adjacent to the hospital, had capacity for sixty-six women. At each division being tapped, a small clinic and dispensary, staffed by a dresser, treated minor injuries and illnesses. The company established a formal nurse training program in 1946 and a course of study for laboratory technicians in 1950. Nine foreign doctors oversaw a medical staff of nearly two hundred Liberian nurses, sanitarians, and laboratory technicians by the late 1950s. Between 1940 and 1960, Firestone's medical services at the Harbel plantations and its much smaller counterparts at Cavalla grew from roughly 300,000 patient visits per year to 500,000.[78]

For some workers, the free medical care that Firestone provided employees was a benefit that outweighed trifling wages. "If you or your child was sick, you took them to the Firestone Hospital for free treatment," remembered Siawa-Geh, who bore ten children on the plantation. "So the little money we were making was big in our eyes because Firestone was taking care of us and our children even during illness."[79] In a country where maternal mortality rates still rank among the highest in the world, access to Firestone's maternity services could be a real draw.

Throughout its history, the Firestone Plantations Company promoted its investment in medical care and research to advertise its goodwill and humanitarian intentions toward Liberia. "Safeguarding the health" of its "rubber workers" was, the company proclaimed, "both an economic necessity and a moral obligation." In a series of promotional films made and distributed in the immediate postwar years, the company brashly credited the "industrial statesmanship of Harvey S. Firestone, founder, and Harvey S. Firestone Jr." for "much of Liberia's progress in medicine and public health."[80]

Behind the company's slick advertising campaign was a darker reality: health care, like much of life on the Firestone plantations, was deeply segregated. Black patients, except when in need of surgery, were confined to the Firestone hospital's ground-floor ward. Thus, when the Honorable Harold Fredericks, Liberia's consul general to Great Britain, was injured in a severe car accident in December 1941, the "highly respectable citizen and responsible Liberian official" found himself denied treatment in the much better upstairs section of the hospital. Monrovia's *African Nationalist* newspaper wondered "what kind of 'Democracy' the United States is fighting for when, in our own country, segregation is being practiced against our leaders." But the existence of a "color bar" in Firestone's Harbel hospital merely scratched the surface of how the company differentially treated and valued Black and white bodies on its plantations.[81]

The study and treatment of malaria reinforced an exploitative and segregated system of health care. Malaria, observed Firestone physician Justus Rice, presented two major problems for the company. Its prevalence among Liberia's population lowered the "general efficiency of labor," and it raised an urgent need for "protection of the white population."[82]

Rice, a young American doctor eager to make money and a name for himself, saw people living on the Firestone concession as reservoirs of tropical disease.[83] The plantation was an ideal laboratory for experimental biomedical research. "Employees are under control," Rice noted, "and are usually housed in camps sufficiently isolated from each other and from native villages to make possible the comparison of treated and control groups."[84] In 1929, he had tested an experimental yellow fever vaccine on three Firestone workers during Monrovia's yellow fever outbreak. The next year, Rice, along with Marshall Barber, a malariologist from the International Health Division of the Rockefeller Foundation, and James Newman of Nigeria's Health Department, embarked on a much larger clinical drug trial aimed at reducing malaria transmission on the plantation.

Rice and his colleagues looked with keen interest upon the antimalarial drug plasmoquine recently developed by the German firm I.G. Farbenindustrie. First tried on the industrial plantations of United Fruit Company, among military troops stationed in British India, and in other settings throughout the tropics, it was known to be toxic or fatal in high doses.[85] It had shown preliminary promise in disrupting the life cycle of the parasite that causes malaria. In the case of *Plasmodium falciparum*, an especially deadly species of the parasite, endemic to Liberia, the drug showed effectiveness in attacking gametocytes, the reproductive cells of the parasitic protozoa, found in an infected person's blood. Gametocytes were critical in the transmission of the parasite from humans to mosquitoes, where a critical step in the parasite's life cycle occurs. Humans that harbored high concentrations of gametocytes, but showed no symptoms of the disease, were hidden carriers of malaria. A mosquito that gorged on their blood and then later bit another person could transmit the disease to Firestone workers, including white personnel. Plasmoquine, by knocking back gametocytes, could potentially break the cycle of transmission. But the drug offered little therapeutic effectiveness to infected individuals.[86]

To test the drug's effectiveness, Rice and his colleagues first drew blood from more than five hundred Firestone laborers and their families to determine the incidence of malaria on the plantation complex. Next, they selected five labor camps—Dressers, Newman, Tabla, Labor, and Moore—located on recently cleared and planted divisions near the Du River, and on a small farm, Flomo Bush. There, Rice's team, with the support of Firestone management, administered plasmoquine to more than 250 men, women, and children.

Rice and his colleagues gave children and adults living in the labor camps the same dosage of plasmoquine. The scientists reported no harmful outcomes, although they presented no clinical evidence to back their claims.[87] The promising results they obtained shaped the medical regimen that Firestone adopted to manage life on the plantations in the war and postwar years, a regimen that underscored how the health of white employees took precedent over that of Liberian laborers.

Domestic workers, the company advised, posed the greatest health threat to white foreign staff. "House servants constitute a reservoir from which the mosquito frequently transfers" malaria "to the employer," a 1941 Firestone operations manual warned. The company insisted that staff ensure servants' compliance: servants were to take with their evening meal a daily dose of quinoplasmoquin, a mix of plasmoquine and quinine, and "be examined periodically for evidence of contagious, infectious and venereal diseases."[88] Daily chemical cleansing of the blood of Black servant bodies with plasmoquine, a drug considered ill-advised for routine use by the Office of the Surgeon General of the U.S. Army, subjected Liberian domestic workers to long-term toxic exposures solely for the protection of white personnel.[89]

Meanwhile, Gene Manis and other white foreign staff took atabrine three times a week to guard against malaria.[90] Recommended for use by the U.S. military in the suppression and clinical treatment of malaria, it was a much less toxic antimalarial drug that alleviated symptoms but did little to prevent spread of the disease. White bodies, in but not of the tropics, were thought to pose little threat of contagion in the racial logics that governed plantation life.

Out on the plantation divisions, where most laborers lived far removed from the housing quarters of white management, different medical protocols applied. Men seeking employment were subject to medical inspections, and detailed medical records were kept on all Liberian overseers and headmen. Any prospective laborer showing signs of elephantiasis, hernia, leprosy, or other affliction was not to be employed. Laborers diagnosed with tuberculosis at the main hospital were immediately dismissed since the disease was "incurable, progressive, and likely to spread infection." Dressers visited the camps daily. They administered quinine twice each week and hookworm treatments once per month, and regularly inspected workers for yaws. Laborers who reported sick or failed to show up to work were also treated. Dressers also conducted in each division a monthly census of men, women, and children and a sanitary inspection of wells, houses, and latrines.[91] Twice yearly, Liberian men, women, and children living on the divisions, which in 1947 amounted to approximately forty thousand people, were immunized against smallpox. Also, "every three months," Manis observed, "the doctor comes out and gives the boys injections to clear up their blood," although what drugs were involved and for what reason is unknown.[92]

The concentrated reservoir of bodies, blood, and parasites contained on the Firestone concession was yet another biological resource for the plantation's extractive economy. During the war years, Harvard University's Department of Comparative Pathology and Tropical Medicine continued building on the connections that Richard Strong had established with the Firestone Plantations Company, furthering its research program and advising the company on disease control. Medical entomologist Joseph Bequaert, a member of the original 1926 Harvard expedition to Liberia, along with his Harvard colleague, David Weinman, and Everett Veatch of the American Foundation for Tropical Medicine, embarked on a massive epidemiological and geographical survey throughout Liberia of human trypanosomiasis, also known as African sleeping sickness. Sleeping sickness, like malaria, compromised the efficiency of labor and, with its potential to spread on the plantation, posed a serious risk to Firestone's labor force. The survey study, commissioned by Firestone, would also in 1944 use its Harbel hospital as a research site, testing on indigenous laborers two new arsenic compounds for the treatment of sleeping sickness.[93]

In 1946, as a memorial to his father and in commemoration of Liberia's upcoming centennial celebration of independence, Harvey Firestone Jr. pledged $250,000 for the establishment of an institute for research in tropical medicine in Liberia. The donation was a direct outgrowth of the mutually beneficial relationships that Firestone had developed with Harvard and other prominent American research universities. President Tubman gifted one hundred acres of land on the Firestone concession adjacent to Robertsfield and the Harbel plantations as the site for the Liberian Institute of the American Foundation for Tropical Medicine.[94] James S. Simmons, former dean of the Harvard School of Public Health, delivered a dedication address at its opening in 1952. The institute was run by a consortium of American universities under the direction of the American Foundation for Tropical Medicine. Tubman's hopes of the institute helping to advance the general health of Liberia's population, however, were quickly dashed. The facility became an enclave of white scientists from a handful of largely American universities who did little if anything to educate or advance the medical and research careers of promising Liberian staff. Its proximity to the Firestone plantations, Robertsfield airport, and a rainforest with a large chimpanzee population offered access to both infrastructure and experimental subjects—both animal and human—in the pursuit of research on malaria, trypanosomiasis, schistosomiasis, and other tropical diseases. Some studies, such as that of parasitologist R.S. Bray, were highly suspect forays into racist science. Bray intentionally infected thirty Liberian staff and residents living in the surrounding area with *Plasmodium vivax*, a strain of malaria not present in Liberia, to determine whether "Negroes" were susceptible to the parasite.[95] Such investigations, both on and off the Firestone plantations, demonstrated the callous disregard with which Western biomedical research subjected people of African descent to experimental exploitation and inequitable medical treatment. Born of plantation slavery, it is a disturbing legacy that endured in the scientific racism and racial inequalities of American health care and in the medical services provided by Firestone in the name of welfare capitalism.[96]

In the transformation of land and ecological relations that built and sustained plantation worlds, Firestone exacerbated certain disease risks and introduced new harms. The making of an industrial landscape was fraught with worker risks. Such occupational hazards, however, posed much less of a concern to the company than did tropical parasites that were a threat to the health of its white staff and to the productive efficiency of labor.

Some risks arising from the industrial ecology of a plantation were biological in origin. The clearing of land, the recruitment of human labor, and the destruction of flora and fauna opened up possibilities for opportunistic insects, along with the parasites they carried, to thrive. The human-loving black fly, *Simulium yahense*, was one. The waterways, critical to the plantation's infrastructure, along with wind breaks and shade furnished by the monoculture rubber forests, offered an ideal habitat for the biting black fly. Most active in the morning, when tappers were at work, *Simulium yahense* found an abundance of human meals on the plantation. As black flies and people moved to the plantation, they brought along a fellow traveler. The parasitic worm, *Onchocerca volvulus*, like its insect vector, flourished in the ecological conditions of the Harbel plantations. Transmitted to its human host via the bite of the black fly, the parasite is one of the leading causes of blindness in sub-Saharan Africa and other parts of the tropical world. On the divisions along the Du River, near where Strong's Harvard expedition originally visited and camped, onchocerciasis, or river blindness, became much more prevalent than elsewhere in Liberia. Sixty years after the first divisions were cleared, the prevalence of *Onchocerca* infection among male laborers living near the Du River averaged 80 percent.[97]

Chemicals that proliferated throughout the plantation complex were another health risk. Chemicals like ammonia were vital to the operation of the plantation. Ammonia, a constant companion in the life of a tapper, was critical to keeping latex in a liquid state. Yet tappers used the chemical without gloves or protective eye gear. It saturated the pores of a tapper's hands, deadened fingertips, and destroyed nails. Once they filled your ammonia bottle, one tapper recalled, you had to close it quickly or, "it may waste on you and burn your skin."[98] Some went blind when the corrosive and caustic chemical got into their eyes. "When it flash in your eye, it spoiled it," Gbe said. "If it is all two of your eyes, it will spoil it."[99]

Many other hazardous chemicals came onto the Firestone plantations in the postwar years. The Second World War had spawned an abundance of new chemical compounds. With them came grand schemes for large-scale industrial agriculture, green revolutions, and feeding a hungry world.[100] Laborers sprayed 2,4,5-T on old rubber trees, then tractors cleared the dead, defoliated vegetation away to make room for new plantings of rubber tree clones. The herbicide had other beneficial effects: it leached into the soil and killed fungi responsible for root rot, a major disease that threatened the health and productivity of Firestone's rubber trees. But the herbicide contains small amounts of a highly toxic environmental pollutant, dioxin. Scientists paid no attention to the chemical's possible health effects on workers or on communities living downstream from the Harbel plantations along the Du and Farmington Rivers.[101]

The fight against black thread, a parasitic fungus that inflicted great damage to the bark of rubber trees, also brought an influx of new chemical compounds onto the plantations. The fungus, *Phytophthora palmivora*, flourishes best during the rainy season. Its mycelia form vertical black threads on a rubber tree's tapping panel, coalescing into patches of dark lesions that, if severe, permanently make that bark region untappable. Because black thread proved particularly destructive to Firestone's prized clone, Bodjong Datar 5, it seriously threatened company profits. The threat prompted extensive research into chemical control. By the 1960s, a new toxic brew of the herbicide, 2,4-D, which stimulated latex production, and the fungicide, captafol, which killed the dreaded black thread disease, was in widespread use throughout the plantations. Tappers smeared the mixture onto the tapping panel by hand. Captafol, which would later be banned for use in the United States because of its carcinogenic effects, also dripped into the collecting cup that tappers wiped clean with their fingers each day.[102]

Little was "natural" about the production of natural rubber in the postwar years. Firestone laborers lived and worked in a plantation world teeming with biological, chemical, and physical risks. During the war years, lawsuits against the company, brought by Liberian workers injured on the job or by surviving families who had lost a loved one in an industrial accident, became more common. The family of Solomon Brooklyn Jr. filed a claim in September 1946, asking for $5,000 in damages after an injury to the worker's foot put him in the Firestone Plantations Hospital where he died of tetanus. The family's attorney accused Firestone physician Dr. K.H. Franz of "gross negligence and experimentalization of human lives." Foreign physicians like Franz, "in search of TROPICAL MEDICAL KNOWLEDGE AND EXPERIENCE un-obtainable in the Americas or Europe," the Liberian lawyer argued, "resort to UNWHOLESOME MEDICAL EXPERIMENTS ON THEIR AFRICAN PATIENTS." In only loosely suturing the wound and failing to give Brooklyn preventative treatment for tetanus at the time of his admission, Franz had displayed "intentional in-humane treatment" toward an employee of the Firestone Plantations Company, the attorney claimed.[103]

In response to increased pressure by the Liberian government, Firestone had put a worker compensation policy in place the same year Brooklyn died. But its death benefit came nowhere close to the damages that Brooklyn's family sought. A worker's family was entitled to an amount that equaled fourteen hundred times that of his day's wages. If Brooklyn had been a tapper, Firestone would have paid out $252 ($3,348 in today's dollars), provided the cause of death was not worker negligence. Had Brooklyn lived, but lost use of his foot, he would have received $126. A hand was worth 700 times more than a worker's wages; an eye, 640 times more. Partial loss of a tapper's sight was valued at no less than $28 and no more than $86.[104]

In the calculus of worker's compensation, Firestone disclosed the value it placed on the lives of Black laborers in the Jim Crow enclave it had imported to Liberia. It was a valuation founded upon structures of racial capitalism rooted in the violent and bloody soil of plantation slavery. Firestone touted its Liberia plantations as an exemplar of modern industry and progress, buttressed by the transformative power and humanitarian benefits of American science and medicine. But in its segregated and unequal treatment of white and Black workers, support of racist science and medicine, and extraction and export of wealth amassed from confiscated lands, Firestone shared more in common with past plantation worlds than it stood apart from them.

# 7

# Cold War Concessions

Lester Walton, as the longest-serving American minister to Liberia, took great pride in his accomplishments advancing friendly relations between the United States and Liberia over a decade. Even before his appointment, he had helped successfully broker the truce between Harvey Firestone Jr. and Edwin Barclay. The Firestone Plantations Company had become the largest employer in Liberia and, in 1944, Firestone's plantation rubber, almost all destined for the United States, accounted for roughly 90 percent of Liberia's $10.5 million in exports. A favorable trade balance had greatly improved the country's ability to pay its debt. Growing revenues meant the Liberian government could look toward investing in health, education, infrastructure, and economic development.[1] During the war years, Walton's vision, advocacy, and diplomatic skills had brought an influx of American dollars, corporate interest, technical expertise, and personnel. American engineers and construction managers from the United States Navy and the Raymond Concrete Pile Company, with the aid of Liberian workers, had begun construction of Monrovia's commercial port and harbor, and new roads for access. Walton could boast that this this project resulted from a $20 million lend-lease agreement that he had helped orchestrate between the U.S. government and Liberia. More so, Walton's plea for American technical assistance to Liberia had led to President Roosevelt's favorable response to President Tubman's request: the dispatch of economic and public health missions to Liberia—teams of Black and white experts in agriculture, economics, public health, medicine, and sanitary engineering—to survey the country's natural resources and assist in improving the nation's economy and health.[2]

Walton hoped to retire "in a blaze of glory" at the end of 1945.[3] But he left Liberia not "on the crest" of achievement but on a wave of controversy. When FDR died in April 1945, Walton, as was customary for diplomats upon a president's election or assumption of office, offered his resignation to President Harry Truman. Before Walton knew anything about it, press reports announced that Truman had accepted his resignation. A flabbergasted Walton wrote to Henry Villard, chief of the State Department's Division of African Affairs. He was mystified as to why Truman, "also a native of Missouri, . . . should find it politically expedient to manifest haste in accepting the resignation of the only Negro in the diplomatic service, whose record . . . had been an excellent one."[4] Meanwhile, an inflammatory story in the *Chicago Defender*, reprinted in Monrovia's *Weekly Mirror*, claimed that Walton, instead of resigning, had been "forced out." The article held that Walton's undoing was a result of the "howl" of African American GIs, previously and currently stationed in Monrovia, who expressed dismay at the treatment of Liberia's indigenous population by the country's "10,000 upper class residents of the coast area." Allegedly, Walton's silence on what some American troops saw as a system of exploitation "for profit" that benefited the "status quo" and, in particular, those in the "Old Guard" of former president Barclay's administration, prompted the need for a change.[5] Walton was furious and hired an attorney to sue the newspaper for libel for publishing "downright lies."[6] When other Monrovia papers came to Walton's defense, the *Weekly Mirror* hit back, asking, if the accusations were false, then why had the issue that ran the article been bought up so quickly by "the majority of that class of Liberians" least able to "spend even a nickel, let alone a dime, on a newspaper"? This, chided the newspaper, was the group of "whose existence Minister Walton had been sedulously ignorant during the ten years of his stay in Liberia."[7]

Although Walton had not been fired but had resigned, some truth sounded in the sensationalist account. Black American soldiers did discuss racism, class, exploitation, and colonialism on the U.S. base in Liberia during the war years. Many expressed dismay at the stark divides between Liberia's settler elite and indigenous people, among them, Ossie Davis. Before becoming an actor, playwright, director, and civil rights activist, Davis had been stationed in 1942 as a scrub nurse at the 25th Station Hospital on the military base adjacent to Roberts Field and the Firestone plantations. It was the first U.S.-commissioned station to be commanded and staffed by Black medical personnel. "I was not only uneasy with the class conflict I felt was brewing in Liberia, I was disturbed by it," Davis explained, recollecting his three years spent in Liberia. "The brotherhood based on race, which I had fully expected, was nowhere to be found," he wrote. "Rather the oppression of one class of people, the native tribes, by another class, the Americo-Liberians, was everywhere in evidence. Had Marx been right—that people as a whole were much more loyal to their class than to their race?" he asked. Davis was even more disturbed at how "easily we became racist and exploiters, treating the natives with that same very superior disdain and disrespect about which we ourselves were constantly complaining to the company commander." Firestone was among the worst offenders, Davis thought. It may have been "only a corporation not a country, like England and France," Davis observed, but Firestone was nevertheless a "colonialist exploiter."[8] On these issues of racial and class divide that structured Firestone's plantation world, Walton had through his years in Liberia been noticeably silent in conversation with his friends, Harvey Firestone Jr., Edwin Barclay, and William Tubman.

That August, Du Bois placed in the *Chicago Defender* a spirited defense of Walton. Du Bois had only contempt for Firestone, but he believed Walton stood "like a rock against race segregation and white rule in Liberia." The "old charge of exploitation of the natives by a Liberian elite" was a cheap shot, argued Du Bois. Even if true, it "would not be one-tenth as bad as the kind of exploitation against natives that is being carried on by whites all over Africa and all over Asia and in much of South America," he reasoned. "There is not time for the social re-organization of a country," wrote Du Bois, "when it is under fire and pressure by white slave drivers," by which Du Bois meant Firestone and the U.S. Navy.[9] In a world dominated by economic and military imperialism in the service of white supremacy, Du Bois put Liberia's sovereignty as an independent Black republic above that of the country's internal class divides that troubled people like Davis.

Edward Dudley, Walton's eventual successor, was less sympathetic to Firestone. Appointed as American minister to Liberia by Truman in 1948, and elevated to ambassador in 1949, Dudley had been a New York assistant state attorney general before joining the NAACP's Legal Defense and Educational Fund, founded and headed by Thurgood Marshall. As assistant special counsel in the 1940s, Dudley had aided the organization's efforts challenging the exclusion of African Americans from graduate and professional programs and fighting for equal pay for Black teachers in Southern public schools.[10] As a diplomat, Dudley initially "restrained himself" from criticizing Firestone in the press, but after three years in Liberia, he confronted the company's racist policies. When white staff at the U.S. Trading Company, a Firestone-owned store, refused to wait on

Mrs. Dudley while extending other discourtesies, Dudley summoned to the American Legation in Monrovia a Mr. Vipond, acting manager of the Firestone Plantations Company. After the ambassador allegedly "dressed down" Vipond, a phone call went from Akron to the State Department. Dudley, in speaking with Vipond, supposedly "accused Firestone of 'transferring' U.S. 'Jim Crow policies' to Liberia" and denounced its segregationist policy of excluding "Negroes from the employee club." Firestone's executive vice-president, Byron Larabee, defended the company's actions. If Firestone adopted a "crusading policy on this matter," Larabee told the State Department, it would jeopardize the company's ability to recruit white personnel. Larabee further complained regarding Dudley that until "a professional Negro" appeared, the company "never had any trouble on these questions." But the questions around Firestone's vast plantation world and segregated enclave, built on white supremacist attitudes and racist policies in a sovereign Black republic, were just beginning.[11]

In 1945, Liberia was catching up with the world and the world was catching up with Firestone. The success of the Firestone Plantations Company heightened recognition, inside and outside of Liberia, of the oppressive forces of racial capitalism and its legitimization of inequality through the construction of racial and ethnic difference, both of which were at play in Liberia. In the postwar years, as civil rights struggles in America, liberation movements in Africa, and labor unrest and fears of communism gained momentum, it became increasingly difficult for the U.S. government to turn a blind eye to the world of racial and class division that Firestone had built.

By the late 1940s, Claude Barnett had strayed from Walton's unflinching support of Firestone in Liberia. In 1947, the enterprising journalist made his first trip to Africa. He was eager to cultivate connections to advance investment opportunities for his small import business devoted to trade in goods from West Africa. He also hoped to further and strengthen ties to West African newspapers and journalists to help the Associated Negro Press expand its news coverage of Africa after the war. Barnett saw both strategies—leveraging Black capital and the Black press—as key to forging a postwar Pan-African solidarity, around capitalism rather than socialism, to support the freedom struggles of people of African descent.[12]

Barnett and his wife, Etta Moten Barnett, traveled "in style" throughout West Africa, including Liberia. A celebrated stage and screen actor, cast as

Bess in the 1942 Broadway revival of George Gershwin's *Porgy and Bess*, Moten Barnett gave concerts in Ghana's capital city, Accra, and other cities they toured. Back at home, Claude Barnett promoted West Africa, and Liberia in particular, as a tourist destination for people of color "tired of Jim Crow travel and facilities" in the United States. "Once you leave American shores, drop your guard against discrimination," Barnett advised readers of the *Negro Digest*. But, Barnett admitted, they had encountered "the inevitable American." "I can never tell whether a Southern white American will behave like a gentleman or a jackass," Barnett noted. "Even in Liberia where Negroes run the government, from dog catcher to president," a white steamship line official they encountered "did not want to publicly accept Negroes as his social equals," wrote Barnett.[13] The same seemed true of Firestone's white management staff. Conversations with Liberians led Barnett to believe that for those working on the Firestone plantations, "real progress upward is blocked and that a little white island or empire has been created in which Liberians are not welcome or cannot enter."[14]

Among Barnett's interests in Liberia was the promotion of investment and professional opportunities for African Americans. Through this pursuit, he would become involved with the Liberia Company, a joint venture between the Liberian government and a group of American financiers. A chance to get "some honest development" carried out in Liberia and break "the monopoly" of Firestone was how Barnett's good friend Frank Pinder, stationed in Liberia as part of the Economic Mission, regarded the Liberia Company. Barnett and Pinder shared a faith in the liberating power of capitalism and both praised the "bi-racial setup" of the Liberia Company's structure, which gave African Americans and Liberians a chance to invest.[15] But the promise of the Liberia Company was short-lived.

Edward Stettinius was the principal mover behind the Liberia Company. A former vice-president of General Motors and chairman of U.S. Steel, Stettinius moved in and out of Roosevelt's administration. He became secretary of state in 1944, then a year later the first U.S. ambassador to the United Nations. Stettinius and his associates feared that capitalism was on the ropes, particularly in Africa. Emory Ross, a Methodist missionary and Liberia Company board member, expressed these sentiments in discussing a new deal for Liberia. "The African," Ross argued, "cannot yet forget his first triple-touch with capitalist society was gunpowder-gin-slavery." Nor, Ross acknowledged, did Africans benefit from later capitalist ventures that were "rigged to strip the African producer and give most of the milk and all of the cream to the distant capitalist society." Given this history, Ross believed Africans were likely to be much more sympathetic to communism, which did not have capitalism's bad past on the continent.[16]

Stettinius at the time viewed Liberia as the American bridgehead to Africa in the fight against communism. The Economic Mission to Liberia that Roosevelt had sent in 1944 had made visible a country rich in iron ore, gold, diamonds, timber, and other natural resources. But the present was doomed to repeat the past unless foreign investment in Africa was put on a different moral and social foundation. The Liberia Company was to be a "new departure in international relations, . . . an experiment to combine in one program the solutions to public welfare and other governmental problems along with the development of the natural resources of the republic of Liberia."[17] In exchange for priority rights to mining and logging concessions to develop the country's rich iron ore and timber reserves, and land concessions to exploit its potential in coffee, cocoa, rubber, and oil palm production, the Liberia Company would guarantee the Liberian government 25 percent of the company's common stock. Another 10 percent of stockholdings was to be held by the Liberian Foundation, a charitable arm of the company to oversee health, education, and training programs.[18]

Both the *New York Amsterdam News* and the *Chicago Defender* published editorials praising the venture.[19] Du Bois was suspicious. "Liberia is taking a second step on a dangerous experiment," he wrote. "The first was the Firestone Rubber concession. The second is the Liberia Company and Stettinius Associates. . . . Its announced board of directors has on it one of the most prejudiced and reactionary admirals ever in the U.S. Navy." Men from the South and from "successful American business" also dominated the board. Du Bois worried about the threat to "Liberia's freedom and independence" if the country simply became "another investment."[20]

The Liberia Company board included prominent names in American business and government with close ties to Roosevelt's administration, including Fleet Admiral William Halsey Jr., the object of Du Bois's scorn; Philip Reed, chairman of the board of General Electric; and Lessing Rosenwald, former chairman of Sears, Roebuck and Co., among others. Barnett, along with Channing Tobias, the first Black director of the Phelps Stokes Fund, were the only two African Americans on the Liberia

Company's founding board. An additional five directors were named by the Liberian government.

Barnett used his board position to advocate for hiring qualified African Americans to fill jobs associated with the company's efforts to stimulate commercial trade with, and private investment in, Liberia. He did not shy from contacting other board members to call out "anti-African" attitudes and condescending behavior among the company's white personnel in Liberia.[21] Stettinius assured Barnett that such behavior would not be tolerated. On one occasion, he asked Barnett to discreetly share names, so they could "go into action and pick out of the barrel the diseased apple, no matter what position that apple may occupy."[22]

Barnett threw his energies into promoting the Liberia Company to potential Black investors and the Black press, for which he was rewarded in company stock. In September 1948, for example, he successfully placed a glossy three-page spread in *Ebony*, showcasing Stettinius's recent trip to Liberia. In words and photos, the piece highlighted a spirit of integration that Barnett believed to be at work in a company that would "unlock vast riches" and "give Liberians a better standard of living." The methods of the Liberia Company, Barnett assured Black readers, "are a far cry from the usual 'imperialist' operations of similar companies of the past." It was a veiled reference to Firestone, which he criticized in the article for paying its Liberian workers an average wage of "only 38 cents a day."[23]

Stettinius's death in 1949 left the Liberia Company without the vision of a committed leader. Whether the Liberia Company would practice new "concepts of partnership and social responsibility," as Stettinius preached, or fall back on old forms of economic imperialism, as Du Bois feared, would never be known.[24] The company foundered for a decade as part of a tangled web of American business interests in the global airline, shipping, and mining industries. In 1962, the Liberian government sold its 25 percent share of the Liberia Company, with a net annual income of $700,000, to the Liberia Development Corporation and dissolved the original agreements.[25]

In the heightened geopolitical tensions that emerged between the United States and the Soviet Union in the aftermath of the Second World War, the African continent became a region of increased interest and concern among two superpowers vying for influence in the world. President Harry Truman's policy of containment, intended to counter the Soviet Union's expanding sphere of power, pitted the Cold War as a battle between free and open, liberal, democratic, capitalist societies and the totalitarian regimes of Communist states. This battle intensified as former colonies gained independence in Africa, Asia, and other parts of the world, their claims to sovereignty bolstered after the Charter of the United Nations, established in 1945, recognized the "equal rights and self-determination of peoples" (even though, in the case of sub-Saharan Africa, the first nation to achieve independence, Ghana, would not do so until 1957). The United States and the Soviet Union jockeyed for position to sway newly independent nations to align on their side of the ideological battle that divided West and East.

Fears that capitalism's exploitative and bloody history on the African continent had planted the seeds for Communist revolution shaped American foreign policymakers' Cold War concerns regarding Liberia, specifically the Firestone plantations. When, in December 1949, Firestone garage mechanics went on strike, setting off a decade of growing worker solidarity and labor unrest on the plantations, those fears heightened. U.S. State Department officials cited "discontentment on the part of certain employees" as a cause. But they also laid the blame on "agitation created by British African subjects from Sierra Leone, the Gold Coast, and Nigeria." They refused to believe that indigenous Liberian workers alone could organize to protest the American corporation's exploitative treatment. Although these officials reported "no Communist influence," they worried that conditions on the Firestone plantations had created a situation "ripe for Communist activity."[26]

The first collective labor action against an American corporation in Liberia originated not on the plantations but at the port under construction in Monrovia by Raymond Concrete Pile Company and the U.S. Navy. In December 1945, workers organized a two-day walkout to protest unfair discrimination in wages, medical care, worker compensation, and canteen privileges. Monrovia's *Weekly Mirror* applauded the action: "It is proof that Liberians are waking up to their rights, and it shows that the age-old belief that Liberians cannot be united is wearing away." The paper denounced the lack of consideration American foreign concessions gave to Liberian labor. Firestone was the worst among them. "At Firestone, where the Liberian Wage Law is not in operation, workers are treated like chattels by their would-be white masters," the *Weekly Mirror* charged. The "only weapon in the hand of the employee" against racial discrimination and inequity in pay, housing, and other working conditions was "TO STRIKE," urged the newspaper, rallying Liberia's incipient working class to action.[27]

A walkout on the Firestone plantations in December 1949 hardly constituted "acts of violence," as a "secret" U.S. government document reported in early January 1950.[28] When the mechanics walked out, accountants, clerks, and clerical staff from Firestone's U.S. Trading Company and Central Office followed suit. Factory laborers and the African medical staff were next. Firestone Plantations manager Ross Wilson claimed that of the sixteen thousand workers employed on the Harbel plantation, only four hundred went on strike.[29] Cooks and stewards also walked out, forcing Wilson's wife to cook and Wilson to wash dishes. Fed up with what he believed to be an illegal action, Wilson drove to the American embassy. He and Ambassador Dudley headed to the Executive Mansion, where President Tubman decided to assemble an executive commission. It included his attorney general, his secretary of agriculture and commerce, the Frontier Force commander, and a Bondiway district judge who was magistrate on the Firestone Plantations.[30]

The commission arrived on the plantations, expecting an angry mob. They found instead "a serene calm." At a schoolhouse, workers assembled and elected representatives to bring their grievances to the commission and management. Wilson at first refused to negotiate. He came to the table only after Tubman threatened his deportation if he didn't cooperate. Worker demands included "better wages, better housing, better hospital care, and better working conditions," as well as better treatment by white management and "immunity from reprisal for taking part in the strike." The commission spent two weeks investigating workplace and housing conditions, pay scales, and medical care on the plantations. It found good cause for the workers' complaints. Commission members recommended to President Tubman the adoption by Firestone of "an eight-hour day for all departments on the Plantations, a 60 percent wage increase for labor, paid vacations," more equitable hospital care, and an end to the construction of worker housing on swampy land.[31]

In early February 1950, amid a commission-negotiated truce, Wilson broke his word. He fired strike leaders and offered workers a raise of 2¢ to their daily wage. Outraged, the workers struck again. Strikers across different sectors of the plantations set rubber trees on fire, destroyed vehicles, and opened "a huge container for latex," dumping the "valuable rubber" into the Farmington River, where it floated down to the Atlantic.[32] More than three hundred "striking laborers used logs and road blocks to disrupt communications" between the plantations and the capital.[33] It was the first incident of violent organized protest in the history of the plantations. Tubman declared martial law, suspending citizens' civil liberties, and sent in "riflemen and machinegun squads" to overpower strikers "armed with cutlasses."[34] Disgruntled laborers returned to work on February 14. After the strike, Tubman appealed to U.S. assistant secretary of state George McGhee for a military adviser and arms to better prepare and equip Liberia's army to deal with labor unrest, which he thought was making the country "vulnerable to foreign doctrines." McGhee promised to "push the matter of military assistance" in Washington to help Liberia protect "against 'Communist agitation'" as it embarked on "its program of development."[35]

No friend of labor, Tubman was the largest independent rubber farmer in Liberia. He had every incentive, economically and politically, to suppress strikes on the Firestone plantations and keep wages low. If Firestone raised wages, Liberia's independent rubber farmers would need to as well, cutting into profits. A handful of Liberians owned rubber estates larger than five hundred acres, employing hundreds of workers. Tubman's four-thousand-acre farm in Totota, on the main road from Monrovia to Gbarnga in the heart of Liberia's rubber corridor, grew coffee, cocoa, and rubber and held a private zoo.[36] Known as Coo-Coo's Nest, Tubman's farm by the 1960s employed more than 250 tappers to harvest latex from two thousand acres planted in clonal varieties, courtesy of Firestone.[37] As rubber prices soared during the Korean War, Firestone's policy of purchasing rubber at wholesale market rates ingratiated the company to Liberian rubber farmers who profited greatly. As strikes on the Firestone plantations and other foreign concessions gained momentum during the 1950s, Tubman, as if in exchange for profits, used his considerable government power to quell labor unrest and maintain "law and order" in his dictatorial state.[38] When, for example, in 1961, mechanics armed "with cutlasses, steel pipes and sticks" organized seven hundred laborers to stop work on the recently granted Salala Rubber Corporation concession, located near Coo-Coo's Nest, Tubman directed his acting attorney general to send men from both the National Police Force and the Liberian Frontier Force to the plantation, and authorized the troops "to shoot and kill" if using tear gas failed to end strike violence.[39] Besides deploying police and military to aid Firestone, Tubman also exerted influence on trade union leadership; in 1959 he appointed his son, William "Shad" Tubman Jr., to head Liberia's Congress of Industrial Organizations.[40]

The first serious strike on the Firestone plantations, which Tubman suppressed in February 1950 using martial law and military might, did little to help labor. Two months after the strike ended, Firestone's Larabee reported to State Department officials that unskilled plantation laborers earned on average 28¢ per day. If true, the strike resulted in a roughly 40 percent increase in wages. But no other worker demands—more equitable housing conditions, better working conditions, better treatment by white management, and no reprisals for strike actions—were met.[41]

Meanwhile, in Akron, Harvey Jr. was focused not on labor unrest but on the golden anniversary celebration of Firestone Tire & Rubber Company's founding. In 1950, his late father's company had surpassed $700 million in sales, and the Liberia plantations had become one of its most profitable subsidiaries.[42] In August, six months after the Harbel plantation strikes, before a crowd estimated in the thousands, Harvey Jr., along with his four brothers, unveiled a gigantic statue of their father: the larger-than-life, bronze-colored patriarch sat in a chair mounted high on a granite block, looking out upon the mile-long industrial complex that was but a part of the Firestone rubber empire.[43] But the unveiling was a masterful deception. Harvey Jr. had commissioned famed American sculptor James Earle Fraser to memorialize his father. When Harvey Jr. learned that Fraser's bronze would not be ready in time, he had the full-size plaster model painted to look like bronze and shipped to Akron for the dedication. Months later, in the dead of night, the plaster model was replaced with the bronze.[44] Both the choice of Fraser, who was recognized for his grand monuments glorifying the history and violence of settler colonialism and American empire, and the ruse spoke to the supreme value the Firestones' empire placed in its public image. The speech, titled "A Great Humanitarian," given at the jubilee by Reverend Walter Trunks of Akron's St. Paul's Episcopal Church, made no mention of Harvey S. Firestone's legacy in Liberia. Cheap land and labor, and high rubber prices, had benefited Firestone immensely. Harvey Jr., buoyed by Tubman's security forces, was not about to bend easily on the wages they paid Liberian "unskilled" labor.

At a time when the U.S. government saw Liberia as an important American beachhead on the African continent in the "battle of ideologies between

Harvey Firestone Jr., President William Tubman, Liberian ambassador Clarence L. Simpson, and two unidentified men admiring James Earle Fraser's statue of the Firestone patriarch in 1954. (Courtesy of Indiana University Libraries.)

the West and the East," Firestone's policies and practices were cause for concern.[45] Shortly after the 1950 strike, State Department officials in Washington impressed upon Larabee that Firestone needed to adopt a "more progressive approach" in its dealings and relationships with "African peoples."[46] White management's intolerant attitudes toward Liberian officials, the "treatment of its native employees," and the lack of training and promotion of Liberians to positions of management were all cited by Ambassador Dudley and others as in desperate "need of reform."[47]

    Firestone's racist attitudes and policies threatened to subvert the U.S. government's foreign policy work promoting public and private investment in Liberia, specifically its plan to showcase Liberia "as a proving ground for President Truman's Point [Four] program."[48] Announced in his inauguration address in January 1949, Truman described "a bold new program for making the benefits of our scientific advances and industrial progress available for the improvement and growth of underdeveloped areas." Truman's speech depicted the world in a struggle between communism, "a false philosophy," and democracy, based on a belief that government was founded to protect "the rights of the individual and his freedom" and that "social justice can be achieved through peaceful change."[49] In countries where the "choice between communist totalitarianism and the free way of life is in the balance," Truman argued, technical assistance and capital investment would "tip the scales toward the way of freedom."[50] But this could only happen if the U.S. government and private enterprise working together could deliver on the promise of capitalism and science—to improve people's lives in lesser developed parts of the world.[51]

When Barnett and Dudley failed in their efforts to secure aid for Liberia through Truman's Marshall Plan, designed to assist the postwar economic recovery of Western European nations, they leveraged their Washington connections to position Liberia as a recipient of Point Four funds.[52] Barnett's 1947 visit to Liberia and the 1949–50 strikes had further chastened his belief in Firestone as Liberia's savior. But in a two-part series he published in the *Chicago World* and other newspapers, Barnett refused to say firmly whether Firestone was "an angel or a devil to Liberia," even as he raised criticisms of Firestone labor policies, including a lack of advancement for nonwhites, that cast the company in an unfavorable light.[53]

Liberia was no stranger to U.S. technical assistance programs. The Economic and Health Missions Roosevelt sent to Liberia in 1944, still in operation in 1950, conducted extensive surveys of the country's health and natural resources and provided scientific and medical expertise. The assistance aided the Tubman administration's development program focused on agriculture, education, health, and economic growth. The U.S. State Department's McGhee regarded the Liberia missions as "principal pilot operations," anticipating a foreign aid approach upon which the U.S. government would soon embark under Truman's Point Four program.[54] By the fall of 1950, Barnett could happily report to the Phelps Stokes Fund's Frederick Rowe that Liberia was the first country slated for Point Four funds on account of "the present program being carried out by the U.S. Economic and Health Missions in Liberia."[55] In December 1950, a formal agreement between the United States and Liberia established a Joint Commission for Economic Development, made up of five American and seven Liberian experts in agriculture, economics, education, public health and sanitation, and other areas. The technical assistance and cooperation plan specified a five- to ten-year economic development strategy, estimated at $32 million and funded through a cost-sharing program of grants and loans provided by the U.S. government and Liberian government revenues.

All told, the U.S. government allocated approximately $36 million in grants and $51 million in development loans to Liberia between 1951 and 1962.[56] Barnett regarded this new venture in international aid as an employment opportunity for African American experts never afforded by Firestone. Oscar Meier, head of the Economic Mission, hoped it would "become one of the best examples of how free and democratic nations can work to the mutual advantage of each other."[57]

The Joint Commission's focus on improving Liberia's agriculture, health, education, and transportation sectors aligned closely with Tubman's professed development goals and unification policies. In his first term in office, Tubman extended voting rights to all citizens of at least twenty-one years of age who owned either real estate in fee simple or a hut in the interior. He also created four new counties out of the former hinterland regions to give them equal status to the five coastal counties occupied largely by settlers. Such acts brought formal political and legal recognition to processes of economic integration and cultural assimilation ongoing since before the founding of the republic.[58] Tubman's investment in and promotion of health services through the technical assistance plan, while he was actively selling concessions for iron ore, rubber, and timber at bargain prices, offered some antidote to the failure of foreign direct investment to much improve the health of Liberians beyond those working the plantations and mines.[59] As more rural people migrated to work on the Firestone plantations and in iron ore mines, the reduction in farm labor necessitated efforts to stimulate agricultural production. Already in 1944 at the start of Firestone's peak employment, the American financial adviser noted "shortages in rice and other foodstuffs," which he attributed to "the drift" of people "from the villages, where they produced their own food, to the plantations and other centers of employment where they do not." The trend, he correctly predicted, would continue without "a compensating increase in production on the part of those who remain in the villages of the hinterland."[60]

Harvey Firestone Jr., as a member of the International Development Advisory Board, commissioned by Truman to offer guidance on the policies and progress of Point Four, quickly became one of the program's most vocal critics. In 1952, addressing a public forum hosted by the *New York Herald Tribune*, Firestone was dismissive of the Point Four approach. If "the most effective means of combatting communism" was to better people's lives in "underdeveloped areas of the world," he declared, the best way to accomplish this was through private capital. Government efforts were best directed not toward technical assistance programs at taxpayers' expense, but instead "toward convincing other governments of the value of making their countries favorable and attractive places for foreign capital." Firestone cited as proof his company's history in Liberia: the company's medical services, school system, labor policies and worker compensation, hydroelectric plant, road infrastructure, and other assets were reasons why "private capital invested in an underdeveloped country can bring great benefits to all." Firestone's undertaking in Liberia, he concluded, "is a proven and tested plan which brings benefits to the investors, which does not cost the taxpayers a single penny, which raises the living standards of the people of the underdeveloped lands and which attacks at its source one of the greatest forces for evil the world has ever known."[61]

Realities on the ground in Liberia—paltry wages, racial inequalities, wealth concentration, labor unrest, land dispossession, and increasing food shortages—suggested otherwise. Earlier that year, Tubman had awarded the rubber mogul the Grand Band of the Order of the Star of Africa for his "deep and abiding interest in the welfare of Liberia."[62] The honor undoubtedly buttressed Harvey Jr.'s exaggerated claims. But it did not convince African Americans like Frank Pinder, working in Liberia under the auspices of Point Four, that Firestone was the country's salvation.

Frank Pinder, senior agricultural specialist on the U.S. Economic Mission to Liberia, landed at Roberts Field on a DC3 military transport plane one early morning in late November 1944. He had come on behalf of the U.S. State Department and the Foreign Economic Administration with a handful of technical experts in agriculture, forestry, geology, and engineering to assist Tubman's administration in a five-year plan of development. Pinder would stay for thirteen years. In that time, he played an instrumental role in the transformation of the Liberian government's agricultural programs. When Pinder arrived, Liberia's Bureau of Agriculture was a small government agency with a minuscule budget of $6,000 per year. Within a decade, largely through his influence, it had become a cabinet-level ministry department with an annual expenditure of nearly $400,000, supported through Liberian government revenues and Point Four funds. By 1957, Pinder had left behind an agricultural program in Liberia that had, in Tubman's words, "not only blossomed and bloomed, but is producing rich fruits a thousandfold." By then, the Department of Agriculture and Commerce, as it was now known, had in place an agricultural extension service that included an experimental research station and eighty-two tree-crop nurseries and demonstration farms, located throughout the country, staffed by more than one hundred technical experts and aides, almost all of whom were Liberian.[63]

Pinder understood the disastrous impact that a one-crop plantation economy could have on people and the land. His parents, caught in the ups and downs of the Bahamas Islands' pineapple plantation economy, had left the small island of Eleuthera in 1895. As a teenager in Key West, Florida, surrounded by Ku Klux Klan violence, Pinder found sanctuary selling citrus fruits and avocados at the roadside stand his two aunts operated on Miami's outskirts. Smitten by agriculture and markets, he enrolled in a college preparatory program at Florida Agricultural and Mechanical University, a historically Black land-grant college in Tallahassee. There, Pinder was mentored by Black instructors, many with ties to Tuskegee, who also worked as Agricultural Extension Service agents and were versed in agricultural cooperatives and marketing. Pinder's first job after college was working for Alachua County, Florida, with Black farmers as a farm demonstration agent. He built a successful program, bringing farmers and their diverse agricultural products—hogs, livestock, citrus fruits, and vegetables—together within agricultural cooperatives, enabling them to sell their commodities at competitive prices in the Northern markets along the East Coast. He led seminars on soil conservation, finance, and home ownership; organized youth into 4-H clubs; and arranged agricultural fairs attended by more than sixteen thousand Black families. Pinder's success caught the attention of Claude Barnett and people in or close to Roosevelt's Black Cabinet, like Constance E.H. Daniels, who championed his appointment in the Farm Security Administration (FSA).[64]

As an FSA agent, Pinder traveled throughout the South working with Black tenant farmers and in migratory farm labor camps. He saw Black farmers caught in the structures of plantation agriculture, perpetuated by a federal, state, and corporate agricultural system that used loans and subsidies to sustain racial discrimination and oppression, often leaving them debt-ridden and landless.[65] At Gee's Bend, Alabama, more than one hundred sharecropper families whose ancestors had worked as slaves on the ten-thousand-acre Pettway cotton plantation were "desolate and destitute," beholden to an absentee landlord and local merchants, whose situation worsened further when the economy collapsed during the Great Depression. The net worth in 1935 of a Gee's Bend family averaged $28.

Roosevelt's Resettlement Administration and its successor, the FSA, purchased the land and offered families low-interest loans for five-acre homesteads, with an option to lease additional lands. Pinder helped shape crop diversification and community education programs and form a farmers' cooperative that included a shared cotton gin and general store.[66]

Pinder's work with Southern Black sharecroppers informed his approach to agriculture in Liberia, where he endeavored "to encourage the Liberian Government to diversify the one-crop rubber economy" that the Firestone concession had instituted.[67] He traversed Liberia's interior, meeting with village chiefs and local farmers, learning of their challenges, and observing their crops. After seven years, he reportedly traveled thirty thousand miles in Liberia on foot and by canoe. Pinder's philosophy of extension eschewed the arrogance and top-down approaches common among white Point Four staff in Liberia. "Old broken down 'ofays,'" Pinder wrote his friend Barnett, using a derogatory term for a white person, "will not get the job done."[68] *Ofay*, which Pinder used often in his correspondence, conveyed his defiance of the racist attitudes of American foreign service personnel who demeaned or would limit his success as an agricultural expert in Liberia.[69] Pinder approached his work with Liberia's rural agriculturists with humility. "I realized that I had come to a people with skills of their own, worthy of the greatest respect," Pinder remarked. "American ideas and skills crossed with native ideas and skills," he observed, "resulted in increased production and an adaptable program free from pride-sapping paternalism."[70]

Evidence of that cooperative spirit and its success showed in numerous Liberian agricultural projects Pinder helped advance. A few months after arriving, Pinder partnered with the head of Liberia's Bureau of Agriculture, Bai Tamia Moore, to develop a pilot program aimed at improving the livelihood of small farmers in Dimeh, a village in the Dei chiefdom, twenty miles from Monrovia. Moore was born to Gola and Vai parents in Dimeh. He was fluent in the indigenous languages of the Gola, Vai, Bassa, and Dei people who inhabited Dimeh and surrounding villages. Moore would later draw upon his intimate knowledge of Liberia's indigenous African cultures and folklore to become one of the nation's most celebrated writers and poets. He was familiar with America as well. He attended public high school in Richmond, Virginia, graduated from Virginia Union University with a BA in biology, and took graduate courses at Howard University before returning to Liberia in 1941.[71]

Respectful of the values, economies, and relationships to land that sustained livelihoods in the region, Moore and Pinder worked with local farmers to develop a plan to bring cash into the community. Together, the American—wise in the ways of Southern Black resistance to evolving regimes of plantation monopoly—and the African—attuned to his people's customary relationships to land tenure and cooperative systems of labor and exchange—put forth a vision of polyculture farming and collective values that ran counter to the plantation.[72] Every effort for the communities was made to build upon and expand rather than replace the crops they valued. They supplied farmers with small farm tools, seeds to grow cash crops, and encouragement to increase the size of rice plantings to help their families get through the hungry season. To expand tree crops in Dimeh and neighboring villages, six hundred thousand cocoa trees, fifty thousand citrus trees, and five hundred trees of new palm varieties were planted. Moore and Pinder also organized a farm cooperative. To transport produce to Monrovia markets before a road was completed, donkeys were used, easing the burden of carrying loads on one's head. Eighty-gallon kettles, furnished by the project, enabled villagers to produce palm oil in bulk more quickly and efficiently. The collective reinvested earnings in an oil press and nut-cracking mill to complete the "factory" cooperative. In a matter of seven years, annual family income saw a fivefold increase.[73]

As he had with Alachua County farmers, Pinder worked to develop American markets for Liberia's agricultural products and expand agricultural trade between the two countries. He focused on palm kernels, palm oil, cocoa, and piassava, tree crops that were an integral part of the lifeways of Liberia's many communities. American soap manufacturers used palm oil, but mostly imported from British and French colonies, and the poor quality of Liberian-grown cocoa prohibited its importation into the United States. In 1947, Pinder successfully arranged the first shipment of 150 tons of palm oil from Liberia to the United States.[74] A year later, he wrote to Barnett that the first shipment of Liberian cocoa that met American standards had been "enthusiastically received on the American market."[75] By 1949 the news was even better. New farming practices, labor saving machinery, and favorable weather conditions, Pinder extolled, brought about "no rice shortage" and a 30 percent increase in agricultural yields, making for Liberia's "biggest food production" year in more than a decade.[76]

But not all went well for Pinder. He confided to Barnett his dismay at "the racial prejudice that has begun to seep through to Liberia." American government programs and Tubman's Open Door policy created a favorable business climate through concessions and tax breaks, resulting in sizable foreign direct investment. With it came an influx of white American managers and technical staff, accompanied by anti-Black attitudes. "I do not intend to be intimidated by such prejudiced 'crackers' and will fight this kind of injustice to the end," Pinder told Barnett. Pinder noted that the "only thing America can point to with pride here is the progress made in agriculture."[77] Many Liberians agreed. An editorial in one Monrovia newspaper singled out Pinder as having "accomplished more single handed than both the Public Health Mission and the Economic Mission combined."[78] While on leave in 1951 pursuing a graduate degree in agricultural economics at Cornell University, Pinder hoped to be reassigned to Liberia. Frederick Patterson, president of Tuskegee and founder of the United Negro College Fund, believed that C. Reed Hill's appointment as U.S. director of technical cooperation in Liberia spelled trouble, for both Pinder and the prospect of increasing the number of African American experts in Liberia through Point Four. "All of this is no doubt a part of the Firestone influence to keep things under his control and permit as little progress as possible," Patterson believed.[79] Pinder's efforts to aid small farmers and diversify the country's agricultural economy threatened Firestone's economic leverage over the Liberian government and the company's need for a plantation's workforce. When Pinder wrote to Dudley about returning to Liberia to continue the Point Four programs he had started, the ambassador wrote back delighted: "We need you like a calf needs his ma."[80]

The appointment in 1952 of John W. Davis as Hill's replacement improved Pinder's situation in Liberia. Davis was a renowned civil rights leader who, as president of West Virginia State College, had helped develop it into a prominent land-grant university. He was a board member of the NAACP's Legal Defense and Educational Fund and worked with Thurgood Marshall in breaking down racial barriers and injustices that African Americans faced in education and employment. Notably, he helped with the landmark 1954 *Brown v. Board of Education* case.[81] Under Davis's leadership, Pinder's programs expanded. A central experimental agricultural station was established in partnership with Liberia's Department of Agriculture and Commerce near Suakoko. The hundred-acre facility contained nurseries, test fields, and demonstration areas and conducted research into commercial vegetable and tree crops, rice cultivation, livestock

Frank Pinder, on the left, meets with Melvin Harris, superintendent of Suakoko
Agricultural Station, and others to inspect improved tomatoes for shipment to
Monrovia, circa 1950s. (Frank Pinder Archival Collection, Meek-Eaton Black
Archives, Florida A&M University.)

and poultry breeding, appropriate farming technologies, and more. Through
Pinder's influence, eight Liberians completed training at American land-
grant colleges in veterinary medicine, agronomy, plant pathology, horti-
culture, entomology, extension education, and related agricultural fields.[82]
Crops that Pinder promoted under the umbrella of agricultural diversification, including palm kernel, achieved sizable production and export
gains. Other projects saw less success, including an effort to make a "rice
bowl" region of Gbedin Swamp in the northeast.[83] During two weeks
in October 1953, U.S. Department of Agriculture agent Wilhelm Anderson traveled with Pinder on the major interior highway from the Firestone
plantations to Suakoko and then Ganta. Anderson marveled at extensive
plantings of tree crops, including "rubber, coffee, cocoa, oil palm, citrus,
and banana" and the increase in swamp rice cultivation, calling the extension program Pinder helped lead "outstanding. It costs little yet is doing
much."[84]

Not everyone agreed. Just months before, Louisiana senator Allen Ellender, as part of a whirlwind 45,000-mile tour of twenty-one African and
Asian nations to assess the merits of Point Four programs, had been in
Liberia less than three days, making a brief visit to a demonstration farm
near Monrovia but deigning to travel to the interior. Ellender was unim-
pressed. "As a possible solution to the chain reaction of hunger, which breeds
discontent and Communism," Point Four was "in need of a thorough over-
haul," he argued. A member of the Senate Appropriations Committee,
Ellender chafed at American citizens "being called upon to" pay taxes to
support projects "spread across the world" and to underwrite "nations
whose debt is far less than our own."[85] The Southern Democrat informed
President Eisenhower that "unless its officials stop giving economic aid
along with advice to under-developed areas of the world," he expected
Congress to kill the program.[86]

In later years, Ellender would come to be known for his outrageous
opinion, in reference particularly to the Black nations of Ethiopia, Liberia, and Haiti, that Black people were incapable of self-governance, embarrassing the Kennedy administration and raising the ire of African
countries and others.[87] Such racist attitudes were clearly on display in his
attack on Pinder's agricultural extension work in Liberia. The senator
claimed that "many Liberian farmers are convinced not of the advantage
of United States methods but of the desirability of avoiding them."[88] Pinder
reached out to Barnett to rebut the senator's accusations with a press release. Barnett zeroed in on Firestone. In an Associated Negro Press release,
Barnett wrote that the outspoken segregationist had spent most of his
time in Liberia "lounging around the Firestone rubber plantation with the
white American personnel up in their exclusive residential section in the
heart of the forest of rubber trees."[89] Ellender had, indeed, nothing but
praise for the Firestone plantations. "If there is a paradise on earth, this is
it," Ellender wrote in his diary, referring to the home of Firestone manager
Wilson, built on top of a hill, not far from the Harbel factory.[90] Ellender
and Harvey Jr. worked in concert against Point Four programs in Liberia.
The Firestone Plantations Company's practice of dumping surplus imported rice on local markets, for example, competed directly with the
smallholder farmers Pinder supported as part of his efforts to combat an
entrenched plantation economy.[91]

Pinder respected and supported the customary relationships to land and
the meanings and values associated with indigenous food crops found among

rural people in places like Dimeh, where he partnered with Africans like Moore. But Cold War economists and American CEOs, who prized economic growth as the metric of success, ignored systems of value and exchange not readily conformable to the linear Western model of development then in vogue.[92] Between 1954 and 1960, Liberia had the second highest economic growth rate in the world. In the early 1960s, a Northwestern University team of economists, commissioned by the U.S. and Liberian governments to evaluate Liberia's economy and recommend policy directions, criticized the agricultural work of Point Four and that of the Liberia Department of Agriculture and Commerce. Agricultural investments and export revenues paled in comparison to those of rubber and iron ore commodities extracted by foreign commercial firms, leading the Northwestern team to castigate the crop diversification strategies pursued by Pinder and his associates. But Firestone's concentrated focus on rubber research and extension earned praise as a model of development. The Northwestern economists blamed Liberia's indigenous farmers; commercial agriculture could not succeed, they argued, without a radical transformation in the economy and life of Liberia's indigenous peoples, whom they labeled "illiterate and backward." The Northwestern economists were puzzled by an agricultural system that was "not so much a technique for producing food as a way of life."[93] But, agriculture *was* a way of life. This is precisely what Pinder, influenced by people like Moore and Liberia's rural farmers, came to understand during his time in Liberia. Plantation agriculture, owned and operated for the purpose of profit, brought unjust violence to some Liberians and their ways of being in relationship to the land, relationships integral to the meanings and values that shaped lives and livelihoods in the country's interior.

In the postwar years, Tubman and his government opened the floodgates to a wave of private foreign investment in Liberia. In 1951, when Firestone rubber accounted for 91 percent of Liberian exports, almost half of Liberia's government income came from plantation revenues. The war and postwar rubber boom proved even more lucrative for Firestone, with net profits from its Liberian rubber plantations estimated at $410 million between 1926 and 1977.[94] In 1956, an act of the Liberian Legislature erected a statue and plaque honoring Tubman for having retired the Firestone loan, "with its humiliating and strangulating effects on the economy of the Nation," four years earlier.[95] Yet the crushing effects of neocolonialism in Liberia did not dissuade Tubman's promotion of his country as a place for foreign capital investment throughout the 1950s. Aiding him was a public relations firm that Walton joined upon returning to the U.S.[96] Tubman's Open Door policy, featuring lucrative tax breaks, low wages, an anti-union bent, and long-term land leases, made Liberia into a patchwork of agricultural, mining, and timber concessions. Eight of the twenty-two concessions granted between 1946 and 1960 were American ventures that also benefited from $40 million in loans from the U.S. government's Export-Import Bank.[97]

B.F. Goodrich was one American company to follow in Firestone's footsteps. It signed a concession agreement with the Liberian government in 1954, ten years into Tubman's presidency and twenty-eight years into Firestone's operations. The agreement, like Firestone's, was laden with controversy. As it had with Firestone, the Liberian government gave B.F. Goodrich authority to, on its own, survey and locate areas suitable for developing agricultural plantations. Some Liberian officials objected to the negotiation's secretive nature and opposed the blanket awarding of six hundred thousand acres of rural land at a tax rate of 6¢ per acre per year.[98] Tubman brought the chiefs, who represented the selected lands, to his home and forced them to accept the agreement terms, which included broad mining, forestry, and agriculture rights.[99] Despite its ambitions, B.F. Goodrich planted only 14,013 acres between 1954 and 1985. But it did survey the entire six hundred thousand acres granted in the 1954 agreement, marking the boundaries of concession lands with cornerstones that would heighten land insecurity and affect the decisions of local farmers for decades to come.

Another American firm to follow Firestone to the West African nation was the Liberia Mining Company. In Western Liberia's Bomi Hills, the Gola people had long known and made use of iron ore deposits that gave the earth a red hue. But these high-grade deposits became known to the American steel industry only when Roosevelt sent U.S. Geological Survey geologists in late 1943. In 1945, Tubman granted exclusive mining rights in an eighty-year lease on up to three million acres of Gola and Vai land to Lansdell Christie, a U.S. military officer assigned to the Roberts Field airport construction project. American steel manufacturer Republic Steel Corporation, along with the Export-Import Bank, provided the bulk of capital needed to set shovels, trucks, and trains in motion.

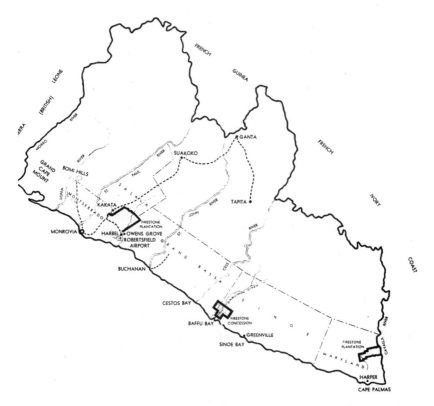

A 1953 preliminary survey map made by B.F. Goodrich showing the Firestone concessions, the Bomi Hills region, and Grand Cape Mount, where the company was seeking its own concession. (B.F. Goodrich Company Records, Archival Services, University Libraries, The University of Akron.)

The concession deal was loudly denounced by Liberian judges, journalists, and other protesters who filed a petition, published in the *African Nationalist*. "Should we now go and cede away vast acreage, and give such sweeping rights over the resources of the country," only to make people "serfs . . . to absentee landlords and foreign concessionaires?" the petitioners asked. The group argued that the terms too much favored the interests of American capital and that the length of the lease jeopardized the welfare of future generations, "for whom we are holding this State in trust."[100] Using Liberia's sedition law, Tubman promptly dismissed the judges and imprisoned petitioner Albert Porte, a teacher and political journalist. In addition, Tubman included the incident among the charges leveled against

Bomi Hills mine area, with piles of iron ore, circa 1950. (Griffith J. Davis Photographs and Films, David M. Rubenstein Rare Book & Manuscript Library, Duke University. © Griff Davis/Griffith J. Davis Photographs and Archives.)

*African Nationalist* publisher C. Frederick Taylor. Those changes would lead in 1950 to Taylor's internment at the Barclay Training Center military base for seventeen years.[101] But the group's prognostication proved correct. In exchange for the company receiving an inordinate share of profits from the sale of $540 million in iron ore extracted from the country between 1951 and 1977, Liberia received a mere $10 million investment.[102]

Initially, Barnett supported the mining project. "On the surface of it I can see nothing wrong with the Christie concession," he stated.[103] But soon it was clear that the Liberia Mining Company employed the same segregationist labor practices as Firestone. In 1951, as Liberian iron ore traveled by rail to the now-open free port in Monrovia and on to American steel factories, Tuskegee's Patterson told Barnett of his concerns regarding the Christie concession. The Tuskegee president on a trip to Liberia saw that Christie had "brought in straw bosses from Europe and everywhere but no Negroes." When confronted about the lack of African American engineers, Christy explained to Patterson, inadequately, that the "mining contract was a short term affair."[104]

By the late 1950s, the immunity that Liberia granted for Jim Crow practices carried out by American firms, particularly Firestone, became more problematic for Tubman. As more young Liberians attended U.S. schools on educational scholarships, funded by climbing Liberian government revenues, their awareness of and displeasure with segregation grew. Many attending Black colleges in the South were "shocked" to encounter racial discrimination.[105] Many also were witness to civil rights struggles sweeping America. In March 1957, Dr. Martin Luther King Jr., whose leadership and commitment to nonviolent resistance in the Montgomery bus boycott had inspired freedom fighters across the world, stopped in Dakar, Senegal, and in Monrovia on his way to Accra. He and numerous other American civil rights leaders had come to celebrate Ghana's political independence from Great Britain and the inauguration of its first prime minister (and president), Kwame Nkrumah. Etta Moten Barnett, again in Accra with Claude, interviewed King. "The birth of this new nation," King told her, "will give impetus to oppressed peoples all over the world."[106] King had linked the civil rights struggles of America with anticolonial movements across Africa and Asia. As president of the first independent state in West Africa, Tubman, who hoped to position himself as a leading statesman helping to guide the future of Africa in a moment of transformational change, could no longer silently sanction racial discrimination and oppression by foreign white capital.

Increasingly, the Monrovia press criticized Firestone's segregationist practices and, even more so, its alleged firing of white employees who married Liberian women, pressuring Tubman to act. In February 1958, the Liberian president introduced into the Liberian Legislature an anti-segregation bill. That Liberia, a Black nation, needed a law against racial discrimination confirms how ingrained were Jim Crow practices in the corporate mining and plantation enclaves spread across sovereign African soil. Firestone protested and sought legal recourse. But eventually the intransigent company largely acquiesced, though it still refused to integrate its plantation schools. Including the children of indigenous workers in classrooms with the children of its foreign employees, Firestone claimed, would jeopardize the education of the white children. Tubman gave in, allowing segregated schools, but Firestone's Larabee was nevertheless livid. Articulating the administration's displeasure with the company's behavior, Eisenhower's special assistant for foreign economic policy warned Larabee that Firestone had a "bad reputation as an employer of Africans," one that "was damaging to the prestige of the United States."[107]

As African leaders like Nkrumah worked to build a decolonized world, they spoke out against the inherent dangers of private capital as demonstrated by the Firestone Plantations Company.[108] At the age of ninety, Du Bois, the elder statesman of Pan-Africanism, was denied a visa by the U.S. government to attend Nkrumah's inauguration. On the eve of Ghana's independence, Du Bois wrote to Nkrumah, "Ghana should lead a movement of black men for Pan-Africanism." A Pan-Africa, he urged, could be built on a "new African economy," one that rejected "subjection to and ownership by foreign capitalists" and instead embraced "a socialism founded on old African communal life."[109] One year later, too frail to travel, Du Bois wrote a speech to be read by his wife, Shirley Graham Du Bois, before the first All-African Peoples' Conference in Accra. Do not surrender to the "fatal mistakes of private capitalism. Either capital belongs to all or power is denied all," Du Bois urged as the torch passed to a new generation. "A body of local private capitalists, even if they are black, can never free Africa; they will simply sell it into new slavery to old masters overseas," Du Bois warned.[110] Perhaps Firestone's history in Liberia, which Du Bois knew intimately, was in the back of his mind as he penned these words.

At the third All-African Peoples' Conference in March 1961, representatives from twenty-one African nations gathered in Cairo and voted to adopt a "Resolution on Neo-Colonialism." The resolution was shaped by Nkrumah's Pan-Africanist appeal, which looked to Africa's future in a federation of independent states united in the fight against racial and class oppression. Echoing Nkrumah and other liberation leaders, the All-African Peoples' Conference denounced the "survival of the colonial system in spite of formal recognition of political independence in emerging countries." Private capital, military aid, and technical support from Western nations had become tools of "indirect and subtle form[s] of domination" to be guarded against.[111] The CIA was anxious about what it described as three days of speeches that "echoed Moscow's propaganda diatribes against the neo-colonialism of the United States and against U.S. domination of the United Nations."[112] Tubman led a bloc of independent African states opposed to building a federation of African countries sympathetic to the interests of the Soviet Union. Two months later the Monrovia group, as it was known, met in Liberia's capital and articulated a more moderate stance on African unity, one based on the economic and social cooperation of politically independent, sovereign African states and much more friendly to the interests of Western nations and private capital.[113]

The friendliness to Western capital that Tubman projected to the outside world belied the growing labor strife and student protests he faced at home. Continuing racial discrimination and growing wealth inequality, spawned by foreign concessions, fueled unrest. The American ambassador to Liberia observed that "a handful of American-owned companies and about 1,000 Americans working in Liberia make more money in Liberia than all Liberians put together."[114] In September 1961, three months after delegates from Cameroon, Nigeria, Sierra Leone, and seventeen other African states had convened in Monrovia, a general strike erupted in the capital. It began at the recently opened Ducor Palace Hotel. Built on a hill above the city, the five-star, eight-story Ducor offered guests luxurious accommodations and the most spectacular views of the Atlantic Ocean in all of West Africa. Racial discrimination against Liberian employees by the hotel's Israeli investment firm prompted protests and walkouts across the city. Tubman blamed the strike, as he often did, on outside agitators and expelled the secretary of the Ghanaian Embassy and a diplomat from the United Arab Republic for government subversion.[115]

Two years later, in July 1963, the largest "no work" action in the country's history shut down Firestone's Harbel plantation. The protests arose when Firestone, having finally agreed to follow the country's minimum wage law and pay tappers 64¢ per day, also announced it would eliminate its rice and palm oil subsidies for workers. It amounted to a significant pay cut for workers. Some twenty thousand tappers on all forty-five divisions stopped work for almost two weeks. Key remembered being pregnant with her son when her husband joined others and "sat down." She feared the repercussions. Soldiers could come and "beat you," she recalled. Also, the Duside hospital closed. "No medicines, no nothing," she said. Firestone had, during the strike, shut down its medical services to Liberian employees. "God blessed me," Key said, thankful the strike had ended before she went into labor.[116]

Firestone also retaliated by suspending its latex purchases from independent rubber farms, numbering more than 2,300 by 1963. As economic pain radiated, the strike escalated. Tubman sent in negotiators and secu-

At a dinner party in New York City in 1961 hosted by Harvey Firestone Jr. for President Tubman, two years before Harvey Jr.'s retirement as CEO of Firestone Tire & Rubber Company. Front row, left to right: Harvey Firestone Jr., President Tubman, Raymond Firestone, and Roger Firestone. (Courtesy of Indiana University Libraries.)

rity forces, trained and supported by U.S. military personnel and funds. One tapper spoke of riding a bus to a strike gathering at the factory. As the bus passed through an entrance gate, soldiers threw in tear gas. Others told of trucks of armed soldiers arriving at the division camps and physically removing those who refused to work. You "can't be on the man's land, occupy his house, and then say you are not going to work," tappers were told.[117] Workers, many armed with sticks and iron bars and a few with shotguns, defended themselves in skirmishes with Liberian government forces. Shots were fired. A worker who was there alleged at least one person died.[118] Firestone agreed to restore its rice and palm oil price subsidies. In a year when Firestone, operating seventy-five plants in the United States and twenty-three countries, saw $60 million in profits and $1.4 billion in annual sales, and Harvey Sr.'s four surviving sons together held $250 million ($2 billion in 2020) worth of company stock, it was a small concession.[119]

In 1963, an era ended as the sixty-five-year old Harvey Firestone Jr. retired as chief executive officer of Firestone Tire & Rubber Company. He and his father had led the company for more than fifty years. That same year, W.E.B. Du Bois, ninety-five years old and a recently naturalized citizen of Ghana, died. He had stood with and against the Firestones in a devil's bargain between an African nation and an American corporation in the ascendant decades of American empire. Forty years before, William Castle looked upon Firestone's entry into Liberia as a strategic opportunity for the United States to gain a larger influence in West Africa. As Africa waxed as a Cold War battleground for the United States and the Soviet Union, Tubman's defense of free market capitalism and embrace of American military and technical assistance had proven Firestone's worth as America's first foothold in Africa, although the company's discriminatory practices would increasingly become a liability for the U.S. government. The plantations had been immensely beneficial to the Firestone empire. Lucrative agreements and clever accounting had ensured that during the years of Harvey Firestone Jr.'s leadership, roughly three of every four dollars made in Liberia found its way to the parent company in the United States.[120] The benefits accrued to Liberia are far less clear.

# Epilogue

Life in Monrovia was bustling in the 1970s. President Tubman's entice-
ment of foreign capital through concessions favorable to investors resulted in immense profits for American companies such as Firestone,
B.F. Goodrich, Republic Steel, and Bethlehem Steel. Foreign direct investments also benefited the capitalist class and petit bourgeoisie of Liberian
society: government bureaucrats, wealthy rubber farmers, real estate investors, entrepreneurs, professors, teachers, and technical experts, among
others.[1] Newfound wealth, American dollars, and an international tourist
trade made Monrovia a vibrant scene of hopping nightclubs, discotheques,
and restaurants, a destination melting pot of musical rhythms, civil rights
activists, and freedom fighters from across the African diaspora. Pan American Airways ran four flights a week between Monrovia, its principal African hub, and New York City. The Liberian capital became known throughout
West Africa as "little America." At The Maze, a small downtown club,
patrons could hear the extraordinary vocal stylings of Nina Simone; the
celebrated artist and activist moved to Liberia in 1974. America had been
her "prison," she told her audience. "Now I'm home," she averred, "now
I'm free."[2] At the E.J. Roye Auditorium, crowds thronged to hear the
Afropop, jazz, and world music sounds of Hugh Masekela and Miriam
Makeba. Partygoers at a private gathering of jet-setter elites might rub
shoulders with Black power advocate Stokely Carmichael (Kwame Ture),
Makeba's husband.[3]

President William Tubman died in office in 1971. As vice-president
William Tolbert assumed the Liberian presidency, he positioned himself as
more sympathetic than his predecessor to African liberation struggles. To
the consternation of the U.S. government, he also was friendly with socialist
states, including the Soviet Union. Believing in the Pan-African fight
against neocolonialism, Tolbert pushed for the renegotiation of concession

agreements as a way to open opportunities for Liberian workers and businesses.[4]

In 1974, efforts to revise Firestone agreements by Stephen Tolbert, the Liberian minister of finance and the president's brother, met with a hostile response from Akron. Raymond Firestone, the second youngest of the Firestone sons, had retired as CEO of the company the previous year, but remained chairman of the board. It would be the last of the Firestone family feuds with the Liberian government. Liberia's finance minister, furthering his brother's push for "Liberianization" of foreign industrial enclaves, pressed Firestone. Demands included affirmative action programs to train and promote Liberian staff, mandatory health and education benefits, preferential procurement of Liberian goods and services, and an obligation to buy independent farmers' rubber according to a specified formula, among others. Tolbert also sought to balance the fiscal lopsidedness of the 1926 agreement. In typical fashion, Firestone dismissed all of the finance minister's requests.[5] Stephen Tolbert was a savvy businessman, with sizable interests in a number of Liberian and Nigerian companies and an estimated wealth of $50 million. He could be as brusque with Firestone as the company was with him. In April 1975, Stephen Tolbert died in a plane crash off the coast of southeastern Liberia.[6] Rumors of foul play circulated, with the Nigerian press suggesting CIA involvement.[7] In May 1976, Firestone came back to the bargaining table and signed a new contract with terms much more favorable to Liberia than those in the 1926 agreement.

President Tolbert's administration, as illustrated by its demands of Firestone, made a concerted effort to break the neocolonial stranglehold on the country. But the Liberian brand of "humanistic capitalism" did little to stem the growing inequalities that divided Liberian society.[8] "Opulent and vulgar wealth existed in the midst of embarrassing ethnic poverty," observed Masekela.[9] A political awakening took hold among Liberian youth. Students from the University of Liberia and Cuttington University organized protests through groups like the Movement for Justice in Africa (MOJA) and the Progressive Alliance of Liberia (PAL). They marched, as described by H. Boima Fahnbulleh, "with the rest of progressive Africa to a dignified future—freed from exploitation, racism and imperialist domination!" Liberian youth denounced foreign capital's rubber, mining, and forestry enterprises. These youth "cast their lot with the poverty stricken masses" and against the "reckless exploitation and parasitism" of an oligarchy they regarded as beholden to foreign interests.[10]

Monrovia, the West African entrepôt, with its luxurious hotels, thriving port, and state-of-the art John F. Kennedy Memorial Hospital, stood as an icon of capitalism's achievements. But in the countryside, where the majority of Liberia's 1.5 million people lived, the wealth and benefits reaped from foreign concessions benefited few. Foreign extractive industries were often built upon the customary lands of Liberia's rural people, with little or no compensation. On April 14, 1979, a mass demonstration organized by the PAL brought thousands of people into Monrovia's streets to protest the Tolbert administration's proposed increase in the price of rice. The government explained that the price increase was necessary to incentivize local rice production. But many saw the move as benefiting a wealthy class of rice importers and large-scale growers, including the president, to the detriment of the nation's rural poor. Government security forces armed with bullets, tear gas, and batons fired into the crowd of unarmed youth. At least forty people were killed. Five hundred more were injured.[11]

The accumulating tinder of inequality, oppression, and resentment became incendiary. In 1980 it erupted in a bloody coup d'état that killed Tolbert. Samuel Kanyon Doe, the leader of the revolt, appointed himself military head of state. Of Krahn heritage, he was the first indigenous person to rule the country, ending the long reign of Liberia's settler elite. Doe, a former master sergeant in the Armed Forces of Liberia, in "A Message to the Nation," declared, "For too long did the masses of our people live in their own country, only to be treated like slaves on a plantation. . . . A handful of families who ruled our nation for 133 years built up their heaven on earth, while the masses of our people continued to live in a hell on earth." The revolutionary song by Nigerian musician Sonny Okosun, "Papa's Land," blasted over the airwaves.[12] It was a reminder of the role land and its contested meanings played in Liberia's history, wherein a weak settler state, eager to preserve its sovereignty and finance its development, granted huge concessions of land and labor to foreign companies even as racial capitalism and empire stacked the cards against its success.

By the dawn of the twenty-first century, war, not promise, would become the image of Liberia seared into the world's collective consciousness. The instability that marked Doe's reign as president left openings for further rebel attacks. Charles Taylor, a charismatic, American-educated Liberian of both indigenous and settler descent, led the major insurgent rebellion. Taylor had in 1985 mysteriously escaped from a prison in Massachusetts, where he was awaiting extradition on a charge of embezzlement within Doe's administration. He next surfaced in Libya. With arms and funds from Libyan dictator Muammar Gaddhafi, Taylor launched an all-out assault on Doe's government in 1989 from neighboring Côte d'Ivoire, where he trained his forces, the National Patriotic Front of Liberia. Unable to take Monrovia from Doe, Taylor instead ruled the country's interior from strongholds on the Firestone plantations and on the outskirts of Gbarnga, the end point of Liberia's rubber corridor.

Liberia descended further into brutal civil war. Taylor took hold of the country's rubber, mining, and timber concessions, to amass weapons and cash to support his growing rebel army. The Firestone plantations, Taylor acknowledged, were the "most significant" revenue source in funding the early days of his rebel insurgency. The plantations also served as a "command post and nerve center" for Taylor's 1992 assault on Monrovia. Public and private-use roads, built by Firestone to move labor from the interior and rubber to the port of Monrovia, became corridors of terror and violence.[13]

Firestone, turning a blind eye to the human rights abuses perpetrated by Taylor, continued to operate the plantations and signed a contract to pay income tax, Social Security pensions, and in-kind contributions of rice and equipment to Taylor's government. Because the start of the Liberian conflict coincided with the end of the Cold War, and the end of Liberia's strategic importance to America in its defense of the free world, the U.S. government refused to intervene in Liberia.

Liberia's natural resources, which had sustained American shareholder profits and fulfilled manufacturer demand, now furnished the cash for continuing war. Taylor was elected president of Liberia in 1997 during a brief peace accord. As president, he again looked to Liberia's natural resources—rubber, diamonds, and timber—to fund both the Liberian army and another he backed, the Revolutionary United Front, the main rebel group fighting in neighboring Sierra Leone's civil war. When a lasting peace came to Liberia in 2003, an estimated 23 percent of Liberia's forests had been harvested and sold to keep arms and cash flowing to Taylor's war machine. More than 250,000 people had lost their lives, more than 1 million people—roughly a third of Liberia's population—had been displaced, and approximately 700,000 refugees had fled the country.

Taylor's role in the Sierra Leonean civil war would be his undoing. He was indicted in 2003 by the Special Court for Sierra Leone for crimes against humanity. He was pressured to resign the Liberian presidency in

2003 and fled to Nigeria. Liberia was traumatized and in ruins. Global development aid had shrunk to $30 million annually, less than two-thirds of what it had been before the civil war. Life expectancy had dropped to forty-seven years. The country's entire infrastructure—roads, electricity, hospitals, schools, water, health care, and sanitation systems—had been destroyed.

From the ashes and blood of war, Liberia rose. In 2005, Ellen Johnson Sirleaf won the Liberian presidential election, becoming the first woman head of state in Africa. Needing capital to rebuild crumbled infrastructure and kick-start the economy, Sirleaf's government looked again for direct foreign investment in its natural resource sector.

Liberia has become a patchwork of foreign concessions for oil palm, timber, and iron ore. In Senii Town, a small village isolated within a vast checkerboard expanse of newly planted oil palm, a middle-aged man angrily recounted to me the loss of everything. The swamps where his grandmother fished, the land where women made farms to earn money to send children to school—all had been taken when his people lost their customary lands to Sime Darby, a Malaysian oil palm company that secured in 2009 a sixty-three-year lease for more than five hundred thousand acres of land from Liberia's government. Sime Darby in Liberia was not a new story, he told me. "We sit on old mats to plait new ones," he reminded those gathered around. This Liberian turn of phrase gestures to the interlaced layers of past and present, to the ways new ideas or situations are built upon old ones. One sits on an old mat woven of raffia palm to braid a new mat for the future. "Firestone is the old mat here," the man argues. "The way the old mat was badly plaited is the same way the new ones are being plaited today."[14]

The recurring narratives of land dispossession, agriculture concessions, foreign direct investment, and failed promises of development in Liberia intermingle and layer upon each other. Concession agreements accrue, one on top of another, like sitting on old mats to plait new. Look beneath what is visible in a concession agreement, and the whole layered history of Liberia's plantation economy is revealed.

The Firestone concession, only partially built on the remains of a previous concession, ignored and erased the claims of rural people to customary land, as the Liberian government made desperate efforts to pay debts and preserve Liberia's sovereignty. The Sime Darby Plantation, likewise, was fashioned from a layered history of new and old land grabs, racial capitalism, corporate greed, corruption, and civil war that shaped and continues to shape people's access—and lack thereof—to land and the wage sector of Liberia's plantation economy. The land granted to Sime Darby in 2009 included part of the 1954 concession granted to B.F. Goodrich. The American tire manufacturer sold the concession in 1987 to Guthrie, a British firm. Guthrie continued to work the plantation through the war years, with intermittent closures, until October 2001, when the company officially ended operations. In 2003, forces of the Liberians United for Reconciliation and Development (LURD), a rebel group opposed to Charles Taylor, seized the Guthrie plantation. The rebels set up their own management team and forcibly recruited experienced tappers to work the holding.[15] Profits from the sale of rubber to Firestone, agreements that were negotiated illegally with LURD rebels from 2003 to 2006, solidified the resistance group's hold over the old Guthrie plantation.[16] When peace came, few LURD members occupying the plantation agreed to the disarmament, demobilization, reintegration, and repatriation process. Considerable efforts were made by the United Nations Mission in Liberia and the Liberian National Police to evict the rebels. But almost two decades after the war, former rebels still on the old Guthrie plantation, leased by Sime Darby, were able to dictate who got jobs on the new oil palm concession. The employment preferences that benefited ex-LURD rebels emerged from the sedimented layers of land dispossession and violence that have cost the region's rural people—whose social and cultural ties to the land extend into the deep past—their own paths to self-determination.

On a May day at the start of the rainy season in 2018, when low-lying clouds bring daily moisture to newly planted crops, women gathered at the Capitol in Monrovia to protest the delay in passing the Land Rights Act. Their placards and banners spelled out the stakes of the land issue for rural women. "Women should have rights to own land individually and collectively," one read. "Women should have equal rights to land and equal participation in governance," read another. A third offered, "40,000 people signed for a pro-poor community land rights bill." Inside, at a hearing of the Senate Committee on Land and Natural Resources, a young woman stood to read a petition signed by more than seventy thousand people from all fifteen counties of Liberia and from other parts of the world, demanding passage of the Land Rights Act. First drafted in 2014, the bill had lingered in the legislature as the worst Ebola outbreak in history swept through Liberia and neighboring Guinea and Sierra Leone. After four years of delay and debate, the bill was passed in September 2018 and signed into law by Liberian president George Weah, inaugurated earlier that year. The Land Rights Act gives legal rights and protection to the majority of Liberia's citizens who live in rural areas and "own their lands collectively according to customary laws."[17] The law was a historic triumph for Liberia's rural peoples, who have for generations witnessed the seizure of their customary lands by the government for foreign concessions. If implemented successfully, with community consultation and informed consent, the law could go far in preventing further injustices and wrongs.

The protracted debate over the law's passage is indicative of the entrenched interests of Liberian elites who have profited from concessions for land and labor. A report issued by the Truth and Reconciliation Commission in 2008 identified inequality in land rights and land access as a major underlying factor that contributed to the country's 1989–2003 civil war.[18] A Governance Commission report that same year concluded that land insecurity in Liberia was a time bomb waiting to explode, and, if unresolved, threatened relapse into another civil war.[19]

As Liberia's plantation economy reshaped life in the region over the course of a century, rural women, as farmers, have endured, perhaps more than any others, the accompanying layers of dispossession and violence. Largely denied employment opportunities on rubber and oil palm plantations and access to customary land, through which they could acquire food security and economic independence, Liberian women have had the most to gain in advocating for land reforms that grant them equal access and rights to land. Unsurprisingly, they were among the most vocal and active of Liberia's citizens in pushing for passage of the Land Rights Act.[20]

Passing along Liberia's rubber corridor on a highway from Kakata to Gbarnga, destroyed during Liberia's civil conflicts and rebuilt by Chinese construction firms, I traveled in 2018 to a remote rural village on the Liberia–Guinea border. We rode upon the same route the Harvard expedition trekked in 1926. With me was Emmanuel Urey Yarkpawolo. When he was young, his family was displaced from Gomue, the village where we are headed, when Taylor's armed rebel soldiers seized the village and customary lands that had belonged to Emmanuel's family and kin for generations. Emmanuel and his family fled to a refugee camp in Guinea, where, hungry for education, the young boy learned to read and write. As a young man, Emmanuel envisioned a means to secure the future of his community, to which he and his kin had returned when peace was restored to the region. In time, this idea matured and was considered and agreed upon collectively by residents of Gomue and the neighboring villages of Kilingan, Malangan, and Bellelah, where more than one hundred children had no access to education. After earning a PhD from the University of Wisconsin–Madison, Emmanuel arrived in Gomue, a village of sixty or so residents, with me in 2018. More than four hundred people had gathered. All had come to celebrate the breaking of ground for a school in the village for area children.

I first traveled to Gomue in 2013, in the heat of Liberia's dry season. On that trip, as Emmanuel and I drove beyond Gbarnga, the pavement became dirt. For several hours, Emmanuel swerved around potholes that could swallow a tire and we drove over hand-built, log-and-plank bridges that required utmost skill to cross. Next, we walked on a footpath through swampland, across creeks, and up to higher ground, past recently hand-cleared secondary forest that awaited planting. After walking an hour, we reached the village, with banana and orange trees growing at its edges, and were enthusiastically greeted by Emmanuel's extended family. Goats and chickens roamed among the people gathering in the village center. A circle formed around Emmanuel's father, the eldest among the villagers, as we sat chatting and paying our respects to a man who, with a wooden stick and raffia mat, had many years ago helped build the government road we'd traveled. Soon, we were led down a path by a file of men in T-shirts and baseball caps, women wearing colorful *lappas*, and young girls and boys, some with a cutlass in hand, to see the village's oil palm nursery.

In this nursery lay the collective vision, hopes, and future of Gomue. Emmanuel had invested in the palm, a high-yield variety brought from Ghana, as insurance to protect the community's right to the land and to establish a smallholder farm. An investment in tree crops was a maturing investment that would support the community. Emmanuel's brother, who had worked for Firestone, had wanted to plant rubber. But rubber, Emmanuel had argued, only has cash value. In a community accustomed to an economy in which labor was traded and relations were forged, strengthened, and repaired through exchanges of items and gifts other than cash, rubber was of limited use. Oil palm had use beyond money in the local economy. One year after I visited the nursery, many men worked together to selectively clear by hand thirty acres of forest, leaving, as is traditionally done, wild palm and other trees, like the cotton tree, which hold special meaning and value. Women took palm seedlings from the nursery and planted them, intercropping with rice. That year's planting proved fortunate: the rice planted saw the community through the Ebola 2014 outbreak that would send the price of rice soaring and cause widespread food insecurity.

By 2018, as the community broke ground for its school, oil harvested from mature palm trees was supporting a labor exchange that helped build a road to Gomue from the main road. Future palm oil exchanges and revenues will also help support the school, which was built over the course of the next two years, largely with donated funds. A planned palm oil processing mill, it is hoped, will greatly increase production efficiency and further increase both exchange value and cash. Pineapple intercropped with palm provides both food for the community and excess crop to sell for cash. The community has begun the process that, if successful, will grant them, through the new land rights law, legal ownership of roughly one thousand acres of customary land. Walking through this land, you see not a palm oil plantation but a cornucopia of subsistence and cash crops, much like the informal and formal economies upon which life revolved in this rural area for many generations. Life in Gomue may not figure into Western valuations of economic success, but it is nevertheless rich with value and meaning.

Driving back to Monrovia along Liberia's still-active rubber corridor, everywhere are small plots with half-built cinder block homes; gardens with peppers, pineapples, or potato greens; or tree crops of planted palm, papaya, banana, and coconut. These patches of utilized land stand in contrast to the plantation.[21] The use of land, demonstrated by buildings or plantings, stands as a signpost of customary rights to land. Such use rights are intended to secure land tenure in contrast to and in defiance of definitions of private property imposed first by Liberia's early settlers, and afterward by the Liberian government, that granted concessions to foreign corporations in exchange for revenue. To what extent Liberian law will stand behind the cultivation of customary land rights remains to be seen. Regardless, the planting and nurturing of subsistence and cash crops, on whatever small plots of land can be claimed, will continue with or without the backing of the state. Of this, one can be sure. Land is life in Liberia. Access to it will not be, nor has it ever been, surrendered easily.

# Acknowledgments

In the course of this project, spanning more than a decade of research and writing, I have accumulated many debts. Numerous scholars, archivists, research assistants, students, government officials, NGO employees, elders, rural Liberian residents, and former Firestone workers have generously shared with me their time, knowledge, and views. They are too many to name here, but collectively, we have brought this book into being. My thanks to all of you.

I must give special thanks to some, though the list is incomplete. Kate Alfin, Michitake Aso, Paul Erickson, Megan Raby, Amrys Williams, and Anna Zeide greatly helped me with their research efforts in the formative stages of the project. Brian Hamilton's masterful sleuth skills helped flesh out characters and events once the book outline came into focus. In its final stages, the book benefited greatly from Ayodeji Adegbite's deeply informed understanding of West African history and sources, and from his critical eye.

I am extremely grateful for the financial support of a number of institutions that made research for this book possible. At the University of Wisconsin–Madison, the William F. Vilas Trust Estate has been a generous benefactor of my work. Grants from the National Science Foundation (SES-1331078) and the Carnegie Corporation of New York, which supported me as an Andrew Carnegie Fellow, assisted in the support of archival and field research in Liberia over a span of eight years. The statements made and views expressed are solely the responsibility of the author.

The Charles Warren Center for Studies in American History at Harvard University and the Rachel Carson Center for Environment and Society offered convivial intellectual environments in which to think, converse, and write at critical junctures in the book's development. At the RCC, Tom Griffiths, Arielle Helmick, Elizabeth Hennessy, Christof Mauch, Ursula Muenster, Azeez Olaniyan, Libby Robin, Helmuth Trischler, Monica

Vasile, Paula Ungar, and many others offered warm companionship and support. A fellowship at the National Humanities Center, made virtual by COVID-19, enabled me to put the finishing touches on the manuscript in a timely fashion.

Few institutions embrace and encourage the kind of interdisciplinarity and public scholarly engagement welcomed at the University of Wisconsin–Madison. I feel incredibly fortunate to be nourished and supported by colleagues in the African Studies Program, the Holtz Center for Science and Technology Studies, the Nelson Institute's Center for Culture, History, and Environment, the Department of Medical History and Bioethics, and the History Department and its graduate program in the history of science, technology, and medicine.

The intellectual shape of the book was transformed by a Sawyer Seminar, "Interrogating the Plantationocene," funded by the Andrew W. Mellon Foundation. To my co-organizers, Monique Allewaert, Pablo Gómez, and Sophie Sapp Moore, and to the many graduate students and visiting speakers who participated in the seminar, I am immensely grateful for the rich conversations and exchanges that greatly deepened my understanding of past and present plantation worlds. To my colleague Monica White, thank you for teaching me so much about community engagement, and Black farming as a practice of resistance and liberation.

My deepest debt is owed to the many people in Liberia who shared their stories, challenged my understandings, watched over me, and confronted my country's past. Stephen Kollison graciously accompanied me on my first trip to Liberia and opened doors to visit the Firestone plantations, on which he grew up. Rufus Karmorh arranged a tour of the plantations and accommodated me in searching traces of its material past. The Honorable Lewis Brown, former Liberian minister of information, culture and tourism, granted permission and access that proved invaluable on many occasions.

The cooperation and collaboration of Philomena Bloh Sayeh, former director-general of the Center for National Documents and Records Agency (CNDRA), and her passion for Liberian history have been inspiring. Out of that partnership—for which I am also indebted to Verlon Stone, who, along with Ruth Stone, has dedicated his life to preserving Liberia's past—an extensive project arose, supported by the Carnegie Corporation of New York, to help organize and process government archival documents. My sincere thanks to Charles Freeman, Mohammed

Nuah, Rita Pschorr, and Koifee Willie Johnson, along with John Sackie, John Yogei, Harwoart Payne, and other CNDRA staff, for the countless hours spent combing through dusty boxes and files as they brought order to the surviving papers of some of Liberia's past presidential administrations. To the Liberian students who took part in our oral history workshop and assisted with interviews, including Robert Cassell, Hawa Kanneh, Charles McCoy, Samuel McIntosh, Sylvester Paye, Emmanuel Sankan, Jammay Smith, and Houmou Sonnie, and to those who helped in its organization, including Bill Allen and Tim Nevin, your work, too, is in these pages. Randal Whitman came to understand the value of his father's photographs and films for the preservation of Liberia's past, and generously donated them to CNDRA and the Liberian Collections Project of Indiana University. They can be found at liberianhistory.org.

Dr. Cecil O. Brandy, former chairman of the Liberia Land Authority, taught me much about the history of Firestone and land rights in Liberia. Joseph Saye Guannu graciously consented to an interview for our film, *The Land Beneath Our Feet*; he saw in historical photographs things I would have never seen or understood on my own. To the late Flomo Barwolor and the other chiefs and elders, some of whom have also passed, I am indebted for the time and patience they took helping a foreigner to understand. To the people of Cotton Tree, Gbarnga, Queezahn, Senii Town, Suakoko, and many other Liberian towns and villages who shared their understanding of Liberia's past with our team, thank you. Without the commitment of Ali Kaba, Silas Siakor, the Sustainable Development Institute, and other NGOs in Liberia committed to land rights, the epilogue in this book would have a quite different ending. Robtel Neajai Pailey kindly critiqued the use of some terms in previous work and pushed me on sources that informed the book.

The incredible members of our core film crew—Alexander (Ush) Wiaplah, James Bayogar, and Sarita West—have been through much together. We forged bonds that continue to connect us across oceans. What a joy it has also been to be blessed by the friendship and voice of Miatta Fahnbulleh; I only hope I have done justice to the past she has known and shared with me.

In its final iterations, this book benefited immensely from the generosity of an amazing group of readers. My sincere thanks go out to Elwood Dunn, Ruth Wilson Gilmore, Cassandra Mark-Thiesen, Patricia Jabbeh Wesley, and Pablo Gómez for your kind and thoughtful comments on the entire manuscript. Neil Maher offered valuable advice during an early draft stage. Heather Swan helped me experiment with different approaches to writing. Rob Nixon encouraged me to trust my instincts regarding what needed saving in the final cut. Samer Alatout offered a friendly ear every time the writing got tough. Sarah Flynn offered editorial input, helping me get to the penultimate draft. To my editor, Marc Favreau, at The New Press, and to my agent, Lisa Adams, thank you for believing in this project, and for your guidance, encouragement, and much-needed editorial interventions along the way. Emily Albarillo at The New Press handled the final stages of production with remarkable care and attention.

My family has supported this project in so many ways over the years. What a gift it was to have my mother live with us in her last year of life. I still hear her words of encouragement each morning as I went to my writing: "May the juices flow." Few writers, I suspect, are as fortunate as I am to have not only a loving and encouraging partner, but a tireless reader and editor, who has little tolerance for fluffy prose. Thank you, Deb, for all you have given to support this journey.

Emmanuel Urey Yarkpawolo has been my guiding light through this project. Our meeting in 2012 transformed not only the direction of this project, but my life. It will take a lifetime to give back what I have received from Emmanuel and his family in America and Liberia; I hope this book is a beginning.

# Notes

## Manuscript Collections

| | |
|---|---|
| AJEP | Allen J. Ellender Papers, Archives & Special Collections, Nicholls State University, Thibodaux, LA |
| BFGR | B.F. Goodrich Company Records, RG 991132, 1870–1981, University Archival Services, University of Akron, Akron, OH |
| CABP | Claude A. Barnett Papers, 1918–1967, Chicago Historical Museum, Chicago, IL |
| CDBKP | Charles Dunbar Burgess King Papers, Center for National Documents and Records Agency, Monrovia, Liberia |
| CDF | Central Decimal Files (RG 59) General Records of the State Department, U.S. National Archives, Washington, DC |
| EPFP | Elizabeth Parke Firestone Papers, University Archival Services, University of Akron, Akron, OH |
| FA-SHC | Firestone Archives, Svend Holsoe Collection, Liberian Collections, Herman B. Wells Library, Indiana University, Bloomington, IN |
| FDRPSF | Franklin Delano Roosevelt, President's Secretary's File, 1933–1946, U.S. National Archives, Washington, DC |
| FRUS | Papers Relating to the Foreign Relations of the United States, Department of State, Office of the Historian, Washington, DC |
| GSP | George Schwab Papers, 2001.7, Peabody Museum Archives, Harvard University, Cambridge, MA |
| HJCP | Harold J. Coolidge Papers, HUG(FP) 78.45, Harvard University Archives, Cambridge, MA |
| LGA-II | Liberia Government Archives II, 1911–1968, Liberian Collections, Herman B. Wells Library, Indiana University, Bloomington, IN |
| LAWP | Lester A. Walton Papers, Schomburg Center for Research in Black Culture, New York Public Library, New York, NY |

LWD            Loring Whitman Diary, Courtesy of Randall Whitman,
               Liberian Collections, Herman B. Wells Library, Indiana
               University, Bloomington, IN
NAACP          History Vault: NAACP Papers, https://proquest.libguides.com
               /historyvault/NAACP
PEML           Papers Relating to Education and Missions in Liberia,
               1925–1929, Boston Athenaeum, Boston, MA
PGWP           Plenyono Gbe Wolo Papers, HUG 4879.405, Harvard University
               Archives, Cambridge, MA
ROAA           Records of the Office of African Affairs Subject File,
               1943–1955, RG59, U.S. National Archives, Washington, DC
RPSD           Richard Pearson Strong Diary, 1926–1927, in Richard Pearson
               Strong Papers, 1911–2004 (inclusive), 1911–1945 (bulk),
               GA 82, Harvard Medical Library, Francis A. Countway Library
               of Medicine, Boston, MA
RPSP           Richard Pearson Strong Papers, 1911–2004 (inclusive),
               1911–1945 (bulk), GA 82, Harvard Medical Library, Francis A.
               Countway Library of Medicine, Boston, MA
WCFP           William Cameron Forbes Papers, bMS AM 1364 (278),
               Houghton Library, Harvard University, Cambridge, MA
WEBDP          W.E.B. Du Bois Papers (MS 312), Special Collections and
               University Archives, University of Massachusetts Amherst
               Libraries, Amherst, MA
WEMC           William E. Manis Collection, African Studies Collection,
               Department of Special Collections and Area Studies, University
               of Florida, Gainesville, FL
WTP-CNDRA      William Tubman Papers, Center for National Documents and
               Records Agency, Monrovia, Liberia
WVSTP          William V.S. Tubman Papers, Liberian Collections, Herman B.
               Wells Library, Indiana University, Bloomington, IN

## Preface

1. Past films in Liberia our crew has produced include *The Land Beneath Our Feet*, directed by Sarita Siegel and Gregg Mitman (Warren, NJ: Passion River Films, 2016), and *In the Shadow of Ebola*, directed by Sarita Siegel and Gregg Mitman (New York: Films Media Group, 2015).

2. See, e.g., Robtel Neajai Pailey, "Slavery Ain't Dead, It's Manufactured in Liberia's Rubber," in *From the Slave Trade to "Free" Trade: How Trade Undermines Democracy and Justice in Africa*, ed. Patrick Burnett and Firoze Manji (Oxford: Pambazuka Press, 2007), 77–83; Save My Future Foundation, *The Heavy Load: A Demand for Funda-*

*mental Changes at the Bridgestone/Firestone Rubber Plantation in Liberia* (June 2008); Uwagbale Edward-Ekpu, "The World's Largest Rubber Company Is Blamed Again for Pollution in a Liberian River," *Quartz Africa*, February 25, 2020, qz.com/africa /1807681/bridgestone-tires-firestone-liberia-blamed-for-river-pollution.

3. Harvey Firestone Jr. to President William Tubman, August 5, 1946, WTP-CNDRA.

4. On imperial ruins, see Ann Laura Stoler, ed., *Imperial Debris: On Ruins and Ruination* (Durham, NC: Duke University Press, 2013).

5. I refer here to the classic text by James Fairhead & Melissa Leach, *Misreading the African Landscape: Society and Ecology in a Forest-Savanna Mosaic* (Cambridge: Cambridge University Press, 1996).

6. The figure varies between 25 and 60 percent or higher, depending on methods. The 50 percent figure is based on Chelsea Keyser, *Good Laws, Weak Implementation*, Police Brief #1, U.S. Agency for International Development (Nov. 2013), http://pdf .usaid.gov/pdf_docs/PA00M7RK.pdf, and Allard K. Lowenstein, *Governance of Agricultural Concessions in Liberia: Analysis and Discussion of Possible Reforms* (International Human Rights Clinic at Yale Law School, 2017), https://law.yale.edu/sites/default/files /area/center/schell/document/liberia_final_2017.pdf, as well as personal communication with Ali Kaba of the Sustainable Development Institute, Monrovia, Liberia.

7. GRAIN, "The Global Farmland Grab in 2016: How Big, How Bad?," June 14, 2016, www.grain.org/article/entries/5492-the-global-farmland-grab-in-2016-how-big -how-bad. On land grabbing as a longstanding process, see Sharlene Mollet, "The Power to Plunder: Rethinking Land Grabbing in Latin America," *Antipode* 48, no. 2 (2016): 412–32.

8. On the afterlife of the plantation, see, e.g., Katherine McKittrick, "Plantation Futures," *Small Axe* 17, no. 3 (2013): 1–15; Clyde Woods, *Development Arrested: The Blues and Plantation Power in the Mississippi Delta* (New York: Verso Books, 2017).

9. *Roe v. Bridgestone Corp.*, 492 F. Supp. 2d 988 (S.D. Ind. 2007).

# 1. "America Should Produce Its Own Rubber"

1. "Rubber Club of America Annual Meeting and Banquet," *India Rubber Review* (January 15, 1917), 17.

2. Quoted in John Tully, *The Devil's Milk: A Social History of Rubber* (New York: Monthly Review Press, 2011), 17.

3. Warren Dean, *Brazil and the Struggle for Rubber: A Study in Environmental History* (Cambridge: Cambridge University Press, 1987).

4. Susanna Hecht, *The Scramble for the Amazon and the "Lost Paradise" of Euclides da Cunha* (Chicago: University of Chicago Press, 2013); Richard P. Tucker, *Insatiable Appetite: The United States and the Ecological Degradation of the Tropical World* (Berkeley: University of California Press, 2000).

5. James Cooper Lawrence, *The World's Struggle with Rubber, 1905–1931* (New York: Harper & Bros., 1931), 12.

6. Joe Jackson, *The Thief at the End of the World: Rubber, Power, and the Seeds of Empire* (New York: Viking, 2008). On Hooker, see Jim Endersby, *Imperial Nature: Joseph Hooker and the Practices of Victorian Science* (Chicago: University of Chicago Press, 2008).

7. Greg Grandin, *Fordlandia: The Rise and Fall of Henry Ford's Forgotten Jungle City* (New York: Metropolitan Books, 2009), and Dean, *Brazil and the Struggle for Rubber.*

8. See Stuart McCook, *Coffee Is Not Forever: A Global History of the Coffee Leaf Rust* (Athens: Ohio University Press, 2019).

9. Charles S. Braddock, "The Future of Rubber in the Far East," *Scientific American* (December 10, 1910), 459.

10. Lawrence, *The World's Struggle with Rubber*, 16.

11. Austin Coates, *The Commerce in Rubber: The First 250 Years* (New York: Oxford University Press, 1987), 178–204. On Ross, see K.G. McIndoe, *The Rubber Tree in Liberia: A Story of the Introduction of Hevea brasiliensis to Liberia* (Dunedin, New Zealand: John McIndoe Limited, 1968).

12. "Rubber in Singapore," *New Orleans Times-Picayune* (September 16, 1917), 67. On Firestone savings, see "British Lead in Rubber," *Kansas City Star* (September 12, 1916), 3.

13. "Far East Attracts Capable Americans," *New Orleans Times-Picayune* (April 18, 1920), 68.

14. "Warning from Mr. Taft, Failure to Protect Americans Abroad Would Be Fatal to Enterprise," *New York Times* ( January 9, 1917), 3. In April 1916, Firestone had already inquired in Washington, DC, whether it was possible to get around the Philippine land laws. See Frank R. Chalk, "The United States and the International Struggle for Rubber, 1914–1941" (doctoral dissertation, University of Wisconsin–Madison, 1970), 18.

15. See Ann Laura Stoler, *Capitalism and Confrontation in Sumatra's Plantation Belt, 1870–1979* (New Haven, CT: Yale University Press, 1985).

16. Riley Froh, *Edgar B. Davis and Sequences in Business Capitalism: From Shoes to Rubber to Oil* (New York: Garland, 1993), 45. On the U.S. Rubber Company, see Shakila Yacob, "Model of Welfare Capitalism? The United States Rubber Company in Southeast Asia," *Enterprise and Society* 8, no. 1 (2007): 136–74. See also H. Stuart Hotchkiss, "Operations of an American Rubber Company in Sumatra and the Malay Peninsula," *Annals of the American Academy of Political and Social Science* 112, no. 1 (1924): 154–62.

17. Harvey S. Firestone, in collaboration with Samuel Crowther, *Men and Rubber: The Story of Business* (Garden City, NY: Doubleday, Page, & Cp., 1926), 14.

18. Firestone, *Men and Rubber*, 23.

19. Alfred Lief, *Harvey Firestone: Free Man of Enterprise* (New York: McGraw-Hill Book Co., 1951).

20. On the history of Chicago as the center of commodities markets, see William Cronon, *Nature's Metropolis: Chicago and the Great West* (New York: W.W. Norton, 1992).

21. Lief, *Harvey Firestone*, 58–62; Michael French, "Harvey Samuel Firestone," in *American National Biography*, ed. John A. Garraty and Mark C. Carnes (New York: Oxford University Press, 1999).

22. On the sights and smells of Akron, see Tully, *The Devil's Milk*, 134–47; Steve Love and David Giffels, *Wheels of Fortune: The Story of Rubber in Akron* (Akron, OH: University of Akron Press, 1999).

23. On Firestone's chair and desk, see James D. Newton, *Uncommon Friends: Life with Thomas Edison, Henry Ford, Harvey Firestone, Alexis Carrel, & Charles Lindbergh* (New York: Harcourt, 1987), 39.

24. Lief, *Harvey Firestone*; Firestone, *Men and Rubber*.

25. Lief, *Harvey Firestone*, 11.

26. Information gathered from U.S. Department of Labor, Bureau of Labor Statistics, *Industrial Poisons Used in the Rubber Industry*, Industrial Accidents and Hygiene Series, No. 7 (Washington, DC: Government Printing Office, 1915); Daniel Nelson, *American Rubber Workers & Organized Labor, 1900–1941* (Princeton, NJ: Princeton University Press, 2014); Love and Giffels, *Wheels of Fortune*.

27. On the history of the assembly line and Ford's place in it, see David Nye, *America's Assembly Line* (Cambridge, MA: MIT Press, 2013). For Model T production numbers, see Bruce W. McCalley, *Model T. Ford: The Car That Changed the World* (Iola, WI: Motorbooks International, 1994).

28. Nelson, *American Rubber Workers*; Lief, *Harvey Firestone*; Firestone, *Men and Rubber*.

29. Firestone, *Men and Rubber*, 137.

30. Lief, *Harvey Firestone*, 112–13.

31. Lief, *Harvey Firestone*, 219.

32. Firestone, *Men and Rubber*, 136.

33. U.S. Census Bureau, *Fourteenth Census of the United States Taken in the Year 1920, Volume 3: Population, Composition and Characteristics of the Population by States* (Washington: GPO, 1922), 784.

34. On Akron's changing demographics, see Nelson, *American Rubber Workers*, 50–55. On car registration, see Federal Highway Administration, Ohio Division, www.fhwa.dot.gov/ohim/summary95/mv200.pdf.

35. Harvey Firestone, "Shall Half the Potatoes Grown Be Lost?," *Fort Wayne Journal-Gazette*, March 2, 1919, Automobile Section, 4.

36. Tully, *The Devil's Milk*, 138.

37. Lief, *Harvey Firestone*, 196; Firestone, *Men and Rubber*, 245.

38. Nelson, *American Rubber Workers*, 23–43; Tully, *The Devil's Milk*, 149–58.

39. Lief, *Harvey Firestone*, 117.

40. Firestone, *Men and Rubber*, 138. On the rubber industry and welfare capitalism, see Nelson, *American Rubber Workers*, 56–61. On Firestone Park, see Love and Giffels, *Wheels of Fortune*, 52–53.

41. On racial exclusion in the Akron housing market, see Kevan Delany Frazier, "Model Industrial Subdivisions: Goodyear Heights and Firestone Park and the Town Planning Movement in Akron, Ohio, 1910–1920" (master's thesis, Kent State University, 1994).

42. Tully, *The Devil's Milk*, 145–46.

43. Joyce Shaw Peterson, "Black Automobile Workers in Detroit, 1910–1930, *Journal of Negro History* 64, no. 3 (1979): 177–90.

44. Nelson, *American Rubber Workers*, 54; Love and Giffels, *Wheels of Fortune*, 114–17. See, also, Stephen L. Harp, *A World History of Rubber: Empire, Industry, and the Everyday* (West Sussex, UK: John Wiley & Sons, 2016) for an excellent historical analysis of issues of race in the control of land and labor by rubber suppliers and manufacturers across the globe.

45. See collection of Harvey Firestone Jr.'s Asheville School yearbooks in EPFP, Box 49. There is also a family photograph documenting the place of Black servants in the Harbel Manor household in Box 52 of this collection.

46. Firestone, *Men and Rubber*, 137.

47. Firestone, *Men and Rubber*, 237.

48. Charles E. Sorensen, *My Forty Years with Ford*, with Samuel Williamson (Detroit: Wayne State University Press, 2006), 18. On the camping trips, see Paul Sutter, *Driven Wild: How the Fight Against Automobiles Launched the Modern Wilderness Movement* (Seattle: University of Washington Press, 2005).

49. On Harvey Jr.'s relationship with Edison and their camping trips, see "Harvey S. Firestone, Jr.," *Nation's Business* (August 1969): 54–59.

50. Mark R. Finlay, *Growing American Rubber: Strategic Plants and the Politics of National Security* (New Brunswick, NJ: Rutgers University Press, 2009), 75–76.

51. "War Aids Rubber Trade: Manufacturers Now Able to Get Larger Supplies," *New York Times* (April 20, 1917), 15.

52. Firestone, *Men and Rubber*, 234.

53. Harvey S. Firestone Jr., *The Romance and Drama of the Rubber Industry* (Akron, OH: Firestone Tire and Rubber Company, 1932), 72.

54. See Lief, *Harvey Firestone*, 155–63; Chalk, "The United States and the International Struggle for Rubber," 35–43.

55. Chalk, "The United States and the International Struggle for Rubber," 31–32.

56. Harvey Firestone Jr., "What About Rubber After the War?," in *Rubber Production and Importation Policy: Hearing Before U.S. Senate, Committee on Banking and Currency, Subcommittee on Rubber*, 80th Congress, March 11, 1947, p. 178.

57. "Firestone Tire Company Makes Good Showing," *The Pioche Record* (December 29, 1922), 1, 6.

58. Quoted in Lawrence, *The World's Struggle with Rubber*, 46.

59. David M. Figart, *The Plantation Rubber Industry in the Middle East*, Department of Commerce, Trade Promotion Series No. 2, Crude Rubber Survey (Washington, DC: Government Printing Office, 1925).

60. See Finlay, *Growing American Rubber*, 55–57; Chalk, "The United States and the International Struggle for Rubber," 44–57; Lawrence, *The World's Struggle with Rubber*, 45–51.

61. "Rubber Men Record Protest to Britain," *New York Times* (February 28, 1923), 9. See also Chalk, "The United States and the International Struggle for Rubber," 55–59.

62. "Firestone Says Rubber Assn. Refused Help," *Syracuse Herald* (May 27, 1923), 3rd sec., 6. Firestone's resignation letter is reproduced in Lawrence, *The World's Struggle with Rubber*, 120–21.

63. "Firestone Urges Rubber Growing," *San Antonio Express* (May 21, 1923), 1.

64. "Harvey Firestone, The American Motorists Should Acquaint Themselves with This Fact and Be as Loyal to Mr. Firestone as Mr. Firestone Has Been to Them," *Standard Sentinel*, August 2, 1923.

65. "An American Crude Rubber Industry," *Steubenville Herald Star*, January 31, 1923.

66. "Explorations for Rubber," *Science* 58 (August 10, 1923), 103.

67. Quoted in Chalk, "The United States and the International Struggle for Rubber," 65.

68. See Firestone testimony in *Crude Rubber, Coffee, etc., Hearings Before the Committee on Interstate and Foreign Commerce, House of Representatives on H.R. 59*, 69th Cong., 1st sess., January 6–22, 1926, p. 252; the rebellion they got caught up in is likely the De la Huerta rebellion. See Sarah Olston, *The Mexican Revolution's Wake: The Making of a Political System, 1920–1929* (Cambridge: University of Cambridge Press, 2018).

69. McIndoe, *The Rubber Tree in Liberia*, 18.

## 2. Reverse Passage

1. On the history of the Mount Barclay Plantation, see McIndoe, *The Rubber Tree in Liberia*; on the early history of the Liberia Rubber Corporation, see Sir Harry Johnston, *Liberia* (London: Hutchison & Co., 1906), 416–25.

2. Hood to Firestone, November 17, 1923, 882.6176 F51/218, 1910–1929, CDF.

3. W.E.B. Du Bois, "Liberia and Rubber," *The New Republic* (November 18, 1925), 326.

4. W.E.B. Du Bois, "Sensitive Liberia," *The Crisis* 28 (May 1924): 10–11.

5. See, e.g., Philip D. Curtin, *The Rise and Fall of the Plantation Complex: Essays in Atlantic History*, 2nd ed. (Cambridge: Cambridge University Press, 1998).

6. Nicholas A. Robins, *Mercury, Mining, and Empire: The Human and Ecological Cost of Silver Mining in the Andes* (Bloomington: Indiana University Press, 2011); Kris Lane, *Potosí: The Silver City That Changed the World* (Berkeley: University of California Press, 2019).

7. The role of plantation slavery in the rise of capitalism has been much debated in the historical profession. The foundation for such claims were laid by C.L.R. James in *The Black Jacobins: Toussaint L'Ouverture and the San Domingo Revolution*, 2nd ed. (1938; repr., New York: Vintage, 1989), and his student Eric Williams in *Capitalism & Slavery* (1944; repr., Chapel Hill: University of North Carolina Press, 1994). In Sidney W. Mintz, *Sweetness and Power: The Place of Sugar in Modern History* (New York: Penguin Books, 1985), Mintz built on this tradition and argued for the importance of the plantation as a model for the industrial factory. A recent resurgence of the argument appears in works such as Sven Beckert, *Empire of Cotton: A Global History* (New York: Vintage, 2015), and Walter Johnson, *River of Dark Dreams: Slavery and Empire in the Cotton Kingdom* (Cambridge, MA: Belknap Press of Harvard University Press, 2013). For an excellent review of this recent literature in the context of the arguments of this earlier Black radical tradition, see Peter James Hudson, "The Racist Dawn of Capitalism," *Boston Review*, March 14, 2016.

8. W.E.B. Du Bois, *The Souls of Black Folk*, 8th ed. (1903; repr., Chicago: A.C. McClurg & Co., 1909), 123, 162.

9. *Constitution of the Republic of Liberia* (1847), reprinted in George W. Brown, *The Economic History of Liberia* (Washington, DC: The Associated Publishers, Inc., 1941), 256. On the complexities of leaving a land of slavery for freedom and how American plantocracies shaped labor systems of production in Liberia, see Lisa A. Lindsay, *Atlantic Bonds: A Nineteenth-Century Odyssey from America to Africa* (Chapel Hill: University of North Carolina Press, 2017).

10. Daniel Webster, "Plymouth Oration," in *The Speeches of Daniel Webster and His Masterpieces*, ed. B.F. Tefft (Philadelphia: Porter & Coates, 1854), 59–111, on 89. On Webster and colonization, see Nicholas Guyatt, "'The Outskirts of Our Happiness': Race and the Lure of Colonization in the Early Republic," *Journal of American History* 95, no. 4 (2009): 986–1011.

11. See, e.g., Bronwen Everill, *Abolition and Empire in Sierra Leone and Liberia* (New York: Palgrave Macmillan, 2013); Tom W. Shick, *Behold the Promised Land: A History of Afro-American Settler Society in Nineteenth-Century Liberia* (Baltimore: Johns Hopkins University Press, 1977); Charles S. Johnson, *Bitter Canaan: The Story of the Negro Republic* (New Brunswick, NJ: Transactions, 1987).

12. For an insightful historiographic analysis of the "moral dialectics" at the core of different interpretations of Liberia's history, see Clarence E. Zamba Liberty, *Growth*

NOTES TO PAGES 35–37

*of the Liberian State: An Analysis of Its Historiography* (Northridge, CA: New World African Press, 2002). Zamba Liberty's key observation, that in the development of the Liberian state "emigrants had to play a dual-power game: maintaining its primacy while externally warding off European powers" (p. 34), greatly informs my own analysis. On settler colonialism, see Patrick Wolfe, "Settler Colonialism and the Elimination of the Native," *Journal of Genocide Research* 8, no. 4 (2006): 387–409.

13. For an excellent analysis of these ambiguities, see Brandon Mills, "Situating African Colonization Within the History of U.S. Expansion," in *New Directions in the Study of African American Recolonization*, ed. Beverly C. Tomek and Matthew J. Hetrick (Gainesville: University Press of Florida, 2017), 166–83, and Brandon Mills, *The World Colonization Made: The Racial Geography of Early American Empire* (Philadelphia: University of Pennsylvania Press, 2020).

14. On Liberia's pre-colonial history, see C. Patrick Burrowes, *Between the Kola Forest and the Salty Sea: A History of the Liberian People Before 1800* (Bomi County, Liberia: Know Your Self Press, 2016).

15. On Sao Boso, see James Fairhead, Tim Geysbeck, Svend E. Holsoe, and Melissa Leach, eds., *African-American Explorations in West Africa: Four Nineteenth-Century Diaries* (Bloomington: Indiana University Press, 2003), 285–87; Warren d'Azevedo, "Phantoms of the Hinterland: The 'Mandingo' Presence in Early Liberian Accounts, Part 1," *Liberian Studies Journal* 20, no. 1 (1994): 197–242.

16. On settler and indigenous conflicts in the early history of Liberia, see Svend E. Holsoe, "A Study of Relations Between Settlers and Indigenous Peoples in Western Liberia, 1821–1847, *African Historical Studies* 4, no. 2 (1971): 331–62. On the original land treaty, see Eric Burin, "The Cape Mesurado Contract: A Reconsideration," in *New Directions in the Study of African American Recolonization* (Gainesville: University Press of Florida, 2017), 229–48. See, also, E. Bacon, *Abstract of a Journal of E. Bacon to Africa: With an Appendix Containing Extracts from Proceedings of the Church Missionary Society in England, for the Years 1819–20 to Which It Printed and Abstract of the Journal of the Rev. J.B. Cates* (Philadelphia: S. Potter & Co., 1821), 14.

17. On the struggles free African Americans faced to obtain full citizenship rights in antebellum America, see Stephen Kantrowitz, *Fighting for Black Citizenship in a White Republic* (New York: Penguin Books, 2012); Martha Jones, *Birthright Citizens: A History of Race and Rights in Antebellum America* (Cambridge: Cambridge University Press, 2018).

18. Tom W. Shick, "A Quantitative Analysis of Liberian Colonization from 1820 to 1840, with Special Reference to Mortality," *Journal of African History* 12 (1971): 45–59. See also Svend E. Holsoe and Bernard L. Herman, *A Land and Life Remembered: Americo-Liberian Folk Architecture* (Athens: University of Georgia Press, 1988).

19. Eric Burin, *Slavery and the Peculiar Solution: A History of the American Colonization Society* (Gainesville: University Press of Florida, 2005).

20. Augustus Washington, "Thoughts on the American Colonization Society, 1851," in *Liberian Dreams: Back-to-Africa Narratives from the 1850s*, ed. Wilson Jeremiah Moses (University Park: Pennsylvania State University Press, 1998), 187, 185. On Washington, see Wilson Jeremiah Moses, "Biographical Sketch of Augustus Washington, in *Liberian Dreams*, 181–83; Shawn Michelle Smith, "Augustus Washington and the Civil Contract of Photography," in *At the Edge of Sight: Photography and the Unseen* (Durham, NC: Duke University Press, 2013), 165–92.

21. Washington, "Thoughts on the American Colonization Society, 1851," 192.

22. Washington, "Thoughts on the American Colonization Society," 187–88.

23. Augustus Washington, "Liberia as It Is, 1854," in *Liberian Dreams*, 204. On Liberia's merchant class, see Dwight N. Syfert, "The Liberian Coasting Trade, 1822–1900, *Journal of African History* 18 (1977): 217–35.

24. Washington, "Liberia as It Is, 1854," 204. For a historical account of nineteenth-century agriculture in Liberia, including the St. Paul River settlements, see William E. Allen, "Sugar and Coffee: A History of Settler Agriculture in Nineteenth-Century Liberia" (doctoral dissertation, Florida International University, 2002).

25. Augustus Washington, "Six Thousand Dollars Better, 1863," in *Liberian Dreams*, 223.

26. Edward W. Blyden, "Travels in Liberia, no. 2," *African Repository* 49 (December 1873): 374.

27. H.W. Johnson, "Letter from Liberia," *African Repository* 43 ( June 1867): 172.

28. Augustus Washington, "Letter from Augustus Washington from the *Colonization Herald*," in *Liberian Dreams*, 217.

29. On the importance of Liberia in the global coffee trade, see Stuart McCook, "Ephemeral Plantations: The Rise and Fall of Liberian Coffee, 1870–1900," in *Comparing Apples, Oranges, and Cotton: Environmental Histories of the Global Plantation*, ed. Frank Uekötter (Frankfurt: Campus Verlag, 2014), 85–112. See also Allen, "Sugar and Coffee," 124–60.

30. Washington, "Letter from Augustus Washington from the *Colonization Herald*," 220.

31. On the collapse of Liberian commodities, see Allen, "Sugar and Coffee," 180–201; Du Bois, "Liberia and Rubber"; McCook, "Ephemeral Plantations," 106–110; Syfert, "The Liberian Coasting Trade," 230–34.

32. See David Kilroy, "Extending the American Sphere to West Africa: Dollar Diplomacy in Liberia, 1908–1926" (doctoral dissertation, University of Iowa, 1995). Cassandra Mark-Thiesen and Moritz A. Mihatsch, "Liberia an(d) Empire? Sovereignty, 'Civilization' and Commerce in Nineteenth-Century West Africa," *Journal of Imperial and Commonwealth History* 47, no. 5 (2019): 884–911.

33. Washington to Roosevelt, September 19, 1907, in *The Booker T. Washington Papers*, vol. 9, *1906–1908*, ed. K. Harlan and R.W. Smock (Urbana: University of Illi-

nois Press, 1980), 337. On Washington's influence on Roosevelt's policies toward Liberia, see Louis R. Harlan, "Booker T. Washington and the White Man's Burden," *American Historical Review* 71, no. 2 (1966): 441–67; Kilroy, "Extending the American Sphere to West Africa," 13–49.

34. "The Liberian Envoys, 'Commissioners from Black Republic Cordially Received by President Roosevelt and Secretary Taft,'" *Washington Bee* (June 20, 1908), 4.

35. Report of the American Commission to the Republic of Liberia, "Affairs in Liberia," Senate Document no. 457, 61st Congress, 2nd Session (1910), 16, 25–26.

36. "The Republic of Liberia, *Washington Bee* (November 27, 1909), 1–2.

37. On Young, see Brian G. Shellum, *African American Officers in Liberia: A Pestiferous Rotation, 1910–1942* (Lincoln, NE: Potomac Books, 2018), 55–88. On Young's friendship with Du Bois, see David Levering Lewis, *W.E.B. Du Bois: A Biography* (New York: Henry Holt, 2009), 124–26; On the 1912 loan, see Kilroy, "Extending the American Sphere," 50–91; George Brown, *The Economic History of Liberia* (Washington, DC: The Associated Publishers, 1941), 167–70. On dollar diplomacy, see Emily S. Rosenberg, *Financial Missionaries to the World: The Politics and Culture of Dollar Diplomacy, 1900–1930* (Durham, NC: Duke University Press, 2004).

38. Quoted in Harlan, "Booker T. Washington and the White Man's Burden," 458.

39. See W.E.B. Du Bois, *Dusk of Dawn: An Essay Toward an Autobiography of a Race Concept* (1940; New York: Oxford University Press, 2007), 61–62.

40. On the impact of World War I on Liberia's economy, see Brown, *The Economic History of Liberia*, 171–74.

41. George Finch to Huntington Wilson, November 20, 1911, 882.51/273.5, 1910–1929, CDF.

42. Du Bois to Hughes, January 5, 1923, in *The Correspondence of W.E.B. Du Bois*, vol. 1, ed. Herbert Aptheker (Amherst: University of Massachusetts Pres, 1973), 160–61.

43. Lewis to President, October 4, 1923, in *The Correspondence of W.E.B. Du Bois*, vol. 1, 278–79.

44. For estimates on slave shipments from the Windward Coast, see C. Patrick Burrowes, *Between the Kola Forest and the Salty Sea*, 269–70.

45. Du Bois recollects his first impressions of Liberia in Du Bois, *Dusk of Dawn*, 59–67. See also Lewis, *W.E.B. Du Bois: A Biography*, 453–59; Hood to Secretary of State, January 17, 1924, 882.00/738, 1910–1929, CDF.

46. Du Bois, *Dusk of Dawn*, 60.

47. See Du Bois, *Dusk of Dawn*, 62–65; Hood to Secretary of State, January 17, 1924.

48. Du Bois to Secretary of State, March 24, 1924, pp. 4, 7, 882.00/737, 1910–1929, CDF.

49. W.E.B. Du Bois, "The Talented Tenth," in *The Negro Problem: A Series of Articles by Representative American Negroes of Today*, ed. Booker T. Washington (New York: James Pott and Co., 1903).

50. Edward W. Blyden, *Liberia's Offering* (New York: John A. Gray, 1862), 74. On Blyden, see Hollis R. Lynch, ed., *Selected Letters of Edward Wilmot Blyden* (Millwood, NY: KTO Press, 1978); Teshale Tibebu, *Edward Wilmot Blyden and the Racial Nationalist Imagination* (Rochester, NY: University of Rochester Press, 2012).

51. Blyden, *Liberia's Offering*, 69–70.

52. Edward W. Blyden to Sir Samuel Rowe, October 22, 1885, in *Selected Letters of Edward Wilmot Blyden*, 353.

53. Edward W. Blyden, *The Three Needs of Liberia* (London: C.M. Phillips, 1908), 35.

54. Blyden, *Three Needs of Liberia*, 2, 34, 14.

55. For an excellent analysis of the ways in which African American and Caribbean immigrants shaped differing Pan-African visions in Liberia, see Caree A. Banton, *More Auspicious Shores: Barbadian Migration to Liberia, Blackness, and the Making of an African Republic* (Cambridge: Cambridge University Press, 2020).

56. Hood to Du Bois, May 7, 1923, WEBDP.

57. Hood to Secretary of State, January 17, 1924, p. 27a.

58. Hood to Du Bois, May 7, 1923.

59. Hood to Du Bois, May 7, 1923.

60. Ronald Harpelle, "Cross Currents in the Western Caribbean: Marcus Garvey and the UNIA in Central America," *Caribbean Studies* 31 (2003): 35–73.

61. "Cheering Negroes Hail Black Nation," *New York Times*, August 3, 1920.

62. "Marcus Garvey (1887–1940): 'Explanation of the Objects of the Universal Negro Improvement Association,'" http://americanradioworks.publicradio.org/features /sayitplain/mgarvey.html.

63. On Elijah Johnson, see Johnson, *Bitter Canaan*, 47–50.

64. Garcia to Honorable President, June 8, 1920, *The Marcus Garvey and Universal Negro Improvement Association Papers*, vol. 2, ed. Robert A. Hill (Berkeley: University of California Press, 1983), 345–47.

65. *The Marcus Garvey and Universal Negro Improvement Association Papers*, vol. 2, ed. Robert A. Hill (Berkeley: University of California Press, 1983–2011), 667, 672.

66. *The Marcus Garvey and Universal Negro Improvement Association Papers*, vol. 2, 667, 672.

67. Open letter from C.D.B. King, *The Crisis*, 22 (June 1921): 53. On Du Bois and Garvey, see Lewis, *W.E.B. Du Bois: A Biography*, 416–34; M.B. Akpan, "Liberia and the Universal Negro Improvement Association: The Background of Garvey's Scheme for African Colonization," *Journal of African History* 14, no. 1 (1973): 105–27; Frank Chalk, "Du Bois and Garvey Confront Liberia: Two Incidents of the Coolidge Years," *Canadian Journal of African Studies* 1, no. 2 (1967): 135–42; Ibrahim Sundiata, *Brothers and Strangers: Black Zion, Black Slavery, 1914–1940* (Durham, NC: Duke University Press, 2003), 48–78.

68. *The Marcus Garvey and Universal Negro Improvement Association Papers*, vol. 9, ed. Robert A. Hill (Berkeley: University of California Press, 1983–2011), 76.

69. "Interview with the Acting President of Liberia . . . by the Commissions of the Universal Negro Improvement Association," March 22, 1921, 882.00/705, 1910–1929, CDF. Quoted in Tony Martin, *Race First: The Ideological and Organizational Struggles of Marcus Garvey and the United Negro Improvement Association* (Westport, CT: Greenwood Press, 1976), 124.

70. W.E.B. Du Bois, "Back to Africa," *Century Magazine* 105 (February 1923): 539.

71. Du Bois to Hughes, January 5, 1923, in *The Correspondence of W.E.B. Du Bois*, vol. 1, 160–61.

72. Marcus Garvey, "The Negro Is Dying Out," in *Selected Writings and Speeches of Marcus Garvey*, ed. Bob Blaisdell (Mineola, NY: Dover Publications, 2004), 182; "The Twelve Greatest Negroes," *Negro World* (August 26, 1922), 4.

73. *The Marcus Garvey and Universal Negro Improvement Association Papers*, vol. 10, ed. Robert A. Hill (Berkeley: University of California Press, 1983–2011), 246–55.

74. "Garvey Followers Barred by Liberia," *New York Times* (August 5, 1924), 21.

75. Elwood Dunn, ed., *The Annual Messages of the Presidents of Liberia, 1848–2010: State of the Nation Addresses to the National Legislature: From Joseph Jenkins Roberts to Ellen Johnson Sirleaf* (New York: De Gruyter, 2011), 664.

76. "Liberia: Black Messiah's Aim," *African World* (August 30, 1924), 198.

77. *The Marcus Garvey and Universal Negro Improvement Association Papers*, vol. 10, 256.

78. "Petition of Four Million Negroes of the United States of America to His Excellency The President of the United States," September 2, 1924, p. 4, 882.5511/10, 1910–1929, CDF.

79. McIndoe, *The Rubber Tree in Liberia*, 21.

80. De La Rue to Castle, March 25, 1924, 882.6176F51/74,1910–1929, CDF.

81. See Hood to Du Bois, November 16, 1925, WEBDP.

82. See Bussell to Castle, June 22, 1924, 882.6176F51/2, 1910–1929, CDF.

83. Dunn, ed., *The Annual Messages of the Presidents of Liberia, 1848–2010*, 667.

84. Copies of the initial agreements are available in Bussell to Castle, June 22, 1924.

85. Hood to Du Bois, November 16, 1925.

86. Du Bois to Firestone, October 16, 1925, in *The Correspondence of W.E.B. Du Bois*, vol. 1, 320–23.

87. W.E.B. Du Bois, "Liberia and Rubber," 329. A number of scholars have pointed to the initial blind spot in Du Bois's thinking regarding Liberia and Firestone, which wasn't apparent in his critique of economic imperialism elsewhere in Africa and around the globe. Cedric Robinson finds it rooted in a "class arrogance exhibited repeatedly by intellectuals of DuBois's class." Cedric Robinson, "DuBois and Black Sovereignty: The Case of Liberia," *Race & Class* 32, no. 2 (1990): 39–50. A similar view is expressed by Ibrahim Sundiata in *Brothers and Strangers*.

88. Castle to Harrison, July 1, 1924, p. 2, 882.6176F51/1, 1910–1929, CDF.

89. Petition to the Senate and House of Representatives of Liberia, 5, 882.5511/15, 1910–1929, CDF.

90. *Philosophy and Opinions of Marcus Garvey, or Africa for the Africans*, vol. 2, ed. Amy Jacques-Garvey (New York: Universal Publishing House, 1925), 397.

91. *The Marcus Garvey and Universal Negro Improvement Association Papers*, vol. 10, 229.

92. "Marcus Garvey and Liberia," p. 10, n.d., Box 9, Executive, Executive Mansion, Subject Files: Garveyism, n.d., LGA-II.

93. Du Bois to President C.D.B. King, July 29, 1924, WEBDP.

## 3. Missionaries of Capital

1. W.E. Burghardt Du Bois, *The World and Africa*, enlarged edition (1946; New York: International Publishers, 2015), 227–28. On racial capitalism, see Cedric Robinson, *Black Marxism: The Making of the Black Radical Tradition* (Chapel Hill: University of North Carolina Press, 2000); Walter Johnson et al., "Race, Capitalism, Justice," Forum 1, *Boston Review* (2017); Ruth Wilson Gilmore, "Abolition Geography and the Problem of Innocence," in *Futures of Black Radicalism*, ed. Gaye Theresa Johnson and Alex Lubin (New York: Verso Press, 2017).

2. "Capitalism requires inequality, racism enshrines it," writes the geographer Ruth Wilson Gilmore in "Abolition Geography and the Problem of Innocence," 240.

3. James C. Young, "An American Rubber Empire Rises in Africa," *New York Times* (December 9, 1926), XX3.

4. On Strong's career in the Philippines, see Warwick Anderson, *Colonial Pathologies: American Tropical Medicine, Race, and Hygiene in the Philippines* (Durham, NC: Duke University Press, 2006). On his involvement in the Manchurian plague epidemic, see Eli Chernin, "Richard Pearson Strong and the Manchurian Epidemic of Pneumonic Plague, 1910–1911," *Journal of the History of Medicine and Allied Sciences* 44 (1989): 296–319; William C. Summers, *The Great Manchurian Plague of 1910–1911: The Geopolitics of an Epidemic Disease* (New Haven, CT: Yale University Press, 2012).

5. On the Harvard expedition, see Gregg Mitman, "Forgotten Paths of Empire: Ecology, Disease, and Commerce in the Making of Liberia's Plantation Economy," *Environmental History* 22, no. 1 (2017): 1–22; Richard P. Strong, ed., *The African Republic of Liberia and the Belgian Congo, Based on the Observations Made and Materials Collected During the Harvard African Expedition, 1926–1927*, 2 vols. (Cambridge, MA: Harvard University Press, 1930).

6. Lady Dorothy Mills, *Through Liberia* (London: Duckworth, 1926), 30–31.

7. LWD, 8.

8. Harold Coolidge Diary, Harvard African Expedition, Vol. II, August 30th–October 14th, 1926–1927, pp. 168–70, Box 1. Diaries, Journals, Notebooks and Other Papers, ca. 1922–1965, HJCP.

9. Strong to Honorable Reed Paige Clark, November 7, 1926, RPSD, 151. See also LWD, 98–99.

10. LWD, 99; RPSD, 146.

11. Firestone to Castle, February 17, 1926, 882.6716F51/146, 1910–1929, CDF.

12. On the Firestone loan, see Frank Chalk, "The Anatomy of an Investment: Firestone's 1927 Loan to Liberia," *Canadian Journal of African Studies* 1 (1967): 12–32, and Kilroy, "Extending the American Sphere to West Africa."

13. Barclay to Minister, May 28, 1925, p. 5, 882.6716F51/43, 1910–1929, CDF.

14. Liberian Secretary of State to American Legation, April 18, 1925, in "A Report on the Relations Between the United States and Liberia," p. 679, 711.82/4½, 1910–1929, CDF.

15. Clifton R. Wharton, February 12, 1926, FRUS, 1926, Volume II, 522.

16. On De La Rue, see Emily Rosenberg, "Ordering Others: US Financial Advisers in the Early Twentieth Century," in *Haunted by Empire: Geographies of Intimacy in North American History*, ed. Ann Laura Stoler (Durham, NC: Duke University Press, 2006), 405–26. On United Fruit, see Jason Colby, *The Business of Empire: United Fruit, Race, and U.S. Expansion in Central America* (Ithaca, NY: Cornell University Press, 2011).

17. Rosenberg, *Financial Missionaries to the World*.

18. De La Rue to Castle, December 21, 1924, pp. 2–3, 882.6176F51/79, 1910–1929, CDF.

19. De La Rue to Castle, July 22, 1924, p. 6, 882.6176F51/11, 1910–1929, CDF.

20. Tredwell to Harrison, January 15, 1925, pp. 6, 1. 882.6176F51/73, 1910–1929, CDF.

21. Castle to Richardson, March 5, 1926, NA, RG 59, 882.6176F51/149, 1910–1929, CDF.

22. Memorandum of a Conversation with Mr. Hines, Secretary to Mr. Firestone, 13 November 1924, p. 2, 882.6176F51/13, 1910–1929, CDF.

23. "Statement of Harvey S. Firestone," January 15, 1926, in *Crude Rubber, Coffee, Etc.*, 254. Details of the loan negotiations are covered extensively in Kilroy, "Extending the American Sphere to West Africa"; Chalk, "The United States and the International Struggle for Rubber."

24. Harvey Firestone to Elmer Firestone, October 1, 1925, Folder 2 of 5, 1926–1940, FA-SHC.

25. "Americans to Found Vast Rubber Empire," *New York Times* (October 15, 1925), 1.

26. See, e.g., Memorandum, William Castle, December 14, 1926, 882.6176F51 /144, 1910–1929, CDF.

27. "Situation Already Causes Concern Abroad," *Firestone Non-Skid* (December 1925), 2.

28. Firestone to Castle, February 18, 1926, NA, RG59, 882.6176F51/147, 1910–1929, CDF.

29. Firestone to Ross, February 16, 1926, NA RG59, 882.6176F51/146; Harvey Firestone to Harvey Firestone Jr., February 16, 1926; Firestone to Firestone Jr., February 13, 1926, 882.6176F51/146, 1910–1929, CDF.

30. De La Rue to Hoffman, February 11, 1926, 882.6176F51/159, 1910–1929, CDF.

31. Harvey Firestone Jr. to Secretary of State, October 16, 1926, 882.6176F51/142, 1910–1929, CDF.

32. "Excerpts from the President's Annual Message delivered 20th October 1926 to the Liberian Legislature," 882.6176F51/142, 1910–1929, CDF.

33. See Chalk, "The United States and the International Struggle for Rubber," 135–38.

34. Harvey Firestone Jr. to Harvey S. Firestone, November 22, 1926, 882.6176F51/142, 1910–1929, CDF.

35. On Castle's interests, see Kilroy, "Extending the American Sphere to West Africa," 364–65.

36. RPSD, 147.

37. Castle to Strong, January 3, 1927, African Expedition—Correspondence, State Department & White House Folder, Box 2, RPSP.

38. RPSD, 146.

39. Secretary to the President to Secretary of Treasury, November 11, 1926, CDBKP.

40. C.L. Simpson, *The Memoirs of C.L. Simpson: The Symbol of Liberia* (London: Diplomatic Press & Publishing Co., 1961), 141.

41. Mills, *Through Liberia*, 28.

42. Wolo to Dickerson, January 9, 1927; Wolo to Dickerson, October 14, 1928, Folder 7, PGWP.

43. "Liberia's National Debt Paid. May the Lone Star Wave Forever . . ." *Liberia Express and Agricultural World* (July 1927), 4; "Firestone Plantation Dompany [sic]," *Liberia Express and Agricultural World* (November 1927), 7.

44. Young, "An American Rubber Empire Rises in Africa," XX3.

45. "Firestone's Project," *Chicago Defender* (January 1, 1927), A1.

46. "Morgan Debaters Lose to Union," *Pittsburgh Courier* (May 4, 1929), 5.

47. "Harvard Expedition off to Africa with Cure for Tropical Diseases," *Boston Traveler*, May 15, 1926, Box 64, RPSP.

48. RPSD, 4.

49. On the Bilibid investigation, see Eli Chernin, "Richard Pearson Strong and the Iatrogenic Plague Disaster in Bilibid Prison, Manila, 1906," *Review of Infectious Diseases* 11, no. 6 (1989): 996–1004; Kristine A. Campbell, "Knots in the Fabric: Richard Pearson Strong and the Bilibid Prison Vaccine Trials, 1905–1906," *Bulletin of the*

*History of Medicine* 68, no. 4 (1994): 600–638. On the place of American science and medicine in the colonization of the Philippines, see Anderson, *Colonial Pathologies*.

50. Paul A. Kramer, *The Blood of Government: Race, Empire, the United States, & the Philippines* (Chapel Hill: University of North Carolina Press, 2006), 309; Anderson, *Colonial Pathologies*; on Forbes's conception of "material development," see Michael Adas, *Dominance by Design: Technological Imperatives and America's Civilizing Mission* (Cambridge, MA: Belknap Press of Harvard University Press, 2006), especially 48–50. On the Philippine currency reforms, see Rosenberg, *Financial Missionaries to the World*; on leprosy eradication, see Michelle T. Moran, *Colonizing Leprosy: Imperialism and the Politics of Public Health in the United States* (Chapel Hill: University of North Carolina Press, 2007).

51. Ellsworth Huntington, *Civilization and Climate* (New Haven, CT: Yale University Press, 1915). On the history of the tropics in Western environmental imaginaries and the construction of ideas of racial difference, see Paul Sutter, "The Tropics: A Brief History of an Environmental Imaginary," in *Oxford Handbook of Environmental History*, edited by Andrew C. Isenberg (Oxford: Oxford University Press, 2014), 162–184.

52. On Strong's Latin America ties, see Marcos Cueto, "Tropical Medicine and Bacteriology in Boston and Peru: Studies of Carrión's Disease in the Early Twentieth Century," *Medical History* 40, no. 3 (1996): 344–64.

53. Thomas Barbour, "Institute for Research in Tropical America," 1, Barbour, Thomas Folder, Box 20, RPSP; Richard P. Strong, "The Modern Period of Tropical Medicine," *American Journal of Tropical Medicine* 17 (1937): 2.

54. The subject of dollar diplomacy and American empire was first taken up by William Appleman Williams and his students at the University of Wisconsin in the 1960s and 1970s. See, e.g., the classic study by William Appleman Williams, *The Tragedy of American Diplomacy*, rev. ed. (New York: Delta, 1962). Frank Chalk, a student of Williams, was the first to explore the history of American foreign relations in Liberia from this perspective. By Chalk, see "The Anatomy of an Investment," and "The United States and the International Struggle for Rubber." See also by Rosenberg: *Financial Missionaries to the World*, and *Spreading the American Dream: American Economic and Cultural Expansion, 1890–1945* (New York: Hill & Wang, 1982).

55. Lovejoy to Strong, February 20, 1925, Office Files: Series 2, Fe—Fo, Firestone Tire & Rubber Co., 1925–1929, RPSP. On the Firestone meeting, see Strong to Firestone, January 2, 1926, Office Files: Series 2, Fe—Fo, Firestone Tire & Rubber Co., 1925–1929, Box 43, RPSP.

56. Shattuck to Strong, June 4, 1926, Office Files: Persons, Colleagues, Staff Continued (Sandground—Shattuck, G.C.), Shattuck, Frederick, Box 23, RPSP.

57. Shattuck to Strong, August 26, 1926; Shattuck to Strong, March 14, 1927, Office Files: Persons, Colleagues, Staff Continued (Sandground—Shattuck, G.C.), Shattuck, Frederick Box 23, RPSP.

58. Young, "An American Rubber Empire Rises in Africa," XX3.

59. Graham Greene, *Journey without Maps* (New York: Penguin Classics, 2007), 42.

60. Young, "An American Rubber Empire Rises in Africa," XX3.

61. Quoted in Mark-Thiesen and Mihatsch, "Liberia an(d) Empire?," 890.

62. Blyden, *Three Needs of Liberia*, 14.

63. On the Berlin Conference, see Matthew Craven, "Between Law and History: The Berlin Conference of 1884–1885 and the Logic of Free Trade," *London Review of International Law* 3, no. 1 (2015): 31–59; Antony Anghie, *Imperialism, Sovereignty and the Making of International Law* (Cambridge: Cambridge University Press, 2007). On its importance in terms of Liberia's internal policies, see Mark-Thiesen and Mihatsch, "Liberia an(d) Empire?"

64. Caree Banton also points to divergent views of Pan-Africanism and Black nationalism among African American and Barbadian immigrants that may have also made Barclay more receptive toward inclusion of Liberia's indigenous population in the emerging nation-state. See Banton, *More Auspicious Shores*.

65. On the hut tax and pacification, see Augustine Konneh, "The Hut Tax in Liberia: The High Costs of Integration," *Journal of the GAH* 16 (1996): 41–60; Yekutiel Gershoni, *Black Colonialism: The Americo-Liberian Scramble for the Hinterland* (Boulder, CO: Westview Press, 1985). On the Frontier Force, see Harrison Oladunjoye Akingbade, "The Role of the Military in the History of Liberia, 1822–1977" (PhD dissertation, Howard University, 1977); Timothy D. Nevin, "The Uncontrollable Force: A Brief History of the Liberian Frontier Force, 1908–1944," *International Journal of African Historical Studies* 44, no. 2 (2011): 275–97. Mark-Thiesen and Mihatsch, "Liberia an(d) Empire?," offer an important argument on how the Berlin conference propelled the Liberian state to reformulate its interior policies.

66. Jo Sullivan, "The Kru Coast Revolt of 1915–1916," *Liberian Studies Journal* 14, no. 1 (1989): 59. See also Ibrahim B. Sundiata, *Black Scandal: America and the Liberian Labor Crisis, 1929–1936* (Philadelphia: Institute for the Study of Human Issues, 1980), 18–19.

67. Strong, *The African Republic of Liberia and the Belgian Congo*, vol. 1, 530.

68. On the history of the Bassa, see William Siegmann, *Ethnographic Survey of Southeastern Liberia* (Robertsport, Liberia: Tubman Center of African Culture, 1969); Burrowes, *Between the Kola Forest and the Salty Sea*.

69. Strong, *The African Republic of Liberia and the Belgian Congo*, vol. 1, 50.

70. RPSD, 160.

71. See the 1926 and 1935 Planting Agreements, which appear as appendices in George Brown, *The Economic History of Liberia* (Washington, DC: The Associated Publishers, 1941), 275.

72. *The Land Beneath Our Feet*, directed by Sarita Siegel and Gregg Mitman (Warren, NJ: Passion River Films, 2016).

73. Porter to Clerks and Overseers, December 30, 1929, Folder 4 of 5, 1926–1940, FA-SHC.

74. Interview with Will-ta D., February 1, 2018.

75. On ecological violence, see Kyle Powys Whyte, "Settler Colonialism, Ecology, and Environmental Injustice," *Environment and Society: Advances in Research* 9 (2018): 125–44.

76. LWD, 12.

77. Harvard African Expedition, 1926–1927 Diary, Vol. 1, June 9–August 30, 106, Box 1, Diaries, Journals, Notebooks and Other Papers, ca. 1922–1965, HJCP.

78. Firestone's public relations made numerous mentions of the medical work of the Harvard expedition as evidence of the "civilizing hand at work." See, for example, James C. Young, *Liberia Rediscovered* (Garden City, NY: Doubleday, Doran & Company, 1934), 57–64.

79. See, e.g., Fairhead, Geysbeek, Holsoe, and Leach, *African-American Explorations in West Africa*.

80. On the conquest of the interior, see Gershoni, *Black Colonialism*.

81. See Timothy D. Nevin, "In Search of the Historical Madam Suakoko: Liberia's Renowned Female Kpelle Chief," *Journal of West African History* 3, no. 2 (2017): 1–38.

82. President Charles D.B. King, "Annual Message from December 22, 1927," in Dunn, ed., *The Annual Messages of the Presidents of Liberia, 1848–2010*, 590.

83. LWD, 91.

84. Strong, *The African Republic of Liberia and the Belgian Congo*, vol. 1, 11.

85. Strong, *African Republic of Liberia*, 57.

86. Sean Foley, "Mount Hermon's African Students, 1898–1918," *Northfield Mount Hermon Journal for the Humanities* 1 (2013): 19–56.

87. See Wolo to Dickerson, June 11, 1919; June 25, 1919; July 29, 1919, Folder 2, PGWP.

88. Wolo to Moody, August 6, 1922; Ross to Dickerson, June 15, 1922; Stokes to Dickerson, May 27, 1922; Folder 4, PGWP.

89. Plenyono Gbe Wolo, "Dr. T.J. Jones' Report on African Education," Folder 1, PGWP.

90. On the school, see Wolo to Dickerson, May 25, 1923, Folder 4; Wolo to Dickerson, June 10, 1923; Wolo to Dickerson, July 6, 1923, Folder 5; PGWP. On Hampton and Tuskegee, see Wolo to Dickerson, April 7, 1915, Folder 2; Wolo to Dickerson, August 26, 1921, Folder 3; PGWP.

91. Wolo to Dickerson, June 30, 1924, Folder 5, PGWP.

92. Wolo to Dickerson, September 19, 1924; Wolo to Dickerson, October 24, 1926; Wolo to Walter, January 12, 1927, Folder 6; Wolo to Dickerson, May 16, 1921, Folder 3; PGWP.

93. Wolo to Dickerson, October 24, 1926; Wolo to Walter, January 12, 1927, Folder 6, PGWP.

94. Strong, *The African Republic of Liberia and the Belgian Congo*, 50.

95. Strong, *African Republic of Liberia*, 56.

96. Strong, *African Republic of Liberia*, 40, 46.

97. James Sibley to George Schwab, August 25, 1927, Box 1, Folder "Correspondence Relating to the Liberian Expedition," GSP.

98. On Schwab, see John Lardas Modern, "Introduction: Duty Now for the Future," *Journal of Nineteenth-Century Americanists* 3, no. 1 (2015): 165–73; David L. Browman and Stephen Williams, *Anthropology at Harvard: A Biographical History, 1790–1940* (Cambridge, MA: Peabody Museum Press, 2013), 357–58.

99. George Schwab, "Bo Zieko Fahtow," Folder "Bo Zieko Fahtow," 23, Box 1, GSP.

100. See, for example, Walter Johnson, *River of Dark Dreams: Slavery and Empire in the Cotton Kingdom* (Cambridge, MA: Belknap Press of Harvard University Press, 2013); Jennifer Morgan, *Laboring Women: Reproduction and Gender in New World Slavery* (Philadelphia: University of Pennsylvania Press, 2004); Caitlin Rosenthal, *Accounting for Slavery: Masters and Management* (Cambridge, MA: Harvard University Press, 2018).

101. Schwab, "Bo Zieko Fahtow," 41.

102. RPSD, 48; Strong, *African Republic of Liberia*, 64.

103. On Madam Suakoko, see Nevin, "In Search of the Historical Madam Suakoko."

104. Strong, *African Republic of Liberia*, 60.

105. Strong to Lowell, November 30, 1926, Office Files, Expeditions Continued, African Expedition—Clippings, Box 30, RPSP.

106. Strong to Lowell, November 30, 1926.

107. Strong to Castle, November 1926, RPSD, 159.

108. See Strong to Taft, January 11, 1928; Taft to Strong, February 3, 1928, Office Files: Congresses, A–Z, Expeditions, African Expeditions—Correspondence, Box 2, RPSP.

109. Strong to the President, February 21, 1928, African Expedition—Correspondence, State Department & White House Folder, Box 2, RPSP; Strong to Forbes, February 4, 1928, Folder 280, bMS Am1364, WCFP.

110. Castle to Strong, February 24, 1928, African Expedition—Correspondence, State Department & White House Folder, Box 2, RPSP.

111. Richard Strong, "Conditions in Liberia," *Boston Herald*, January 14, 1928.

112. LWD, 84.

113. Sundiata, *Brothers and Strangers*, 97–139.

## 4. An American Protectorate?

1. James Kilgallen, "Edison Observes Birthday," *Times Herald* (February 11, 1929), 1.

2. "Edisoniana," *Time*, February 25, 1929; L.C. Speers, "Prepared to Honor Hoover with Edison," *New York Times* (February 11, 1929), 8.

3. On the breaking of the Stevenson Act, see Chalk, "The United States and the International Struggle for Rubber," 162.

4. James Kilgallen, "Discusses Situation in Rubber," *Olean Evening Times* (February 26, 1929), 15.

5. "American Interests in Rubber Planting Projects Are Going into Many Corners of the World," *Rubber Age* (July 25, 1930), 416–20.

6. James Kilgallen, "Harvey S. Firestone Offers His Opinions on Business, Success," *Olean Evening Times* (February 25, 1929), 1.

7. Kilgallen, "Discusses Situation in Rubber," 15.

8. John Loomis to His Excellency, September 30, 1929, 882.51A/74, 1910–1929, CDF.

9. On the retrenchment, see William Francis to Secretary of State, December 27, 1928, 882.6176F51/270, 1910–1929, CDF. On the downturn in profits, see "Firestone Tire and Rubber," *Rubber Age* (December 25, 1929), 308–9.

10. Harvey Firestone Sr. to Harvey Firestone Jr., October 27, 1928, Folder 2, FA-SHC.

11. Francis to Secretary of State, December 27, 1928.

12. See Mariola Espinosa, *Epidemic Invasions: Yellow Fever and the Limits of Cuban Independence, 1878–1930* (Chicago: University of Chicago Press, 2009).

13. Sidney De La Rue to Henry Carter, June 24, 1927, 882.6176F51/238½, 1910–1929, CDF. On differential mortality rates, see George H. Ramsey, "Yellow Fever in Senegal with Special Reference to the 1926 and 1927 Epidemics," *American Journal of Epidemiology* 13, no. 1 (1931): 129–63.

14. Andrew Sellards to Dr. Strong, October 21, 1927, Folder 2, Sellards, A.W., Box 23, RPSP.

15. Francis to State Department, Extract of Dispatch No. 278 of April 17, 1929, from the American Legation at Monrovia, Liberia, in Clifton Wharton to Secretary of State, September 23, 1929, 882.124A/64, 1910–1929, CDF.

16. Francis to State Department, Extract of Dispatch No. 278 of April 17, 1929; John Loomis to Henry Carter, July 12, 1929, 882.124A/64; Justus Rice to Yellow Fever Commission, May 3, 1929, 882.124A/64, 1910–1929, CDF.

17. Richard Strong to Harvey Firestone Jr., February 7, 1929, Office Files: Series 2, Fe—Fo, Firestone Tire & Rubber Co., 1925–1929, RPSP. On Hindle's vaccine, see Edward Hindle, "A Yellow Fever Vaccine," *British Medical Journal* 1, no. 3518 (1928): 976–77.

18. See Corwin to Martin, April 10, 1929, Monrovia Radiogram, Office Files: Series 2, Fe—Fo; Firestone Tire & Rubber Co., 1925–1929, RPSP; Francis to State Department, Extract of Dispatch No. 278 of April 17, 1929; Rice to Yellow Fever Commission, May 3, 1929.

19. Memorandum of Telephone Conversation Between Mr. Marriner and Mr. Harvey Firestone Jr., June 29, 1929, 882.124A/48, 1910–1929, CDF.

20. Esme Howard to Henry Stimson, July 3, 1929, 882.124A/37, 1910–1929, CDF.

21. See Espinosa, *Epidemic Invasions*.

22. Clifton Wharton to Secretary of State, August 19, 1929, p. 5, 882.124A/56, 1910–1929, CDF.

23. On health metaphors that shaped the work of U.S. financial advisers, see Rosenberg, *Financial Missionaries to the World*.

24. See, e.g., Adell Patton, "Liberia and Containment Policy Against Colonial Take-Over: Public Health and Sanitation Reform," *Liberian Studies Journal* 30, no. 2 (2005): 40–65.

25. Porter to Ross, January 16, 1930, Folder 4, FA-SHC.

26. McIndoe, *The Rubber Tree in Liberia*, 24.

27. Reber Jr. to Secretary of State, February 3, 1931, 882.6176F51/298, 1910–1929, CDF.

28. Chalk, "The United States and the International Struggle for Rubber," 163–75.

29. "Firestone Tire and Rubber Earns $7,726,870 in Year," *Rubber Age* (December 25, 1929), 308–9; Lief, *Harvey Firestone*, 268–73; Newton, *Uncommon Friends*, 52–57.

30. On the introduction of *Pueraria*, see McIndoe, *The Rubber Tree in Liberia*, 27.

31. McIndoe, *The Rubber Tree in Liberia*, 38.

32. "Americans to Found Vast Rubber Empire," *New York Times* (October 15, 1925), 1, 4.

33. William Castle to William Francis, June 21, 1928, 882.5048/1, 1910–1929, CDF.

34. Castle to Francis, June 21, 1928.

35. Raymond Buell, "Liberia," August 29, 1928, p. 29, 882.5048/9, 1910–1929, CDF.

36. Raymond Leslie Buell, *The Native Problem in Africa*, vol. 2, 2nd ed. (1928; Hamden, CT: Archon Books, 1965), 831.

37. Buell, "Liberia," 32.

38. Strong to Castle, September 26, 1928, African Expedition—Correspondence, State Department & White House Folder, Box 2, RPSP.

39. President C.D.B. King to Secretary of State, August 30, 1928, 882.5048/7, 1910–1929, CDF.

40. Francis to Castle, March 7, 1929, p. 82.

41. Information about this incident gathered from William Francis to William Castle, March 7, 1929, 882.5048/19, 1910–1929, CDF; Johnson, *Bitter Canaan*, 179.

42. Adam Hochschild, *King Leopold's Ghost* (Boston: Houghton Mifflin, 1998).

43. For differing arguments about whether Firestone was the motivation behind the State Department's decision to confront the Liberian government on accusations of slavery and forced labor, see Ibrahim Sundiata, *Black Scandal*; Sundiata, *Brothers and Strangers*; and Arthur J. Knoll, "Firestone's Labor Policy, 1924–1939," *Liberian Stud-*

*ies Journal* 16, no. 2 (1991): 49–75. My own analysis agrees with Sundiata's definitive account of Liberia's forced labor crisis.

44. Buell, *The Native Problem in Africa*, vol. 2, 834.

45. Morris to Walker, December 4, 1925, 882.6176F51/140, 1910–1929, CDF.

46. De La Rue to Castle, December 10, 1925, 882.6176F51/136, 1910–1929, CDF.

47. Morris to Walker, December 4, 1925. On Walker's alleged power, reach, and number of wives, see Richard P. Strong Diary, 56–57, typescript, 1926–1927, RPSP.

48. Charles S. Johnson to Assistant Secretary of State, October 1, 1930, p. 17, 882.5048/349, 1910–1929, CDF.

49. Circular Number 7, June 17, 1927, Executive, Interior Department, General Records, Central Province, 1927–1941, n.d., Box 9, LGA-II.

50. Francis to Castle, March 22, 1929.

51. On Twe, see Johnson, *Bitter Canaan*, 166–67; E. Elwood Dunn, Amos J. Beyan, and Carl Patrick Burrowes, *Historical Dictionary of Liberia*, 2nd ed. (Lanham, MD: Scarecrow Press, 2001), 339–40. On Twe and Francis, see Francis to Castle, March 22, 1929.

52. Francis to Castle, March 22, 1929.

53. William Francis to His Excellency, June 8, 1929, Diplomatic No. 311, 882.5048/41, 1910–1929, CDF. On Francis's life, see Douglas R. Heindrich, "A Citizen of Fine Spirit," *William Mitchell Magazine* 18, no. 2 (2000): 2–6; Paul D. Nelson, "William T. Francis, at Home and Abroad," *Ramsey County History* 51, no. 4 (2017): 3–12.

54. "W.T. Francis Recovering in Liberia," *New York Times* (July 4, 1929), 15; "W.T. Francis Dies of Yellow Fever," *New York Times* (July 16, 1929), 18.

55. "Wm. T. Francis, Minister to Liberia, Taken by Death: Fever Claims W.T. Francis in Liberia," *Chicago Defender* (July 20, 1929), 1. See also "W.T. Francis Laid to Rest in Nashville," *Chicago Defender* (August 24, 1929), 3.

56. Strong to Castle, July 11, 1929, 882.124A/41, 1910–1929, CDF.

57. Castle to Strong, July 15, 1929, p. 3, 882.124A/41, 1910–1929, CDF. The most authoritative account of the Liberian labor scandal, the League of Nations investigation, and its impact in Liberia and the African diaspora can be found in Sundiata's *Black Scandal* and *Brothers and Strangers*.

58. See, e.g., Castle to Harvey Firestone Jr., November 9, 1929, 882.5048/114, 1910–1929, CDF.

59. Castle to Stimson, September 18, 1930, 882.00/820, 1910–1929, CDF. Quoted in Sundiata, *Brothers and Strangers*, 143.

60. Francis to Castle, May 17, 1929, 882.5048/36, 1910–1929, CDF.

61. Faulkner to His Excellency the President, July 6, 1925, CDBKP.

62. See, e.g., "Candidate for President in Liberia, Here," *Afro-American*, July 20, 1929. Charles S. Johnson wrote sympathetically about Faulkner in his *Bitter Canaan*, 161–63. See also Nnamdi Azikiwe, *Liberia in World Politics* (1934; Westport, CT: Negro University Press, 1970), 184–87; Simpson, *The Memoirs of C.L. Simpson*, 150–52.

63. Francis to Wilson, May 17, 1929, 882.5048/36, 1910–1929, CDF.

64. Stimson to AM Legation, June 5, 1929, 882.5048/20, 1910–1929, CDF. Francis confirms the cablegram from Stimson was received on June 7, 1929. See Francis to Secretary of State, June 14, 1929, 882.5048/41, 1910–1929, CDF. For the letter to Barclay, see Francis to Excellency, June 8, 1929, Diplomatic No. 311, 882.5048/41, 1910–1929, CDF.

65. Barclay to Minister, June 11, 1929, p. 2, 882.5048/41, 1910–1929, CDF.

66. Renee Colette Redman, "The League of Nations and the Right to Be Free from Enslavement: The First Human Right to Be Recognized as Customary International Law—Freedom: Beyond the United States," *Chicago-Kent Law Review* 70 (1994): 759–800.

67. Barclay to Minister, June 11, 1929, p. 2.

68. *Report of the International Commission of Enquiry into the Existence of Slavery and Forced Labour in the Republic of Liberia* (Monrovia, Liberia, August 1930), 6.

69. Henry L. Stimson to Mr. President, October 24, 1929, p. 3, 882.5048/105A; Castle to Carter, November 18, 1929, 1910–1929, CDF.

70. Scott to Mr. Secretary, November 5, 1929, 882.5048/123, 1910–1929, CDF.

71. Memorandum to Castle, November 18, 1929, 882.5048/130, 1910–1929, CDF.

72. Charles S. Johnson, "Famous Sociologist Asks, Answers Some Key Questions for Negroes," *Chicago Defender* (September 26, 1942), A32.

73. Richard Robbins, *Sidelines Activist: Charles S. Johnson and the Struggle for Civil Rights* (Jackson: University Press of Mississippi, 1996), 209. On Du Bois's critique, see also Marybeth Gasman, "W.E.B. DuBois and Charles S. Johnson: Differing Roles of Philanthropy in Higher Education," *History of Higher Education Quarterly* 42 (2002): 493–516; Lewis, *W.E.B. Du Bois: A Biography*, 471–72.

74. Charles S. Johnson to James P. Moffitt, December 30, 1929, 882.5048/204, 1910–1929, CDF.

75. Quoted in John Stanfield, "Introductory Essay," in Johnson, *Bitter Canaan*, xxvi.

76. Johnson to Assistant Secretary of State, October 1, 1930, p. 37, 882.5048/349, 1930–1939, CDF.

77. Johnson to Assistant Secretary of State, October 1, 1930, pp. 20–22.

78. Quoted in Phillip James Johnson, "Season in Hell: Charles S. Johnson and the 1930 Liberian Labor Crisis" (doctoral dissertation, Louisiana State University, 2004), 265.

79. *Report of the International Commission of Enquiry into the Existence of Slavery and Forced Labour.*

80. *Report of the International Commission of Enquiry*, 83–84.

81. *Report of the International Commission of Enquiry*, 84.

82. Simpson, *The Memoirs of C.L. Simpson*, 154.

83. Johnson, *Bitter Canaan*, 95.

84. Johnson, *Bitter Canaan*, 130.

85. Charles S. Johnson, "Myth Makers and Mobs," *Opportunity* 1 (April 1923): 3. For an excellent analysis of Johnson's scholarship on race relations, see Patrick J. Gilpin and Marybeth Gasman, *Charles S. Johnson: Leadership Beyond the Veil in the Age of Jim Crow* (Albany: State University of New York Press, 2003).

86. Quoted in Johnson, "Season in Hell," 248.

87. *Report of the International Commission of Enquiry*, 84–85.

88. Reber to the Secretary of State, September 11, 1930, 882.5048/300, FRUS, 1930, vol. 3, 350.

89. Reber to the Secretary of State, September 25, 1930, 882.5048/308, FRUS, 1930, vol. 3, 352. See also Reber to the Secretary of State, September 21, 1930, 882.00/844, FRUS, 1930, vol. 3, 351.

90. Memorandum of telephone conversation with Harvey Firestone Jr., May 26, 1931, 882.01/24, 1930–1939, CDF.

91. "King Must Quit: Liberia Aflame; Slavery Exposé Stirs Citizens," *Afro-American* (November 15, 1930), 1. See also Azikiwe, *Liberia in World Politics*, 201–6.

92. Reber Jr. to the Secretary of State, October 13, 1930, 882.00/850, FRUS, 1930, vol. 3, 361.

93. Quoted in Azikiwe, *Liberia in World Politics*, 199–200.

94. Secretary of State to the Chargé in Liberia (Reber), November 3, 1930, 882.5048/321, FRUS, 1930, vol. 3, 365.

95. The Department of State to the Liberian Consulate General at Baltimore, November 17, 1930, 882.5048/347, FRUS, 1930, vol. 3, 371.

96. Azikiwe, *Liberia in World Politics*, 206.

97. Memorandum of telephone conversation with Harvey Firestone Jr., May 26, 1931.

98. Simpson, *The Memoirs of C.L. Simpson*, 158.

99. Reber to Secretary of State, January 21, 1931, 882.01, Foreign Control/16, FRUS, 1931, vol. 2, 661.

100. Reber to Secretary of State, January 23, 1931, 882.01, Foreign Control/16, FRUS, 1931, vol. 2, 667.

101. Quoted in Azikiwe, *Liberia in World Politics*, 249.

102. Secretary of State to the Minister in Switzerland, February 21, 1931, FRUS, 1931, vol. 2, 671.

103. The Minister in Liberia (Mitchell) to the Acting Secretary of State, July 24, 1931, FRUS, 1931, vol. 2, 689–90.

104. Memorandum of the Government of Liberia on the Report of the Experts Appointed by the Council of the League of Nations, Annex I (a), in *Request for Assistance Submitted by the Liberian Government*, League of Nations, C469.M.238, 1932, VII, 58.

105. Report of the Experts Designated by the Committee of the Council, Annex I, in *Request for Assistance Submitted by the Liberian Government*, League of Nations, C469.M.238, 1932, VII, 14.

106. Report of the Experts Designated by the Committee of the Council, 14.

107. The Consul at Geneva (Gilbert) to the Secretary of State, February 6, 1932, 882.01 Foreign Control/207, FRUS, 1932, vol. 2, 700.

108. The Secretary of State to the Consul at Geneva (Gilbert), January 13, 1932, 882.01 Foreign Control/185a, FRUS, 1932, vol. 2, 687.

109. Radio Address by the Honorable Henry L. Stimson, Secretary of State, May 9, 1931 (Washington, DC: U.S. Government Printing Office, 1931), 7.

110. Memorandum by the Chief of the Division of Western European Affairs, 882.01 Foreign Control/187, FRUS, 1932, vol. 2, 690.

111. Draft of Detailed Plan of Assistance Prepared by the Experts, Annex II, in *Request for Assistance Submitted by the Liberian Government*, League of Nations, C469.M.238, 1932. VII, 62–67.

112. Harvey Firestone to Honorable Herbert Hoover, September 26, 1932, 882.6176 F51/356½; MacVeagh to Secretary of State, July 10, 1934, 882.6176 F51/411, 1930–1939, CDF.

113. Quoted in Chalk, "The United States and the International Struggle for Rubber," 194.

114. Memorandum: Liberia, November 23, 1933, 882.6176 F51/398½, 1930–1939, CDF. On the strategic play by Barclay in this act of the Liberian Legislature, see Simpson, *The Memoirs of C.L. Simpson*, 178–83.

115. Memorandum by the Chief of the Division of Western European Affairs (Moffat) of a Conversation Between the Secretary of State and Mr. Everett Sanders, January 26, 1933, FRUS, vol. 2, 886.

116. The Ambassador in Great Britain (Mellon) to the Secretary of State, January 25, 1933, 882.01 Foreign Control/476, FRUS, vol. 2, 884–85.

117. The Secretary of State to the Minister in Switzerland (Wilson) at Geneva, January 31, 1933, FRUS, vol. 2, 892.

118. Firestone to Honorable Herbert Hoover, February 10, 1933, 882.6176 F51/356½, 1930–1939, CDF.

119. Firestone to Secretary of State, February 9, 1933, 882.6176 F51/356½, 1930–1939, CDF.

120. Memorandum: Liberia, November 23, 1933, 882.6176 F51/398½, 1930–1939, CDF. See also "Conspiracy to Oust Barclay Heard in Court," *Afro-American* (April 9, 1932), 21.

## 5. Contested Development

1. Minutes of the Joint Meeting of the Advisory Committee on Education in Liberia and the Trustees of the Booker Washington Agricultural and Industrial Institute of Liberia, December 17, 1932, p. 2, 882.421/108, 1930–1939, CDF.

2. Minutes of the Joint Meeting of the Advisory Committee, 3–4.

3. Minutes of the Joint Meeting of the Advisory Committee, p. 3.

4. On the Phelps Stokes Fund, see Eric Yellin, "The (White) Search for (Black) Order: The Phelps-Stokes Fund's First Twenty Years, 1911–1931," *The Historian* 65, no. 2 (2002): 319–52; Sarah Dunitz, "Expanding Educational Empires: The USA, Great Britain, and British Africa, circa 1902–1944" (doctoral dissertation, Columbia University, 2017). On Anson Phelps and the founding of Liberia College, see Thomas W. Livingston, "The Exportation of American Higher Education to West Africa: Liberia College, 1850–1900," *Journal of Negro Education* 45, no. 3 (1976): 246–62.

5. W.E.B. Du Bois, "Negro Education," *The Crisis* (February 1919), 173, 177–78. On Du Bois and Jones, see Donald Johnson, "W.E.B. Du Bois, Thomas Jesse Jones, and the Struggle for Social Education, 1900–1930," *Journal of African American History* 85, no. 3 (2000): 71–95. See also Mark Ellis, *Race Harmony and Black Progress: Jack Woofter and the Interracial Cooperation Movement* (Bloomington: Indiana University Press, 2013), 38–61.

6. For an excellent analysis of how Jones's ideas matched with Firestone's needs in Liberia, see Donald Spivey, "The African Crusade for Black Industrial Schooling," *Journal of Negro History* 63, no. 1 (1978): 1–17.

7. Carter Woodson, "Whites Plan to Exterminate Tribes and Make Africa White Man's Country," *Afro-American* (April 11, 1931), 12.

8. Carter Woodson, "Thomas Jesse Jones," *Journal of Negro History* 35 (1950): 107. See also Pero Gaglo Dagbovie, *"Willing to Sacrifice": Carter G. Woodson, the Father of Black History, and the Carter G. Woodson Home* (Washington, DC: National Park Service, 2012).

9. Edward H. Berman, "Tuskegee-in-Africa," *Journal of Negro Education* 41, no. 2 (1972): 99–112; Donald Spivey, *The Politics of Miseducation: The Booker Washington Institute of Liberia, 1929–1984* (Lexington: University Press of Kentucky, 1986). On the exportation of Tuskegee to Africa, see Andrew Zimmerman, *Alabama in Africa: Booker T. Washington, the German Empire, and the Globalization of the New South* (Princeton, NJ: Princeton University Press, 2010).

10. Minutes of the Meeting of the Members of the Board of the Booker Washington Industrial and Agricultural Institute, November 10, 1928, 882.42/Washington, Booker/1, 1930–1939, CDF.

11. James Sibley to Anson Phelps Stokes, June 1, 1929, 882.32/Washington, Booker T./9, 1930–1939, CDF.

12. Address of W.T. Francis, U.S. Minister, Liberia, at the Founder's Day Exercise of the Booker Washington Industrial and Agricultural Institute, Kakatown, Liberia, March 17, 1929, 882.42/Washington, Booker/1, 1930–1939, CDF.

13. Sibley to Walkins, December 27, 1926, PEML.

14. Report of R.R. Taylor upon the Booker Washington and Agricultural and Industrial Institute at Kakata, Republic of Liberia, October 1929, 882.42/Washington, Booker/13, 1930–1939, CDF.

15. Harvey Firestone Jr., *The Romance and Drama of the Rubber Industry* (Akron, OH: Firestone Tire & Rubber Co., 1932), 110.

16. Booker Washington Agricultural & Industrial Institute of Liberia, Report of Principal Paul W. Rupel, Covering the Three Years of His Administration, September 1935 to September 1938, p. 7, 882.42/Washington, Booker/31,1930–1939, CDF. In 1938, there were 120 students enrolled, 2 of whom were girls. Of that number, only 11 were enrolled in the agriculture program.

17. Lester A. Walton, "Liberia's New Industrial Development," *Current History* 30 (April 1929): 108–14, on 109, 108, 113.

18. On Walton's life, see Susan Curtis, *Colored Memoires: A Biographer's Quest for the Elusive Lester A. Walton* (Columbia: University of Missouri Press, 2008).

19. On Moore, see Arthur Johnson and Ronald M. Johnson, "Away from Accommodation: Racial Editors and Protest Journalism, 1900–1910," *Journal of Negro History* 62, no. 4 (1977): 325–38.

20. Quoted in Sundiata, *Brothers and Strangers*, 207.

21. Lester A. Walton, "Lester Walton Affirms Its Title to a Capital 'N,'" *New York Times* (May 10, 1913), 10. See also Walton, "Appeal for the Negro: Lester A. Walton Asks the Dignity of a Capital for His Race," *New York Times* (April 26, 1913), 10.

22. Walton to Barnett, January 23, 1933, Folder 7, Box 187, CABP.

23. Walton to Barnett, February 15, 1933, Folder 7, Box 187, CABP.

24. Barnett to Walton, February 22, 1933, Folder 7, Box 187, CABP.

25. On their behind-the-scenes publicity efforts, see, e.g., Barnett to Walton, February 22, 1933; Walton to Barnett, March 2, 1933; Barnett to Walton, March 16, 1933; Barnett to Walton, May 9, 1933; Barnett to Walton, June 28, 1933; Folder 7, Box 187, CABP.

26. Walton to Barnett, March 14, 1933, Folder 7, Box 187, CABP. See also Barnett to Walton, March 16, 1933, Folder 7, Box 187, CABP.

27. For an excellent analysis of divided opinion across the African diaspora on the matter of the League investigation and accusations, see Sundiata, *Brothers and Strangers*; Rodney A. Ross, "Black Americans and Haiti, Liberia, the Virgin Islands, and Ethiopia" (doctoral dissertation, University of Chicago, 1975),

28. On Schuyler, see, e.g., Danzy Senna, "George Schuyler: An Afrofuturist Before His Time," *New York Review of Books Daily*, January 19, 2019. www.nybooks.com

/daily/2018/01/19/george-schuyler-an-afrofuturist-before-his-time/; Oscar R. Williams, *George S. Schuyler: Portrait of a Black Conservative* (Knoxville: University of Tennessee Press, 2007).

29. George Schuyler, "Views and Reviews," *Pittsburgh Courier* (February 3, 1934), 10.

30. William N. Jones, "Day by Day," *Baltimore Afro-American*, June 23, 1934.

31. George Schuyler, *Black and Conservative* (New Rochelle, NY: Arlington House, 1966), 110.

32. Schuyler, *Black and Conservative*, 160.

33. George Schuyler, "Views and Reviews," *Pittsburgh Courier* (January 20, 1934), 10.

34. See, e.g., Lester Walton, "America, Save Liberia!," *New York Age* (June 2, 1934), 6.

35. Chiefs to Hon. Secretary of the League of Nations, August 6, 1932, Folder Executive Mansion, Domestic Correspondence—Departmental Central Province, Gbanga District Commissioner, 1931–1943, Box 1, LGA-II. In Liberia, a *palava* is a traditional meeting where disputes are settled.

36. Barnett to Walton, February 22, 1933, Folder 7, Box 187, CABP.

37. W.E.B. Du Bois, *The Crisis* (October 1932), reprinted as "Du Bois Takes Pointed Issue with President," *Pittsburgh Courier* (October 29, 1932), A1.

38. Dorothy Detzer, *Appointment on the Hill* (New York: Henry Holt & Co., 1948), 130–31.

39. Quoted in Ross, "Black Americans and Haiti, Liberia, the Virgin Islands, and Ethiopia," 115.

40. Du Bois to Harvey S. Firestone, October 26, 1925, WEBDP.

41. W.E.B. Du Bois, "Liberia, the League, and the United States," *Foreign Affairs* 11, no. 4 (1933): 682–95, on 684.

42. W.E.B. Du Bois, "The African Roots of War," *The Atlantic* (May 1915): 707–14, on 713. See also Walter Rodney's classic work, *How Europe Underdeveloped Africa* (1972; repr., Baltimore: Black Classic Press, 2011).

43. "Winship Is Named Envoy to Liberia," *New York Times* (February 28, 1933), 10.

44. Detzer to White, June 8, 1933, WEBDP.

45. The Special Commissioner for Liberia (Winship) to the Secretary of State, May 12, 1933, FRUS, 1933, vol. 2, 912–13.

46. The Special Commissioner for Liberia (Winship) to the Acting Secretary of State, June 9, 1933, 882.01 Foreign Control/573, FRUS, 1933, vol. 2, 915. On Firestone's support of the pamphlet, see Ross, "Black Americans and Haiti, Liberia, the Virgin Islands, and Ethiopia," 132–34.

47. Henry L. West, *The Liberian Crisis* (Washington, DC: American Colonization Society, 1933), 13–14, 29, 22, 34.

48. The Special Commissioner for Liberia (Winship) to the Acting Secretary of State, 915.

49. White to Roosevelt, Telegram, June 7, 1933, WEBDP.

50. Du Bois, "Liberia, the League, and the United States," 695.

51. Louis Grimes to Walter White, June 23, 1933, NAACP Branch Files (Foreign), Liberia, July 1933 Folder, Papers of the NAACP, Part 11: Special Subject Files, 1912–1939, Series B: Harding, Warren G. through YWCA.

52. Du Bois, "Liberia, the League, and the United States," 682.

53. Statement of Du Bois at State Department on July 31, 1933, 1–2, NAACP Branch Files (Foreign), Liberia, August 1933 Folder, Part 11: Special Subject Files, 1912–1939, Series B: Harding, Warren G. through YWCA. For an excellent account of the NAACP/WILPF alliance in response to the Liberian crisis, see Sundiata, *Brothers and Strangers*, 173–79, and Ross, "Black Americans and Haiti, Liberia, the Virgin Islands, and Ethiopia," 115–97.

54. Statement of Du Bois at State Department on July 31, 1933, 5–6.

55. Du Bois to Detzer, August 28, 1933, WEBDP.

56. The Under Secretary of State (Phillips) to President Roosevelt, August 16, 1933, 882.01 Foreign Control/620a, FRUS, 1933, vol, 2, 924–25.

57. The Acting Secretary of State to the Chargé in Liberia (Werlich), August 22, 1933, 882.01 Foreign Control/625a, FRUS, 1933, vol. 2, 928.

58. Barnett to Roy, August 5, 1933, Folder 7, Box 187, CABP.

59. Walton to Barnett, July 31, 1933, Folder 7, Box 187, CABP.

60. Walton to Mr. President, September 24, 1933, Folder 2, Box 8, LAWP.

61. Roy to Barnett, September 9, 1933, Folder 7, Box 187, CABP.

62. Firestone to the Secretary of State, September 22, 1933, 882.01 Foreign Control/657, FRUS, 1933, vol. 2, 934–36.

63. Walton to Barnett, February 14, 1934, Folder 7, Box 187, CABP.

64. Christy Jo Snider, "The Influence of Transnational Peace Groups on U.S. Foreign Policy Decision-Makers During the 1930s: Incorporating NGSO into the UN," *Diplomatic History* 27, no. 3 (2003): 377–404; Sundiata, *Brothers and Strangers*, 173–84.

65. "Joint Resolution Authorizing the President of Liberia to Complete Negotiations in Connection with the League Plan of Assistance to Liberia," January 14, 1934, Folder 2, Box 8, LAWP.

66. Walton to Barnett, January 18, 1934, Folder 7, Box 187, CABP.

67. George Arthur Padmore, *The Memoirs of a Liberian Ambassador: George Arthur Padmore* (Lewiston, ME: Edwin Mellen Press, 1996), 42.

68. Walton to Barnett, May 7, 1934, Folder 7, Box 187, CABP.

69. Lester Walton, "America, Save Liberia!," *New York Age* (June 2, 1934), 6.

70. Du Bois to Walton, June 14, 1934, WEBDP.

71. See Chalk, "The United States and the Internal Struggle for Rubber," 209–11.

72. The Secretary of State to the Chargé in Liberia (MacVeagh), July 20, 1934, FRUS, 1934, vol. 2, 802–3.

73. Report by Mr. Harry A. McBride, Special Assistant to the Secretary of State, Upon Conditions in Liberia," October 3, 1934, 882.01 Foreign Control/915, FRUS, 1934, vol. 2, 806–15, on 812–13.

74. The President of Liberia (Barclay) to Mr. Harry A. McBride, Special Assistant to the Secretary of State, August 28, 1934, 882.01 Foreign Control/915, FRUS, 1934, vol. 2, 815–21.

75. John MacVeagh to Secretary of State, July 10, 1934, p. 2, 882.6176 F51/411, 1930–1939, CDF.

76. Quoted in Chalk, "The United States and the Internal Struggle for Rubber," 211.

77. March 23, 1935 Evening Conference, Folder 3, Box 1, FA-SHC.

78. For the final agreements, see "Agreement Between the Government of Liberia and the Finance Corporation of America, Signed, March 16, 1935," 882.6176F51/411$^5$/$_{11}$, 925–34; "Agreement Between the Government of Liberia and the Firestone Plantations Company, Signed March 20, 1935," 882.6176F51/411$^{10}$/$_{11}$, FRUS, 1935, vol. 1, 940–43.

79. The Secretary of State to the Chargé in Liberia (Hibbard), June 8, 1935, 882.01/48a: Telegram, FRUS, 1935, vol. 1, 949–50.

80. Walton to Barnett, June 20, 1935, Folder 7, Box 187, CABP.

81. See, e.g., "Indorsers of Lester A. Walton for Post of United States Minister to Liberia," Box 7, Folder 187, CABP.

82. Walton to Barnett, July 13, 1937, Folder 7, Box 187, CABP.

83. "Walton to Seek Conciliation of Liberian Groups," *New York Herald Tribune*, July 4, 1935.

84. Du Bois to Walton, July 9, 1935, WEBDP.

85. Walton to Barnett, January 20, 1936, Folder 7, Box 187, CABP.

86. Firestone Plantations Company, *Views in Liberia* (Chicago: Lakeside Press, R.R. Donnelley & Sons, 1937).

87. Walton to Barnett, March 3, 1936, Folder 7, Box 187, CABP.

88. Walton to Foster, November 21, 1937, Folder 10 "Correspondence, 1937," Box 8, LAWP.

89. Walton to Barnett, November 26, 1935, Folder 7, Box 187, CABP.

90. Amos Sawyer, *The Emergence of Autocracy in Liberia: Tragedy and Challenge* (San Francisco: Institute for Contemporary Studies, 1992) similarly points to Firestone's support of independent rubber farmers as an important factor in the concentration of wealth and political power among Liberian elites.

91. See Interoffice Memo from D.A. Ross to HSF Jr., May 11, 1933, Firestone Papers, Folder 4, Box 1, FA-SHC.

92. Twe to Faulkner, November 19, 1931, 882.6176F51/310, 1930–1939, CDF. See also Dr. F.W.M. Morais, "The Firestone Plantations and Their Meaning to the Aborigines of Liberia," *Voice of the People* (October 1931), 1, 4. On Twe, see Tuan Wreh,

*The Love of Liberty . . . The Rule of President William V.S. Tubman in Liberia, 1944–1971* (London: C. Hurst & Co., 1976), 48–57.

93. See Interoffice Memo from D.A. Ross to HSF Jr., May 11, 1933, Firestone Papers, Folder 4, Box 1, FA-SHC.

94. Edwin James Barclay, "Second Inaugural, January 6, 1936," in *The Inaugural Addresses of the Presidents of Liberia: From Joseph Jenkins Roberts to William Richard Tolbert, Jr., 1848 to 1976*, comp. and ed. Joseph Saye Guannu (Hicksville, NY: Exposition Press, 1980), 300–304.

95. Minutes of November 10, 1937 Conference Incl Barclay, Cooper, HSFJr, Folder 4, Box 1, FA-SHC.

96. Padmore, *The Memoirs of a Liberian Ambassador*, 26–27.

97. See "Excerpts of Memorandum of Meeting w. Pres. Barclay, Feb. 20, 1936," Folder 3, Box 1, FA-SHC.

98. "Firestone Development in Liberia," 882.6176 F51/439, April 28, 1937, 1930–1939, CDF.

99. See "Harbel Bridge Officially Opened," July 12, 1937, 882.6176 F51/441; Walton to Secretary of State, "Firestone Makes Marked Progress in Liberia," January 5, 1938, 882.6176 F51/450, 1930–1939, CDF.

100. McIndoe, *The Rubber Tree in Liberia*, 59–60.

101. "Republic of Liberia, Export Data, 9-26-40," Folder 2, Box 1, FA-SHC; "Liberia Balances Budget, Envoy Reports on Return, *New York Herald Tribune*, February 10, 1938.

102. Walton to Du Bois, April 12, 1937; Du Bois to Walton, May 28, 1937, WEBDP.

103. Brown, *The Economic History of Liberia*, 205.

104. Brown, *The Economic History of Liberia*, vii–viii.

105. Interview with Loma Flowers, October 28, 2017; George Brown, "Biographical Essay," April 20, 1965, courtesy of Loma Flowers.

106. For an excellent account of the milieu in which Brown was immersed in London, see Marc Matera, *Black London: The Imperial Metropolis and Decolonization in the Twentieth Century* (Berkeley: University of California Press, 2015). See also Robinson, *Black Marxism;* Minkah Makalani, *In the Cause of Free: Radical Black Internationalism from Harlem to London, 1917–1939* (Chapel Hill: University of North Carolina Press, 2011).

107. Quoted in Matera, *Black London*, 250.

108. Azikiwe, *Liberia in World Politics*, 396.

109. Brown, *An Economic History of Liberia*, 76.

110. Brown, *An Economic History of Liberia*, 69–106.

111. Brown, *An Economic History of Liberia*, 102–3.

112. Brown, *An Economic History of Liberia*, 103, 106, 216.

113. Brown, *An Economic History of Liberia*, 218–19.

114. Brown, *An Economic History of Liberia*, 231. For reference to the original title of his book, see "Historians to Discuss the Negro in the International Situation," *New York Age*, August 24, 1940, 10.

115. Brown, *The Economic History of Liberia*, 227, 207.

116. Brown, *The Economic History of Liberia*, 231.

## 6. Plantation Lives

1. "Cruiser Boise Visits Monrovia," *Weekly Mirror* (November 4, 1938), 1.

2. Villard to Secretary of State, November 6, 1938, pp. 6–7, 811.3382/54, 1930–1939, CDF.

3. Walton to Murray, January 25, 1941, Folder 16, Correspondence, 1939–1943, Box 8; Hon. Lester A. Walton, United States Minister to Liberia, *Remarks on the Occasion of the Formal Opening of the American Legation Building*, March 31, 1941, Folder 11, Box 13, LAWP.

4. "U.S., Liberia Sign Friendship Treaty," *New York Amsterdam News*, September 10, 1938.

5. Villard to Secretary of State, November 6, 1938, pp. 3–4.

6. "Harvey Firestone Dies in Florida," *Evening Star* (February 7, 1938), 3. See also "Harvey Firestone Is Dead in Florida," *New York Times* (February 8, 1938), 21.

7. Harvey Firestone Jr., "The American Way," *India Rubber World* 103 (November 1, 1940): 31–32.

8. Figures are from "Crude Rubber," Rubber Manufacturers Association, Inc., May 10, 1943, p. 3, Folder Crude Rubber, 1943, Box 90 (JF-1), BFGR.

9. On the history of the U.S. effort to secure rubber supplies during World War II, see Mark R. Finlay, *Growing American Rubber: Strategic Plants and the Politics of National Security* (New Brunswick, NJ: Rutgers University Press, 2009); Paul Wendt, "The Control of Rubber in World War II," *Southern Economic Journal* 13, no. 3 (1947): 203–27. For industry accounts, see Harvey Firestone Jr., "What About Rubber After the War?," *Saturday Evening Post* (March 4, 1944), 12–13, 60, 63, 65; Otto Scott, Bill Mulligan, Joseph Del Gatto, and Ken Allison, "The Division of Rubber Chemistry: Catalyst of an Industry, Part III," *Rubber World* (December 1966), 83–96.

10. "Firestone's Total Sales Reach New High Record," *Rubber Age* (January 1941), 264. The estimated number of trees is drawn from acreage figures, with 110–125 trees per acre serving as the optimal planting standard.

11. Walton to Hull, May 22, 1941, Folder 16, Correspondence, 1939–1943, Box 8, LAWP.

12. See Joint Strategical Planning Committee to Joint Planning Committee, May 7, 1941, Safe File: West Africa, Series: Safe Files, 1933–1945, FDRPSF.

13. Guy Richards, "U.S. to Establish Bases in Liberia to Block Nazi Menace in Africa," *Daily News*, September 13, 1941.

14. Scott et al., "The Division of Rubber Chemistry," 90.

15. Figures are from "Africa," *India Rubber World*, April 1944, 103–4.

16. Firestone Jr., "What About Rubber After the War?," 63.

17. American Chemical Society, *United States Synthetic Rubber Program, 1939–1949* (Washington, DC: ACS Office of Communication, 1998).

18. The film, "Liberia—Africa's Only Republic," was directed by Charles Morrow Wilson, who at the same time would also publish *Liberia* (New York: William Sloane Associates, 1947), which reads like an advertisement for Firestone in Liberia. For publicity on the film, see "Firestone Liberian Film Preview," *India Rubber World* (January 1948), 520. Parts of the film are available at www.youtube.com/watch?v =H1sMNvzDEV0".

19. W.E.B. Du Bois, "The Wind of Time: Lester Walton's Resignation," *Chicago Defender* (August 4, 1945), 13. The number of Liberian workers fluctuated in the 1940s and 1950s from 25,000 to 30,000; white managers fluctuated from 125 to 175. For figures, see Wilson, *Liberia*, 133–34; Wayne Chatfield Taylor, *The Firestone Operations in Liberia* (Washington, DC: National Planning Association, 1956), 65; Robert M. Clower, George Dalton, Mitchell Harwitz, and A.A. Walters, *Growth Without Development: An Economic Survey of Liberia* (Evanston, IL: Northwestern University Press, 1966).

20. Gene Manis to Mother and Beth, January 1940, pp. 16–18, WEMC.

21. For an early, powerful critique by Liberian scholars on the Firestone plantations and foreign concessions, more generally, as enclaves in Liberia, see Dew Tuan-Wleh Mayson and Amos Sawyer, "Capitalism and the Struggle of the Working Class in Liberia," *Review of Black Political Economy*, 1979, 140–58. For more recent theoretical discussions of the enclave and foreign concessions, see, e.g., Ann Laura Stoler, *Carnal Knowledge and Imperial Power: Race and the Intimate in Colonial Rule* (Berkeley: University of California Press, 2010); Hannah Appel, *The Licit Life of Capitalism: US Oil in Equatorial Guinea* (Durham, NC: Duke University Press, 2019).

22. Employment Contract, November 20, 1939, WEMC. On the average American income, see Diane Petro, "Brother, Can You Spare a Dime? The 1940s Census: Employment and Income," *Prologue Magazine* 44, no. 1 (2012), www.archives.gov /publications/prologue/2012/spring/1940.html.

23. Manis to Mother and Beth, January 1940, 20. Descriptions of the Firestone bungalows are compiled from Manis's letter; Taylor, *The Firestone Operations in Liberia*, 81–82; and my own visits to these homes in Liberia.

24. William I. Vass, "Special Pamphlet #1, Plantation, Rubber: General Information, New Development, Maintenance Work," Firestone Plantations Company, 1956, Box 1, FA-SHC.

25. Manis to Mother and Beth, January 1940, p. 21.

26. See., e.g., *Planter's Punch*, January–February 1946, v. 7, no. 1, Folder 2, Correspondence, 1945–1946, Box 13, LWP; *Planter's Punch*, March 1 and 15, 1941, and

"Minstrel Show" program: "Firestone Overseas Club Presents the Greater Minstrel Shows, 9:30 p.m., Sept. 27, 1941. Clubhouse," WEMC.

27. Kenneth McIndoe, *Planter's Punch*, January–February 1946, v. 7, no. 1, p. 9, Folder 2, Correspondence, 1945–1946, Box 13, LAWP.

28. Walton's archive contains evidence of invitations to events on the plantations. See, e.g., H.W. Hirlman to Walton, July 29, 1938, Folder: Correspondence, July 1938, Box 9; "Program: Inspection and Entertainment for Legislature and Invited Guests, Firestone Plantations, Saturday, December 7, 1940," Folder 4: News clippings re Liberia, 1938–1945, Box 15, LAWP.

29. See, e.g., Taylor, *The Firestone Operations in Liberia*, 82.

30. "Preliminary Survey of Liberia, November 1953," Box D3-3. Not catalogued. Folder Liberia 1953–1955, BFGR.

31. Elza Schallert, "West Africa Patterns Inspire Work of Woman Ceramist," *Los Angeles Times* (February 26, 1955), 10.

32. Esther Warner, *New Song in a Strange Land* (Boston: Houghton Mifflin Co., 1948), 20.

33. Esther Warner, *Seven Days to Lomaland* (Boston: Houghton Mifflin, 1954), 82.

34. Warner, *New Song in a Strange Land*, 41.

35. This betrayal of trust was shared with me by Dr. Joseph Saye Guannu, interview, June 25, 2012. On Harley, see Winifred J. Harley, *A Third of a Century with George Way Harley in Liberia* (Newark, DE: Liberian Studies Association in America, 1973); George Way Harley, *Native African Medicine, With Special Reference to Its Practice in the Mano Tribe of Liberia* (Cambridge, MA: Harvard University Press, 1941).

36. Arthur I. Hayman and Harold Preece, *Lighting Up Liberia* (New York: Creative Age Press, 1943), 182.

37. Hayman and Preece, *Lighting Up Liberia*, 65, 99, 239.

38. Harry McAlpin, "Engineer's Attack on Liberia Policy Draws Fire of U.S. State Department," *Chicago Defender* (January 23, 1943), 6.

39. Hayman and Preece, *Lighting Up Liberia*, 56.

40. Hayman and Preece, *Lighting Up Liberia*, 62.

41. Hayman and Preece, *Lighting Up Liberia*, 55.

42. See *General Information for the Information and Guidance of Staff and Families of Firestone Plantations Company and Affiliated Companies in Liberia*, June 15, 1941, p. 25, WEMC (hereafter referred to as *General Information for the Information*).

43. Hayman and Preece, *Lighting Up Liberia*, 57.

44. Wolo to Dickerson, January 9, 1927, PGWP.

45. Kpelle was confirmed the lingua franca of the plantations in numerous interviews I did with retired Firestone workers and management.

46. Wilson, *Liberia*, 152.

47. Wilson, *Liberia*, 116.

48. Helm's biographical information is from *Planter's Punch*, January–February 1946, v. 7.

49. Harvey Firestone Jr., "Dedication of Liberian Institute," p. 3, January 11, 1952, Box 11, Folder 19, Texts of Walton's addresses re Liberia, 1939–1952, LAWP.

50. See, e.g., G.P. Spangler and K.G. McIndoe, "Full-Spiral Tapping of Hevea brasiliensis—II," *India Rubber World* 2 (March 1949), 723.

51. Comparative wage rates are available in Jules Charles Horwitz, "A Case Study of the Firestone Tire and Rubber Company in Liberia" (master's dissertation, University of Chicago, 1959), 72. On Akron wages, see "Firestone Grants Wage Increase," *Rubber Age* (June 1948), 352.

52. Gbe R. interview, January 30, 2018. I have used fictitious Kpelle names as pseudonyms to protect the identities of Firestone workers we interviewed.

53. Gwi B. interview, January 30, 2018.

54. Manis to Mother and Beth, January 1940, 21.

55. On the details of the stand map, see William Vass, "Special Pamphlet #3, Plantation, Rubber: Bringing a Plantation into Production," pp. 2–3, Box 1, FA-SHC.

56. William Vass, "Special Pamphlet #1, Plantation, Rubber: General Information, New Development, Maintenance Work," p. 11, FA-SHC.

57. On the parallels of the task as a management practice in plantation slavery and the industrial workplace, see Rosenthal, *Accounting for Slavery*, 201–3.

58. Jaweh-teh M. interview, February 12, 2018.

59. A number of tappers I spoke with referred to the importance of ammonia in keeping "latex awake." For a description of ammonia and its importance in the industrial ecology of rubber, see A.T. Edgar, *Manual of Rubber Planting (Malaya), 1958* (Kuala Lumpur: The Incorporated Society of Planters, 1958), 470–75.

60. "Firestone's Liberia Production," *Rubber Age* (December 1945), 413.

61. On figures for natural latex imports, see "U.S. Imported 660,386 Tons of Natural Rubber in 1949," *Rubber Age* (February 1950), 556.

62. Namolu D. interview, February 1, 2018.

63. Maximum wage scale rates are drawn from *General Information for the Information*, June 15, 1941, 31, EMP.

64. Key S. interview, January 31, 2018.

65. Lomalon F. interview, February 1, 2018.

66. Siawa-Geh S. interview, January 30, 2018.

67. John Payne Mitchell, "Firestone in Liberia" (master's dissertation, Boston University, 1951), 47.

68. Firestone promotional film, www.youtube.com/watch?v=H1sMNvzDEV0.

69. Firestone promotional film.

70. Pa S. interview, June 20, 2012.

71. Frederick Helm, "The Tom Tom Times," *Planter's Punch*, January–February 1946, v. 7, 3.

72. U.S. Department of Labor, *Summary of the Labor Situation in Liberia* (Washington, DC: Bureau of Labor Statistics, 1959), 9. In 1963, Portugal filed a complaint against Firestone and the Liberian government under articles of the International Labor Organization that prohibited the use of compulsory or forced labor for the benefit of private individuals or companies. See *Report of the Commission Appointed Under Article 26 of the Constitution of the International Labour Organisation to Examine the Complaint Filed by the Government of Portugal Concerning the Observance by the Government of Liberia of the Forced Labour Convention, 1930* (No. 29), *Official Bulletin* (Geneva, April 1963). See also Christine Whyte, "A State of Underdevelopment: Sovereignty, Nation-Building and Labor in Liberia, 1898–1961," *International Labor and Working-Class History* 92 (2017): 24–46. For the continuation of coerced labor under Tubman's administration, see Cassandra Mark-Thiesen, "Of Vagrants and Volunteers During Liberia's Operation Production, 1963–1969," *African Economic History* 46, no. 2 (2018): 147–72.

73. Na-Fallon T. interview, February 12, 2018.

74. Settlement figure is from Clower et al., *Growth Without Development*, 160.

75. On Firestone's school system, see Clower et al., *Growth Without Development*, 160–67; Taylor, *The Firestone Operations in Liberia*, 104–7; Jaweh-the M. interview, February 1, 2018.

76. Gwi S. interview, January 30, 2018.

77. In 1963, Forbes reported that Firestone's gross profit from its Liberia plantations could "run to 150% over cost" and provided the company with 10 percent of its total net income. Under optimal conditions, the company could have made 200 percent profits off its Liberia plantations. See "Firestone's Bid for the Top," *Forbes* (February 15, 1963), 22–25, and "Firestone's Lively Corpse," *Forbes* (February 15, 1963), 24–25.

78. See, e.g., *History of the Firestone Health Services, Liberia* (n.d.), Box 1, FA-SHC; Clower et al., *Growth Without Development*, 160; Taylor, *The Firestone Operations in Liberia*, 73–75; *Medicine in the Tropics* (Firestone Plantations Company, 1948, 23 minutes), www.youtube.com/watch?v=RgPYyhmM85Q&index=95&list=PL7dF9e 2qSW0bv--6anMWu-gq7LlVpUhBX&app=desktop

79. Siawa-Geh S. interview, January 30, 2018.

80. *Medicine in the Tropics.*

81. Comments, *African Nationalist* 4 (December 20, 1941): 2.

82. Marshall A. Barber, Justus B. Rice, and James Y. Brown, "Malaria Studies on the Firestone Rubber Plantation in Liberia, West Africa, *American Journal of Hygiene* 15, no. 3 (1932): 601–33, on 623–24.

83. See, e.g., Justus B. Rice, *My Number Two Wife* (New York: Meredith Press, 1968), 12.

84. Barber et al., "Malaria Studies on the Firestone Rubber Plantation," 602.

85. See, e.g., H.B.F. Dixon, "A Report on Six Hundred Cases of Malaria Treated with Plasmoquine and Quinine," *Journal of the Royal Army Medical Corps* 60, no. 6 (1933): 431–39; Paul F. Russell, "Plasmochin, Plasmochin with Quinine Salts and Atrabine in Malaria Therapy," *Archives of Internal Medicine* 53, no. 2 (1934): 309–20.

86. On plasmoquine's development, see David Greenwood, "Conflicts of Interest: The Genesis of Synthetic Antimalarial Agents in Peace and War," *Journal of Antimicrobial Chemotherapy* 36, no. 5 (1995): 857–72.

87. Barber et al., "Malaria Studies on the Firestone Rubber Plantation."

88. *General Information for the Information*, 4.

89. Office of the Surgeon General of the Army, "The Drug Treatment of Malaria, Suppressive and Clinical," *Journal of the American Medical Association* 123 (September 25, 1943): 205–8.

90. See Manis to Mother and Beth, 20. Manis's description was consistent with the protocol outlined in Firestone's 1941 operations manual.

91. *General Information for the Information*, 26–28.

92. Manis to Mother and Beth, 21. The smallpox immunization program is discussed in *Medicine in the Tropics*.

93. See George C. Shattuck, *Tropical Medicine at Harvard, 1909–1954* (Boston: Harvard School of Public Health, 1954), 54–56; Everett Veatch, Joseph C. Bequaert, and David Weinman, "Human Trypanosomiasis and Tsetse-flies in Liberia," *American Journal of Tropical Medicine and Hygiene* 26, Suppl. 5 (1946): 1–105; David Weinman and Karl Franz, "Early Results of the Treatment of African Trypanosomiasis with Two New Arsenical Preparations (Melarsen Oxide and 70A) Preliminary Report," *American Journal of Tropical Medicine* 25 (1945): 343–44; David Weinman, "The Treatment of African Sleeping Sickness with Two New Trivalent Arsenical Preparations (Melarsen Oxide and 70A)," *American Journal of Tropical Medicine* 26, Suppl. 5 (1946): 95–105.

94. Firestone Jr. to Tubman, August 5, 1946, WTP-CNDRA.

95. R.S. Bray, "The Susceptibility of Liberians to the Madagascar Strain of *Plasmodium Vivax*," *Journal of Parasitology* 44, no. 4 (1958): 371–73. See also R.S. Bray, A.E. Gunders, R.W. Burgess, J.B. Freeman, E. Etzel, C. Guttuso, and B. Colussa, "The Induced Infection of Semi-Immune Africans with Sporozoites of *Lavernia Falcipara* (-*Plasmodium Falciparum*) in Liberia (Preliminary Report)," WHO/Mal/349, July 27, 1962, WHO Library. The lack of training of Liberian staff is an issue that came up in interviews with Dr. Fatorma Bolay and Dr. Emmet Dennis, current and former directors of the Liberia Institute of Biomedical Research, which took over the operation of the Liberian Institute for Tropical Medicine facility in 1971. A brief history of LITM is discussed in David McBride, *Missions for Science: U.S. Technology and Medicine in America's African World* (New Brunswick, NJ: Rutgers University Press, 2002), 180–82, and Patton, "Liberia and Containment Policy Against Colonial Take-Over."

96. See, e.g., Rana A. Hogarth, *Medicalizing Blackness: Making Racial Difference in the Atlantic World, 1780–1840* (Chapel Hill: University of North Carolina Press, 2017); Harriet A. Washington, *Medical Apartheid: The Dark History of Medical Experimentation on Black Americans from Colonial Times to the Present* (New York: Doubleday, 2006).

97. Milan Trpis, "Consequences of Vector Behavior in Epidemiology of Onchocerciasis on the Firestone Rubber Plantations in Liberia," *American Journal of Tropical Medicine and Hygiene* 74, no. 5 (2006): 833–40; Victor K. Barbiero and Milan Trpis, "The Prevalence of Onchocerciasis on Selected Divisions of the Firestone Rubber Plantation, Harbel, Liberia," *American Journal of Tropical Medicine and Hygiene* 33, no. 3 (1984): 403–9; Victor K. Barbiero and Milan Trpis, "Transmission of Onchocerciasis by Local Black Flies on the Firestone Rubber Plantation, Harbel, Liberia," *American Journal of Tropical Medicine and Hygiene* 33, no. 4 (1984): 586–94.

98. Na-Fallon T. interview, February 12, 2018.

99. Gbe R. interview, January 30, 2018.

100. Edmund Russell, *War and Nature: Fighting Humans and Insects with Chemicals from World War I to Silent Spring* (Cambridge: Cambridge University Press, 2001); Nick Cullather, *The Hungry World: America's Cold War Battle Against Poverty in Asia* (Cambridge, MA: Harvard University Press, 2010).

101. On the use of 2,4,5-T and other chemicals on the Harbel plantations, see J. Schreurs, *Black Thread Disease, Control Measures and Yield Stimulation in Hevea Brasiliensis in Liberia* (Wagenigen, Netherlands: H. Veeman & Zonen N.V., 1982). On Agent Orange, see Institute of Medicine (US) Committee to Review the Health Effects in Vietnam Veterans of Exposure to Herbicides, *Veterans and Agent Orange: Health Effects of Herbicides Used in Vietnam* (Washington, DC: National Academies Press, 1994). On the toxic violence of plantations, see Malcom Ferdinand, "Bridging the Divide to Face the Plantationocene: The Chlordecone Contamination and the 2009 Social Events in Martinique and Guadeloupe," in *Neoliberalism in the Caribbean and French Antillean Uprisings of 2009*, ed. Adlaï Murdoch (New Brunswick, NJ: Rutgers University Press, 2019); Vanessa Agard-Jones, "Bodies in the System," *Small Axe: A Caribbean Journal of Criticism* 17, no. 3 (2013): 182–92.

102. Schreurs, *Black Thread Disease*; J.M. interview, February 2, 2018.

103. Dupigny-Leigh to Brownell, November 16, 1946, WTP-CNDRA.

104. Larabee to Cassell, June 11, 1946; Firestone Plantation Company Workers' Compensation Policy, June 27. 1946; WTP-CNDRA.

## 7. Cold War Concessions

1. John A. Dunaway, *Republic of Liberia, Annual Report of the Financial Adviser, 1944*, Folder 5, Box 11, LAWP.

2. For a summary of Walton's accomplishments as American minister to Liberia, see Lester A. Walton, "Negroes in the U.S. Diplomatic Service," *New York Amsterdam*

*News* (December 10, 1949), 33, 46; "Liberia Loses Great Friend in Walton's Resignation," *African Nationalist*, February 23, 1946. On the economic and public health missions, see McBride, *Missions for Science*.

3. Walton to Villard, May 19, 1945, Correspondence 1944–45, Folder 7, Box 11, LAWP.

4. Walton to Villard, May 19, 1945.

5. "Lester Walton Recalled," *Weekly Mirror*, August 17, 1945. Reprinted from Alfred Smith, "GI Howl on Liberia Ousted Diplomat," *Chicago Defender*, June 16, 1945.

6. Walton to Nan, July 6, 1945, Correspondence, 1944–1945, Folder 7, Box 11, LAWP.

7. "What Is a False Accusation? And Who Is Unfair?," *Weekly Mirror*, September 14, 1945.

8. Ossie Davis and Ruby Dee, *With Ossie and Ruby: In This Life Together* (New York: William Morrow, 1998), 129–30, 133.

9. W.E.B. Du Bois, "Lester Walter's Resignation," *Chicago Defender*, August 4, 1945.

10. "Edward R. Dudley, 93, Civil Rights Advocate and Judge, Dies," *New York Times* (February 11, 2005), C14; John Kirk, "The NAACP Campaign for Teachers' Salary Equalization: African American Women Educators and the Early Civil Rights Struggle," *Journal of African American History* 94, no. 4 (2009): 529–52.

11. "Secret, Memorandum of Conversation," Participants: Byron H. Larabee, Firestone; MM. Feld and Farmer, AF, November 29, 1951, Folder 10, Box 1, RG 59, Lot 56D 418, ROAA. On the history of resistance to segregation on the Firestone plantations, see Adell Patton Jr., "Civil Rights in America's African Diaspora: Firestone Rubber and Segregation in Liberia," *Canadian Journal of African Studies* 49, no. 2 (2015): 319–38.

12. For an excellent study of Barnett and the Associated Negro Press, see Gerald Horne, *The Rise and Fall of the Associated Negro Press: Claude Barnett's Pan-African News and the Jim Crow Paradox* (Urbana: University of Illinois Press, 2017).

13. Claude A. Barnett, "Tourist in Africa," *Negro Digest* (September 1948), 72–76, on 72, 75.

14. Barnett to Wilson, July 18, 1950, Folder 1, Firestone Plantations Company, 1925–1958, Box 190, CABP.

15. Pinder to Barnett, October 18, 1947, Folder 1, Frank Pinder, 1938–1951, Box 186, CABP.

16. Emory Ross, "A 3-Way Venture by the Stettinius Associates-Liberia, the Liberia Company, and the Liberia Foundation," p. 2, November 15, 1948, Folder 2, Liberia Company, November 1948–January 1949, Box 191, CABP.

17. "Plans Announced for the Liberia Company," Telegram, September 26, 1947, Folder 3, Liberia Company, 1946–1947, Box 190, CABP.

18. "The Liberia Company," October 28, 1947, Folder 3, Liberia Company, 1946–1947, Box 190, CABP.

19. See, e.g., "The Liberia Company," *Chicago Defender*, October 11, 1947; A.M. Wendell Malliet, "World Fronts," *New York Amsterdam News*, May 1, 1948.

20. Lillian Scott, "U.S. Company to Exploit Liberian Resources in Deal with Government," *Chicago Defender*, October 4, 1947.

21. Barnett to Embree, November 30, 1948, Folder 2, November 1948–January 1949, Box 191, CABP. See also Blackwell Smith, February 14, 1948, Folder 4, Liberia Company, January–April 1948, Box 190, CABP.

22. Stettinius to Barnett, December 6, 1948, Folder 2, Liberia Company, November 1948–January 1949, Box 191, CABP.

23. "Liberia Company," *Ebony*, September 1, 1948, 56–57.

24. Edward Stettinius, "The Untapped Potential," June 5, 1948, 20, Folder 5, Liberia Company, May–June 1948, CABP.

25. "Tax Agreement Entered into by the Government of the Republic of Liberia, Liberia Development Corporation, and the Liberia Company," 1962; "Statement of Income and Earned Surplus for the Year Ended December 31, 1961," Folder 5, Liberian Company, 1952–1966, Box 191, CABP. See also F.P.M. van der Kraaij, *The Open Door Policy of Liberia: An Economic History of Modern Liberia* (Bremen, Germany: Selbstverlag des Museums, 1983), 84–99.

26. ANE—Mr. Berry, Mr. Sims, "Strikes of Firestone Plantations, Liberia," January 10, 1950, Liberia 1950, p. 4, Firestone, Box 1, Lot 56D 418, ROAA.

27. "Labour Strike Hits Raymond Concrete Pile Company, Is Orderly Conducted," *Weekly Mirror* (December 21, 1945), 1, 3.

28. ANE—Mr. Berry, Mr. Sims, "Strikes of Firestone Plantations, Liberia."

29. Wilson to Hon. C. Abayomi Cassell, December 17, 1949, Folder Firestone Plantations Company Correspondence (1944–1970), WVSTP.

30. Mitchell, "Firestone in Liberia," 50–55. Mitchell was the secretary on the investigating commission appointed by Tubman.

31. Mitchell, "Firestone in Liberia," 52, 54, 58. See also The Ambassador in Liberia (Dudley) to the Secretary of State, January 13, 1950, p. 5886, 876.062/1-1350L Telegram, FRUS, 1950, vol. 5.

32. Mitchell, "Firestone in Liberia," 58. See also Conger-Thompson to Tubman, February 5, 1950, Folder Firestone Plantations Company Correspondence (1944–1970), WVSTP.

33. "Liberia's Gov't in Hot Spot," *New York Amsterdam News* (February 18, 1950), 1.

34. "Liberia Proclaims State of Emergency," *New York Times* (February 15, 1950), 14.

35. "Liberia Asks U.S. for Army Adviser," *New York Times*, March 2, 1950.

36. On the size of Tubman's Totota farm, see Wreh, *The Love of Liberty*, 25. On the acreage holdings of independent rubber farmers, see Clower et al., *Growth Without Development*, 285–87.

37. Progress Report for May and June 1967, Folder Farm Account Reports and Statements, 1946–1990, WVSTP.

38. On increasing labor unrest in the 1950s, see Dew Tuan-Wleh Mayson and Amos Sawyer, "Labour in Liberia," *Review of African Political Economy* 6, no. 14 (1979): 3–15.

39. Tubman to Mr. Secretary, September 22, 1961, WTP-CNDRA.

40. Mayson and Sawyer, "Labour in Liberia," 11.

41. Memorandum of Conversation, by Mr. Harold Sims of the Office of African and Near Eastern Affairs, April 14, 1950, 110.15 MC/4-1450, p. 1718, FRUS, 1950, vol. 5.

42. Kraaij, *The Open Door Policy of Liberia*, 64. Firestone's after-tax profits from its Liberia operations between 1956 and 1960 totaled approximately $13 million per year. See Clower et al., *Growth Without Development*, 169.

43. See, e.g., *Firestone Non-Skid*, August 15, 1950; Edward S. Babcox, "The Harvey S. Firestone Memorial," *Tire Review* (August 1950), 29, 32–33.

44. Joyce Dyer, *Gum-Dipped: A Daughter Remembers Rubber Town* (Akron, OH: University of Akron Press, 2003), 89–90.

45. Department of State Policy Statement, Liberia, January 10, 1951, p. 1276, FRUS, 1951, vol. 5.

46. Memorandum of Conversation, by Mr. Harold Sims of the Office of African and Near Eastern Affairs, April 14, 1950, 110.15 MC/4-1450, pp. 1718–1719, FRUS, 1950, vol. 5.

47. Memorandum of Conversation, by Mr. Harold Sims (April 14, 1950), 5917.

48. Department of State Policy Statement, Liberia (January 10, 1951), 1276.

49. President Harry S. Truman, Inaugural Address, January 20, 1949, Harry S. Turman Library and Museum, www.trumanlibrary.gov/library/public-papers/19/inaugural-address.

50. Truman to Rockefeller, with Related Material, November 24, 1950, The Point Four Program Collection, Official File Series, Harry S. Truman Library & Museum, www.trumanlibrary.gov/library/research-files/harry-s-truman-nelson-rockefeller-related-material.

51. On the U.S. Cold War strategy of development, see, e.g., David Ekbladh, *The Great American Mission: Modernization and the Construction of an American World Order* (Princeton, NJ: Princeton University Press, 2009); Nick Cullather, *The Hungry World: America's Cold War Battle Against Poverty in Asia* (Cambridge, MA: Harvard University Press, 2010).

52. See, e.g., Barnett to King, September 21, 1949, Barnett to Meier and Pinder, August 20, 1950, Folder 1, Point 4 Program (Liberia), Box 192, CABP.

53. "Firestone Plantations—Angel or Devil to Liberia," *Chicago World* (1950), Folder 1, Firestone Plantations Company, 1925–1958, Box 190, CABP.

54. McGhee to Wilbur, July 28, 1949, Folder 10, 1949, General Economic Reports, Liberia, RG59, Lot 56D 418, Box 1, ROAA.

55. Barnett to Rose, September 19, 1950, Folder 1, Point 4 Program (Liberia), Box 192, CABP. Liberia's importance as a model of Point Four has been underappreciated by U.S. history scholars.

56. Figures are from Clower et al., *Growth Without Development*, 360–61; McBride, *Missions for Science*, 186.

57. Oscar W. Meier, "Liberia's Expanding Economy," *Foreign Agriculture* 15 (February 1951): 31.

58. On Tubman's policies, see Elwood Dunn, *Liberia and the United States During the Cold War: Limits of Reciprocity* (New York: Palgrave Macmillan, 2009).

59. See McBride, *Missions for Science*, 173.

60. Republic of Liberia, Annual Report of the Financial Adviser, 1944, pp. 17–18, Folder 5, Box 11, LAWP.

61. Harvey Firestone Jr., "Private Enterprise and Point Four," *Vital Speeches of the Day* (1952), 92–94.

62. *Liberia and Firestone* (Harbel, Liberia / Akron, OH: The Firestone Plantations Company, 1954[?]), 21.

63. "A Tribute from the President of Liberia to Mr. Frank E. Pinder," October 9, 1957, Folder 2, Frank Pinder, 1952–1959, Box 186, CABP. For snapshots that give a sense of Pinder's accomplishments in Liberia, see *Point Four Pioneers: Reports from a New Frontier* (Washington, DC: U.S. Government Printing Office, 1951); "Agricultural Outlook," *Liberia Today* 7 (December 1958), 69–73; International Cooperation Administration News, December 2, 1957, Folder 2, Frank Pinder, 1952–1959, Box 186, CABP.

64. Frank E. Pinder II, *Pinder: From Little Acorns* (Tallahassee: Florida Agricultural and Mechanical University Foundation, 1986).

65. Pete Daniel, *Dispossession: Discrimination Against African American Farmers in the Age of Civil Rights* (Chapel Hill: University of North Carolina Press, 2013); Monica White, *Freedom Farmers: Agricultural Resistance and the Black Freedom Movement* (Chapel Hill: University of North Carolina Press, 2018).

66. See Pinder, *Pinder*, 59–60. On the Gee's Bend project, see John Beardsley, "River Island," in *Gee's Bend: The Women and Their Quilts* (Atlanta, GA: Tinwood Books, 2002), 22–35.

67. Frank Pinder, "Point Four—A New Name for An Old Job!," n.d., Folder 1, Frank Pinder, 1938–1951, Box 186, CABP.

68. Frank Pinder to Claude Barnett, February 15, 1952, Folder 2, Frank Pinder, 1952–1959, Box 186, CABP.

69. My thanks to Monica White for helping me to understand the significance of this term in Pinder's resistance politics.

70. Pinder, "Point Four—A New Name for An Old Job!," 8–9.

71. On Moore's biography, see Bai T. Moore Papers, 1919–2004, Liberia Collections, Indiana University, http://webapp1.dlib.indiana.edu/findingaids/view?doc.view =entire_text&docId=VAC1412.

72. On cooperative traditions in Southern agriculture as forms of resistance to evolving regimes of plantation monopoly, see Clyde Woods, *Development Arrested* and

White, *Freedom Farmers*. Jean Casimir coined the word *counter-plantation* in rethinking the history of Haiti and the sovereignty of its peasantry in the countryside. See, most recently, *The Haitians: A Decolonial History*, trans. Laurent Dubois (Chapel Hill: University of North Carolina Press, 2020).

73. Bai T. Moore, "A Preliminary Report on the Dimeh Project," June 27, 1950, Folder 1, Point Four Program (Liberia), 1947–1953, Box 192, CABP; *Point Four Pioneers*; *The Point Four Program: A Progress Report* 6 (May 1951): 3–5.

74. Pinder to Barnett, October 18, 1947, Folder 1, Frank Pinder, 1938–1951, Box 186, CABP.

75. Pinder to Barnett, January 15, 1948, Folder 1, Frank Pinder, 1938–1951, Box 186, CABP.

76. Pinder to Barnett, September 1, 1949, Folder 1, Frank Pinder, 1938–1951, Box 186, CABP.

77. Pinder to Barnett, May 16, 1950, Folder 1, Frank Pinder, 1938–1951, Box 186, CABP.

78. "Laurels For:," *The Friend* (October 11, 1947), 4.

79. Patterson to Barnett, January 17, 1951, Folder 1, Frank Pinder, 1938–1951, Box 186, CABP.

80. Dudley to Pinder, May 8, 1952, Folder 2, Frank Pinder, 1952–1959, Box 186, CABP.

81. See, e.g., the tributes to Davis by Charles Wesley and Hugh Gloster in *Journal of Negro History* 66 (Spring 1981): 78–80.

82. See Pinder to Barnett, February 26, 1954, Folder 2, Frank Pinder, 1952–1959, Box 186, CABP.

83. Palm kernel exports increased from zero in 1945 to $1.5 million in 1955. See "Reporting on 12 Years of Progress," *Liberia Today* 5 (January 1956): 2. On the Gbedin swamp rice project, see *Liberian Swamp Rice Product: A Success* (Washington, DC: United States Foreign Operations Administration, 1955).

84. Wilhelm Anderson, "Report on Visit to Liberia, October 12 Through October 23, 1953," Folder 1, Point 4 Program (Liberia), 1947–1953, CABP. See also Clayton Orton, *Agriculture of Liberia* (Washington, DC: United States Foreign Operations Administration, 1954).

85. "Ellender Has Some Reports," *Daily Chronicle* (DeKalb, Illinois), October 30, 1953, p. 19.

86. "Ellender Sees Congress Action on Point 4 Plan," *Daily Advertiser* (Lafayette, Louisiana), October 9, 1953, p. 7.

87. "Liberian Asserts Ellender Hurts Brotherhood Cause, *New York Times* (June 24, 1963), 2. For the larger context of the challenges that racial discrimination in the U.S. posed for American foreign relations, see, e.g., Thomas Borstelmann, *The Cold War*

*and the Color Line: American Race Relations in the Global Arena* (Cambridge, MA: Harvard University Press, 2002), and Brenda Gayle Plummer, *Rising Wind: Black Americans and U.S. Foreign Affairs, 1935–1960* (Chapel Hill: University of North Carolina Press, 1996).

88. "Ellender Hits at Liberian Aid," *Pittsburgh Courier* (March 20, 1954), 5.

89. The quote is from an ANP press release accompanying Barnett to Pinder, March 10, 1954, Folder 2, Frank Pinder, 1952–1959, Box 186, CABP. See also Pinder to Barnett, February 26, 1954, Folder 2, Frank Pinder, 1952–1959, Box 186, CABP.

90. AJE Diary 1953, Liberia, p. 33, Box 1517, AJEP.

91. On Firestone's dumping of rice imports on local markets, see Niels Hahn, "The Experience of Land Grabbing in Liberia," in *Handbook of Land and Water Grabs in Africa: Foreign Direct Investment and Food and Water Security*, ed. Tony Allan, Martin Keulertz, Suvi Sojamo, and Jeroen Warner (London: Routledge, Taylor & Francis Group, 2013), 71–87.

92. On the making of "economic growth" as a scientific object, see Michelle Murphy, *The Economization of Life* (Durham, NC: Duke University Press, 2017). See also Julie Livingston, *Self-Devouring Growth: A Planetary Parable as Told from Southern Africa* (Durham, NC: Duke University Press, 2019).

93. Clower et al., *Growth Without Development*, 244. For an excellent, critical historiographical analysis of the Clower study, see Liberty, *Growth of the Liberian State*.

94. Kraaij, *The Open Door Policy of Liberia*, 64. Rubber production figures are from Clower et al., *Growth Without Development*, 146, 154.

95. Taylor, *The Firestone Operations in Liberia*, 57.

96. On Walton's public relations work for Tubman, see, e.g., Walton to Tubman, October 9, 1951, and Benham to Tubman, n.d. Folder 5, Correspondence with William Tubman, 1950–1953, Box 19, LAWP.

97. Clower et al., *Growth Without Development*, 37.

98. See Kraaij, *The Open Door Policy of Liberia*, 120.

99. For additional details, see Emmanuel Urey, "Political Ecology of Land and Agriculture Concessions in Liberia" (doctoral dissertation, University of Wisconsin–Madison, 2018).

100. John Robert Badger, "World View: Liberia's Future," *Chicago Defender* (March 2, 1946), 15.

101. Kraaij, *The Open Door Policy of Liberia*, 167; Wreh, *The Love of Liberty*, 88–89.

102. Kraaij, *The Open Door Policy of Liberia*, 168–69.

103. Barnett to Phillips, May 13, 1946, Folder 3, ANP + WNS Business Dealing, 1930–1964, Box 188, CABP.

104. Patterson to Barnett, January 17, 1951, Folder 1, Frank Pinder, 1938–1951, Box 186, CAPB.

105. "Liberians Report Bias in U.S.," *Chicago Daily Tribune* (December 28, 1960), 3. For an excellent analysis on how liberation struggles in Africa and the civil rights movement in the U.S. impacted Liberia, see Patton, "Civil Rights in America's African Diaspora."

106. Interview by Etta Moten Barnett, March 6, 1957, in *The Papers of Martin Luther King, Jr., Volume IV: Symbol of the Movement, January 1957–1958*, ed. Clayborne Carson et al. (Berkeley: University of California Press, 2000), 146. See also Kevin K. Gaines, *American Africans in Ghana: Black Expatriates and the Civil Rights Era* (Chapel Hill: University of North Carolina Press, 2006).

107. Quoted in Patton, "Civil Rights in America's African Diaspora," 334.

108. In his classic book, Walter Rodney devotes a number of pages to Firestone in discussing American capitalism and the exploitation of Africa. See Rodney, *How Europe Underdeveloped Africa*, 192–93.

109. W.E.B. Du Bois, "A Future for Pan-Africa: Freedom, Peace, Socialism," *National Guardian*, March 11, 1957, reprinted in W.E.B. Du Bois, *The World and Africa* (New York: International Publishers, 1965), 296.

110. W.E.B. Du Bois, "The Future of Africa," reprinted in Du Bois, *The World and Africa*, 308–9.

111. AAPC, *All-African People's Conference: Resolution on Neo-Colonialism*, Cairo, 1961. Reprinted in *Africa: The Politics of Independence and Unity* (Lincoln: University of Nebraska Press, 2005). The literature on the history of Pan-Africanism(s) is large. See, e.g., Sidney J. Lemelle and Robin D.G. Kelley, eds., *Imagining Home: Class, Culture, and Nationalism in the African Diaspora* (New York: Verso Books, 1994); Toyin Falola and Kwame Essien, eds., *Pan-Africanism, and the Politics of African Citizenship and Identity* (New York: Routledge, 2014); Hakim Adi, *Pan Africanism: A History* (London: Bloomsbury Academy, 2018).

112. CIA, "The All Africa Peoples Conference in 1961," November 1, 1961, CIA-RDP78-00915R0013003200009-3, p. 8.

113. See, e.g., "Surrender of Sovereignty Declared Unrealistic," *Liberian Age* (May 11, 1961), 1, 8; Dunn, *Liberia and the United States*, 61–63.

114. Quoted in Dunn, *Liberia and the United States*, 45.

115. *U.S. Army Area Handbook for Liberia* (Washington, DC: U.S. Government Printing Office, 1964), 321, 382. Martin Lowenkopf, *Politics in Liberia: The Conservative Road to Development* (Stanford, CA: Hoover Institution Publications, 1976), 101.

116. Key S. interview, January 31, 2018. On the strikes, see Lowenkopf, *Politics in Liberia*, 102–3; Patricia A. Schechter, *Exploring the Decolonial Imaginary: Four Transnational Lives* (New York: Palgrave Macmillan, 2012), 159–63.

117. Gwi S. interview, January 30, 2018; Dee B. interview, January 31, 2018.

118. Interview with Saphana K., January 30, 2018. On independent confirmation of shots fired by Firestone management, see Richards to Tubman, August 12, 1963; Tubman to Acting Attorney General, August 16, 1963, WTP-CNDRA.

119. "Harvey S. Firestone Jr. Dies at 75," *Rubber & Plastics News* (June 18, 1973), 8; "Firestone's Bid for the Top," *Forbes* (February 15, 1963), 22.

120. Kraaij, *The Open Door Policy of Liberia*, 64.

## Epilogue

1. On Liberia's class structure during the decade of the 1970s, see George Klay Kieh Jr., "Dependency and the Foreign Policy of a Small Power: An Examination of Liberia's Foreign Policy During the Tolbert Administration, 1971–1980" (doctoral dissertation, Northwestern University, 1986).

2. Radio recording of Nina Simone in *What Happened, Miss Simone?*, directed by Liz Garbus (Netflix, 2015). See also Katherina Grace Thomas, "Nina Simone in Liberia," *Guernica*, June 19, 2017, www.guernicamag.com/nina-simone-in-liberia/.

3. For a vivid picture of Monrovia's chic scene in the 1970s, see Hugh Masekela and D. Michael Cheers, *Still Grazing: The Musical Journey of Hugh Masekela* (New York: Crown Publishers, 2004).

4. See Niels Hahn, "US Covert and Overt Operations in Liberia, 1970s to 2003," *Air & Space Power Journal—Africa and Francophonie* 5 (2014): 19–47; Dunn, *Liberia and the United States*, 87–137.

5. Kraaij, *The Open Door Policy of Liberia*, 77–83.

6. "Stephen Tolbert and Five Associates Killed in Plane," *Jet* (May 15, 1975), 15.

7. Brooks Marmon, "Murder and Mayhem in Liberia: What America Wrought in the Country America Created," *Pambazuka News*, February 2, 2017.

8. Quoted in H. Boima Fahnbulleh, "Preface," in *Voices of Protest: Liberia on the Edge, 1974–1980*, ed. H. Boima Fahnbulleh (Boca Raton, FL: Universal Publishers, 2004), v.

9. Masekela and Cheers, *Still Grazing*, 258.

10. H. Boima Fahnbulleh, "Repression in Liberia," in *Voices of Protest*, 2; Fahnbulleh, "Preface," in *Voices of Protest*," vii.

11. Union of Liberia Associations in the Americas, Inc., "Mass Killing in Liberia," in *Voices of Protest*, 281–84; Gwei Feh Kpei, "The Struggle Continues (Movement for Justice in Africa), March 1979," 317–37, in *Voices of Protest*.

12. Doe's "Message to the Nation" is quoted in Jairo Munive, "A Political Economic History of the Liberian State, Forced Labor, and Armed Mobilization," *Journal of Agrarian Change* 11, no. 3 (2011): 357–76, on 367. "Papa's Land" played on Liberia's national radio station for almost two months after the coup.

13. T. Christian Miller and Jonathan Jones, "Firestone and the Warlord: The Untold Story of Firestone, Charles Taylor, and the Tragedy of Liberia," ProPublica, November 18, 2014. On Firestone and Taylor, see also Stephen Ellis, *The Mask of Anarchy: The Destruction of Liberia and the Religious Dimension of an African Civil War* (New York: New York University Press, 2006). While much ink has been spilled on the

causes of Liberia's civil war, for an explanation that effectively grounds it in the ethnic tensions that arose out of the settler and then neo-colonial state, see George Klay Kieh Jr., *The First Liberian Civil War: The Crisis of Underdevelopment* (New York: Peter Lang, 2008).

14. Interview with James B., July 4, 2013.

15. Stephen Archibald, *Feasibility Study into the Rehabilitation & Reintegration of Unregistered Ex-Combatants, Guthrie Rubber Plantation, Liberia, September–December 2006* (Landmine Action Liberia, 2006). On the links between plantation labor and mobilization of combatants in the civil war, see Munive, "A Political Economic History of the Liberian State." On the impact of the Sime Darby concessions on rural livelihoods, see Urey, "Political Ecology of Land and Agriculture Concessions in Liberia."

16. Nicholai Hart Lidow, *Violent Order: Understanding Rebel Governance Through Liberia's Civil War* (Cambridge: Cambridge University Press, 2016).

17. Rachel Knight and Ali Kaba, "The Land Rights Act Victory in Liberia Means the Work Has Just Begun," Thomson Reuters Foundation News, October 23, 2018.

18. Truth and Reconciliation Commission of Liberia, *Final Report of the Truth and Reconciliation Commission of Liberia (TRC): Volume I: Preliminary Findings and Determinations* (Monrovia, Truth and Reconciliation Commission, 2008).

19. Alaric Tokpa and Joseph Asunka, *Land Disputes in Liberia*, n.d., 6.

20. On agriculture, women's rights, and the Land Rights Act in Liberia, see, e.g., Moses M. Zinnah, Mulbah S. Jackollie, Emmett Crayton, and Olive B. Cisco, *Gender Assessment of the Policy Environment in Relation to the Cocoa, Oil Palm, Rubber and Timber Value Chains in Liberia*, Proforest's Production Landscape, February 2020. Some of the material on the history of Sime Darby and women's land rights arose from collaborations with Emmanuel Urey, as well as field research for his doctoral dissertation, which he graciously shared with me.

21. Sylvia Wynter's observation of the dichotomy between plantation and plot and the latter's importance as "a source of cultural guerilla resistance to the plantation system" offers a fruitful line of inquiry in pondering rural people's response to Liberia's plantation economy. See Sylvia Wynter, "Novel and History, Plot and Plantation," *Savacou* 5 (1971): 95–102.

# Index

Page references in *italics* refer to illustrations and their captions.

Salala Rubber Corporation, 218
Sao Boso (King Boatswain), 36
Schuyler, George, 147–49
Schwab, George, 96, 188
Scott, Emmett, 41–42, 123, 124
Selassie, Haile, 174
Sellards, Andrew, 105–6
Shattuck, Frederick Cheever, 74, 80–81
Shattuck, George, *64*; Cheek-Shattuck
    incident, 65, 66, 74–75
Sherman, Reginald, 115
Siawa-Geh (Firestone worker),
    197, 201
Sibley, James, 107, 142–44
Sierra Leone, 242
Sime Darby, 243–44
Simmons, James S., 205
Simone, Nina, 239
Simpson, Clarence L., 75, 127, *220*
*Simulium yahense* (black fly), 205
Singapore, 5–6
Sirleaf, Ellen Johnson, 243
Sisler, Louis E., 10–11
slavery, 32, 34, 62; Convention of
    1926 on, 116, 122; in Liberia,
    League of Nations Commission
    report on, 126
sleeping sickness (human trypanosomia-
    sis), 205
smallpox, 87–88
Smith, James Skivring, Jr., 174
Sorensen, Charles, 20
Sottile, Antoine, 122
Soviet Union, 215–16
Spain, 115
Stettinius, Edward, 213–15
Stevenson, James, 22
Stevenson Restriction Act (Britain,
    1922), 22–26, 101–2
Stimson, Henry, 118, 123, 130–31,
    135, 137

Stockton, Robert Field, 36
Strong, Richard Pearson, 62–63, *64,*
    77–80; in Cheek-Shattuck incident,
    65–66, 74–75; on H. Firestone, Jr.,
    73; on Harvard African Expedition,
    97–98; on indigenous population, 85,
    92, 94–97, 188; on Liberian forced
    labor, *98,* 98–100, 112, 114, 120;
    meets with H. Firestone, Sr., 80–81;
    in the Philippines, 78–79; on yellow
    fever vaccine, 106
Suakoko, Madam, 97
Sumatra, 7
Supreme Court (U.S.), citizenship
    denied to Black people by, 37
swidden agriculture, 84–85
Swinehart, James, 11
synthetic rubber (GS-R), 178

Taft, William Howard, 1, 41–42, 99
tappers working for Firestone, 188–96,
    *189, 191, 195, 196*
Taylor, C. Frederick, 233
Taylor, Charles, 241–43
Taylor, Robert, 143, 144
Theiler, Max, *64,* 87–88
Thomas, John, 13
Tobias, Channing, 214
Tolbert, Stephen, 240
Tolbert, William, 239–41
True Whig Party (Liberia), 121, 148
Truman, Harry S: foreign policy of,
    215–16, 220–23; Walton's resignation
    accepted by, 210
Trunks, Walter, 219
Truth and Reconciliation Commission
    (Liberia), 245
trypanosomiasis (African sleeping
    sickness), 205
Tubman, William, 184, 187, *220;* death
    of, 239; Harvey Firestone, Jr.,

# About the Author

Gregg Mitman is the Vilas Research and William Coleman Professor of History, Medical History, and Environmental Studies at the University of Wisconsin–Madison. An award-winning author and filmmaker, his recent books and films include *Breathing Space: How Allergies Shape Our Lives and Landscapes* and *The Land Beneath Our Feet*. He lives near Madison, Wisconsin.

# Publishing in the Public Interest

Thank you for reading this book published by The New Press. The New Press is a nonprofit, public interest publisher. New Press books and authors play a crucial role in sparking conversations about the key political and social issues of our day.

We hope you enjoyed this book and that you will stay in touch with The New Press. Here are a few ways to stay up to date with our books, events, and the issues we cover:

- Sign up at www.thenewpress.com/subscribe to receive updates on New Press authors and issues and to be notified about local events
- Like us on Facebook: www.facebook.com/newpressbooks
- Follow us on Twitter: www.twitter.com/thenewpress
- Follow us on Instagram: www.instagram.com/thenewpress

Please consider buying New Press books for yourself; for friends and family; or to donate to schools, libraries, community centers, prison libraries, and other organizations involved with the issues our authors write about.

The New Press is a 501(c)(3) nonprofit organization. You can also support our work with a tax-deductible gift by visiting www.thenewpress.com/donate.